ALSO BY GERALD ASTOR

THE BLOODY FOREST:
BATTLE FOR THE HUERTGEN:
SEPTEMBER 1944–JANUARY 1945

THE GREATEST WAR:
AMERICANS IN COMBAT, 1941–1945

TERRIBLE TERRY ALLEN:
COMBAT GENERAL OF WWII—
THE LIFE OF AN AMERICAN SOLDIER

WINGS OF GOLD:
THE U.S. NAVAL AIR CAMPAIGN IN WORLD WAR II

SEMPER FI
IN THE SKY

SEMPER FI IN THE SKY

THE MARINE AIR BATTLES
OF WORLD WAR II

GERALD ASTOR

PRESIDIO
PRESS

BALLANTINE BOOKS
NEW YORK

A Presidio Press Trade Paperback Original

Copyright © 2005 by Gerald Astor

Published in the United States by Presidio Press, an imprint of
The Random House Publishing Group, a division of
Random House, Inc., New York.

PRESIDIO PRESS and colophon are
trademarks of Random House, Inc.

ISBN: 0-89141-877-6

Printed in the United States of America

www.presidiopress.com

2 4 6 8 9 7 5 3 1

Book design by Joseph Rutt

This book is intended as a tribute
to those who have served their country,
specifically those from Marine Corps aviation.
I also want to honor my wife Sonia
who has in her own way, along with her creativity
as an artist, demonstrated a rare quality of courage.

CONTENTS

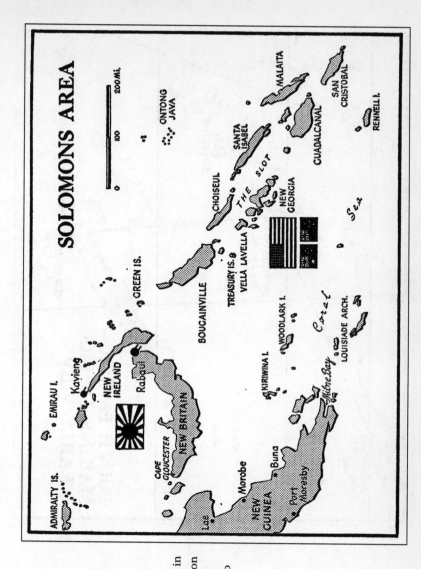

SOLOMONS AREA

Marine aviation operated in the South Pacific's Solomon Islands before moving up through the Philippines to Iwo Jima and Okinawa.

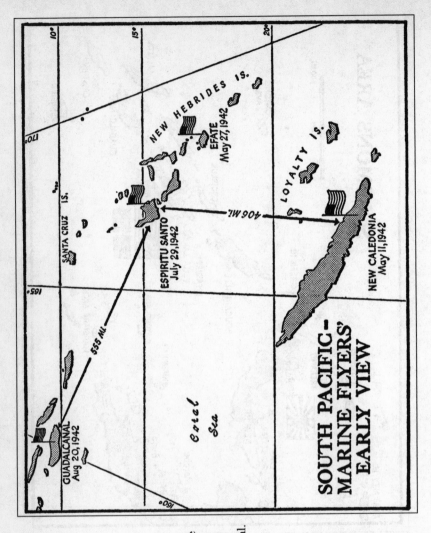

SOUTH PACIFIC—
MARINE FLYERS'
EARLY VIEW

The first Marine air bases were
located at Efate and Espiritu
Santo from where aircraft and
airmen traveled to Guadalcanal.

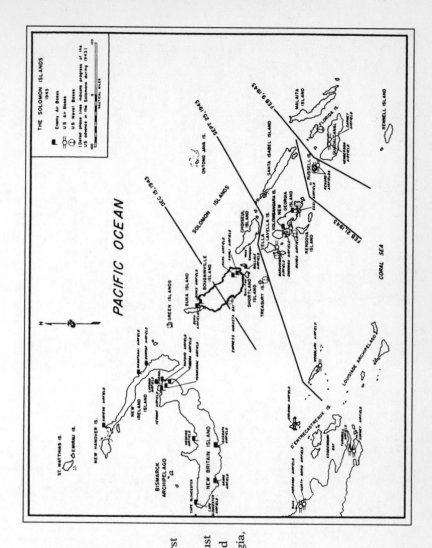

From Henderson Field, the first base on Guadalcanal which opened for operations in August 1942, Marine aviation followed the foot soldiers to New Georgia, then Bougainville.

SEMPER FI
IN THE SKY

ONE

TAKING WINGS

Even before the Wright brothers lifted off from the sands of Kitty Hawk, North Carolina, in 1903, both the Army and Navy had begun to take an interest in the military possibilities of flying machines. By 1907 the Army had created an Aeronautical Division within the Signal Corps, and the Navy ordered its first aircraft to be delivered in 1911. That same year Alfred Austell Cunningham—an army veteran of the Spanish-American War, "a confirmed aeronautical enthusiast" (as he said after a 1903 balloon ride), and a commissioned Marine lieutenant at age twenty-seven—on his own while stationed in Philadelphia, leased a purported airplane for twenty-five dollars a month. He christened it *Noisy Nan* because of the racket created by the engine.

Unfortunately the contraption lacked the essential requirements of aerodynamics. Powered by an obstreperous four-cylinder motor, it lacked sufficient muscle to lift its wings, fuselage, and pilot off the ground. Only after as much as an hour of cranking would the engine sputter to life, enabling the plane to careen down the field without ever achieving flight. Cunningham created a bump at the end of the runway that jolted the machine as much as fifty feet into the air but *Noisy Nan* refused to continue on its own, content to settle back to earth. "I called her everything in God's name to go up," said Cunningham. "I pleaded with her. I caressed her. I prayed to her and I cursed that flighty Old Maid to lift up her skirts and hike, but she never would."

When he abandoned *Noisy Nan* as a lost cause, Cunningham joined a local flying club and the members lobbied for a Marine airfield. Congress took notice, and the Marine Corps commandant of the day silenced the clamor by assigning Cunningham to flight school under the auspices of the Navy. On August 20, 1912, he soloed after two hours and forty minutes of instruction; Marine aviation had its first pilot. Cunningham continued to learn the art of flight for another year before he asked for ground duty "because my fiancee will not consent to marry me unless I give up flying."

By 1915, however, the bride apparently relented, because Cunningham again received the designation of "naval aviator" and, with several others, notably Lieutenant Bernard L. Smith, sought to expand Marine horizons. Cunningham actually attempted the first catapult takeoff from a warship while it was under way. The catapult proved insufficient to the task, hurling Cunningham and his Curtiss flying boat into the water, an accident that broke his back. Another daredevil, Captain Francis T. Evans, confounded the experts when in 1917 he successfully looped a seaplane twice and then brought it out of a deliberate spin. Bernard Smith worked with Navy fliers to perfect a method to drop bombs from a plane and as an attaché in Paris spent three years visiting the World War I fronts to observe aerial warfare.

With the Great War ravaging Europe and the airplane becoming another, albeit limited, weapon, the military establishment in the United States took notice. The Naval Appropriations Act of 1915 allowed naval aviation forty-eight officers and ninety-six enlisted men, with the Marine Corps, under a formula of four to one, authorized twelve officers and twenty-four enlisted men. The bill provided 50 percent extra pay to aviators for hazardous duty. Cunningham assumed command of an aviation company for a Marine Corps advance base force and interviewed all candidates for aviation service.

After the United States entered World War I, Cunningham sailed to Europe to study British and French aviation. He flew on photographic and bombing missions. Upon his return to the States he submitted a plan to the Secretary of the Navy for aircraft attacks upon submarines and their bases. In the last days of July 1918 the First Marine Aviation Force, with Squadrons Seven, Eight, and Nine, arrived in France and became part of the Navy's Northern Bombing Group. Shortly after taking up station, the Aviation Force began unpacking crated boxes containing American-made De Havilland 4 bombers. Unfortunately the wood spars of the wings were warped, many control wires were too short, the engines required extensive overhauls, and bombsights and airspeed indicators had to be requisitioned. While waiting for functioning DH-4s, Marine pilots underwent some training with the French and British, and a few Americans flew missions in Royal Air Force (RAF) fighters, Sopwith Camels.

Among the airmen was Francis P. Mulcahy, a son of Irish immigrants, a native of Rochester, New York, and a classmate of football celebrity Knute Rockne at Notre Dame, from where he graduated in 1914. In 1917, before the United States entered the war, Mulcahy, already in the Army, had applied, unsuccessfully, for flight training. When he heard that commissions in the Marines were available, Mulcahy pleaded with Notre Dame's Father Cavanaugh to aid him. On the strength of the priest's recommendation, Mulcahy obtained his transfer as well as the opportunity to fly under civilian instructors working for the Signal Corps.

Shipped to France, Mulcahy earned a Distinguished Service Medal after he and two other pilots dropped food and bread to an isolated French regiment. The trio of DH-4s skimmed the battlefield at a hundred feet, making four trips under intense machine-gun, rifle, and artillery fire. Mulcahy said he never feared antiaircraft, mainly because of the limited range of such weapons.

On September 29, 1918, Mulcahy, with Gunnery Sergeant Thomas McCulloch in the rear seat of a DH-4, engaged in a shootout with enemy planes. Recalling the sudden attack by the German aircraft, Mulcahy said, "I was alone, maneuvering as best I could. They filled the damn thing with bullets. It was the nastiest kind of crackling sound. One went through McCulloch's flying suit. This old plane had a wind-driven propellor, two of them, because they had two main tanks to suck the gas from the tank to the carburetor. One bullet must have just barely missed my head because it hit one of those things and put it out of commission. The engine stopped. I thought, Oh, oh, here I go in Germany, Holland or something with no engine. Then I thought, I'll try the other tank. And whoop—she jumped. They must have been very much surprised when we didn't go down."

Even more discomfiting to the enemy, McCulloch actually shot down one of the Fokkers, becoming the first of the Marine contingent to register a victory. The official records claim only four enemy planes shot down by Marines, but the number may be slightly higher. Subsequently Lieutenant Ralph Talbot with Corporal Robert G. Robinson allegedly downed three enemy planes in duels on October 8 and 14, with Robinson seriously wounded in the stomach and leg. Both received the Medal of Honor. Not until October 14 did the Marines drop their first bombs, 2,218 pounds' worth, by Squadron Nine on a railroad junction. By the time of the November 11 armistice, the Marines reported four pilots KIA and three wounded—but sixteen from the overseas air arm died of influenza.

The achievements of Marine aviation's 282 officers and 2,180 enlisted men in France during World War I were minor, but the corps now held a franchise for air warfare. However, policy dictated that Marine fliers serve ground duty tours. Lieutenant Colonel Thomas C. Turner, a former machine-gun company commander who used his spare time to learn to fly with Army pilots and was a spit-and-polish disciplinarian, assumed command of the airmen. As officer in charge, he ruled as a benevolent despot, and his superiors, impressed by his demeanor and achievements, granted him a waiver for a hearing defect. During his term, flying was a high-risk duty; in 1922, of seventeen new officer pilots, nine died in crashes. The following year, out of eleven additions, four were killed.

Robert Sherrod, in his *History of Marine Corps Aviation in WWII*, recalled a conversation with a flier from that era who told of a candidate for aviation in 1924 being asked whether he wanted a three-, four-, or five-year tour. "What's the casualty rate?" he asked. "Oh, about 25 percent a year." The volunteer answered, "Put me down for five years and I'll be 125 percent dead when I return to the line."

Turner coped with ever-declining appropriations during the 1920s as the number of aviators fell to as few as 43 in 1921 and then rose in small increments to a mere 132 by 1930. Probably the only reason the figure climbed at all during the decade lay in the Marine presence in Santo Domingo, Haiti, and Nicaragua. A six-plane squadron, in 1919, joined a regiment of Marines stationed in Santo Domingo (leathernecks had been there since 1914) to strafe "bandits" or perhaps rebel groups, perform reconnaissance, and, with a specially modified De Havilland, evacuate wounded from deep in the interior of the country.

Revolution in the Carribean island nations of Santo Domingo (now the Dominican Republic) and Haiti and Central America's Nicaragua intermittently brought in Marine Corps ground troops and some aviation units. The Fourth Air Squadron under Captain Harvey B. Mims, in 1919, with seven seaplanes and six Jenny airplanes, arrived in Port-au-Prince, Haiti. For fifteen years the aviators would support efforts by local soldiers and a Marine brigade to suppress insurgencies. It was in Haiti that Lieutenant Lawson H. M. Sanderson, unhappy with the hit-or-miss techniques of aerial bombardment, manufactured a bomb rack using a burlap sack and a sight from a rifle barrel. He practiced on a range, diving at an angle of forty-five degrees, and reported, "The accuracy was astounding." His squadron mates adopted the method, and glide-bombing, as it was called, became standard practice. Others would refine the techniques. Supposedly a keen student of a demonstration at an air race was the German aviator Ernst Udet. Upon his return home he designed the Stuka dive-bomber, a fearsome weapon during the early years of World War II.

When the Marines intervened in Nicaragua in 1927 they brought an aerial observation squadron led by Major Ross E. Rowell. He had learned to fly by paying for private lessons. Rowell's initial requests for entry as a naval aviation pilot (NAP) had been denied; not until 1923, at age thirty-nine, did Rowell get his wings. As the situation in Nicaragua worsened, a second squadron arrived, with Rowell taking overall charge.

On the evening of July 15, 1927, revolutionaries headed by Augosto Sandino attacked an outpost at Ocotal manned by thirty-seven Marines. The leathernecks repulsed the Sandinistas, but Ocotal lay 125 miles from the capital city of Managua and any reinforcements would need ten days to trek through the mountainous jungles. Apparently Marine headquarters was unaware of the desperate situation. Two pilots, Lieutenant Hayne D. Boyden and Marine Gunner Michael Wodarczyk, while on patrol, discovered the plight of the besieged Americans. Wodarczyk sprayed the Sandinistas while Boyden landed in a field and, in Spanish, interrogated a Nicaraguan for information. Boyden then took off, and he, too, strafed the rebels.

The airmen returned to Managua and reported to Rowell. The major then led a five-plane flight of De Havillands, which spotted the insurgents. According to Rowell's statement to a Navy history unit, "I led the attack and dived out of column from 1,500 feet, pulling out at about 600. Later we ended up diving in from 1,000 and pulling up at about 300. Since the enemy had not been subjected to any form of bombing attack, other than dynamite charges thrown from the Laird-Swallows by the Nicaraguan Air Force [a two-plane organization], they had no fear of us. They exposed themselves in such a manner that we were able to inflict damage which was out of proportion to what they might have suffered had they taken cover." Estimates of the casualties ranged from fifty to two hundred, with many dead.

For six years, Marine airmen battled against Sandino's forces. Wodarczyk, who was nicknamed the "Polish Warhorse" and had been a gunnery sergeant in France during World War I, had part of his tail shot off by rifle bullets in one encounter. His bombs, dropped from a very low altitude, killed a top Sandinista. In a single day he led his patrol through three intense engagements, flying for seven hours. A bullet wounded one of his observers, another passed through his parachute pack, and he completed twenty-five missions against the enemy, more than anyone in the squadron. He was named to receive a Distinguished Flying Cross. His designation as "student naval aviator" posed a problem. Regulations specified that a Marine could not qualify as a "naval aviator" unless he had attended flight school at Pensacola. But graduation from there awarded a commission. Men like Wodarczyk, skilled mechanics who learned to fly without formal training, lacked the kind of education that would enable them to serve as staff officers, exercise command responsibilities, and supervise military operations. All of the armed services, anxious to enroll more aviators, had hit on the notion of enrolling skilled enlisted men as pilots. Because they were not commissioned, the rosters remained within the authorized number of officers.

According to Mulcahy, one Major Edwin H. Brainard, a former aide to the Secretary of the Navy and at the time head of Marine aviation, went to Admiral William A. Moffett, chief of the Bureau of Aeronautics, and said, "Admiral, this is ridiculous. Here's a man who is going to get the DFC. Why does he have to go to Pensacola? He's already fighting the war in Nicaragua."

Moffett agreed. "Okay, we'll make him a Marine aviator." Wodarczyk received his naval aviator wings and his medal in the same ceremony. (The phenomenon of enlisted pilots continued into World War II, when it was gradually phased out.)

In the jungles of Nicaragua another Marine aviator achieved fame for his daring rescue of the wounded. Christian F. Schilt, an Illinois farm boy, had attended a polytechnic school in Indiana before enlisting in the Marine Corps two months after the United States entered World War I. As an enlisted man he served with a seaplane squadron assigned to antisubmarine patrol in the Azores. He earned his wings and commission in 1919 and did tours in Santo Domingo and Haiti before receiving orders to Nicaragua.

He recalled the tactics. "The ground forces sometimes gave us directions where to go or we'd locate them [the rebels] and drop a bomb on them or shoot our machine guns. Quite frequently we saved the ground forces from being severely attacked." It was a primitive display of tactical support for infantry.

After the guerrillas ambushed and surrounded two columns of Marines, killing four and wounding another sixteen, Schilt became part of an effort to save the embattled ground forces. "There wasn't any field there to go in and do anything. We dropped tools—pick axes, shovels and stuff like that so they could clear off an area big enough for a small plane to land. It took them about three days to do that and I think we had about 400 feet there.

"Maj. Rowell assigned me to the mission of getting in there. I made ten trips and brought out all the seriously wounded and the commanding officer." Schilt used an O2U Corsair biplane that did not have brakes. To stop him after a landing, said Schilt, Marines on the ground grabbed on to the wings. "One time they stopped one [at] the precipice, a 2,000 foot drop. On takeoff they'd have two men on each wing and they'd hold it back while I revved up the engine and would signal them to let go." During these moments on the ground, snipers took potshots at the plane, holing it on several occasions. Schilt's feats brought him a Medal of Honor.

Samuel S. Jack, born in 1905 on an Arizona ranch, applied to the Naval Academy "looking for an education." He enjoyed his four years in Annapolis but during summer cruises suffered bouts of seasickness. From the Class of 1927, Jack became one of twenty-six graduates to choose service in the Marine Corps. While in the first weeks of flight school Jack was pulled out for a tour in Nicaragua, but he returned to Pensacola to complete his training. "Of the 16 that began with me," said Jack, "eight got wings, four of whom were killed within four years."

He flew O2U planes in Nicaragua. "Navy castoffs," said Jack, a complaint that lasted well into World War II. His duties in Central America often involved scouting for the bandits or searching for leatherneck ground patrols that had lost contact with headquarters. Because of the thick vegetation the hunters flew as close to the ground as possible, sometimes barely skimming trees that stuck up 100 to 150 feet. The aircraft communicated with friendly ground forces by dropping notes to them.

Jack often found his efforts frustrated by the erratic functioning of weapons. Poor synchronization caused forward machine guns to bite into propellers. When he discovered an enemy pack train moving out, he unloosed his small bomb load. "I think out of the nine I dropped, eight were duds. That wasn't very effective, and my gunnery sergeant [in the observer seat] got off about one round with the Lewis gun and it jammed. In clearing the thing he dropped [a part] over the side." Jack drew one small satisfaction: "By diving on the pack train we got the mules scattered."

Frank Croft, a 1923 academy graduate, said, "After the summer cruise, I decided I did not like the Navy. I was put on report day after day because the Navy did not look kindly on my request for Marine duty." Croft admitted he was something of a nonconformist, even being arrested after a night of carousing following receipt of his commission. Fortunately for him he faced a friendly judge advocate who apparently honored a precept from the period: "You know you're not a true Marine until you've had a general court-martial and a dose of gonorrhea."

He arrived in Nicaragua in 1931 as a member of VM-3. The squadron flew amphibians, capable of setting down on rivers and small fields. "Many times we'd haul five Nicaraguan soldiers, standing up, in one of those amphibs. They had to stand because there wasn't room otherwise because they had their rifles and their packs. Those planes got airborne at 75 knots and top speed was about 80 knots." With no air-to-air radio, Croft explained, "We carried a little blackboard in the cockpit. We always went in two planes—never single—in case one had a forced landing or was shot down. To communicate back and forth, you took this little blackboard and you wrote a message in chalk on it and then you'd fly up alongside the other plane and hold the board outside of the fuselage. Then the other fellow would answer you."

On one flight in a Curtiss F8C-1, Croft, accompanied by another plane, tossed a payroll off at an appointed site and then continued toward a field near Quilali to pick up a wounded member of the native Nicaraguan forces. "I had never been there, had never seen it. [I] had to go in a very narrow canyon, no other way to approach; otherwise you went over a tremendous precipice. I went in downwind, crossed a bridge in a creek in the middle of the field, saw the end of the field coming, so I ground looped and stopped.

"I loaded up this wounded man, had them hold my wings at the end of the grass strip and I got off and back to Managua. That

F8C-1 was so underpowered that it could barely get off the ground under any condition. I never knew they were shooting at me from both sides." Later, Croft learned that this was the same place where Christian Schilt earned his Medal of Honor for performing the same feat, although Schilt's mission required ten trips.

Frank H. Schwable, son of a career Marine officer who had served during the Boxer Rebellion in China and the Philippine Insurrection, spent some of his boyhood years in Santo Domingo, where in 1918 his father was on duty. "Senior officers had orderlies. An orderly had a tent and lived right in our backyard. I used to go out and roughhouse with those guys. They taught me how to field strip a rifle and pistol, the .45, and how to clean them, how to hold them, how to handle them, how to aim—everything excepting how to shoot.

"They also taught me, through observing them, spit and polish. They were always shining the brass buttons and Dad's shoes and boots. They really instilled me with the spirit of spit and polish, the Marine Corps pride in your uniform, pride in the outfit. I was born a Marine and I knew I was going to be a Marine." A posting for his father to Philadelphia enabled the youth to tour the Navy yard there, where he became familiar with ships. He frequently visited the naval aircraft factory. "They were experimenting with arresting gear for carriers. They had an automobile with a hook drive up the road, and they would have wires across, very much like they do with current arresting gear, with sandbags all lined up in the road. The farther you went, the more sandbags you picked up until you finally stopped. They had one of the early catapults out on the dock and were experimenting shooting airplanes off the catapult.

"[This] is where I got my first ride in an airplane. I hung out, I guess about a year and a half in the factories. I was there with my tongue hanging out, dying for a ride. Finally some officer [Al Williams, a Navy pilot specializing in experimental work and air races] gave up and offered me a ride in an airplane. Of course I had to get clearance from my family in case of an accident and the family [said,] 'Uh, uh, no soap.' I got them to promise me if I ever got another offer that they would sign it. About six months later, Williams offered me a ride. Mother and Dad signed and that was in one of those seaplanes, a Curtiss F.5L. They put me right up in the very nose. I'll never forget the sensations of flying but I didn't see anything because I didn't have a helmet, I didn't have any goggles and the wind was coming in my eyes. I remember the sensations of taxiing, taking off, flying, landing. I was an aviator from then on. I was sold."

Schwable entered the Naval Academy, graduating in 1929 as a second lieutenant in the Marines. He pinned on wings in 1931, embarking for Nicaragua in 1932. During his tour there he received the Nicaraguan Cross of Valor for meritorious service in attacks on armed bandits and helping ground troops search for survivors of crashes in the jungle. "I dropped a few bombs and fired a machine gun a few times," remarked Schwable, "but you could never see the bandits."

Some Marine fliers became casualties of these small wars. The Sandinistas captured, tortured, and murdered two of them; several others fell victim to noncombat crashes. At the same time, the aviators expanded their responsibilities by establishing air transport units that hauled cargo in the Corsairs, De Havillands, and trimotor Fokkers.

During the late 1920s, in the Far East, Marines flew mostly reconnaissance missions in the vicinity of Tientsin while below, warlords, Communist forces, and a government under Chiang Kai-shek battled for control of China. Tommy Turner's reign as aviation commandant ended abruptly in 1931 when he impetuously rushed to inspect damage to a new amphibian after its left wheel sank into soft sand. He walked into a still-spinning propeller. Roy S. Geiger, Marine Aviator No. 5, a veteran of the World War I experience in France, replaced him.

In one respect the tiny Marine aviation units between the world wars gained an advantage over their contemporaries in the other branches of the armed forces. They accrued some battlefield knowledge dealing with ground support and bombing during their missions overseas. However, they remained as ignorant of air-to-air combat as other U.S. fliers.

A signal influence upon the future of Marine aviation came with the 1933 establishment of the Fleet Marine Force assigned to seize bases for naval operations. That assignment lifted the Marines out of the traditional duty of firefighters dispatched on an emergency basis to trouble sites and provided a mission that dominated World War II activities. With the ground forces committed to amphibious assaults, the airmen would concentrate upon preinvasion bombardment and tactical support for the landing teams. The new policy enunciated a secondary mission for the Marines: replacement squadrons for carrier-based naval aircraft. During the 1930s, Marine fliers qualified as carrier pilots. At some point in World War II, however, the Marine command made the mistake of abandoning carrier training, forcing the fliers to depend upon land bases. That would limit their role until late in the war when the policy changed.

A stepchild in the past, the air arm was given a somewhat more independent status within the corps upon the creation of the Fleet Marine Force. However, the Navy continued to be the source for aircraft and equipment, an arrangement that often meant Marines received second-best stuff the Navy no longer deemed desirable or else what was available after the parent service had filled its needs.

When he returned from Nicaragua for stateside duty, Frank Schwable participated in exercises designed to meet the mission of support for the Fleet Landing Force. From the airfield at Quantico he practiced dive-bombing on the Potomac River while landing craft chugged through a smokescreen. He engaged in maneuvers at the islands of Culebra and Vieques during experiments with amphibious landings. Late in November 1941, after a stint in the Aeronautics Division's Plans Section, designated a naval observer, he traveled to Cairo and London. He had just left Singapore, bound for Karachi, when the Japanese attacked Pearl Harbor.

In one of its more singular bounces, football brought Harold William Bauer into the Marine Corps and aviation. From a family of three sons and two daughters born to German immigrants, Bauer grew up in Kansas and then Nebraska, where his father held the job of railroad station agent. As a high school student Bauer starred in football, track, and basketball. Only the third alternate candidate from his congressional district, in 1926, Bauer still entered the U.S. Naval Academy. (His two younger brothers followed him to Annapolis.)

As a plebe he combined his athletic talent with sufficient scholarship to stand 56th in a class of 528. In the varsity backfield during the following years, Bauer, a six-foot two-hundred-pounder, ran, passed, drop-kicked, and blocked for a highly regarded squad. But as he realized that his indulgence in sports had begun to erode his grades, Bauer dropped basketball and lacrosse. He also earned some nicknames. At the academy he regularly attended chapel led by a minister informally christened "Holy Joe," and midshipmen referred to Bauer as "another Holy Joe." He added to the lore by telling associates that he owed his square jaw and dark complexion to his Native American blood. "Holy Joe" became "Indian Joe," perhaps a tribute to Mark Twain's fictional character. Newspaper accounts of a football game against the University of Pennsylvania called him "Indian Joe Bauer," but in later years the ethnic reference disappeared, and even to his family he became simply Joe Bauer.

When he graduated in 1930, Bauer allegedly chose a second lieutenant's commission in the Marines because he believed that might improve his opportunities to play football. He was correct; after his basic officer training he received an assignment to Quantico, Virginia, where he played on the corps team. He spent two springs at Annapolis assisting as a coach for basketball and lacrosse.

Married in 1932 to Harriette Hemman, Bauer applied for aviation training and qualified for his wings in 1935. Early on he demonstrated great skill as a fighter pilot, instructor, and tactician. Inevitably he received a promotion to a responsible position, becoming executive officer of VMF-221. He and the squadron were preparing to ship out from San Diego for overseas duty on December 7, 1941.

Among the small contingent of Marine pilots in the 1930s was Bob Galer. Son of a Seattle fire captain, Galer, born in 1913, attended the University of Washington. An all-American basketball player, he enrolled in the Navy's Reserve Officers Training Program because "I thought it was the best-looking operation at the university." He said he first considered aviation a career after Charles A. Lindbergh, in 1927, completed the first successful solo nonstop flight across the Atlantic.

Galer's years in college coincided with the depths of the Great Depression. "The maritime union struck," he recalled, "and broke the city of Seattle. My dad was supporting three sons in school and they paid him in scrip that was only good for food and a few other things. We never had any money. We all turned out to be strikebreakers. We took jobs on the docks." The Galer boys supplemented their income by managing fraternities. "We had to join different ones [to get] free room and board."

Galer took his degree in industrial engineering in 1935, and his basketball talent helped enlist him in the Marines. "The Marine major in charge [of the ROTC unit] was trying to recruit me to come to Quantico to play basketball. He was talking about a regular commission, and I checked it out to find out when I could start to fly. With a regular commission, you'd have to wait about two years. But at the same time, the Army colonel from the ROTC had a son whom he thought he'd get a regular commission. But his son got turned down. He [the colonel] asked if there was any way he could get his son a regular commission. A Marine at headquarters said, 'There's one possibility. A guy named Galer who's been lined up also put in for flying.' " The upshot was a trade-off that made the colonel's son a second lieutenant while Galer became an aviation cadet.

He soloed in the open-cockpit "Yellow Peril" biplane at Sand Point, Washington, before moving on to Pensacola, where the instruction qualified him in seaplanes, amphibians, dive-bombers, and fighters. (Among Galer's "running mates" at Pensacola was another University of Washington alum, Gregory "Pappy" Boyington, who would achieve fame and notoriety during the war.) Halfway through the course Galer grabbed an opportunity for a regular commission, which entitled him to live in officers' quarters rather than the cadet barracks.

From Pensacola he headed to Quantico, where the question of whether he would pilot a dive-bomber or a fighter arose. Galer said he preferred to fly a fighter because "it flew faster and you could play better." According to Galer, "Theoretically, to get into fighters, you had to play polo. I told them I could play polo if necessary and I got into fighters. Then I went to the first polo practice and they understood that I had never played." The squadron commander, Tex Rogers, allowed Galer to continue in the cockpit of the F4B-4, a Boeing-manufactured biplane.

The squadron regularly appeared at air shows, and Rogers led them in nonreg stunts known as hotdogging. The squadron commander happened to be courting a young woman who lived near Quantico. "We'd take nine airplanes," recalled Galer, "be up practicing for an air show, and end up flying between her house and the barn." At this time Marine fliers still learned how to take off and land on carriers. Galer and his mates eventually qualified in that skill at San Diego. Moreover, adhering to the doctrine that every Marine should be versed in the arts of an infantryman, the aviators put in time at the rifle range.

After a tour in the Caribbean that involved working with amphibians as well as fighters, Galer, in February 1941, joined VMF-2 at the Ewa base on Oahu in the Hawaiian Islands. "We flew Brewster Buffalos [F2A-3s]. It was a dog. It was not a popular plane but we all had them. We chased the Army Air Corps [simulated dogfights] and did night work."

Among the ground crews servicing the Ewa-based aircraft was Kentucky native Strimple C. Coyle, known to his friends as Jim. "My father," said Coyle, "was station master for the railroad in the little town of Reeseville, Texas and then became a telegrapher for an oil company. I was born at Una, Texas, July 31, 1920. We moved to Fort Natchez and lived well; my father would rent a limousine for a drive. But he died when I was nine and by 1929 the family was desperately poor. We were so poor when [the] Depression began we didn't even know there was a Depression."

To survive in the depths of poverty, Coyle shuttled from one family to another, dropped out of school in the ninth grade, and at seventeen enrolled in the Civilian Conservation Corps (CCC), a government program that housed, fed, and paid young men who worked to build the country's infrastructure. "I was in heaven in the CCC," said Coyle. "It was a way out for me." He tried to return to his Texas roots and resume his schooling but gave it up. "I saw a poster saying 'Join the Marines, See the World.' I filled out a card, and in 1939 was sworn into the Corps."

Following boot camp in San Diego, he became part of the Aviation Detachment stationed at North Island. Through the Marines, he took courses enabling him to acquire his high school equivalency and even some college credits. Orders assigned him to the fighter squadron VMF-2, which included Bob Galer, Pappy Boyington, and Captain Henry "Baron" Elrod, among others.

Coyle recalled his first experience aboard an aircraft carrier. "We were having carrier qualifications for our pilots on the *Saratoga*. I was 'an airplane pusher,' working on the flight deck. They would take off from the stern flying forward. When they came back in, they would land and keep the engines running. We'd push them forward as far toward the bow as we could, until all planes had landed and then push them back to the stern to prepare for next take. They also had elevators take a plane down into the bowels of the ship for work.

"Captain Elrod was a section flight leader. As his three planes came in, we pushed the first two into slots, into the center and starboard. I was on side of deck next to the edge and when Elrod's plane came he was to be pushed to the port side. Elrod was very rough on his airplanes; he'd gun it, then jerk it around. His tail wheel caught in a little drainage gutter. I was trapped between the wing and edge of deck of the *Saratoga*. Instead of being patient and allowing us to lift the plane out of the rain gutter, he gave it full power. He blew me off the deck of the carrier. It was about 50 feet down to the water but there were nets spaced [alongside] and fortunately he blew me into a net. All I had to do was climb back up on deck.

"In January, 1941, our squadron transferred to Ewa Mooring Mast near Pearl Harbor. Ewa Mooring Mast had previously been used for Navy blimps on sea patrol. [When we arrived] there was not much there, coral, sisal plants and a small strip. Over a period of time we developed that into operational field. We had many accidents in those days. In June, 1941, Major Fife was leading a training flight from Ewa to a Maui air base. Flying at about 9,000 feet, at night, dark, as they approached Maui, Fife lost visual contact with leading elements of flight because they entered an overcast, I believe Major Putnam was CO at that time. He was leading the flight. They became separated and were unable to make contact again. First Lieutenant William Faris, Second Lieutenant Werner Hagemann Jr., Second Lieutenant Clyde Story were lost when they didn't return with the flight.

"Not long after that we were given Brewster Buffalos. The pilots had a really bad time of it trying to fly that thing. We had three planes in front of the ordnance shack while one of our pilots was coming in for a landing, doing what we call bumper drills, preparing for carrier qualification. He lost control of his plane, crashed into two or three Brewster Buffalos sitting out in front of the ordnance shop and which mechanics were working on. I lost several of my buddies. They were burned to death."

James G. Law, born in Brooklyn, New York, in 1920, grew up in poverty. "My father left us when I was about four years old. He was a World War I vet and was disabled by mustard gas in France." At sixteen Law had graduated from high school, working part time to help support the family, and he learned a bit about auto mechanics and plumbing from a relative. After a year on a shipping department job, paid twelve dollars for a six-day week, he enlisted in the First Marine Corps Reserve Battalion. "I participated in weekly drill periods with the Marine Corps Reserve and two weeks each year at Quantico, Virginia Marine Base. The pay for a private was $21 per month with 20 cents taken out for medical care. For each Reserve drill night, we received 70 cents (no taxes or Social Security were deducted)." When he achieved the rank of private first class, his pay went up to a dollar a day for drills.

In November 1940 President Franklin D. Roosevelt declared a period of national emergency, and a number of National Guard and Reserve units were ordered to active duty. The outfit that included Law received its orders to report. After two months of field training at Quantico, he sailed to Guantanamo Bay, Cuba. "I was assigned as a squad leader and as we marched along dusty roads, up and down hills and maneuvered through the fields, I kept watching the Marine aircraft in the air above us, and I wished I could be up there."

He applied for a transfer to aviation duty, a request that sat poorly with his first sergeant, who stuck him with thirty days of mess duty. When he finished that stint, he again sought assignment to aviation. That earned him another month in kitchens until the top kick finally relented and helped him draft an application. When it was approved, Law checked in with the First Marine Air Group's Headquarters and Service Squadron.

"I was excited to be around Marine aircraft, even though most of them appeared to be obsolete. Many of them were fabric covered bi-planes." Still, he learned to repair hydraulic cylinders, controls, and brakes, how to splice steel cables, and other tasks. By the summer of 1941 the corps had begun to receive new planes—Grumman F4F Wildcat fighters and Douglas SBD Dauntless dive-bombers. By July 1941, with the influx of more and more recruits, Law made sergeant.

"There were many signs that the days of peace were running out. We were ordered to give all our aircraft, which were bright aluminum, a coat of camouflage paint. The top half of the planes were painted dark blue to make them less visible from above when flying over water. The lower half were light grey to blend in with the sky. We also installed self-sealing fuel tanks in many of the planes. Another safety feature to protect pilots was the installation of armor plates around the pilot's cockpit. We had a big holiday meal on Thanksgiving in November. Things were quiet but we had the feeling that it would not be for long, as we listened to the news broadcasts on the radio."

That ominous sense seemed not to have permeated the atmosphere in Hawaii. While diplomatic relations with Japan deteriorated toward the end of the year, Galer saw no changes in the Ewa routines. "There was practically no mention of trouble with Japan." Noting that the aircraft were all lined up, wingtip-to-wingtip, on the Saturday before the Pearl Harbor attack, Galer remarked that there was no suggestion they should be scattered. Nor was there any discussion about the quality of Japanese planes or pilots. "The first lieutenants weren't advised. We were too busy chasing girls and playing."

Jim Coyle, however, said he was more aware of the gathering storm. "I knew we would be at war with Japan. We were already fighting in the Atlantic with submarines [U.S. Navy warships were escorting convoys to England]. We had war games. We knew it was going to happen. It was common talk."

Under the charter promulgated in 1933, Marine aviation slowly expanded, although Congress during the Great Depression kept the armed forces on a sparse diet of appropriations. By the end of 1941 the qualified pilots numbered 425 and the World War I Jennies composed of wood and fabric had given way to single-winged, all-metal fighters and bombers. On the other hand, dependent upon the Navy for its equipment, the Marines would begin World War II relying on the obsolete and highly vulnerable Brewster Buffalo. Navy pilots climbed into the cockpits of F4F Grumman Wildcats, far superior planes although weaker in some respects than the Japanese opposition. The Marines had a single advantage over both their colleagues in the Navy and Army. Between the world wars they alone had flown under conditions that resembled one type of combat: attacking targets on the ground, strafing, bombing, and dealing with fire from below. To be sure, no Americans, except a handful of volunteers enrolled in the RAF, engaged in aerial combat or against an enemy with sophisticated antiaircraft.

TWO

PEARL HARBOR AND WAKE ISLAND

In his book *Devilbirds*, Marine Corps combat correspondent John De Chant reported that on December 7, 1941, "In a cottage at the abrupt little Ewa Beach on the western shore of Oahu, Captain Dick Mangrum, a Marine dive-bomber pilot, thumbed through the comic strips of the Honolulu paper. He shrugged off the muted sounds of machine-gun firing. The Fleet was always holding some kind of light-weapons exercise. Strange, though, that this one was so early on a Sunday morning. Then bomb explosions mingled with the soft, distant snapping of the gunfire. Thinking how damned odd that was, Mangrum looked out and saw a tight formation of planes flying low along the beach, right past his front door in the direction of Pearl Harbor. They had bright-red meatballs on their wings."

When the Japanese attacked, VMF-2 had been redesignated as VMF-211 with the squadron located in three different places: Ewa, Wake, and Midway islands. The Ewa complement consisted of six officers and forty-seven enlisted men, manning ten F4F-3s—early versions of the Grumman Wildcat—and one SNJ-3, a Texan trainer. At the Wake Island Group eleven officers and sixteen enlisted men operated twelve F4F-3s. The Midway Group of seventeen officers and eighty-two enlisted men had not yet received their planes.

Bob Galer, as a fighter pilot with VMF-2, part of Marine Air Group (MAG) Twenty-one, had spent ten months at Ewa flying an F2A-3 Brewster Buffalo in training exercises. "On the night of December 6," recalled Galer, "I went to a party at a big house. Two of us stayed there on Saturday night to play golf the following day. On Sunday morning we had a Bloody Mary, and we were out on the lanai, and *Bingo!* The war started.

"We were overlooking Pearl Harbor. We could see the bombs, and three minutes after it started we knew it was the Japs because they came by with the red ball painted on the sides. We took off for Ewa, and as we went by Pearl City, they strafed everything. Trying to dodge, we drove into a cane field and got stuck. We commandeered a taxi and reached Ewa. There was very little damage there, other than to all of the airplanes. We didn't have one operational plane."

Jim Coyle, a corporal in the Ordnance Section, remembered, "That Sunday morning most of our people were on liberty after being paid on Friday. I had duty that weekend and was standing out in front of the barracks when a buddy, named Smits, and I first saw the aircraft flying overhead. We saw them going toward Pearl Harbor, and the next thing they were all over us. We thought it was the Army on maneuvers, coming in low, firing their guns. We thought it was fake ammunition, blanks, but they dropped some small bombs, 100 pound bombs that exploded on the field. They were firing at people coming out of barracks.

"Sisal plants surrounded the field. When the bullets hit the sisal plants, it sounded like gunfire all over again. They were strafing the barracks and strafing us. My buddy and I said, what is that? Look at those red fireballs on the fuselage and on wings, red ball on rudder, red stripes around the fuselage. They were coming in so low, we could see the Japs. The gunners were just grinning at us while firing at us.

"We finally got the message. We ran into the barracks and got our rifles. But a few weeks before our personal ammunition was taken away from us and they took the ammunition out of the guns in planes. They put it all in an ammo dump behind barbed wire across the field. We ran over to the guard tent at the gate. They had two boxes of bandoliers of ammunition, they gave us one, we went back, found a hole in the coral and got in and began firing at Japanese as they came over.

"No one seemed to be in control, most of our officers were on liberty except those with specific duties. Smits and I decided to go down to the end of the runway in case they tried to land parachute troops. That's where we were when the second attack began. We said, when they come in, take one shot each, as everyone comes across. We were very methodical, I guess we had pretty good training.

"I heard that Mrs. Elrod [the wife of Captain Henry Elrod, who nearly blew Coyle into the sea] lived at Pearl City. Capt. Elrod was now with a detachment on Wake Island. Mrs. Elrod was the daughter of the Navy captain or admiral, and when she met Hank he was an enlisted man in the Marine Corps. They fell in love and got married. Hank became an officer and a pilot. She was a very special lady. She came to the base to find out what was happening. She was parked at the gate, ran to her car, took out a .45 automatic, stood in middle of the street, firing at those Japanese planes."

Just as at the Army's Hickham and Wheeler fields, all of the Marine planes had been parked wingtip-to-wingtip, providing easy targets for the raiders. Confirming Coyle's sense of chaos, Galer said, "We were running around like chickens with their heads cut off. We came through the gate and we were issued rifles and told to get where they were building a swimming pool. There was a hole and there were about a dozen Marines in there. We'd shoot volleys at the strafers coming by."

Richard Mangrum described the Pearl Harbor raids that cost his squadron just about all of their aircraft as "a real first-class strafing attack. . . .We were all extremely angry at the time. We felt that war was imminent and an acute sense of embarrassment that we were caught literally with our pants at half mast. I think many of us had a whole admiration, not a grudging one, for the professionalism of the Japanese force and a rather complete amazement that they were as effective as they were. Our knowledge was sketchy of the Japanese, and I supposed in the junior ranks we reflected much of the general popular opinion that by no means could the Japanese be as efficient as we nor could they carry out operations of that nature with the tremendous effectiveness that they did."

So with this rude awakening to the realities of the Japanese strength, as pilots, navigators, aerial gunners, and radiomen plugged away at the marauders with Springfield '03 rifles in Hawaii, began the introduction of Marine Corps aviation to World War II. By the time the first wave of Japanese carriers disappeared, Marine Air Group Twenty-one commander Lieutenant Colonel Claude A. "Sheriff" Larkin not only had no more flyable planes but also nursed shrapnel wounds in both legs and one hand. Some ten to fifteen minutes later about thirty Aichi Vals, dive-bombers, swooped down upon Ewa and—with the U.S. aircraft obviously demolished—bombed the buildings and sprayed machine-gun bullets at Marines scurrying for cover or attempting to defend their turf.

Master Technical Sergeant Emil Peters and Private William Turner manned a .30-caliber machine gun in a parked, wrecked dive-bomber. A burst into the belly of one Val skimming the field drew smoke, and the plane crashed beyond the runway. Other attackers retaliated against the pair in the SBD, and the torrent of bullets fatally wounded Turner. A third and final run by enemy fighters doused Ewa with their machine guns, killing a sergeant shooting at them with a rifle. As the last of the Japanese disappeared, Larkin counted three dead, one dying, and thirteen wounded. Of his forty-eight assorted fighters, dive-bombers, and utility planes, he had only a single transport, temporarily at Ford Island for repairs, not totally wrecked or severely damaged.

The destruction of Marine aviation might have been even worse had not some thirty-two fighters and bombers—including a dozen new F4F-3 Grumman Wildcat fighters—traveled to Wake Island's narrow airstrip, with fourteen Brewster Buffalos ferried by the carrier *Saratoga* to further strengthen that outpost. In addition, the *Lexington* bound for Midway Island bore eighteen of VMSB-231's dive-bombers. Combined with aircraft still stationed in the continental United States following the opening salvos of World War II, Marine aviation possessed a paltry force of some 150 planes.

At Quantico, Virginia's, Turner airfield, Jim Law recalled lying on his bunk, listening to a football game on the radio. Soon he and three other Marines would meet "four young ladies who lived in an apartment in D.C. We were promised a super home cooked meal and then a party.

"All of a sudden, the game broadcast was interrupted with the announcement that the naval base at Pearl Harbor had been bombed by the Japanese Navy. I bounced off my bunk, hardly believing what I had just heard. Word spread through the barracks like wildfire. Although we knew we were preparing for war, we didn't expect it to happen like this.

"In less than five minutes, a bugler sounded general quarters and assembly. We fell into formation in front of the barracks. The duty officer of the day made the short announcement which I will always remember. He said, 'Gentlemen, we are at war— you will govern yourself [sic] accordingly. You will all report immediately to your duty stations.' We were out of our civilian clothes, into our working uniforms and on the flight line in a couple of minutes.

"In spite of what had just happened a few minutes ago, everything seemed to be well organized. We were ordered to start the engines on all aircraft that were in operating condition. They were all quickly taxied or towed and dispersed over the whole field. Planes were always kept fueled, but we topped off all the fuel tanks. Roving teams of two-man armed guards covered the field, circling the parked aircraft.

"Reports kept coming on the radio about the damage and casualties in Hawaii. We all knew that this is what we had been training for—we just didn't think it would happen this way. But we were angry and raring to go.

"The First Marine Air Wing was ready to go. All the wooden crates and boxes that we had for shipping tools, equipment, generators, etc. had been saved and were ready to be packed. They were all marked and identified as to squadron and also what was in the boxes. During the night of 7 December 1941, these boxes were brought out of the warehouses that they were stored in and stacked next to the hangars. We didn't know where we might be going but we assumed it would be some place and soon."

During the first days and weeks after the bombing, extreme

frustration gripped Marine pilots like Galer who had no flyable airplanes. "We were kind of helpless. Every man I knew wanted to get a shot at the bastards," he said. But for the moment he and the others in Marine aviation met for briefings and concentrated on improving their skills as foot soldiers, learning to dig better trenches and sharpen their aim with rifles.

Joe Bauer re-created his memories of the days leading up to Pearl Harbor and immediately after in what became his war diary. ". . . we never doubted a minute that we would eventually be at war with somebody, but somehow we felt that it just couldn't happen till the summer of '42. We also felt quite certain that we were going to be allowed to be with our families [he had both a wife and a young son] for several more months before any emergency might arise to drag us away. The USS *Saratoga* was scheduled to leave San Diego for Honolulu about 9 Dec. And so far we were not included on her passenger list.

"About that time, the lid blew off! We received orders to go to Honolulu on 8 Dec. aboard the USS *Saratoga*. That gave us exactly one week to get our personal affairs squared away, get our squadron gear together and get packed. It was a very hectic week, I can assure and as you no doubt remember was climaxed by the news that Japan made a surprise attack on Oahu."

The devastation at Pearl Harbor stunned Bauer. "Imagine seeing 6 or 8 battleships either capsized or sitting neatly on the bottom of the harbor, 2 or 3 cruisers in the same fix, destroyers and other ships destroyed, hangars burned and airplane remains littered about like a junk heap."

For other Marine aviators, however, the assault upon Pearl Harbor was only a prelude to their confrontation with the Japanese. Guam, encircled by the other Mariana Islands with Japanese bases on them, fell swiftly on December 9 and 10. As the Imperial forces began to overwhelm the defenses in the Philippines, tiny Wake Island, named for a British sea captain from the eighteenth century, two thousand miles due west of Honolulu and one of the farthest outposts of the United States in the Pacific, awaited its turn. Pan American Airways, which in 1935 inaugurated its China Clipper service, had secured rights to use Wake as one of its sites for landing, refueling, and even temporarily housing passengers. Simultaneously, alongside construction crews for the airline, the U.S. Navy began to convert Wake into an island bastion.

Unlike Guam, surrounded by Japanese-held islands, Wake stood in total isolation, nearly a thousand miles from its nearest neighbor. The theory behind the decision to fortify and defend Wake, enunciated by Admiral Husband E. Kimmel, Commander in Chief, Pacific, from his Pearl Harbor headquarters, held that Wake was key to any attempt by the Japanese to expand eastward into the Pacific. A stout defense of Wake would force the Japanese to commit substantial assets, exposing their ships to the American fleet. What Kimmel and his like-minded strategists had not taken into account was the catastrophic destruction on December 7 that befell the U.S. Pacific Fleet. There was no armada to sally forth against a Nipponese thrust.

Army troops, the remnants of a Marine battalion evacuated from China, small elements of the Asiatic fleet, and Air Corps personnel defended the Philippines. Wake, actually the largest of a coral atoll that included Wilkes and Peale islands, at the start of December 1941 hosted a Marine garrison of about four hundred; a seventy-five-man Navy contingent, mostly to service the naval air station; and almost twelve hundred civilian workers hired to construct the facilities for Pan Am and fortifications. Captain Henry S. Wilson supervised a five-man team from the Army, operating an Army communications radio van that would assist B-17s traveling to the Philippines.

Arriving at Wake on December 4, having taken off from the carrier *Enterprise*, were twelve F4F-3 Wildcats, the newest fighter additions to the arsenal that belonged to Marine aviation's VMF-211. Although far more effective machines than the pitiful Buffalos, the first Wildcats had neither protective armor for the pilots nor self-sealing gas tanks. The bomb racks did not accommodate the ordnance at Wake. Identification Friend or Foe (IFF) devices had not yet been installed, and Wake itself lacked radar. The Grumman fighter was equipped only with a mechanical system for raising or lowering its landing gear. Pilots cranked a chain mechanism with one hand while controlling the stick with the other. Wildcats also posed an inherent problem when land-based. The high, narrow-tracked gear elevated the wing, making the aircraft vulnerable to crosswinds during takeoffs and landings. As a result, pilots, particularly inexperienced ones, coped with a tendency to ground loop. Aircraft carriers limited this problem by turning in an appropriate direction when launching or receiving their planes.

Furthermore, none of the fliers on Wake had more than thirty hours of experience in the F4F-3. The narrow strip hacked into the coral and scrub and could accommodate only one takeoff at a time. Revetments or shelter for planes remained on the drawing board. The initial forty-seven ground crewmen brought to Wake included only two airplane and engineer mechanics; the remainder specialized in ordnance.

In the first days after VMF-211 touched down at Wake, Major Paul Putnam, the CO, dispatched his fliers on patrols and practice bombing and strafing runs. Major Walter Bayler, with the Marine unit establishing the air base, wrote a note to his wife on Sunday, December 7 (Wake is on the western side of the International Date Line from Hawaii) remarking, "It's a beautiful spot. . . . and so utterly peaceful."

On December 8 at 6:30 A.M. on Wake, the Army's Captain Wilson telephoned the airfield radio trailer. John De Chant reported the sergeant on duty as mumbling, "I can't believe what I'm hearing" while he held the earphones to the mouth of the phone. Wilson listened to a Morse code transmission from Hawaii—"SOS. SOS. Japs attacking Oahu. This is the real thing. Hickham Field and Pearl Harbor under attack," ending with the tocsin, "This is no drill!" Bill Sloan, who interviewed the Army radioman Sergeant Ernest Rogers for his book *Given Up for Dead*, said Rogers hopped into a motorcycle sidecar; the driver brought him to Wilson with the message. A sailor on duty at the Wake Navy radio shack copied a similar report from Pearl Harbor.

Wilson alerted the Marine commandant, Major James P. Devereux, and the entire garrison scrambled for their duty stations. Putnam put up a flight of four Wildcats, led by Captain Henry

"Baron" Elrod, which roamed a southern sector until their gas ran low and another echelon of four replaced them in the sky. A Pan Am Clipper, having taken off at dawn for Guam, was recalled, and its pilot agreed to help search the area. None of the Wake aviators saw anything untoward.

Just before noon, however, the men on Wake heard the roar of multiple motors. Out of a rain squall came two dozen aircraft, dead-on for the island. At three thousand feet they crossed the reef that girded Wake and systematically pounded the atoll. The deluge of bombs and the hail of machine-gun bullets killed or wounded seven pilots and twenty-one of the ground crew, wiping out seven of the Wildcats on the ground and damaging one. Gas dumps erupted in flames, and the raid wrecked the meager repair sheds. Elrod's air patrol landed, having fruitlessly searched a sector that did not cover the bombers' route. One F4F-3 struck debris, damaging the propeller. Wake's air force now numbered only four planes.

Putnam and Bayler studied their maps and concluded that the marauders took off from the Marshall Islands. They plotted the most likely time and direction for the next waves. On Tuesday, December 9, Elrod and three others attempted to engage twenty-seven twin-engine Mitsubishi Nell bombers. Technical Sergeant William J. Hamilton, one of two enlisted pilots, in tandem with Lieutenant Dave Kliewer dove on a nine-plane element. The Marines slashed through the formation spraying .50-caliber bullets, but the Nells stolidly droned on course. The Grummans wheeled, tearing through the enemy a second time and then a third. One bomber started to wobble and burn. Hamilton and Kliewer poured more bullets into the bomber, which crashed into the sea. This first knockdown by Marine fighters, however, did not seriously interfere with the attack, which blasted buildings, anti-aircraft positions, and even the well-marked hospital. The raiders killed or wounded dozens from the Marine garrison and the civilian workforce.

The Japanese struck again on December 10, arriving right on the schedule predicted by Major Putnam, showing up just before 11:00 A.M. They devastated Wilkes Island, igniting a monster explosion in the construction team's dynamite stores, which in turn blew up much of the antiaircraft and coastal battery ammunition cached on Wilkes. On this occasion Henry Elrod, diving upon the bombers, scored two kills.

The inevitable surfaced the following day. Before dawn, lookouts peering seaward from the Wake beaches with binoculars picked out faint blinks of light and some indistinct shapes. Devereux, who knew no U.S. task force could be in the vicinity, squinted into the darkness with night glasses, and he realized an invasion fleet was approaching his tiny enclave. A pair of Wildcats on reconnaissance reported fourteen ships, light cruisers, destroyers, smaller gunboats, and transports.

When the lead ships steamed within forty-five hundred yards of the shore, Wake's coastal guns greeted them. The cruiser *Yubari* reeled from four hits, and a battery on Wilkes put a shell into the destroyer *Hayate*, apparently detonating its fuel and ammunition and causing a huge fireball that killed every one of the 167 sailors. Two rounds damaged a second destroyer, another cruiser absorbed a hit on a turret, and the artillery heavily damaged or even sank one transport. The invaders scattered. A duel ensued between a single functioning gun on Peale and three destroyers, with the American gunners registering several hits before the Japanese broke off the engagement and joined a general retreat.

Out of range of the batteries on Wake, the Japanese were stunned to suddenly find themselves under attack by the four remaining Wildcats, each armed with two hundred-pound bombs— slung under the wings in a homemade rack devised by pilot Herb Freuler—and fully loaded .50-caliber machine guns. Although Japanese submarines had reported the presence of American combat aircraft, the Japanese strategists had not bothered to provide air cover for their ships. Putnam himself led three captains, Elrod, Freuler, and Frank "Duke" Tharin. Working together, Elrod and Tharin focused on the two cruisers, *Tenryu* and *Tatsuta*. They hit both vessels before hurrying back to the landing strip to be rearmed.

In the central command shack, Major Walter Bayler listened to the radio messages between the two pilots as they went after the destroyer *Kisaragi*. "Hey, Duke, see that big fat son of a bitch straight ahead?" Elrod asked Tharin.

"I see him," answered Tharin. "Let's get him."

After an interval during which Bayler heard the crackle of machine-gun fire, Elrod shouted, "You hit him, Duke. You hit him with your second. Look at the smoke!"

Tharin responded, "You didn't do so bad yourself. Your first one rattled his rivets." Actually, the pair made four round trips seeking to blast the destroyer. Only one of their bombs actually struck the destroyer. But it was enough. A fire belowdecks could not be contained despite desperate efforts by the crew to extinguish the blaze. Lieutenant John Kinney, who had relieved two of the Wildcat pilots, was about to start his bomb run on the *Kisaragi* when the destroyer's depth charges detonated, hurling fire, men, and debris into the air as it foundered.

Immediately after the remainder of the enemy flotilla scurried away, the report to the Pacific Fleet Command from the senior Wake officer, Navy Commander Winfield Scott Cunningham, carried the customary padding for coded messages: "SEND US STOP NOW IS THE TIME FOR ALL GOOD MEN TO COME TO THE AID OF THEIR PARTY CUNNINGHAM MORE JAPS . . ." Unfortunately the extraneous words included what author Sloan said was a private joke by the Navy radio officers. A public relations zealot instantly hailed the embattled Marines of Wake as requesting, "Send us more Japs." After the war Cunningham, who had very little to do with the actual defense, and Devereux vigorously denied ever desiring to see more of the enemy.

The first effort to vanquish Wake had been rebuffed, but the tiny Marine air arm was down to its last two planes. During Elrod's passes at the enemy ships, machine-gun bullets riddled his F4F-3. On his final flight, with an oil line severed, the Baron desperately headed back to Wake. His sputtering engine carried him only as far as a boulder-strewn beach where he crash-landed. Amazingly he survived without injury, but the plane was beyond repair. Herb Freuler, in his badly shot-up fighter, managed a deadstick landing on the airstrip, but the wounds to his engine rendered the aircraft unflyable.

The days of VMF-211 dwindled. Kliewer, scouring the offshore waters, claimed he caught an enemy submarine charging its batteries on the surface. He strafed the U-boat and dropped his bombs from so low an altitude that the explosions scorched his fuselage and shrapnel punctured his wings. The target submerged rapidly. Back on Wake, Kliewer informed Paul Putnam of the action, and the Marine commander took off to investigate. All he could find was a large oil slick. Whether Kliewer actually destroyed a sub was never confirmed, although the Japanese would later question captured Americans about a missing submarine.

Tharin, on a routine dusk patrol, came upon a lone four-engine Mavis bomber. It dropped its ordnance and then started a strafing run. Tharin dove on the Mavis and riddled it with .50-caliber bullets before the plane burst into flames and then crash-landed in the water. The Marine returned to Wake and picked up some bombs, intending to destroy the still-floating aircraft, but when he came back it had slid under the ocean.

The Japanese continued to hammer the island from the air. The Marines kept their two Wildcats going by cannibalizing parts from the wrecked planes. Freuler, although hobbled by diarrhea, devised a system for transferring oxygen from storage tanks, stored for construction projects, into the small bottles used by aviators. John Kinney and William Hamilton, when not in the air, helped rebuild engines and replace parts.

During one raid a bomb fell directly upon an unfinished revetment with its Grumman. As the enemy planes departed, Kinney and Hamilton with several others sprinted toward the burning Wildcat. Two men began unbolting the still-intact engine while others hurried up with a hoist to lift it free. Despite the intense heat from the blaze, they succeeded, and Kinney, driving a tractor, hauled the engine to one of the Wildcats that needed a new motor.

As early as December 10, Admiral Kimmel in Honolulu—recognizing the precarious status of Wake and its strategic value for retaining island bases at Midway, Palmyra, and Johnston—drafted a plan to resupply and reinforce Wake by means of a task force that would include an aircraft carrier. Ultimately, on December 15, Task Force Fourteen set out for Wake with the

Saratoga, bearing VMF-221 plus many Navy fighters, a small galaxy of destroyers, cruisers, and a seaplane tender packed with Marines. They could not reach Wake before December 23.

Joe Bauer with VMF-221 was under no illusions about the dire fate he faced. ". . . news we received upon landing at Pearl Harbor—namely that we were to go to Wake—sorta stunned me. I felt very sorry for the Marines at Wake and wanted to go to their aid but at the same time I could see the futility of it all. Wake would fall to the Japs whenever they wanted to make the necessary effort. It could not be protected by our surface vessels due to its distance from Pearl Harbor. We felt the Wake garrison should be evacuated rather than send more lambs to the slaughter. . . . We left Pearl Harbor aboard the USS *Saratoga* feeling that we were to be sacrificed but we were determined to do our bit for our country and were proud to be able to serve her even for such a small thing as Wake Island. The general frame of mind then was that we knew it was curtains but we felt a sense of pride in our position for being called on to aid the gallant defenders of Wake and were completely resigned to our fate."

So depressed was Bauer that on December 24 he wrote what he believed was a farewell, addressed "Dearest Little Family," which included his wife Harriette and Dolly, a sister who lived with them. ". . . I don't think there is much doubt that you and Billy [his son] will soon be on your own. Please don't take it too hard. Buckle down and face it as inevitable. . . . You might as well move to Waco until the war is over, and then do whatever you like. Try to get some sort of a job to keep yourself occupied. Raise Billy to be a man and not a Mama's boy. Make him earn money as soon as he is physically capable. That is very important!"

Bauer instructed his wife about changes of address, reminded her that she should "Take care of the insurance, and it will take care of you." He advised her to seek legal advice for settling problems and warned she should be careful "they do not take you for a ride. You have been the most wonderful little wife any man could ask for and have been forced to put up with a very disagreeable husband. Please forgive all of this as I really love you and Billy with all my heart. Dolly, you have had to put up with a lot of grief in your life due to certain fatal mistakes [unknown]. Do try to keep Harriette from making similar ones."

After asking the recipients to pass word to his parents on how much he loved them and convey his remembrances of others, he finished, "I only wish I could go to my grave knowing I had lived a more generous and serviceable life."

At the same time, the Japanese, bruised by the treatment of their first invasion fleet, organized a new task force that would reinforce the assault on Wake with a pair of carriers. The two task forces raced toward the objective, and the Japanese finished first. On December 21 their flattops had steamed to within two hundred miles northwest of the island, well within range of their fighters and dive-bombers. The American warships were still some six hundred miles east, too far to help the beleaguered. Whether Wake could have held out until Task Force Fourteen entered the battle became moot. President Franklin D. Roosevelt, in consultation with his Navy Secretary Frank Knox, had relieved Kimmel because of the disaster at Pearl Harbor. The temporary Pacific chief, Admiral William Pye, never sanguine about the Wake rescue mission, canceled the operation. To the great surprise and relief of Bauer, on Christmas Day, VMF-221 was dropped off at Midway Island to reinforce that garrison.

Actually, several days before Bauer had penned his final thoughts home, a new and final phase to the Wake Island saga debuted on December 22. Speedy fighters and dive-bombers from the Japanese carriers blasted the atoll, zooming by so fast that the ground gunners could hardly track them with the standard three-inch antiaircraft weapons. Only the .50-caliber machine guns could harass the waves of attackers.

When the hammer fell on December 22, Freuler and Davidson met a stream of bombers, accompanied by fighters, obviously from a carrier. Freuler shot down two bombers before he caught a bullet in his shoulder. He staggered back to the field, touching down just as his engine expired. His companion, Davidson, last seen diving on a Zeke fighter with another Zeke on his tail, disappeared.

The flying days of VMF-211 on Wake were over. Putnam, Elrod, and the other survivors reverted to infantrymen for the final defense of Wake. On the night of December 22, the first of the Japanese soldiers established a beachhead on Wake. A handful left from VMF-211, led by Paul Putnam and Henry Elrod, stubbornly yielded ground while fighting with submachine guns, rifles, and pistols. David Kliewer and Sergeant Robert Borquin from the squadron ground crew, with several others, holed up at the airfield fending off enemy soldiers. As the invaders overran American positions in the early morning of December 23, Cunningham decided to surrender. Devereux, reluctant initially, agreed to pass the word to the isolated pockets of resistance. When he reached the sector near the airfield where the survivors of 211 had made their stand he saw Putnam, his face bloodied from a bullet to his jaw. Elrod—who had halted one advance by the Japanese using a submachine gun and then firing a captured Japanese weapon—lay dead in a gun pit, clutching a hand grenade. He became the first Marine of World War II to receive a posthumous Medal of Honor. Kliewer and Borquin and their team, who had planned to detonate charges that would destroy the airstrip, also gave up when Devereux reached them.

The survivors from the squadron, along with the others from the military and civilian ranks on Wake, now began a three-and-a-half-year prison camp ordeal.

THREE

DISASTER AND VICTORY AT MIDWAY

While the defense of Wake slowly crumbled and the twelve Wildcats of VMF-211 fell victim to enemy guns and bombs, Marine aviation Colonel "Sheriff" Larkin at Ewa on Oahu had no airplanes to direct. Ewa played host to an Army Air Corps squadron for a few days until Wheeler Field could be repaired. VMF-221 from the *Saratoga* stayed for one night before the carrier bore it off on the aborted run to reinforce Wake. Larkin used the time to add and lengthen runways and erect buildings that were well dispersed in the event the Japanese called again. Larkin salvaged some of his damaged F4F-3 fighters, only to have the Navy expropriate them. Desperate Marine pilots sought air time in a few rickety, early versions of the Douglas Dauntless dive-bombers.

Larkin's ambitious program followed news that he would soon welcome the First Marine Air Wing. Ross Rowell, the veteran of the Nicaragua expedition, and in 1941 director of Marine Corps aviation, wrote Larkin an optimistic note: "It may sound insane, but I am grateful for every plane destroyed on the ground. It will help us to build up a fit fighting outfit in the long run. The house is not on fire yet." Rowell ordered Larkin to divide his incoming squadrons in such a fashion that only three or four experienced pilots would serve in a unit, noting "the RAF error of washing out the major portion of our talent in the first battle. If we fail to prepare for a long war now, we will never win it." Rowell, unlike many of his contemporaries, had no illusions about how tough and extended would be the battle against the Japanese.

The fall of Wake opened the way for the Japanese to attack the Midway atoll, thirteen hundred miles from Honolulu. Admiral Ernest J. King, who became the Chief of Naval Operations on December 31, halted any speculation that Midway might be written off with an order to his new Pacific commander, Admiral Chester Nimitz, to retain a line from Midway to Samoa to Fiji to Brisbane "at all costs." Midway beyond all others would provide the Japanese with a stepping-stone in a march toward Hawaii, although postwar research indicates that there were no plans to expand that far east. However, Midway in the hands of the enemy would certainly render any effort by the United States to roll back the conquests of the Nipponese much more difficult.

Midway consists of two islands. Sand, the larger one, housed the naval air station and the Sixth Marine Defense Battalion. Eastern Island served as the Marine air base. When the first bombs crashed down at Pearl Harbor, Midway lacked any land-based air protection, although the *Lexington* was at that moment sailing toward Midway with VMSB-231, a scout-bomber squadron. When word of the Japanese attack reached the *Lexington,* it reversed course and VMSB-231 airplanes took off in a vain search for the raiders. On that night a Nipponese cruiser and destroyer approached Midway and hurled a number of shells. A Marine shore battery patiently waited until the vessels steamed within forty-five hundred yards of the shore. Using searchlights to pinpoint the foe, the Marine guns scored several hits, and the Japanese retired. An air strike by Japanese planes from carriers returning from their Pearl Harbor triumph had been canceled because of poor weather. The need for air support in the assault upon Wake diverted two flattops from hitting Midway. As a consequence, Midway would pass five months not seriously molested, preparing for a Japanese thrust.

On December 17, seventeen dive-bombers from VMSB-231—having been at sea and within flight distance of Midway ten days earlier—now, guided by a PBY patrol boat, took off from Hawaii in the longest mass, over-water, single-engine flight to date. All arrived safely on the island. The First Marine Air Wing promised to Larkin by Rowell, traveling from the East Coast of the United States, halted in California for a reorganization that activated four MAGs, albeit they had few planes among them. When the new aircraft did reach Hawaii, Bob Galer and his colleagues could only check-fly them before the planes shipped to Midway Island, where Lieutenant Colonel William J. Wallace had formed VMF-221 and VMSB-241 into Marine Air Group Twenty-two.

In March 1942, now a captain, Galer received orders to take one other pilot and perhaps three enlisted men to tents across the field where he would organize VMF-224. A shipment of the despised Buffalos gave Galer's squadron the semblance of a fighter squadron, and he, along with Captain John L. Smith, commander of VMF-223, flew to nearby Kauai to practice night fighter tactics. On the night of March 3–4 several Japanese flying boats had conducted a harmless raid; if a repeat performance occurred, Galer and company were to confront the enemy. However, VMF-224 saw no interlopers in Hawaiian airspace.

It was on Midway, however, that the Marine fliers would next encounter the Japanese. The first contingent of dive-bombers that made the long over-water trip coped with primitive aviation facilities on Eastern Island. Radio communications were still being installed, and ground support was minimal. During the weeks immediately after Pearl Harbor mechanics and others ordinarily charged with servicing aircraft took up positions to defend the Midway beaches. During January, when Lieutenant Colonel Wallace took overall command of the two resident squadrons, VMSB-241 and VMF-221, civilian contractors constructed revetments to protect the planes while aircrews patrolled and practiced intensively. Technicians began to learn the intricacies of a primitive radar system. Workers built propeller and machine shops.

In March a four-engine "snooper" approached Midway. Four fighters intercepted the slow-moving but heavily armed flying boat. They knocked it out of the air, although Sergeant Bob Dickey, one of the enlisted pilots, felt the sting of the victim's guns. Wounded and bleeding profusely, his instrument panel shot up after attacking from underneath the tail, he brought his Brewster

Buffalo home to a smooth landing. Along with his congratulations for a job well done, Wallace issued a bottle of bourbon to the victors.

That small triumph aside, the development of Marine aviation sputtered. Rowell, with the Second Wing in San Diego, wrote to Larkin, "I have now accumulated 35 second lieutenants in various stages of advanced training. . . . If . . . you want some half-baked flyers, send me a dispatch to that effect." Higher-ups accepted the novices, shipping them to Ewa and Midway to complete their instruction at these sites, closer to the battle zone.

While the Marines struggled to strengthen their air arm, in the Coral Sea on May 7 Navy pilots met their Japanese counterparts in the first sea battle exclusively fought in the air. When the engagement broke off, the United States counted one heavy carrier, the *Lexington*, sunk; another, the *Yorktown*, was seriously damaged. The enemy also destroyed a destroyer and an oiler. The Imperial Navy lost a light carrier, and heavy damage to a heavyweight flattop rendered it out of action for months. Because the Japanese mistakenly believed that two U.S. flattops, a battleship, a cruiser, and a destroyer lay at the bottom of the Coral Sea, they discounted their own losses and a huge fleet plowed toward the next objective, Midway. The armada, under Vice Admiral Chuichi Nagumo, included carriers to launch aerial attacks on the island and to defend against raids on the fleet, along with capital ships to bombard Midway; bringing up the rear came transports packed with troops for an invasion.

Intelligence, having broken the code, and therefore privy to Japanese dispatches, determined that the long-expected attack on Midway was imminent. Reinforcements arrived at the Marine base in the form of two Marine rifle companies, five more antiaircraft batteries, and some light tanks. For the aerial defenses, the Navy flew in sixteen PBYs slated for reconnaissance duty and half a dozen TBFs with torpedo capability. A batch of Army Air Corps B-25s and B-17s further packed the atoll. Lieutenant Colonel Ira L. Kimes succeeded Wallace. Major Floyd B. Parks led the Marine fighters while Major Lofton R. Henderson commanded the dive-bombers. By the end of May the Marine Midway air arsenal included twenty-seven dive-bombers—SBD-2s and SB2Us—along with twenty-eight fighters, twenty-one F2A-3s (Brewster Buffalos), and seven F4F-3s (Grumman Wildcats). The allotment indicated how Marine aviation functioned as a Navy stepchild. The parent organization now operated only F4F Grumman Wildcats, handing down to the Marines their F2A-3 Brewster Buffalos, also known as "Flying Coffins." The Buffalo was no match for the Japanese Zero under any circumstances. Nor were the VMSB-241's eleven SB2U-3 dive-bombers—Chance-Vought Vindicators, nicknamed "Vibrators" and "Wind Indicators"—adequate. The surfaces of the SB2U-3 sometimes crumbled during dives, and the plane was prone to ground loops. Navy carrier squadrons only piloted the SBD-2 Douglas Dauntless, a superior aircraft, itself scheduled to be supplanted by Grumman's SB2-C Helldiver. At almost the last minute, the Marines had acquired seven Wildcats. One of them was assigned to Captain Marion F. Carl.

Born on an eighty-cow dairy farm in Oregon, Carl entered Oregon State University in 1933 as a student in mechanical engineering. After taking a year off, he returned to school. "When I graduated in 1938 my degree was in mechanical engineering, [with an] aeronautical option." Although his four years of ROTC qualified him as a second lieutenant in the Army Corps of Engineers, Carl, who had taken private lessons and spent about twenty hours in the cockpits of Piper Cubs, had applied for flight training. Turned down because the Army had filled its quota, Carl, although on active duty with the Army, approached the Navy, which accepted him as a cadet.

He began his instruction in an eight-man class at Sand Point, Seattle. "There was a Marine officer there, a very sharp-looking Marine captain—boots, britches, the whole thing. He nailed me and said, 'You're the only one in this class that qualifies to be a Marine.' All the rest of them had less than a college degree. The Navy was accepting them with two years of college. That started me out in the Marine Corps."

As with all Marine pilots, he learned his craft under Navy auspices, leaving Sand Point for Pensacola after ten hours of training. At the Florida base he flew twin- and single-engine seaplanes and then his first fighter, the primitive Boeing model. After he received his wings and commission, Carl became an instructor. Finding that work "boring," Carl hooked a ride to Washington, DC, and persuaded an officer at Marine Corps to transfer him to a new outfit in formation at San Diego.

"It was my first fighter squadron," said Carl, "and they had Grumman Wildcats. They only had them for a short time before the Navy took them back because they were running short of Brewster Buffalos in exchange. In the latter part of November [1941] we were given orders to move to Hawaii. The whole squadron, airplanes and all, were to board the *Saratoga* and head out there. We were scheduled to leave San Diego on December 8, 1941. We shoved off right on schedule. We stopped at Pearl Harbor for two nights and then we joined a task group and kept going. We were within 400 miles of Wake Island when Wake fell. They diverted us then to Midway."

For five months the two Marine squadrons on Midway practiced gunnery and bombing, while the fighters all sharpened their skills for the anticipated dogfights. A shortage of gasoline limited training. During this period Carl, along with the others in VMF-221, flew Brewsters, but toward the end of May the Navy delivered the seven Wildcats and Carl's division switched to them. VMSB-241 was also seriously handicapped, even though it had received eighteen SBD-2s, the latest dive-bombers to roll off the Douglas assembly lines. Ten of the pilots had arrived at Midway a bare week before the coming confrontation with the enemy, and only three of this complement had ever logged time in a Dauntless.

Not everyone from VMF-221 deposited by the *Saratoga* stayed at Midway. Six fighter pilots as well as another six from the scout-bomber squadron received orders to report to Honolulu. Among those ticketed for Hawaii was Joe Bauer, now promoted to major and assigned to take over a new fighter squadron.

As the showdown approached, four U.S. carriers, including the hastily repaired *Yorktown*, steamed at full speed toward Midway, where they would be pitted against an equal number of enemy flattops. But the first to launch would be the Japanese, and the first to feel the blows of the Japanese and to attempt to defend their turf would be the small band of land-based fliers.

On June 4, at 4:00 A.M., loudspeakers on the Japanese carrier *Akagi* announced, "Aviators, assemble," and the fliers attended their final briefing before manning their aircraft thirty minutes later. On Midway six of the F4Fs and twenty of the Brewsters from VMF-221 had begun patrols designed to alert the garrison of hostile forces approaching the atoll. Even before the enemy appeared, mechanical problems scratched one Wildcat and one Buffalo. While the fighters hovered near Midway, PBYs and B-17s searched for oncoming Japanese. On the ground the Army B-17s and B-26s, a handful of Navy torpedo bombers from VT-8, and all of VMSB-241 awaited a sighting that would call them into action.

After Carl and five other F4Fs prowled about the sky for less than an hour with no sighting of the Japanese, Colonel Kimes summoned them back for refueling. Unfortunately, as four of the fighters landed, one slid into the sand while taxiing to the revetment, burying its landing gear. Furthermore, two Marine pilots, Captain Francis P. McCarthy and Second Lieutenant Roy A. Corry Jr., never received the recall message and continued to bore through hundreds of square miles of empty sky over the ocean. That reduced the Wildcat portion of VMF-221 to only three operational planes available for immediate duty when the enemy finally showed.

Within a few minutes of the return to the Midway base, one of the scouting PBYs radioed word of carriers approaching and another Catalina crew reported forty-five planes on a course for Midway. The Sand Island radar picked up blips from incoming aircraft and, upon this information, the air alarm sounded. To make certain his forces got off the ground, Kimes dispatched a pickup truck whose siren alerted pilots standing by planes with idling engines.

Major Floyd Parks led VMF-221's first division—eight Buffalos and the three Wildcats—into the air to meet the attackers. The other half of the fighter group also took off but were vectored to an area where they could combat aircraft coming from a different direction. Radio had finally contacted McCarthy and Corry, and the pair quickly came back for refueling. Meanwhile the VMSB-241 dive-bombers under Henderson and his executive officer, Major Ben Norris, sought the Japanese carriers. The Army B-17s and B-26s, along with the Navy torpedo planes, made a similar effort, but there was no coordination among the various American thrusts at the enemy fleet.

Marine Captain John F. Carey, one of the F4F pilots, apparently spied the raiders first, calling out on his radio, "Tally ho! Hawks at Angels Twelve [altitude twelve thousand feet]!" The message notified not only his companions but also listeners at Midway. With that news, plus the radar readings, Kimes ordered fighters prowling another sector to join in the defense. To the amazement of the Marines, subsequently reported Kimes, the formidable mix of 108 fighters and bombers from the Japanese carriers approached at twelve thousand feet, two thousand beneath the trio of Wildcats flown by Carey, Carl, and Lieutenant Clayton Canfield. Because the Japanese apparently believed Midway knew nothing of their approach, the Zeros assigned to protect the bombers were actually *beneath* the latter. Carey would later claim the fighter cover was not below the bombers but behind them. Whatever their position, the Marines thus received one free pass against the bomber formations before the Zeros could interfere.

"We were the first to encounter the incoming flight," said Carl, who noted that his flight had become separated from the Brewster contingent. "We initiated an attack, and it turned into kind of a dogfight. There was supposed to be six of us, but there were only three. There was radio silence. We were not allowed to transmit. All we could do was listen. I was a section leader and I had put Canfield on Carey's wing." (Carey's original partner was the pilot who mired his plane in the sand.)

"We made an overhead pass on the dive-bombers coming in, which means you're meeting them head on. It was a perfect setup for what we called an 'overhead' which is the safest and most deadly approach you can come up with. We were trained for that. Carey and Canfield were coming right straight down on them, and when they pulled out, which is natural, they were going in the same direction as the dive-bombers. I considered that a mistake.

When I completed my pass, I rolled 180 degrees and went the op-posite direction because I could see all these damn Zeros. It took me about five seconds to figure out that if I had pulled out head-ing for the island, I was going to have Zeros all over me. If I went away from the island, since they were covering the bombers, they probably wouldn't follow me.

"I came back around and climbed back up. I was figuring out what the hell I was going to do when I got jumped by a lone Zero. He put a few holes in my airplane and I decided I would try to out-maneuver him. I discovered that was a waste of time. The damned Zeros were so quick. I dove into a cloud and when I hit the cloud, I chopped the throttle all the way back. When I came out the other side, he was ahead of me. I pulled the trigger—he was down below me—and at the same time I pushed the nose over to get the sight on him. All four of my guns jammed! Because at the same time I shoved over and pulled the trigger, all the am-munition went to the top of the cans and all four guns just plugged up. He got off scot-free. If I had waited a second, let things stabilize for a moment and then pulled the trigger, every-thing would have been all right. I was pretty green. I didn't know any better. We didn't continue the fight. He knew he had lucked out.

"I came back over the field and I watched the fight going on down there. I was off by myself, waiting for the action to end. Fi-nally when everything was over, three Zeros were all that was left. They weren't together [but] strung out in a long column, maybe 200 to 300 yards between them. I bounced the rear one and shot him down. I had manually charged the guns, managed to get three out of the four working."

According to Carey, he swept down upon a lead dive-bomber and his machine guns exploded the Aichi although a bullet smashed through his windshield. As he attempted a tight turn, a rear gunner in one of the bombers stitched his plane; bullets struck both of his legs. Canfield, on Carey's wing, picked out an-other target "until it exploded and went down in flames."

As Zeros started to head in their direction, Carey, in agony be-cause of his leg wounds, followed Canfield through cloud cover to

Midway. Canfield's landing gear folded as he touched the runway, and the Wildcat skittered over the ground. He barely had time to jump from the wreck into a trench as the Japanese dive-bombers started to unload. Right behind Canfield, Carey staggered onto the field. With both tires blown and lacking the strength in his wounded limbs to apply brakes, Carey slid off the runway and smashed into a revetment. Two Marines yanked him from the cockpit and into the revetment as the bombs started to explode.

Carl had his first aerial victory, but neither he nor the other two Wildcat pilots inflicted any serious damage to the dive-bombers. "Carey and Canfield got the hell shot out of them," remarked Carl. "They both got back, but Carey never flew again. Both of the planes ended up on the runway as a pile of junk."

For those following Major Floyd Parks into battle, the outcome would be deadly. Lieutenant Darrel Irwin, wingman for the Fourth Division leader, Captain Robert Curtin, said he glimpsed the Parks group make an overhead approach and then never saw them again. The only pilot in Parks's division to survive, Second Lieutenant Charles S. Hughes, aborted his attack when the engine of his Brewster malfunctioned, causing him to land the defective machine just before enemy dive-bombers arrived.

An Air Corps liaison officer, Major Joseph K. Warner, believed he saw Parks after he bailed out. "As soon as his shoot [sic] opened the Japs were at him, and didn't let up even when he landed on the reef. This enemy is cold blooded in every respect of the word though I disagree with the expression that a Jap will ram his plane into another or take undue chances. Don't let anybody fool you, the Jap wants to live every bit as much as we do and this was proven time and again." Warner's comments about the Japanese ethos, included in a Marine historical monograph on the corps at Midway shortly after the battle, predated by more than two years the appearance of the first kamikazes, and seemed to be aimed largely at inciting fury against the enemy; they were based on no personal knowledge.

Actually, a pair of torpedo boats attempted to rescue the downed pilot, but the reef blocked their way. They did rescue Captain Herbert T. Merrill from the Second Division. When flames enveloped Merrill's Buffalo, although severely burned around his face, neck, and hands, he stayed at the controls long enough to reach the atoll's lagoon. Then he resorted to his parachute and splashed down in the water. One of those boats that had vainly tried to help Parks came near enough for a sailor to swim past the jagged rocks and coral and help Merrill to safety.

The squadron executive officer, Captain Daniel J. Hennessy, commanded the Second Division, and he along with three others from the unit succumbed to the Japanese gunners. Only Merrill and Captain Phillip R. White lived through the day. After he swooped down on the bomber formation without tangible results, White shook off a Zero and then caught up with a bomber leaving the scene. He sprayed it with machine-gun bullets and watched as it "made an easy left turn into the water." When White climbed into the clouds he came upon another enemy aircraft. He plugged away at it, probably registering some hits, but—having run out of ammunition—he headed back to Midway to rearm and refuel.

The Third Division of Captain Kirk Armistead vectored in upon the stolid V-formations of the enemy dive bombers, using the head-on approach from a steep angle above the targets. Armistead said, "I saw my incendiary bullets travel from a point in front of the leader, up thru [sic] his plane and back through the planes on the left wing of the Vee. I continued my dive, and looking back, saw two or three of those planes falling in flames. . . . After my pullout, I zoomed back to an altitude of 14,000 feet. . . . I looked back over my shoulder and about 2,000 feet below and behind me I saw three fighters in column, climbing up towards me, which I assumed to be planes of my division. However, they climbed at a very high rate and a very steep path. When the nearest plane was about 500 feet below and behind me I realized that it was a Japanese Zero fighter. I kicked over in a violent split S and received 3, 20mm shells, one in the right wing gun, one in the right wing root tank and one in the top left side of the engine cowling. I also received about 20, 7.7 rounds in the left aileron which mangled the tab on the aileron and sawed off a portion. I continued a vertical dive at full throttle, corkscrewing to the left, due to the effect of the damaged aileron. At about 3,000 feet, I started to pull out, and managed to hold the plane level at an altitude of 500 feet." He fled to Midway, only to find it under heavy assault. For a number of anxious minutes he hid by staying out of the sunlight and finally touched down.

His second in command, Captain William C. Humberd, bagged an Aichi but discovered a pair of Zeros hot on his tail. He threw his plane into a dive as a lone enemy pursued him. Humberd reported, "I descended to water level trying to gain distance on the fighter staying with me. I stayed at water level with full throttle gaining distance slowly until I decided the distance was great enough to turn on the plane in which case we met head on. I gave a long burst when we were about 300 yards distant and the plane caught on fire and out of control dived in the water." Back at Midway he obtained emergency repairs to his flaps and landing gear, as well as replenishing his gas and ammunition. He had just taken off again when Midway air control ordered all fighters to return to base.

Second Lieutenant Charles M. Kunz, behind Armistead, saw two of the enemy planes shot down, probably destroyed by the flight leader and Humberd. In his pass he fired on another bomber, which wobbled off in flames. He picked off a second one when a fighter rocked his Buffalo with a stream of bullets that laced his wing and the cockpit. One slug grazed his head. Dizzy and nursing a badly damaged plane, Kunz brought his disabled machine to the field. He was hustled off to the aid station.

A pair of second lieutenants, William V. Brooks and William B. Sandoval, wingmen for Humberd and Armistead, felt the bite of the Japanese machine guns. Brooks steered toward Midway, and antiaircraft fire from the Marines on the ground drove off his tormentors. With his Buffalo riddled by bullets, Brooks prepared to land but suddenly noticed two planes apparently engaged in a dogfight. He hurried over to help a presumably beleaguered American only to realize the Japanese had staged a sham battle to entice him. Brooks quickly retreated, exchanging fire with one of the Zeros while on a course to the Midway field. As he started his approach he spied two more enemy fighters savaging Sandoval's hapless Buffalo. Even though only one of his machine guns still fired, Brooks hastened to aid his colleague, but he arrived too late with too little, and Sandoval plunged into the water.

Marine pilots Francis McCarthy and Roy Corry in their Wildcats, having belatedly heard the word to return for replenishment, joined the fracas after Carey's F4F-equipped division first encountered the waves of Japanese aircraft. Instead of a passel of bombers to attack, they endured the attention of eight enemy fighters. McCarthy blasted one but then, afire himself, fell out of the sky. Corry, while dodging three attackers, knocked down a Zero and then caught up with an Aichi leaving the scene for its carrier. He delivered a short burst, and the dive-bomber crashed into the sea.

The first assault by aircraft from the Japanese flattops left relatively minor damage, partly because of the actions of VMF-221. The attacks on the assortment of dive- and level-flight bombers reduced their number by half. The Japanese admitted losing a total of nine planes, crediting six to interceptors and three to the island's AA. The figures are less than those claimed by the defenders, but the Japanese also described thirty-four of their planes as damaged.

That said, the first strike at Midway effectively eliminated the ground-based air defense. Fifteen of VMF-221's twenty-five pilots were gone, along with their thirteen Brewsters and two Wildcats. Six of the surviving pilots were wounded. Furthermore, of those fighter aircraft that had returned to Midway, only two were considered operational. That anyone had been able to land on the island after that initial raid was only because the Japanese, expecting to successfully invade Midway, wanted to preserve the runways for their own aircraft.

Pacific Fleet commander Admiral Chester Nimitz had emphasized that the best defense for Midway would lie in offensive actions by its airplanes. His directive said, "BALSA'S [the code name for Midway] air force must be employed to inflict prompt and early damage to the Jap carrier flight decks if recurring attacks are to be stopped. Our objectives will be first, their flight decks rather than attempting to fight off the initial attacks on BALSA. . . ." Following that strategy, immediately after the fighters took off to intercept the oncoming Japanese, Midway launched its strike aimed at the enemy carriers. The attack included the Navy's half a dozen torpedo-bearing TBFs and four Army B-26 Marauders, which carried tin fish—ordnance never before used by the medium bombers. When these Americans came in sight of the Japanese carriers, fighters zoomed up to meet them. The Navy and Army aircrews withered under the attacks. A single TBF struggled home to Midway, with one gunner dead and another wounded. The Japanese shot down two of the B-26s, and their gunnery lacerated the pair that made it to their base.

At the same time, the twenty-seven dive-bombers of VMSB-241 also bound for Nagumo's flotilla broke into two groups: sixteen Dauntlesses (the newer SBD-2s) under Major Lofton R. Henderson, and eleven aged SB2U Vindicators led by Major Benjamin Norris. Henderson's flight sighted the enemy first, and he ordered runs on a pair of carriers whose flight decks sported the traditional red circle (meatball) insignia. Because too many of his pilots had little experience in dive-bombing, Henderson directed a glide-bombing approach. From an altitude of eight thousand feet, the formation of bombers would slide to four thousand feet and then, in an every-man-for-himself approach, enter a power glide to five hundred feet or less for the bomb release. While that may have better suited his unit, the maneuvers made for easier targets for the Japanese fighters that had roared off the carrier decks to meet the threat and for the thunderous antiaircraft thrown up by the fleet.

The enemy planes, some with retractable landing gear and other older models with fixed wheels, deployed in two levels and showed great skill in coordinated attacks. They picked off the lead American, Major Henderson. Even though Henderson's wing burst into flame, he managed to drop his bomb, which exploded in the water near one of the flattops. His plane then crashed into the Pacific. Behind Henderson, Captain Elmer Glidden, the SBD Second Division commander, automatically took charge.

While his companions started to fall all about him, Glidden believed he saw several hits, but in fact no ordnance actually struck any of the carriers. First Lieutenant Daniel Iverson Jr. pulled away from his target observing a carrier with "almost an entire ring of fire from the flight deck." Fighters collected about his tail, and a bullet severed his throat microphone. He escaped to make a wobbly landing at Sand Island, where the ground crew counted 210 holes in his SBD. Others from VMSB-241 absorbed horrific punishment from the carrier defenses. Half of the sixteen SBD-2s, with their crews, disappeared. Two dive-bombers managed water landings near enough to Midway for a patrol plane and a torpedo boat to rescue crewmen.

The slower dozen SB2U-3 Vindicators skippered by Major Norris lagged about fifteen minutes behind Lofton's group. Apparently the first team of fighters had worked over the Dauntlesses, for those who met Norris and his pilots performed much less effectively, failing to shoot down any of the group, although one machine-gun burst killed Private Henry L. Starks, who was manning a rear machine gun. Such was the dearth of trained personnel that the hapless Starks had never even fired a machine gun in the air.

The Japanese warships, although not initially scoring any victories, drove the attackers to a position where a run at the carriers required passage over the entire fleet. That discouraged Norris from seeking out the carriers; instead he instructed his companions to drop on a battleship. Again, the best the raiders could achieve was a series of near misses. Two Vindicators were lost over the Japanese fleet and another two, including the one with the body of Starks, ran out of gas in the vicinity of Midway. PT boats retrieved the Marines aboard.

At the time the patrolling PBYs first found the Japanese flotilla on June 3, the Army B-17s had roared off on a hunt. The long-range Flying Fortresses found the warships. But their high-altitude bombing runs only disturbed the fish. The attempts by the land-based Midway air arm had not contributed an iota to what Nimitz had demanded.

With VMF-221 out of action, its complement, including the able-bodied flight personnel, assisted other elements of the Midway defense. The remnants of VSMB-241 stood by for another mission. In those first hours the U.S. fleet still desperately steamed under forced draft toward the island; Rear Admiral Raymond Spruance, commander of Task Force Sixteen, one of the two U.S. fleets dispatched to save Midway, calculated that by 9:00 A.M. his flattops would be within the comfortable range of one hundred miles from the enemy. But as word of the air assault upon Midway reached Spruance, he decided that if he waited, he might lose his best opportunity to deal the Japanese a mighty blow, catching them with their planes aboard as they prepared for a strike against his fleet. However ineffective the aerial defense of Midway, the minor injuries inflicted upon the first wave by VMF-221, the ground AA, and the futile dive-bomber attack by VMSB-241 convinced the Japanese chief of the First Air Fleet, Vice Admiral Nagumo, to order a second air attack before bringing up his big ships and the transports. It would prove a critical decision in determining the outcome of the battle for Midway.

The next effort to halt the Japanese armada came with the carrier-based Navy torpedo planes of VT-8, which, with six aircraft stationed on Midway, was minus six of its complement. VT-8 operated the lumbering TBD Devastator. Due to the early launch ordered by Spruance, the 175-mile range guaranteed the Devastator could not make it back to the flattops. Its hundred-miles-per-hour speed while delivering the frequently defective Mark IV Torpedo rendered the plane most devastating to its occupants. When VT-8 arrived over the Japanese fleet, the gunners on the ships and the fighters in the sky engaged in the equivalent of a live fire drill, knocking down every single TBD. However, because Nagumo had decided to bombard Midway again rather than go after the U.S. fleet, the decks were crowded with aircraft loaded with bombs to smash the Midway installation, rather than torpedoes that could have rocked the U.S. fleet. Instead, with some Japanese fighters engaged in the destruction of VT-8 and coping with a modest amount of air cover from Navy F4Fs, while others aboard the carriers were being gassed, American dive-bombers, in the hands of pilots well trained in the proper techniques, dropped from the sky. With no aerial opposition, they hammered the Japanese flattops, inflicting massive damage.

During the day, after the Japanese had also pounded the *York-*

town—which eventually succumbed to a submarine's torpedo—twelve planes from VMSB-241, divided equally between SBD-3s and SB2Us, left Midway for a night attack on an enemy carrier reportedly blazing 180 miles out. They could not locate the alleged target, and while endeavoring to find their way home through squalls, Ben Morris in a Vindicator vanished.

On the following morning Kimes received an order to send his dive-bombers after two Japanese battleships spotted 140 miles from the atoll. Again an even dozen aircraft left the base on Eastern Island and in less than an hour came upon broad oil slicks, presumably deposited by the battleships. Following the spoor they pounced upon the vessels—actually the heavy cruisers *Mogami* and *Mikuma*. Captain Marshall A. Tyler in the faster SBD section dove on the already badly damaged *Mogami*. Then the section of Dauntlesses plunged through a maelstrom of AA but escaped injury. Their bombs, however, struck no closer than near misses.

Captain Richard Fleming, slightly wounded twice on the previous day, led his section of SB2Us on a glide-bomb approach at the second ship, the *Mikuma*. Intense flak met them, and Fleming's engine gave off smoke. Captain Leon M. Williamson saw the burning plane crash on the cruiser's aft turret. According to a Japanese officer, the flames, sucked into the air intake of the starboard engine room, ignited gas fumes in a conflagration that killed many sailors. Captain Akira Soji aboard *Mogami* later said, "I saw a dive bomber dive into the last turret and start fires. He was very brave." Americans present at the scene doubt that Fleming intended a suicidal act, but in any event he became the first Marine pilot to earn a Medal of Honor. (Henry Elrod's was awarded in 1946 after the facts of the Wake defenses were learned.)

In the Battle of Midway the Japanese saw four carriers sunk, as well as hundreds of skilled pilots and planes lost. The American victory turned back any opportunity for the Japanese to expand farther east across the Pacific, and many historians called it the turning point in the war, although three more years of hard combat would ensue. Marine aviation had played a role, but the airmen were justifiably bitter about having to fight the foe with such obviously inferior equipment. Captain Phil White said, "The F2A-3 [Brewster Buffalo] is *not* [his italics] a combat airplane. The Japanese Zero fighter can run circles around the F2A-3. It is my belief that any commander who orders pilots out for combat in an F2A should consider the pilot as lost before leaving the ground. It is inferior to the planes we are fighting in every respect. The F2A-3 has about the same speed as an Aichi 99 Val Dive Bomber."

Kunz, with a crease across his forehead from a bullet, said, "The [Zero] has been far underestimated. As for the F2A-3, it should be in Miami as a training plane, rather than be used as a first-line fighter."

Another observer commented that when two Brewsters met Zeros, "both looked like they were tied on a string while the Zeros made passes at them." The Nimitz strategy of offense against the enemy fleet rather than defense of Midway may have implicitly determined the weak fighter protection, including the deployment of the obsolete Brewster Buffalos afforded the island. If so, both VMF-221 and VMBF-241—which assaulted the enemy fleet without benefit of fighter cover—paid a high price in blood for that approach.

Lieutenant Colonel Ira L. Kimes, in command of the Midway Marine air force, compiled doleful statistics: fifteen fighter pilots, eleven dive-bomber pilots, and twelve rear-seat gunners dead or missing in action. Another seventeen airmen were wounded. VMF-221 counted between thirty-seven and forty-three enemy shot down and claimed direct bomb hits on two carriers and two battleships.

Navy and Marine fliers were united in their fury at any credit claimed by the Army Air Corps for the defeat of the Japanese at Midway. The rancor generated over different accounts of who did what would fester in the highest circles of command and among the lower echelons actually engaged in subsequent battles. At the same time, Sheriff Larkin, appalled by the sacrifice of Marine airmen condemned to the ancient SB2Us and the F2As, drafted a report on the inadequacies of his aircraft. Rather than have the information pass through the slow-moving official channels, he wrote to Rowell, "I gave Jim Roosevelt [then a Marine major] a folder of the action on Midway to take to his Dad [the president]. In about two weeks if you are ordered as president of a general court-martial to try one fellow named Larkin—soften your heart."

Larkin never faced any tribunal, and after the war James Roosevelt said he thought Larkin's personal account "resulted in considerable improvement in the situation shortly thereafter."

It was around the time of Midway that Captain Frank T. McCoy Jr. of the Army Air Corps first devised names to denote the different Japanese aircraft. The nomenclature tacked male ones on fighters and female on bombers. The Mitsubishi-manufactured Zero fighter became the Zeke. Other fighters were Nate, Oscar, Rufe, Pete, Tony, Frank, and, late in the war, Jack and George. The twin-engine bomber received the name Betty, and the Aichi dive-bomber was known as Val. Other bombers became Lily, Sally, and Nell, with the Kawanishi four-engine patrol bomber an Emily. By December 1943 the entire South Pacific Command had adopted the system.

FOUR

CACTUS SPROUTS

Rebuffed at the Battle of Midway, the Japanese gave up notions to extend their control in the Pacific Ocean toward Hawaii and instead focused on consolidating holdings closer to home. In particular, the Japanese looked to the Solomon Islands, a chain of heavily jungled, sometime mountainous islands in the Southwest Pacific off the coast of New Guinea. The Battle of the Coral Sea, a victory for the Japanese with the sinking of the carrier *Lexington*, nevertheless discouraged them from an invasion of Port Moresby on New Guinea. However, after seizing Bougainville and New Georgia on the northwestern reaches of the archipelago, the Nipponese headed for Tulagi and Guadalcanal at the southeastern edges. Possession of this pair could interfere with shipping to Australia and jeopardize portions of New Guinea still held by the Allied forces. In pursuit of these objectives, a month before the Battle of Midway, Japanese troops had already landed on Tulagi.

Aware of the strategic value of the Solomons, U.S. naval forces, directed by Chief of Naval Operations Admiral Ernest J. King, had hastily begun building bases on the closest islands to Guadalcanal, the New Hebrides outposts of Espiritu Santo and Efate. King convinced his military colleagues that these would provide the first rung on the ladder that would climb through the Solomons and then the Bismarck Archipelago en route to the Philippines and Japan itself. On April 4, 1942, the Joint Chiefs of Staff created a divided command in the Pacific Theater. General

Douglas MacArthur, now in residence in Australia after escaping from the Philippines in March, received suzerainty over the southwest, a territory that included Australia, New Guinea, both the Bismarck and Solomon archipelagoes, and the Philippines. Admiral Chester Nimitz took charge over the remainder of the Pacific, a huge chunk of ocean speckled with the likes of the Gilbert, Marshall, Caroline, Mariana, Palau, Bonin, and Ryukyu islands all the way to the China coast and the doorstep of Japan itself.

The U.S. strategists discussed a number of plans to begin a rollback of the Japanese Empire, mindful that the task of winning in Europe drew priority for military assets. MacArthur proposed a strike at Rabaul, the huge base being constructed by the Japanese on New Britain in the Bismarcks. The Navy, which would be expected to provide fighter cover plus the warships and transports for an amphibious venture, protested it could not meet the needs. Instead, the admirals and Marine generals targeted the Tulagi–Guadalcanal area. Although the charter placed the Solomons under MacArthur's jurisdiction, not only did the Navy's strategy win acceptance, but achievement of the goals was vested in naval command.

Originally Tulagi, the biggest port in the Solomons and the site of the capital, figured as the most important objective. But after aerial reconnaissance discovered the Japanese building an airfield on Guadalcanal that poked toward the New Hebrides bases, the Americans shifted their interests to that steamy piece of real estate. The Fleet Landing Force mission for the Marines and the obligation of the leatherneck air arm to support the endeavor would debut at Guadalcanal.

An amphibious force of nineteen thousand officers and enlisted men was committed for an invasion of these Solomon outposts. MacArthur contributed Air Corps B-17s for reconnaissance and interdiction of Rabaul-based enemy aircraft, but the burden of protecting the landings and then hammering any defenders would fall upon Navy warships and aviation.

The New Hebrides base at Efate, code-named Roses, lay 707 miles from Guadalcanal. Jim Coyle recalled that on March 14, 1942, he was among 150 enlisted Marines with one officer, Captain John K. Little, a reservist serving with MAG-24 headquarters squadron, who boarded a ship bound for Efate. They brought with them nineteen trucks and two bulldozers, plus a generous supply of picks and shovels. On the island they joined with five hundred soldiers from the Army's newly formed Americal Division—and, according to Coyle, fifty convicts from the local jails—to build an airfield. On April 30 the air station at Vila was declared operational. Major Harold W. Bauer subsequently brought his VF-212 with twenty-one F4F-3s to Efate. August 2 saw the arrival of VMO-251, led by Lieutenant Colonel John N. Hart, an observation squadron that used a modified Wildcat equipped with wing tanks for long-range sorties while retaining machine guns for dogfights.

On July 12, 1942, the Marine Fourth Defense Battalion, Navy Seabees, and Army engineers and soldiers arrived on Espiritu Santo, also in the New Hebrides but, much more conveniently, 150 miles closer to Guadalcanal. They, too, constructed an airfield amid the jungle and coconut trees. The base operated under the code name Buttons.

The island also became home for Marine Air Group Eleven, including Staff Sergeant Jim Law, as a member of the maintenance crews for F4Fs and SBDs. They had sailed on a former commercial liner, the SS *Del Brazil,* in comparative comfort with "real good chow" served by civilian cooks. Life on Espiritu Santo, however, was more difficult. "There was no natural water supply," explained Law. "The top five feet was soil but below that was solid coral. I spent a few hours taking my turn about 30 feet below the surface with a jackhammer, chopping into the coral and hauling it to the top in buckets with an attached rope. We finally hit water at about 40 feet down. The temperature down in the hole must have been well over 100 degrees and the diggers got relieved regularly.

"It was only a couple of days before the runways were usable and some of the fighter and dive bomber squadrons of MAG-11 flew in from an airfield located on the other end of the island. In short order, we had an operating airbase."

On August 7, 1942, following the usual softening-up barrages from warships and carrier planes, the loudspeakers on transports in the Sealark Channel of the Solomons bleated, "Land the Landing Force!" Over the side clambered First Marine Division leathernecks to create separate beachheads on four islands, Tulagi, Gavutu, Tanambogo, and, most important, Guadalcanal. The first three places, some twenty miles north of Guadalcanal, harbored fifteen hundred defenders who literally fought almost to the last man, killing 108 Marines and wounding another 140 before the islands could be declared secure.

Intelligence reported five thousand Japanese soldiers garrisoned on Guadalcanal but actually there were only six hundred fighting men and fourteen hundred laborers. The Japanese were caught without effective shoreline defenses, and the Marines moved inland far enough to capture the airstrip being built by the enemy. However, the Japanese command in Rabaul reacted swiftly to the news of the American invasion of the island. Airplanes hurried to attack the ships and Marines. Navy fighters from carriers desperately fought them off at considerable loss— almost 30 percent of the Wildcats on the first day. Vice Admiral Frank Jack Fletcher, in charge of the task force assigned to serve the amphibious operations, apparently panicked when he realized his carriers were in grave danger from the Rabaul-based bombers. He reneged on his promise to cover the invasion force and removed his three carriers, leaving the troops and warships still on station unprotected by aircraft. The raids would continue without letup for days. The two Marine aviation units were stationed too far away to contribute directly to the battle for Guadalcanal. They could only protect the bases in the New Hebrides.

When a Japanese task force fell upon the American-Australian screening force off Savo Island, they sank the cruisers *Astoria*, *Quincy*, *Vincennes*, and *Canberra* while seriously damaging the *Chicago*. Had the Japanese warships ventured farther they could have wiped out the transports and cargo ships unloading men and supplies. Vital matériel lay heaped on the beaches, but no enemy aircraft dropped bombs that could have denied the Marines the wherewithal to fight. As it was shortages of barbed wire, ammunition, food, and other items threatened the survival of those ashore.

Major General Alexander A. Vandegrift, commander of the
Marines on the island, had immediately ordered his First Engineer Battalion to complete the airfield begun by the enemy. Henderson Field, named in honor of the dive-bomber pilot killed at
Midway, needed extensive work, although the Japanese had already tested it. Their lighter planes did not require a hard surface
or a long runway. In fact, the construction gangs worked from
both ends toward the middle. After the Marines seized the strip, a
huge hole about two-thirds of the way along needed some five
thousand cubic yards of dirt. The bulldozers of the engineers remained offshore, still stowed on the ships. In a monumental effort, by August 12, the men—working with hand shovels and
captured enemy trucks—managed to ready Henderson Field for
aircraft.

In addition to a basic runway surface, the field required a service component for the aircraft and communications. A Navy unit
known as Cub-1, about 120 sailors, most of them fresh out of aviation technical schools, with one officer, Ensign George Washington Polk, stepped ashore on August 15. The executive officer of
VMO-251, Major Charles Hayes, acting as representative of Rear
Admiral John Sidney McCain, Commander Aircraft, South Pacific, had overall charge of the air arm's ground support. Said
Hayes, "We had some light bombs, ammunition and hand tools.
The men had for their own accommodation just what they could
carry on their backs. We . . . unloaded on the open beach and
tried to get the field ready to accept aircraft. Of course we had no
equipment and it was about all we could do to get these sailors
shaken down and teach them how to live under those conditions.
But we did get the essentials of the shops and communications set
up and actually began to operate the aircraft as soon as they arrived." (After the war, Polk became a journalist, and his murder in
Greece became a cause célèbre.)

In effect, Hayes became the operations officer of Henderson
Field. He had benefited from some earlier schooling based upon
the knowledge of Marine aviators sent to Europe and Asia as observers of aerial warfare. In particular, the Marines drew upon

Britain's Royal Air Force, which developed the fighter-director concept.

But the immediate problem for those holding Guadalcanal was a shortage of aircraft. The initial plan counted on the carrier *Long Island* to ferry the portions of Marine Air Group Twenty-three, amounting to half of two fighter and two dive-bomber squadrons, close enough to Guadalcanal for them to fly to Henderson. The forward echelon of the group consisted of VMF-223, commanded by Captain John L. Smith, and VMSB-232, under mustachioed Major Richard C. Mangrum. Smith, a native of Oklahoma, had graduated from the University of Oklahoma in 1936 with an ROTC commission as a second lieutenant in the Army Field Artillery. However, he had resigned within two months in favor of the same rank in the Marine Corps. Having completed the required ground assignments, Smith entered flight training in 1938 and pinned on his wings a year later. Mangrum, who graduated from the University of Washington in 1928, received his Marine commission one year later after flight training.

Nearly all of the pilots in both squadrons were recent graduates of flight school and without carrier training. Most of the dive-bomber crews had never practiced their trade. At the last moment, the squadrons received the latest versions of the Wildcat and the Dauntless with unfamiliar equipment. To throw these raw, partially schooled airmen into the battle would condemn most of them to an early death without effectively thwarting the Japanese. Rear Admiral John S. McCain, in command of aircraft in the South Pacific, upon hearing of a delayed arrival by MAG-23, flatly said, "I need fighter planes at Guadalcanal now."

Mangrum said he received word of his assignment to the Guadalcanal operation early in July. "On the 5th of July in Colonel Claude Larkin's office, I shall never forget being admonished that this was of the utmost top secrecy and that no one, NO ONE!, even my executive officer or no one else in my squadron was to be told where we were going. We were to be ready for combat, ready for departure on the 1st of August and no one was to be told where we were going.

"I left the colonel's office and went back to my squadron's head-quarters where I was greeted by my sergeant major, and the first question he asked me, he said, 'Major, where's Guadalcanal?' And it had been practically a closed gate [secure premises] since Pearl Harbor."

Mangrum welcomed about a dozen new pilots, fresh out of flight training in Pensacola. "Looking at their flight log books, I was appalled to discover that none of them had much over 200 hours in the air and two had slightly less than 200 hours of flying of all types in the air, and none in the aircraft with which we were equipped. We had one solid month of working as hard as we could, day and night, to try to bring these people up to some de-gree of combat effectiveness."

Henry W. Hise typified one of the novices with MAG-23. He had completed his flight school course in the middle of May and had compiled 206.2 flight hours when he reported to an advanced carrier training group at the San Diego naval base, in June 1942. "I didn't fly much there. My log book shows 6.2 hrs in an SNJ-3 [a scout trainer]. Three times I flew myself. The operation there was very small. I became educated to the life style of Naval aviators which was much better than that of Marine lieutenants."

Toward the end of the month he and other Marine aviators sailed to Hawaii and took up station at the Ewa base, where he lived in tent city. "I reported in to Marine Air Group 23, assigned to newly forming squadron flying SBD-2s. I'd never touched the aircraft, and the closest I [had] flown was the [Northrop] BT-1, one of the first dive-designed bombers with split brakes, perfo-rated flaps. It was grossly underpowered, climbed at 85 knots; the damn thing cruised at 90, glided at about 90.

"Richard C. Mangrum was the squadron commander, tall, slim and handsome. I thought of him as immensely experienced; I was, as they put it, green as a red blackberry. We had three veter-ans of Midway, Danny Iverson, Bruce Prosser and Tom Moore.

"I was made assistant materiels [sic] officer, buildings and grounds. I knew nothing about the job. As we prepared for the Guadalcanal Operation, the first thing we did was check out the SBD-2 aircraft. I was given the handbook to read. Then they sat

you down and went over the controls, location of things, the unusual features—hydraulic pump, for wheels and flaps. The airplane
had 750 horsepower, twin .30 caliber machine guns in the rear and
a gunner, and radio system in the rear. We had a hand mike to communicate back and forth to the gunner and to talk over the air.

"We began flight operations for all the new second lieutenants.
Prosser and Mangrum checked you out. I got my first flight one
day after my 22nd birthday, 8th July 1942. From the 8th of July to
31 July I flew 60 flights. They kept us at it, morning, noon and
night. During this period we learned to fly the airplane, tactics,
used formation of a step down Vee, in columns. Mangrum was an
excellent aviator. I was so young and ignorant, not really able to
assess the training. Danny was my flight leader. As a veteran of
Midway, he was somewhat pessimistic about our chances. During
the Marine attack against cruisers [off Midway] they lost half of
the flight to Zeros. Danny, who got only one gear down when he
came back to Midway, faithfully relayed to us that we second lieutenants were doomed to die because the Japanese could fly rings
around us.

"Tom Moore who'd been at Midway was equally pessimistic.
He had been separated from his flight over the great big blue Pacific and fortunate to have enough gas to turn and get back to
Midway. Bruce Prosser was never much of an optimist, always
seemed to have weight on his shoulders. He was not given to face-
tious remarks, very closed mouthed, appeared somewhat unhappy about what we were going into."

The dour predictions failed to daunt Hise and his colleagues.
"The attitude among the second lieutenants was, 'things can't
really be as bad as these Midway veterans said.' We were going to
do our damnedest to stay alive. The atmosphere was one of quiet
desperation. I had not been prepared for this in my training. It
differed from anything before in my life. After the Coral Sea problems and the fight at Midway, we were resolved to sell our lives
dearly. We hoped at least to shoot down one or two Japanese
planes or sink a ship."

As glum as the veterans were about the future, Mangrum's
pupils learned how to dive-bomb, with a technique described by

Hise. "You fly to the target at 90 degrees from the direction from which you wanted to dive. The leader would waggle his wings, go up and over to the left or right, turn 90 degrees, push the aircraft into a 60 or 70-degree dive, come back on the brakes, pull the throttle back. At about 2,000 to 3,000 feet over the target you would release the bomb. Then you would level out at 1,000 feet."

In their practices the squadron attacked a rock on the western side of Maui. They also embarked on a hasty effort to carrier-qualify. They started with field practice, mixed in with the instruction on dive-bombing. Noel Gayler, an accomplished Navy fighter pilot, served as the landing signal officer. Hise packed in fourteen periods of bounce drills—landing, taking off, and then landing again in the prescribed space. On July 31 Hise and the others flew out to sea for the final exam, setting down on the carrier *Hornet.*

"I made my first approach," said Hise, "and got a cut [a signal that his approach was acceptable] and I got the aircraft on the ship. I [saw] this figure rushing up to me, slapping one thumb up against the palm of his other hand, to lift the hook, and he violently waved me to taxi forward. I goosed it, which I had been instructed to do. They pushed me back, gave me a turn up power signal, I ran the aircraft up to what I thought was enough power, 35 inches of manifold pressure. I went down the front of deck, nearly fell into the water, came around again, got another cut, came around for a third cut. I was the first guy through. They sent me out to orbit in front of the ship at about 30,000 feet, goofing around. I damn near spun in."

As commandant of VMF-223, however, John L. Smith felt that many of his youngsters were unready for combat. In fact, just before the scheduled sailing, the fighter pilots received the latest Grumman, the F4F-4, the newest of the Wildcats, with unfamiliar two-stage superchargers. Smith also fretted over the reduced time spent training with oxygen masks. (Similarly, VMSB-232 turned in its reconditioned SBD-2s for spanking-new SBD-3s equipped with self-sealing tanks and armor plate.) Instead of embarking all of the original members of VMF-223 on the *Long Island,* arrangements were made for the carrier to stop at Efate and swap some of the less proficient fliers for the more experienced and better-trained pilots of Joe Bauer's VMF-212.

Mangrum fretted over the size of his complement. "I left for the Solomons with 12 aircraft and 15 pilots, only three spare pilots. The real requirements of military operations extend around the clock, and it was later decided that a full squadron would be 18 aircraft with 53 pilots in order to provide depth."

There were no alternate pilots to recruit for the dive-bomber squadron, which departed from Hawaii on August 2. Hise, who had no idea where they were headed, described the *Long Island*, a converted collier, as having the watertight capacity of a bathtub. If hit by a torpedo it would have gone down quickly. On the initial leg of the voyage, the carrier plodded along at eight knots per hour, without any escort and a fat target for submarines. But Hise said he and his mates were blissfully unaware of the ship's vulnerability. With all of the planes packed onto the flight deck, there would be no room for takeoffs. Instead they would be individually catapulted into the air.

"As we got deeper and deeper into South Pacific," said Hise, "we second lieutenants would get out at night and watch the tremendous stars, impressed by the presence of the Southern Cross. As we approached the equator, they held a big celebration shellback ceremony [a naval tradition upon crossing the equator], we received subpoenas to Davy Jones' Court of Raging Main. They had a big tub of water, they would dump you in. True to his spirit, Marion Carl [assigned to the fighter squadron] led an insurrection of pollywogs and threw a bunch of the ship's company into the pool."

After the pause at Efate, the cruiser *Helena* and a destroyer assumed escort duty. "The big day finally arrived," remembered Hise. "We were finally going to be launched to some strange island, none of us had ever heard of, Guadalcanal. I thought what a strange name. We got ready to go, I put my parachute and a machete into the airplane. Wearing a .45 caliber pistol on my web belt I got into the aircraft, and they were shooting us off [a] catapult. They had already launched a number of aircraft, almost 90 degrees to the midline of the boat. The aircraft was held by a hold-back ring in the deck. On the catapult, a guy stood by the wing, waving two fingers around and around. You turn loose the brake, run the aircraft up to full power. He drops his arm, you feel like a bug just hit with a fly swatter. The gun power of the cat imparted its greatest part of force in its initial bolt. It slammed my head back against the head rest. During the initial shock you were warned to stick your elbow in your guts, so you wouldn't yank back on the stick. The recipe didn't work for me, my elbow didn't hold and I pulled up on the stick, the nose came up smartly, then pushed over. [I was] winging my way just above the waves but I finally got up, a little shook by this experience, and took my place alongside Mangrum.

"We had launched late in the afternoon of August 20, [since we] wanted to get into Guadalcanal before dark. The Japs had been bombing them at night. As we came up what later became known as the Gut, Florida Island was off to the north and Guadalcanal to the south. The hills were higher than I anticipated, about 8,000 feet. The air strip was a gravel strip. As I came around and looked in front of me I saw a whole lot of greenery in front of me, enormous trees at the end of the strip. I made a three point landing, the power came off. To my amazement there were Marines lined up and down the strip, cheering. I taxied off, over this hard ground. I had forgotten to open my cowl flaps, engine got up to about 206 degrees, as hot as it should be. We got our twelve birds, the advance echelon of 232. I was number three to land. The fighters arrived behind us. They had been maintaining cover in case Japanese Zeros came by."

The incoming airmen were quickly directed to their bivouac area, near Pagoda Hill. It was so designated because of a rough-hewn building erected by the Japanese as their headquarters. Atop it was something that resembled a pagoda and provided its name. For the Americans, the place served as the air traffic control center. The code name for Henderson became Cactus.

The embattled inhabitants of Guadalcanal depended upon a network of coast-watchers, planters, and other civilians hidden in the many islands to provide advance warning of oncoming Japanese planes or ships. After observing the enemy aircraft, coast-watchers would radio a description of the approaching raiders in time for the planes at Henderson to take off and gain enough altitude to compensate for the superiority of the Japanese fighters. Because the enemy code had been broken, the Americans also benefited from intelligence gleaned through intercepts of Japanese radio messages. The range of Cactus's radio extended a mere twenty miles, although those installed in aircraft could report back from as far away as one hundred. Later the field would possess a radar system capable of detecting airplanes en route to Guadalcanal.

"That night," said Hise, "we set up our sleeping bags [carried in their parachute bags] in captured Japanese tents. They didn't have any sides, just a top and were set up in a coconut grove close to our aircraft. The first night all hell broke loose not too far away [about three thousand yards off]. The Japanese tried to cross the river on red beach. I believed they killed about a thousand Japanese. [A somewhat exaggerated figure, since the entire attack force numbered about nine hundred.] In blissful ignorance I thought this must be like this all the time, all night gun fire and shelling, but I got some sleep."

Hise remembered great confusion during the first bombing raids. "Everyone was running around like a chicken with its head cut off. Nobody knew what to do. The Japs would bomb the strip about a half mile from us. Mangrum seemed somewhat agitated, striding about. I lay down in the palm grove, in a depression about one foot deep. I lay there and looked up at the sky and here come the Japs right down the strip, in a Vee. They were silver aircraft, at about 7,000 feet in perfect formation with level bombing. The bombs came marching down the strip. I could hear them shrieking and then ground shaking explosions. It was quite impressive, black smoke and crap flew up from the vicinity of the runway. I concluded my protection inadequate. I needed a little deeper hole.

"The next day we had a Zero strafe the airfield. It was quite exciting, the first time I'd ever seen a belly tank on [an] airplane, very novel indeed. Everybody in camp that could fire a weapon was shooting into the air. Shortly after here comes an F4F smoking. Half of these guys on the airfield were firing at him, one guy with a .45 shooting at him. I thought it the stupidest thing I ever saw."

Marion Carl, a veteran of the Battle of Midway where he had accounted for one enemy plane, occupied the cockpit of a VMF-212 Wildcat and, like Hise, on August 20 touched down at Henderson Field. Carl, as executive officer, ranked third in the squadron, with Smith at the top and Captain Rivers Morrell as the second in command. "When we arrived," Carl recalled, "we found the place pretty primitive. We slept under tents. I think it was the second night I was there (Hise claimed it was the first) we were lying right there in the sack and you could see the tracers going back and forth. It looked like they were only out there about 200 yards. It's what they called the Battle of the Tenaru." Early Marine histories labeled the site of the combat as the Tenaru River but in fact their maps misidentified the stream, Alligator Creek.

The fighting along the creek stretched into the daylight hours, and the fighter pilots of VMF-223 engaged in their first action on Guadalcanal, strafing the Japanese. The ground support, the first effort of this type since the Nicaragua days, fulfilled the requirement established in the directive that established the Marines as "the fleet landing force."

Shortly after noon, the Marines jousted with half a dozen incoming Japanese planes off Savo Island to the north. John Smith scored the first victory when he knocked down a Zero, but the enemy and the ground conditions sapped the U.S. strength. One shot-up fighter crashed when landing. A blown tire during takeoff brought heavy damage to a dive-bomber, and two other aircraft needed extensive repairs.

To create a reserve of pilots, the command arranged for half a dozen or so from VMF-212 to join the small group already on Guadalcanal. Among the reserves was Charles M. Freeman, a native of Rochester, New York. Freeman, known among his mates as Mel, said, "My father was a newspaper man. Almost from a boy I loved everything about flying. There was great excitement when Lindbergh flew the Atlantic, and we had some pictorial books of flying. I looked at pictures, made model airplanes. My father had good connections with people with airplanes, and I was always mooching free rides." The senior Freeman's employer, the Gannett newspaper chain, owned several airplanes.

The younger Freeman was at the University of Pennsylvania when the war broke out in Europe. He reasoned, "If America were going to get in a war then I better learn to fly. At the frat house, the headline in the newspaper said '50,000 pilots, 50,000 airplanes.' I had worked my tail off [all] summer in a root beer factory, making some money. Dad said I could take some of the money, $50, when I went back to college, to start in the CPT [Civilian Pilot Training] program, I was then a junior, 21 years old.

"As a senior, I took the advanced program, graduated from that. In Jan. '41 I wanted to quit school. The Navy was on campus recruiting pilots, had a real good program. They showed the movie *Flight Command*, with Navy pilots landing on carriers. I signed up with [the] Navy to become a pilot. A few days after I graduated, they sent me to Floyd Bennett Field, spent a few weeks there then went to Pensacola.

"I could see that as a Navy pilot you could end up a patrol plane pilot, do cruiser observation. I wanted to be a fighter pilot and you could transfer from the Navy to the Marines. When I was near the finish of training, I transferred. On December 7th, we'd been out the night before, raising hell in the barracks. I remember walking down the hall, some guy had a radio on, and hearing they're attacking Pearl Harbor. We were ordered to get to the airplanes and disperse them, some were flown away. The whole idea was to spread them out. I was in the war, not yet commissioned but I had finished my training. A few days later I was commissioned."

As the corps organized for war, Freeman sailed to Hawaii, where at Ewa in March 1942 he was assigned to VMF-212. "My first experience with [Lieutenant] Colonel Joe Bauer came after work. We were standing around, and a guy by the name of Red [Lawrence] Taylor, who ended up being my bunkmate and was one of the first guys killed, was drinking beer. Joe walked in, and we were all kind of being respectful. He reached over, took the beer can out of Red Taylor's hand and threw it against the wall. 'From now on, you drink water. The party is over! We are going to go to war. You are going to be the best pilots.' " Despite Bauer's restriction on potables, alcoholic beverages figured prominently in the coping mechanisms of many aviators, including those in the Marines.

Bauer, whom subordinates sometimes called "Coach," taught Freeman and the others the basics of the Thach Weave. Unlike the pessimists who predicted to Hise and others they were doomed, Bauer denigrated fears of being shot down. "Before you get your feet wet, you're in a rubber boat. When you reach the shore the natives will take care of you, and then in a couple of days you'll be back here." While teaching combat maneuvers, Bauer often flew a slow-moving SNJ trainer against students in Wildcats, artfully gyrating through the sky while the novices struggled to get on his tail or keep him in their gun sights. He constantly explained the essentials of a dogfight and, on the ground, diagrammed problems and solutions on a blackboard.

Freeman recalled, "He whipped us into shape. We were starting to switch to the F4F. The Navy gave us the ones that were beat up. [The lament over receiving secondhand Navy castoffs was a constant.] Ewa was still shot up but two or three weeks after that we were told to get our gear together. We were leaving, went aboard the *Hornet*. We were passengers; our planes were hung on the overheads. Navy pilots did any flying.

"Down near New Caledonia, we heard reports there was battle going on somewhere [Coral Sea]. On May 5th, we launched, not knowing a damn thing about where we were going. I was the junior officer pilot of VMF-212. We flew in formation finally (first time with these airplanes), came over the town of Noumea [New Caledonia], didn't really know where the field was. Flew north over town, just about out of fuel, finally located the air strip, got in and got the airplanes down. It was the longest over-water hop of a fighter squadron at the time."

In these anxiety-ridden days before the Battle of Midway, Freeman recalled, "We were expecting to be attacked. I don't remember seeing more than 2 or 3 antiaircraft guns. We flew our tails off, one to three hops a day, trying to get in condition. We had a sergeant pilot [there were a total of three in VMF-212], a tall gangly guy and some of his behaviors were a little weird. During one flight, there was a bridge near the airport. He tried to fly under that bridge [but] didn't quite make it, bounced the airplane on the other side, pushed in the belly, managed to get airborne and head it into the airstrip. Bauer could have killed him. He took his wings away on [the] spot, told him he'd never fly an airplane again. He kept him in the squadron as a strip worker. [Bauer] said, 'We can't lose one single airplane with foolishness. You'll get all the chances you want to be a hero.' He had a real idea about the war." Bauer actually gave the miscreant another chance but after he damaged a second airplane, he was restricted to ground service.

Freeman continued, "We finally got the word we were going to Efate. They said the field was ready, but it was not much of an airfield. They were still working on it. We had been practicing short field landings. Our officers told us we had to land in the first 50 feet of the field. It was very peaceful and quiet. One bad scare came while we were there. Patrols picked up a big Jap fleet heading south, that was going to pass by the New Hebrides. We went on alert; the idea of 16–18 planes fighting off a determined Jap attack on New Hebrides didn't look like anybody would survive. We had pretty high respect for the Zeros. How could you keep on fighting if they sent on wave after wave. I remember sitting in my plane in [the] dark, engine warmed up. I was going to be in the first flight. Waiting for the signal was pretty scary. I had some pretty long patrols going north. We began to feel war was passing us by when they opened up Santos [Espiritu]; we were the most experienced and best squadron but they held us back."

The opportunity for pilots in 212 suddenly appeared. "They wanted five or six reserve pilots for VMF-223. Bauer got us together and told us about landings on Guadalcanal. 'I'm sure every one of you wants to go, so you're all volunteers. We're going to draw cards to see who gets to go.' I never won a thing in my life but I drew one of the lucky cards, to get to join 223 on Guadalcanal. Bob McLeod, Red Taylor, John Massey, Tex Hamilton, we were on standby, we could do anything we wanted to do. The next day [August 21] we were on our way up, on an AVD [a destroyer transport] loaded with gas and mines. It got to torpedo junction where you make a left-hand turn—sure enough right above our heads, a couple of bombers. We couldn't tell who it was, but they did not drop any eggs on us. About that time the lookout yelled, 'torpedo!' and there was sure enough a torpedo coming at us. We went down at the bow, at flank speed, that thing went under the stern. Really close.

"We were waiting for dark to start up toward the beach. They put us over the side in rubber boats with our parachute bags. It was dark as a son-of-a-bitch, no lights anywhere. They put us ashore. I wasn't ten or fifteen feet up that beach and there was some shooting. A guy grabbed me and said lay down, I fell down, lay there, in the dark until they got us into jeeps.

"We went through a grove. Every once in a while we'd stop. Then they said we can't go any further tonight. We slept there, with parachute bags and clothes we had carried. I flew for the first time the next day. On the following morning, we got bombed, my first time under fire. That is a horrible experience. We were on the air strip and they were after the air strip. We hadn't even gotten the slit trenches dug. I ran for a bunch of trees back of the air strip. You could hear 'em [the bombs] whistling down. I dove in between a couple of big trees with big high roots. A guy at another tree sat up and a piece of shrapnel cut him in half, cut his guts out. I was convinced the only real safety was in the air. I didn't want to be on the ground.

"There were snipers around in trees, right near where we were. I can remember Massey, a terrible cigarette smoker, the first or second night the son of a bitch rolled over, lit a cigarette. I loved Massey but I yelled, 'Turn that out!' Anyone who lit up at night was just coaxing a sniper."

While Freeman tried to adjust to life on Guadalcanal, Richard Mangrum sought to improve the capabilities of his squadron in both scouting and attacking. Mangrum arranged for a portable lighting unit to illuminate a third of the runway at night and parked a jeep with its headlights on at the far end of the takeoff strip. After an episode of after-dark shelling by the enemy, Mangrum said they began nocturnal missions. "I took a three-plane section off and we climbed out and there was a sliver of moon left. Standing around the end of Florida Island, we could make out Japanese ships and we attacked them."

He continued, "The first bomb I ever dropped on a Japanese was at 2 o'clock in the morning. We couldn't tell if we hit or had done them any damage whatever, and the next morning we found some oil in the area, but it was meaningless. I think it certainly gave the Japanese something to think about, that we finally had a capability of some sort, perhaps not too effective at night."

Despite the best efforts of the valiant construction crew, potential disaster hung over even routine operations. Carl reported, "We didn't have much of a field there then. Henderson Field was pretty much pitted. We lost some planes on landings and takeoffs, particularly if we tried to take off at night, as we did a couple of times. We also seemed to be right on the borderline for fuel and ammunition most of the time. Sometimes we had supplies for only 24 hours. Particularly at the time of the Battle of Savo Island, the Navy was skittish about bringing anything in there. So we had to get it by air and some days we would have only six airplanes in commission." Two days after the Marine airmen took up station, five Army P-400s—a version of the P-39 Airacobra—from the Sixty-seventh Fighter Squadron reinforced what became known as the Cactus Air Force. Subsequently more planes and pilots from the Sixty-seventh settled in at Cactus.

Hise remembered, "The whole damn thing, flight operations conducted there [was the] blind leading the blind. The second day we were there, we launched but I didn't go. They heard some Japanese ships were coming. [The planes] went off, were gone a couple of hours, found nothing. The first flight I made [occurred after] coast watchers radioed down to us. They had spotted Japanese coming out of Rabaul. They ran up a white flag [as a signal] to save our aircraft. We'd all get in our birds and fly away and after the Japanese had come and delivered attack, we'd land."

Charles "Fog" Hayes, as operations officer, said that during the first few days while the fighters took off to meet raiders, the ground crews "man handled" the SBDs back into the coconut groves to get them out of sight of the Japanese. "We found as things progressed that one of the best ways of protecting the scout bombers when we got word of an attack coming down the Slot was to get them in the air and fly them around to the other side of the island and bring them back when the attack was over. The Japanese were operating at extreme range and while they could make it down [to Guadalcanal] they couldn't stay very long."

As good an account as the defenders of Guadalcanal rendered, they suffered a steady attrition through combat or accidents. When the Japanese shot up Captain Rivers Morrell a few days after the squadron began operations, Marion Carl moved up. He and John Smith took turns leading the fighter flights. Meanwhile the Japanese, recognizing the growing threat to their plans by the Americans on Guadalcanal, organized a task force to deliver troops protected by a fleet that included three carriers and three battleships.

As the flotilla steamed toward Guadalcanal, Rear Admiral Frank Jack Fletcher prepared a reception that featured the carriers *Saratoga* and *Wasp*, hosts to Navy fighters, dive-bombers, and torpedo bombers. At Cactus the tiny band from VMF-223 and VMSB-232 rose to greet a raid of fifteen bombers, shepherded by twelve fighters from the carrier *Ryujo*. Marion Carl led the interceptors. He personally destroyed two bombers and a Zero. Lieutenant Zenneth A. Pond, Lieutenant Kenneth D. Frazier, and Marine Gunnery Sergeant Henry B. Hamilton (an enlisted pilot, one of the temporary replacement pilots drafted from VMF-212) shot down a pair apiece. Altogether the Marines accounted for sixteen aircraft, and the Japanese attack from the air never reached its target. However, three Marine pilots vanished, presumably crashing into the water, and one flier managed to bail out over Tulagi and return to the squadron. Meanwhile the Navy air assault upon the enemy fleet sank the *Ryujo* and splashed as many as seventy-five of the foe.

For their part, the Japanese hit the *Enterprise* with three bombs. Still, the damage to the American carrier brought an unexpected boon to the Cactus Air Force. Navy Lieutenant Turner Caldwell, low on gas and dubious about trying to board the *Enterprise*, chose to lead his eleven SBDs to the comparative safety of Henderson Field. For more than a month these dive-bombers would operate from Guadalcanal.

The success of the Americans in the air did not deter the

Japanese commander from his objective: the landing of ground forces on Guadalcanal. Mangrum recalled that a few of his planes were in the air that night but at about three o'clock in the morning, Intelligence advised that a Japanese task force was approaching, with an assault upon the beachhead by enemy carrier planes expected by daylight. Said Mangrum, "There was a feverish operation to get our aircraft that had been operating during the night refueled and rearmed. This was extremely slow because of the lack of facilities. It was barely completed by daylight."

With an attack expected imminently, Mangrum launched his SBDs at daylight. "Unfortunately, there was a squall area over the Florida straits and we simply could not get through with the kind of equipment we had in those days. We had to return, rearm and refuel. We took off again. By that time some of that squall area had moved on and we could get through. So now it's middle of the morning and we hadn't yet been attacked, fortunately."

Hise dated August 25 as his first real operation and ended up flying right wing on Mangrum. He noted that some of the dive-bombers under the Navy's Turner Caldwell were part of the American contingent. A handful of fighters from Guadalcanal, augmented by Wildcats from the *Enterprise,* accompanied the SBDs. "Away we went, to the north and west," said Hise. "We climbed up to about 12,000 feet. I had the aircraft in blower [supercharger] and looking across this blue Pacific I could see the clouds marching across in columns, white and puffy. I was getting tired, in the danged airplane a long time. The fighters had up and left. They had run low on fuel. There off to port a few miles ahead, three columns of ships were steaming in formation, heading generally towards Guadalcanal. I was greatly excited, anticipated momentarily attack by Zeros, having lost fighter cover. I thought they're going to be on us in a minute. We approached these ships; looked like classic dive bombing going down on a target at Maui. Mangrum came up on these ships, 90 degrees to the ships' travel, heading west. He made a high speed approach, waggled his wings, and over he went. Baldy [Lieutenant Lawrence Baldinus] went and I kicked the airplane up and over and put the nose down, thumbed down the flaps, pushed back the throttle, started rolling the left tab because of the lack of torque as it comes to idle. You've kicked the old bird over so you're swinging on the bell, floating off the seat. Once I got the aircraft established in the dive, I was busy looking for the biggest ship. I resolved this might be my last day on earth. I saw the biggest one and Baldinus had the same thought as I did. He was right in front of me. It turned out we were diving on a cruiser. You don't stay long in a vee, starting at 10,000 feet and diving at about 240 knots at the bottom. I was coming up fast on the guy. I reached the point to drop my bomb. I thought I had everything right, pulled the bomb release and came back on the stick and added a little power, got a little gray— this was before G-suits—made a right turn. I did something you're not supposed to do. I didn't dare not to see what I did. To my great disgust there were no great black balls of fire. I could see a half a circle in the water beside the ship, but not a spark. I advanced full power and got my flaps up. I joined up on Baldinus because I was concerned about being alone with Zeros about. Second, I didn't know the way home, only a vague notion, I had no precise heading, I was pretty much out of it, in my infancy in flying, Baldinus was a most accomplished flyer with more hours than several second lieutenants combined.

"Mangrum had missed. He had not gotten lined up and made a second run. I thought this above and beyond. The flight was successful. We all went home. I didn't think we did anything, but I found I was credited with hitting a cruiser. Baldinus got credited with sinking the cruiser. We were the two guys who had dived on the vessel. [Official records indicate the warship was only damaged.] It was just great we had made this run and didn't lose anyone. I'm sure we turned them back at the very minimum."

In addition to the flagship cruiser hammered by Baldinus and Hise, the combined efforts of the Marines and Navy, along with bombs dropped by an Army B-17, burned a large transport, sank one destroyer, and damaged a second. Two Marine rear gunners shot down floatplanes. More important, the assault persuaded the task force to abandon its attempt to bring fresh troops to fight the defenders on Guadalcanal.

Mel Freeman, the replacement pilot from VMF-215 who

reached Guadalcanal by sea, said, "In the morning we were told who we would fly with, what airplane we were assigned to and who was going to be our first wave. At that stage, you checked your airplane. We didn't try to launch everything at once. There was our first wave, then a reserve to protect the guys when they were landing in case there was a second group [of enemy aircraft following the initial raiders] behind them. The idea was to make the attack, get in there and go after the bombers. We were told to forget the fighters. You can't win, can't fight 'em, and that's not what we're after, the fighters can't do any harm; we were there to protect Guadalcanal. The bombers can do harm. Our objective was always get the bombers.

"There was a red alert the next day. We got our first big scramble with Marion Carl. In the scramble to take off, you would try to take off in sections. In the air everybody just joined up on everybody else, and tried to stay together. If you had time to fly formations you did, but not if you didn't.

"The attack came from the west. We climbed and tried to get into position, if we could get word fast enough. The coast-watchers were just fantastic, but we never really had enough time. Very few times were we in position—getting to 30,000 feet. We couldn't get up there. At 30,000 you didn't really have a fighting machine and couldn't fly that smooth. The air was so light, if you made a sharp turn, you lost a lot of altitude.

"The first battle I was in, I was pretty far back—as a second lieutenant I was the junior man and was usually way back. By [the] time the first wave got to bombers in position to attack 'em, they had made a turn toward the north. They had already lightened, dropped their bombs. They were nose down and going. I could see Marion Carl. Bombers were over here on my left, I'm looking at Carl up at the top, several hundred feet higher, I was probably almost at the tail end of the line, the fighters had come in. We always would hold up for fighters and go for the bombers. When he [Carl] peeled off, he made one of the most damn beautiful overhead runs I ever saw. The twin engine Bettys were getting away from us. I made my run on one. I came in and misjudged him. I was at about a 45 degree angle to him, I was able to put my bullets ahead of his right motor, pretty sure I hit him, that engine started to smoke. I later claimed a probable on him. I didn't see him blow up.

"I peeled off and was going forward trying to get more speed to come back up as they were pulling ahead of us. Down below I saw a torpedo bomber, looked very much like our TBD, a three-man crew, a big greenhouse canopy. He was down below. I came in on him and the tail gunner really let me have it, but I think I got him. I know I killed that gunner. When I pulled up over that [plane] he was hanging over the side. I looked down and that Jap pilot and middle guy were just looking up at me. I could see their faces. I was afraid I would overrun him, I peeled off and turned around to like come back at him again. A Japanese fighter came around and was really bearing down on me. We exchanged shots head-on. He went over my head. I don't know what happened to him. He kept going.

"This is my first blood, first battle, I had never shot to kill. I had this thought, 'What are you doing?' I was feeling, all I wanted to be was an airplane pilot and here I am in an airplane trying to kill someone. After I made that run on the second bomber, and the Zero made his run on me, I was looking ahead. A Grumman fighter came by, spinning, smoking, partly on fire, I kept hoping someone would bail out but he never did. It was Red Taylor. We had been very good friends. He was a big ole boy from Berkeley, University of California football team.

"I didn't know at the time it was Taylor. I went back to [the] field and landed. It's a really weird but very exhilarating feeling . . . you survived your first combat, I thought I had done pretty well. I felt really good about what I was doing. Every sort of crisis or emergency, I was cool, I don't know why I [did] not fall apart or flap in the face of emergency.

"I flew a couple more battles, patrols, strafing missions. We were feeling desperate, hoping the ground troops would hold the line. I realized that if we don't hold these bastards off we're going to be pushed into the sea. Every night those Jap ships came down that slot and threw big shells. One day I went back to where our camp was, nothing was left of my tent, I didn't have anything. I hated that shelling, it was terrible. During the day, we were on alert or trying to fight. At night we were getting shelled, getting sniped. Fatigue was something, always tired. Tired and hungry. Food was crappy. We ate as well as anybody—they weren't treating us better. Last days on Guadalcanal I couldn't keep food down. I practically lived on cocoa.

"Three or four days after that first battle, I was in another fight. I was flying John Smith's wing. My plane had been hit, had a hole in it, so I couldn't get the altitude. I was flying this thing but my battle was over. I was around 23,000 feet, I was in an upside down spin, down to 8 or 9,000 feet. I'd been on oxygen and I couldn't get out of this upside down spin, I had heard talk, way back, all those stories when you sit around hangars . . . get your foot on the stick, give it a good fast kick to get out of an upside down spin. I took off my oxygen mask and my throat mike, unhooked my safety belt, and I did kick the stick. The next thing I was out of that spin.

"I called on the radio and said, 'I'm in a bad spot, I'm going to have to jump. Try to get the boats out.' The damn airplane was falling fast. I must have been at about 5,000 feet. I pulled the rip cord but I was over the water. As I got down to the water I was too weak to get up and unsnap my parachute. I was too weak from lack of oxygen. The damn parachute was like a sail. I was under the water, on the verge of drowning. I had my cartridge belt, gun, water bottle [dragging me down]. Plus, there were sharks around. I was a swimmer in college. Finally I managed to get [an] arm free, pulled one of the valves on my life jacket, slowed me down and I popped to the surface. Not too far away was a boat, landing craft.

"That was my last flight on my first tour. I had lost an airplane. They had more pilots than planes. They sent me back in a DC-3 to Efate. I felt bad about losing [the] plane. I wasn't ashamed but felt bad." Freeman had been on Guadalcanal for less than a week.

FIVE

CACTUS BUDS

On August 26, a day after a Japanese task force abandoned an attempt to disembark troops on Guadalcanal, sixteen twin-engine bombers, escorted by a bevy of fighters, renewed the effort to knock out operations at Henderson Field. Somehow the raiders avoided the Marine fighter patrols and dumped about fifty bombs on the base. They ignited two thousand gallons of scarce aviation gasoline, and the conflagration exploded several American thousand-pounders stored on the ground, adding to the devastation. Shrapnel ripped into parked aircraft and damaged the communications shack.

However, Marine Wildcats caught up with the enemy as they headed home. Marion Carl became the first Marine ace when he shot down a pair. Three of the recruits from VMF-212 at Efate demonstrated the wisdom of their selection. Captain Loren D. Everton, a twenty-nine-year-old who had been a pilot since the age of seventeen when he'd barnstormed with an ex-Marine flier, splashed three bombers. Henry "Tex" Hamilton, ranked as a Marine gunner and one of the few enlisted pilots, with seven years at the controls, registered two victories. Lieutenant John H. King scored one. Altogether the Cactus defenders claimed thirteen Japanese planes destroyed.

On the ground, in the air, and from the sea, the two sides slugged away toe-to-toe in a near-incessant atmosphere of bloody combat. Henry Hise said, "Guadalcanal was not boring. It was hairy." There was little in the way of creature comforts to alleviate the stress. The basic diet included dehydrated potatoes, Spam— World War II's signature facsimile of ham—and some captured rations. Hise recalled, "I didn't much care for the food. I was omnivorous, a billy goat. I had a cast iron gut and could eat almost anything. The food was what you would call miserable. They were feeding us twice a day. The ships had done such a lousy job of unloading, harum scarum. We were eating canned Jap food, and some Australian sheep's tongue which was one of the most obnoxious items. Candy, like LifeSavers, was pretty good. We used captured cookware, I had a Japanese blue metal bowl. I had never drunk coffee before. I'd fill up that bowl with coffee and pour in a lot of condensed milk. The camping facilities used bedrolls in Japanese tents. We dug straddle trenches for latrines and pissed on palm trees when one was handy. There was not much in the way of bathing facilities. We went down to the river, soaked and washed. It was the only bath I had on Guadalcanal. I was full of sweat, dust and grime. I paddled around in the water and came back to camp much refreshed. The sanitation was not too good." Dysentery became a common complaint, and the ubiquitous bloodthirsty female anopheles mosquito infected many with malaria.

The omnipresent black dust of the Solomons, stirred up by activity on the ground and the Japanese bombs, fouled engines, which required almost incessant cleansing. The field itself remained a hazard, almost an obstacle course for anyone seeking to leave the ground or land. Hise remembered, "My job was to disperse the aircraft. To move the planes further away we made a primitive bridge with crossties and coconut logs. Being extremely green, while pulling aircraft around with trucks, none of us knew what we were doing. With a rope around the landing gear, one truck lurched forward and damaged the plane. We should have had someone in [the] cockpit to operate the brakes. We had to manually fuel planes with gas [using hand pumps and fifty-five-gallon drums]. Sometimes we had to help load our own bombs." During the first weeks of operation, there were no bomb hoists, forcing the ground crews and pilots to trundle the ordnance to the aircraft and then lift it by sheer muscle power to the racks.

"When it rained," said Hise, "to taxi you'd need almost take off power to get to the end of the runway. Soon as aircraft got on soft ground they sank up to the hubs." Historian Bob Sherrod described a takeoff as resembling "nothing more than a fly trying to rise from a runway of molasses."

Hise described a typical experience. "Almost invariably about 11 o'clock every day—it was a rare day they missed—one time when the white flag had gone up, we were trying to get our aircraft going and get out of there. I went out there to number 25. We had a guy named Bell [ground crew]. Bombs had straddled him and made a Christian out of him. He jumped up on the wing with an inertial starter, then gave the required number of twists. He yelled, 'Lieutenant, you've got it!' and jumped off the wing and started looking for a foxhole. We started out taxiing. It was a bit precipitous. The field was strewn with bomb craters, some of them deep and a few shallow ones from daisy cutters [a type of bomb] that threw shrapnel out parallel to the ground. It was tough going in the dust. When I got to the end of the runway, I got a wheel in [a] bomb crater about 18 inches deep and we were stuck. I put on full power but there was no pulling out. I concluded we were about 75 feet off the end of the runway. It was no place to be. [My gunner] and I jumped out and secured the aircraft. Near a hangar used to service fighters, I found a hole with a sun shade above it. I was pooped from events, but nothing was happening, I lay back and went to sleep. I was in deep slumber when all of a sudden I heard bombs falling. The never to be forgotten high shrill noise woke me up and I looked up at the plane overhead. The bomb hit no more than 50 yards away, really shook the ground. The noise impressed me.

"The hangar had been set afire, some ammunition was exploding, an F4F sitting in the hangar was unscathed. We milled around there, watching aircraft burn. I always admired the way those Jap pilots would fly formation, amazed those guys would fly three aircraft on either side of the leader. Particularly after they dropped bombs. My airplane wasn't holed, no damage, and was pulled out of the hole by a truck."

While the Japanese air arm attempted to ravage the American

positions almost daily during the daylight hours, they also sought to harass the defenders with nighttime sorties, the original "Washing Machine Charlies" or "Louie the Louses" who assassinated sleep with sporadic after-dark bomb drops. The sound of the unsynchronized motors of twin-engine bombers gave rise to the *Washing Machine Charlie* moniker, to differentiate it from the single-engine *Louie the Louse*. The noisy nocturnal stabs from the air were augmented by shells lobbed from submarines or destroyers lurking offshore. More ferocious bombardment by warships would occur later.

On one occasion Henry Hise happened to be serving as the eyes of the Marines. "I went out with old Danny [Iverson] on a search, going up the channel between the islands towards the Russells, Santa Isabel on one side and the Russells on the other side. It was late afternoon and the cans [enemy destroyers] would come down at night and shell the place. It was hard on sleep and nerves. Old Danny and I were out steaming along at 130 knots, about 1,000 feet off the surface. Up ahead we saw these four ships with the sun, blood red behind them. They were beautifully silhouetted.

"Having gone through recognition classes as a naval aviation cadet I recognized them as Japanese destroyers but old Danny didn't. We normally flew without radios, I couldn't say anything, Danny had his gunner start blinking at these guys with the Aldis lamp [a portable signal light]. They blinked back with guns; they started shooting at us. Old Danny put on all the power he had, I stuck it to my airplane, poured the coal to number 25, I was very proud I had my own airplane. Danny was running at take off power, I was falling behind. He goes up atop a small layer of clouds and he dives through the clouds on these ships below 7,500 feet. I armed my 500-pound bomb which I had hung myself the night before. We also gassed our planes ourselves. We didn't know any better coming through that hole in the clouds. It helped them [provided a range]. They armed their fuses accordingly.

"I was looking down on one, 90 degrees to me. I established my dive. All of them were firing at me; it just scared the hell out of me. This was the first time I was doing it myself with the full attention of four Japanese cans. I got down to about 2,500 feet and I cut my bomb loose, I'm sure I missed that guy. I couldn't find Danny, and went back to Guadalcanal, reported to Pagoda Hill. Danny . . . didn't get lined up. He tried a second time and still couldn't get lined up and drop his bomb. The important thing was we reported we found them. We had located these people. They didn't shell us that night, maybe Danny and I scared them off."

Early in the struggle for Guadalcanal, some Japanese prisoners persuaded Lieutenant Colonel Frank Goettge, an Intelligence officer, that a number of their compatriots, wandering in the bush, beset by disease, and near starvation, could be induced to surrender. Instead of taking a heavily armed patrol, Goettge, with one of the prisoners as a guide, led a group with limited firepower into the jungle. They were ambushed and slaughtered. Only three of the twenty-four Marines survived. Word of the incident spread through the ranks, with predictable reactions.

Hise said he went to look at about thirty Japanese captives contained behind a barbed-wire fence. "They were held like so many cattle, completely open to the sunshine. The Marines usually preferred to kill them. I had no more sympathy for them than gorillas. I had fallen into the spirit of the times. It was a dehumanized enemy. I thought of them like cockroaches, masturbating before God. Merciless as we were, they were damn lucky to be alive, without a whole lot of kindness. The convention [Geneva protocol regarding treatment of war prisoners] was not so rigorously adhered to. Pearl Harbor was so recent, the strangeness of the Japanese and what happened to Goettge's patrol."

Despite the terrible pounding of vessels seeking to reinforce their garrison on Guadalcanal, the Japanese persisted. On August 28 still another expedition of four destroyer-transports left Rabaul with thirty-five hundred soldiers, bound for the embattled island. This time it was a patrol from the *Enterprise* that spotted the ships steaming down the Slot. "We launched our SBDs, about eight aircraft," said Hise. "Four Navy guys got off ahead of us. We went over Florida past Savo on our left. A pretty good distance out I saw ships on the surface, little ships, like miniatures. We were at 10,000 feet. They were blinking, firing. I was flying off the left of Iverson's wing, I was bouncing around trying to get Iverson's attention.

"Mangrum saw these ships and I saw planes diving on the lead can. The Navy pilots were diving on them, I saw an explosion on the bow of one several miles away. Just in front of the bridge. I lost sight of them when our flight was turning and I found myself diving and at a 90 degrees direction this can was traveling with a great big wake, obviously a lot of power. I had a pretty good dive angle. The aircraft felt fine and I got the brakes down, in good style. Atop the dive I had lagged a little [waiting his turn after] Iverson and Mitchell. I led this can, hoping for it to run under my bomb. I dropped my bomb and pulled up. I took a look, to see what I had done. I had led them too much, got a beautiful hit in the water right out in front of them.

"I later learned that Mitchell who had followed Iverson had never broken his dive and gone into the water. As I left for home I saw a Japanese destroyer. I had charged my guns, the .50 calibers in the fuselage, synchronized to fire through the prop. I was approaching off its starboard side aft at a 45 degree angle, I got the nose down and I started my left side machine gun, my first experience with aerial gunnery in an SBD. It was going pop, pop, pop, about that fast. I had a go strafing that Japanese ship, very briefly. I ended up flying over the bow at about 200 feet. I picked up some of my companions. As I did, off to my left I saw the ship that I'd seen hit before we dived had sunk, except for the forward portion of the ship. It was one of the most delightful sights I had seen. I couldn't have been any more pleased with any turn of events. I went on greatly enthusiastic. We had really sunk a ship. I later found out that the Navy had done it. It was claimed by us that we sunk three of four destroyers which I really can't believe. We landed about dark; the entire flight had taken two hours."

Richard Mangrum, while proudly reporting the successes in interdicting the Japanese, said that after several daylight fiascoes the Japanese "got smart. They came racing down there during hours of darkness." They modified their tactics even further when they realized that their antiaircraft tracers at night revealed their position. "The Jap very soon discovered that if he just laid doggo, and showed no lights whatever, we were almost totally ineffective. Couldn't find him against any low visibility at all. By the time a pilot had pushed over in his dive, he would lose him again and we simply had no point of aim. They did in fact land a number of troops in this fashion.

"[Still] it became more and more expensive for the Japanese to attempt this kind of operation and their next tactic was to try to run troops in small craft from the Shortland Islands area down through the Slot, lying doggo against the shoreline, heavily camouflaged during daylight hours and then proceeding on during hours of darkness. Eventually, a great many of them got to Guadalcanal that way.

"We discovered this concept and went after them. We found literally hundreds of these boats in various places along Choiseul Island and other little indentations in the shoreline. They'd be pulled up, several of them, side by side, hastily covered with limbs and branches. They were very hard to see and I'm sure we didn't see all of them. But we saw many. Unfortunately, we didn't have the proper type of armament against targets of that nature. The only bombs we had were demolition bombs with fuzing for ships. We'd come down time and again and put a bomb right through a good-sized landing barge and of course blow it to hell, but probably not hurt the one 20 feet from it. That airplane had no strafing capability that was worth a damn. A great many troops were stopped from ever getting to Guadalcanal. On the other hand, a great many of them got to Guadalcanal."

The intensity of battles between the troops on the ground mirrored that in the air. On August 29 raiders sifted through the protective screen of Marine fighters and dumped their bombs on the field. As the enemy turned for home, the Marines claimed to have destroyed four bombers and four fighters. In contrast with his opposite number at VMO-251, John Smith packed in as many missions as his VMF-223 subordinates. He had already emulated Carl, achieving the status of ace. On August 30 a report from a coast-watcher of large flocks of both fighters and bombers bound for Guadalcanal ignited a frantic scramble. Eight Marines in their Wildcats headed toward the stratosphere to gain an altitude advantage, while their eleven Army Air Corps companions in P-400s could only climb to twenty thousand feet, the uppermost height possible for the Airacobra. The air defense had mustered every flyable plane in the arsenal.

Ordinarily the protocol dictated focus on the bombers, but Smith and his associates saw twenty-two Zeros swooping down upon the Army fighters. With two Americans already dangling in parachutes, Smith ordered an immediate attack upon the Zeros. Within the space of a few minutes, the squadron commander shot four fighters out of the sky, Marion Carl brought down three aircraft, and even the battered P-400s accounted for a pair, albeit losing four planes with two of the pilots able to walk back to Cactus. From the raiding force a total of fourteen aircraft failed to survive. Only three of the Airacobras remained air-worthy, and their obvious inferiority to the Japanese fighters wrought a decision to restrict them to ground support missions.

Among the early casualties was dive-bomber pilot Henry Hise. "The last experience I had on Guadalcanal," said Hise, "we had had a scramble to get away from Japanese aircraft. That morning and then in the afternoon [August 30] Leo Smith's Squadron [VMSB-231] arrived. The CO [Major] Leo Smith and his Exec [Captain] Ruben Iden got word from Pagoda Hill of ships landing troops on the beach. That night I got the job to go with Smith and Iden to go down and look for Japanese. We used bottles of Saki [captured Japanese wine] with wicks to light a flight path down [the] runway. We got a very poor briefing and away we went.

"We joined up successfully, turned out lights, flying step down, I was right side, Iden on the left, about 7,000 feet, pretty high to see anything. I was unable to watch [the] shoreline I was so busy flying the airplane, stumbling along at a considerable distance down the beach, when, to my surprise, Smith waggled his wings and over he went in dive. Iden followed. I was much perplexed that these guys were diving on non-existent ships, I was danged if I was going to dive on non-existent targets. I had gone ten or twelve minutes when I did see a ship coming to the beach, nose in. I decided I would go in as a dive bomber with brakes but then glide bomb. I got the bomb armed, with my nose aimed at him. It was quite a dilemma. I wasn't sure it was Japanese. Hell, it could be one of ours. I pulled on the bomb release. It wouldn't release, I thought I'm going to hit the water. I horsed the aircraft out of there.

"A Japanese ship opened up on me with a tracer. Fraley [Private F. L., his rear gunner] opened up back on ship with his twin 30s. The tracers looked like they were barely crawling up at you and then as they got near, they went zip, by you in a flash. I was relieved to have them shooting at me. If they were Americans they wouldn't shoot at me which was completely wrong.

"I got probably one bomb off just past the stern. I could see I missed it, I went home, kept the water on my right, land on my left. I landed, brought the aircraft in, taxied it over to its parking spot. A jeep took me to report to [MAG-23 executive officer Lieutenant Colonel] Charlie Fike and I said I had seen a ship, probably landing troops and had a go at it. The jeep carried me back to our camp. I was going back to bed, I was so tired, 7–8 hrs flying that day and we'd been there about ten days. I was ready to lay down [to] rest when they sent a weapons carrier to pick me up because they wanted to debrief me further. [Second Lieutenant D. V.] Rose [from VMSB-232] was there. He had been out somewhere. [Second Lieutenant R. W.] Vaupel [from VMSB-231] got up with [the] driver. The weapons carrier had no cab, just seats. Rose and I were in the back end. He was a fine guy, a veteran of Midway. We were starting out across the kunai grass at Henderson Field when a Mavis [four-engine Japanese flying boat] started a bomb run, traveling from west to east, dropping his bombs. You could hear the bombs whistling. The first explosions were a dull red flash and then smoke and dust would obscure it, like a muzzle flash of a gun. The bombs were marching down the runway in our direction. The kid driving the truck floor-boarded it. Being a semi-rational being, I realized this was the worst thing. The Japs were dropping daisy cutters, shrapnel to burn or damage aircraft and kill people.

"Vaupel was yelling jump, the bombs were coming down the runway, we were off to seaward side of the runway which was still lit with flare pots. The truck was picking up speed, Rose jumped off the left side. I stepped over and bailed out to the left, I don't think I cleared the fender, I remember rolling in a somersault position across the ground. I found myself laying prone, flat on my belly, I knew I had hit hard. I thought I'd get up—if you can get up and walk, like in football, you'd be okay. The best I could do was raise myself up on [an] elbow. Pretty soon someone came out and hollered, 'Anybody hurt?' I yelled 'I am.'

"They lay a stretcher beside me. I eased myself on it, lay on my belly, I wasn't hurting that much but I spent a miserable night on a canvas cot. With great effort I could turn over. There was no X-ray machine to see how badly I was hurt. I thought in a couple of days I'd get up. In a couple of days, I got the notion things were getting a little more serious. Other people were being hurt. During a severe fire fight, while Prosser was visiting me, a Marine contemporary of his had been shot in the arm. To my surprise this guy was happy as hell, because it was a ticket out of there.

"I got an idea something pretty seriously happened to me when I hadn't urinated for a day and a half. Ole Doc Roe came in with what I thought was a pretty novel idea. They catheterized me. They had a bombing raid and brought a fellow in who'd been hit in the face with shrapnel. He had a great big bloody bandage where his jaw should be. They took us down into a dugout, carried me on a flat canvas stretcher. They set me up like a can of lard on a shelf."

Referring to the soldier wounded in the jaw, Hise recalled, "This boy's eyes were bulging, hands shaking, couldn't talk, sitting on a stool in the middle of this dugout. He got hold of a piece of paper and wrote something on it—'will I be all right?' and the doctor said of course. Then the doctor said to a corpsman, 'Keep this man sitting up.' When the corpsman went out at night, in the darkening interior where you could barely see, this ole boy was gasping and gurgling. He slumped down, instead of sitting erect. Pretty soon he was horizontal, then he quit, he was dead. I couldn't keep that old boy alive. I had to quit worrying about him and start worrying about myself when we had shelling that night, close enough to make the ground tremble and dirt trickle around our dugout. My heart was going a mile a minute wondering whether you're going to be buried alive.

"The next day they took me on a Stokes stretcher [formed in the shape of a human]. I had a blood blister from internal bleeding on my back. They took me down to the strip. They were not flying any non-combat aircraft and were gonna evacuate me in a B-17. They stuffed me in through the gunner's window, starboard side, and lay me down on the floor. Away [we] went, down to Espiritu Santo. I got cold. We flew at 7,000 feet. I was as dirty as mud. I hadn't shaved and medical care was almost non-existent. Without an X-ray they didn't know the extent of my injury. I was taken out to the USS *Curtis,* a seaplane tender, with a sick bay. As I looked up at the ship, from a rocking boat, a couple of navy types—one boy got me by [my] feet and the other under the shoulders. My gut spasms, which were involuntary, had my knees come up to my head. I thought why not lift me by the middle. I couldn't stand to be lifted head and heels. I cursed those guys and they gave me a little more care. On the ship in sick bay, they put me on a soft bed. Damned if it didn't nearly kill me. My back sagged and I was really in agony. I would have been better off on a hard cot.

"I was there with a bunch of guys who were hurt as bad as I was. One ole boy there with gas gangrene in the gut area died next day, another who broke his neck in a swimming accident, hitting his head in the Lunga River [on Guadalcanal], died. There was a doc evacuated for morphine addiction. He sat on a top bunk, crocheted all the time—a very novel cat. One ole boy, Kenneth Kirk, had his front teeth missing. Flying down to Efate over the ocean, he had a midair collision that killed the other pilot. Kirk bailed out and had a broken leg.

"These guys came in with their machine and tried to X-ray me for about three days, with me complaining bitterly about the way they were treating me. They really didn't know what was wrong with me for about three days. Finally, they told me I had a broken pelvis, broken right pubic arch, and a damaged lumbar vertebra, knocked off the sides of it. I was getting pretty fractious. I had always thought I was a pretty macho guy, nothing was going to bother me. I was taking little white pills, codeine. I'd get my arm stuck underneath me when I turned over on my belly. They literally put my ass in a sling, a canvas raised my middle but I received no relief.

"Apparently, the Japanese Navy was believed to be coming down to the area. They sounded General Quarters, sick bay was below the water line, way below decks. They blacked out the ship and I heard them dogging down the doors above us. We were in total darkness. [It was frightening] knowing you're down there and couldn't walk. Luckily, I was not claustrophobic. We bitched enough about it. Next time the [Japanese warships] came they wrapped a canvas sling around my rump, put me back in the Stokes stretcher and away we went up the ladder. An ole doc, a navy doctor, shot me with morphine. He broke out one of those little ole toothpaste tubes with a needle on the end of it, stuck me, squeezed that whole thing in me. Then I didn't give a damn, copacetic . . . I was lying out on that deck, looking out at the night sky. I thought everything was the roses, really the berries."

To handle the increasing number of patients, a medical facility was constructed on the beach at Efate. Hise endured a rough ambulance ride that triggered bursts of agony. "They put us in tents. They brought in these burn cases, from flash fires, off the *Wasp* and who looked like tar babies. Their features had swelled. In black face, their lips swelled up, fingers looked like black bananas. Their heads looked like bowling balls. They put tannic acid on them and they were in agony. I thought for the first time I'm well off. I admired one ole kid. During his pick up [after the *Wasp* sank] a can had come along. He was sucked into [the] screw and got a pretty good cut across his back. He was in pretty bad shape but still horny as hell. An ignorant young American at death's door, and still the ole sex drive continued working."

Hise and others were evacuated on a Dutch ship for a two-day voyage with him "on another shelf." At New Caledonia he boarded the *Solace*, a hospital ship. "I felt, boy, this is absolutely great. I was in a bed that could roll up, with ropes I could haul myself up, I was pretty comfortable. I had clean sheets. These ole boys shaved me, the first time since I had been hurt 10 days earlier. It was confirmed, a busted pelvis, broken vertebra. From then on everything was pretty much easy. We made it to an Auckland [New Zealand] hospital."

As Hise indicated, the tiny Cactus Air Force welcomed reinforcements on August 30 when two more squadrons from MAG-23, commanded by Lieutenant Colonel William Wallace, arrived amid an attack by enemy planes that succeeded in sinking a U.S. destroyer-transport, the *Colhoun*. The newest organizations included nineteen fighters from VMF-224 led by Major Bob Galer and a dozen dive-bombers under Major Leo R. Smith. At day's end Guadalcanal counted eighty-six pilots and sixty-four functioning aircraft, including ten from the Navy and the three surviving Airacobras. Two days later, Seabees equipped with a pair of bulldozers joined the effort to improve Henderson Field and scratch out a second small strip, designated Fighter One.

Within a few days the entire command structure at Henderson Field took on a new look. Brigadier General Roy S. Geiger, an aviator whose experience dated to World War I, and commander of the First Marine Air Wing, set up shop in the Pagoda to personally take charge of the air campaign. As his chief of staff he brought with him Colonel Louis E. Woods, and between them they brought some order to what had been a rather chaotic operation. Geiger lifted morale with news that MAG-14 had begun the process of shipment to Guadalcanal, where it would relieve the battered remnants of MAG-23.

At the same time as Henderson Field added to its strength, the Japanese also committed another thirty-six fighters and twenty-seven medium bombers to buttress their campaign to oust the Americans from the island. Although Admiral McCain requested more help from the Army and the Navy, those services insisted they could spare neither fighters nor carrier-based planes. Bob Galer noted that during his time at Guadalcanal there were never enough F4Fs available as a reserve. Nor did the pilots have intelligence or weather briefings before taking off. "You knew they were coming and you looked out to see whether it was raining or not."

Three days after coming to Guadalcanal, the virgins of VMF-224 scrambled with some veterans of VMF-223 to confront a forty-plane raid. Galer demonstrated his proficiency by shooting down a pair. According to Galer, "Normally, without other instructions, you'd go for the bombers. We found particularly that if you hit the lead bomber, they might all drop their bombs. That resulted several times in them bombing their own side."

The twin-engine Bettys, the most common type of bomber, packed a fair amount of defensive firepower, particularly the twenty-millimeter cannon or stinger in the tail. "The tail gunner couldn't shoot up," noted Galer, "so as you'd roll over and come down, you'd be particularly safer than coming up from behind. In one of those big melees, after it started, all that theoretical stuff broke down.

"Altitude was important. If I didn't have the altitude, I'd go up, but I preferred the altitude. We'd roll over and come down on them. We could pick up enough speed that even if the Zeros led down on us, if we had timed it right we could beat them. Then we'd come back out and fight them. You had a four-plane division. You could protect each other's tails to a degree. That protection [the Thach Weave], after about three minutes of fighting, was scattered all over."

Occasionally the mission shifted. "The boss at the Pagoda would say, 'The number one priority on this mission is ships,' and they'd hang a couple of bombs on us as well as the ammunition for the machine guns."

In these early days of aerial combat fighters did not carry camera guns. Galer said, "Usually the ships we were protecting would report that '[so-and-so] shot down two Jap airplanes here,' and you'd get credit for it." Sometimes other pilots could confirm a claim, but as in all theaters of World War II, fierce competition for the title of "ace" exaggerated successes. Flight leaders, explained Galer, had the advantage since they led the first pass at the targets.

On September 9 Marion Carl and his colleagues sortied upon word of incoming bombers. The marauders mistakenly overflew Henderson, enabling the defenders to gain plenty of altitude before falling upon their prey. "While I was attacking them," remembered Carl, "I was shot down by a Zero. I never even saw the guy that did it. I bailed out at 22,000 feet. I landed in the water and I had a life vest, that's all. Clayton Canfield was in the same flight and he got shot down too, but he got picked up immediately by a destroyer. When I hit the water, there wasn't anything near me. I treaded water for about four hours. I was only about half a mile or so offshore. I tried to swim ashore, but there was a current there. I just wore myself out, getting nowhere. It's pretty hard to swim when you've got your shoes on and you're packing a .45 and so on. Finally, a native came out in a dugout canoe. He circled me a few times; he was going to make sure I wasn't Japanese. His American name was Steven but he couldn't speak English.

"He finally let me climb in the boat and we went ashore. He promptly took me to a fellow by the name of Eroni, who was a native doctor but not a native of that island. He was a Fiji boy with the equivalent of about a high school education, could speak English very well and was trained to administer medicine to the natives. He had sulfas and he'd perform even a simple operation if he had to. He was good at setting bones and things like that. I stayed with Eroni, his wife and child, a little girl."

Carl learned he was about twenty miles from Henderson Field and his host had a fourteen- to sixteen-foot boat. "It had one of these little single-lungers, about a five-horse, single cylinder job. I tried to get it running but it wouldn't start. We decided to walk back. He said, 'Okay, I'll take you.' He was a rugged little fellow. He started walking and I thought that I was in good shape, but I sure had trouble keeping up with him."

The night before, Carl had heard and even seen the flashes from a bombardment of the base by Japanese warships. "We got part way back towards the base and we started running into lots of natives coming towards us. The Japanese had landed some troops between where I was and the base and the natives were all fleeing. As soon as we ran into them, we realized that there wasn't any chance of me getting through the lines.

"I came back to where the boat was and went to work on the engine. There wasn't anything wrong with the boat and I got it running. That night, we waited until about two or three in the morning—we figured we wanted to hit the beach up there about dawn. We didn't want to be going up the straits and run into any of the Japanese, and yet we wanted to get there about daylight.

We had to time it just right so that when we passed that part of the beach where the Japanese were, it would still be dark. Yet we didn't want to get up there too early, because the damned fleet might be coming down and doing some more shelling."

Altogether Carl had been missing for five days, and during that period the offshore bombardment had drastically altered the scenery. "I could hardly recognize the place. We were camped under a grove of palm trees. All the tops of all those palm trees were gone!" He was further taken aback when he entered his tent. "All of my gear had been divided up and somebody was in my bunk! I had to kick him out. He happened to be a member of VF-5 and they had been in there temporarily. [Members of the twenty-four-plane Navy squadron were refugees from the *Saratoga*, disabled by a torpedo.] It was standard practice in those days. Because everybody was scratching even for clothing, food sometimes."

While Carl was out of action, the indefatigable John Smith surpassed him in victories, sixteen to twelve. General Roy Geiger, pleased with the rescue of Carl, had summoned him to headquarters, where he twitted him about Smith's successes. "What are we going to do about that?" Geiger supposedly asked. Carl snapped, "Goddammit, General, ground him for five days."

If such moments of levity occurred, they were overshadowed by the parlous state of the aircraft and their pilots. While the Japanese absorbed fearful losses, they still shot down enough Americans and destroyed or badly damaged enough aircraft to reduce the U.S. assets on Guadalcanal to marginal limits. Almost equally injurious, weather and the sodden, pitted field cost lives and wrecked aircraft. On a single day, September 8, a collision on the strip smashed two fighters, another crashed on landing, a fourth nosed over in the mud, and one blew up after it slewed into the ground during takeoff. Altogether that day, six fighters morphed into junk and two more required extensive repairs.

Combat fatigue was responsible for some accidents, and in other cases errors of navigation and identification marred search missions. Inevitably there were those who had lost their nerve. While Hise was aboard the *Solace*, Leo Smith, the CO of VMSB-

231, appeared, diagnosed with combat fatigue after flying the single mission that was Hise's finale. According to author Thomas G. Miller in his book *The Cactus Air Force*, Bob Galer scorned some of the veterans of VMF-221 who flew at Midway as "almost worthless." (Miller specifically noted Marion Carl and John Dobbin as exceptions.) Galer also took exception to another top officer. "The squadron commander of one of the dive-bomber squadrons thought he was so important that he shouldn't be risked. That didn't help. The colonel toured around the camp area and he allowed as how, if the Japs took the field, he was going to drive his jeep and put to sea. I told him in words of one syllable, 'Get the hell out of my camp and don't come back.' And he got out and he didn't come back."

Mel Freeman said, "We had one guy who was a real coward, a big loud mouthed son of a bitch, an all American football player. He just was plain chicken and in that first group I was in. He hurt his knee in a jeep accident, he got taken out, right away [about six days after arrival]. Then the son of a bitch, in complete violation of security, wrote some letters to *Time* magazine, in which he was a great hero." The offender subsequently was shipped back to the United States.

On the other hand, the majority showed an esprit de corps that overshadowed the few slackers. Said Galer, "Mostly the gang was ready, willing, and available. If you had dysentery . . . when you landed, you got out of the airplane and got into a jeep or some vehicle or you'd walk over and undress in the stream to take a bath." Galer, who endured the discomfort of dysentery along with a mild case of malaria, remarked, "To add to the difficulty, even on the ground you didn't have any toilet paper. You had a Sears and Roebuck catalog if you could find one. It wasn't nice. We didn't have much medicine in the first month."

Responsible for the air defense, Admiral McCain had pleaded for additional squadrons, and while the top echelons felt they could not spare wholesale transfers from other areas, it was a standard practice to fly in men and machines to replace losses of personnel and aircraft. Roy Spurlock, assigned to VMO-251 stationed at Espiritu Santo, had been flying patrols to protect that base against a possible attack when he and several others from the squadron received orders to deliver a batch of new planes to Guadalcanal.

Spurlock detailed the path that led him to Henderson Field. "I got into the Marine Corps because I was brought up in a military atmosphere. My father had been discharged from the army in 1919, he had been a second lieutenant but was too late for WWI. I loved to wear pieces of his uniform and one of my father's assistants on his job was an ex-Marine, an old China hand. I read books about war, *Fix Bayonets* by Ernest Tomlinson and *Old Gimlet Eye*, Lowell Thomas's biography of General Smedley Butler of the Marines.

"I had completed two years of college at Eastern Kentucky Teachers College in 1940 and transferred to the University of Kentucky. Things were heating up quickly around the world, and as a student of history, it seemed obvious to me we would soon be in the thick of it. I applied for a Marine Aviation Cadet appointment. I reported to Anacostia, December 16, 1940. I was 20 years old. After 30 days [of flight instruction] I was able to solo and accepted for appointment as a cadet."

Spurlock passed through the various schooling programs, all under Navy auspices, that produced Marine pilots. He learned to handle the already obsolete biplane dive-bombers and fighters. After he graduated and pinned on his wings, he became aware of the recruiters for Claire Chennault's American Volunteer Group in China, later known as the Flying Tigers. "They gave us a very attractive offer, $1,200 in gold deposited in any bank if we would go over and join the Flying Tigers. You were required to resign your commission and sever relations with the United States government. I just couldn't see kicking the U.S. government and Marine Corps in the teeth after all they'd done to make me a pilot, so I turned it down."

In December 1941 Lieutenant Spurlock reported to San Diego and the Second Marine Aircraft Wing. Ultimately assigned to VMO-251, Spurlock traveled to Espiritu Santo in early August 1942. "Cadres of fighter pilots went up to Guadalcanal as part of fighter command, but the squadron itself was not ordered to

Guadalcanal." Spurlock denied the assertion by Sherrod that VMO-251 lacked proficiency, insisting that the aeronautical skills, the gunnery scores while shooting at target sleeves, and the quality of personnel made the squadron's airmen believe "We had the best in the Marine Corps." He concluded that military politics influenced decisions on who would man the planes on Guadalcanal. Spurlock did admit there was an impression that the squadron was not pulling together because of friction among some of the top elements. "Major Hart [the CO] did not like to fly and he directed that his exec, Major Charles Hayes, serving as his operations officer, not fly. That could have had some effect upon decisions."

On September 10 Spurlock graduated to Guadalcanal. "I was in there with five or six planes when we flew some planes off the *Hornet*. We took off from Espiritu Santo, in the backseat of SBDs. While qualified to land on carriers, we had not done that lately. Therefore, the Navy flew us to the *Hornet*. During our stay on the ship we ate a lot of ice cream, had hot showers on ship [luxuries not ordinarily enjoyed at Espiritu Santo]. We flew F4Fs off the carrier and landed on Guadalcanal.

"My timing was perfectly right about the first part of Sept. 10–11th. The Japanese seemed to favor attacking about the 12th of the month, go hammer and tongs. When they got their noses bloodied, they'd sort of slack off from the ground attempts that continuously tried to retake the airfield. We got up there right in the middle of a bloody battle. The Japs were sending down Zeros and bombers, anytime they could get enough of them together. The Japs owned the seas around Guadalcanal in the night. We could stay only because we had the airfield during the day. Destroyers and cruisers frequently shelled the perimeter and air strip.

"The foxholes on Guadalcanal had no roofs when we first moved in. It quickly became obvious this wouldn't cut it, Jap cruisers were slinging shells into the palm trees where the slits were. You'd dive into a slit trench and shells, lightly fused, would hit palm trees and go off in a terrific explosion. They would fling shell fragments down into slit trenches. It was not long before the palm trees got pretty ragged and we got roofs over the slit trenches. I had a good friend who during a night attack when there were no roofs, laid face up. He said, 'If I'm going to get killed I may as well watch it.' There was a sudden crash and something tore at his leg. He thought he lost his leg and felt down, felt blood but instead of a bloody stump, he found a coconut had hit him right on the knee cap. He wasn't permanently damaged but limped around for days.

"While I was in Guadalcanal in September, the Japs tried to throw us off the island. We were saved by the artillery, Chesty Puller's 7th Marines and Merritt Edson's Raiders. We were on the airfield, where we had to spend the night, laying in foxholes, with no cover over the foxhole, cruisers and destroyers shelling [the] airfield. I could see shells exploding in the trees blowing up on the field, machine guns firing all around where Japs were attacking. We had pack howitzers, 75 mms and a few 105 mm howitzers. The brunt was on the pack howitzers, firing all night long. You could hear the section chiefs shouting out commands, then bangs over in the coconut groves where the Japs were attacking. Fear is a funny thing. I was wearing a cotton khaki shirt, khaki pants, and all of a sudden my knees began to twitch. It had never happened before to me. I couldn't stop them."

Actually, the furious Japanese attacks against the American lines defending Henderson Field came perilously close to overrunning the Marines. During the Battle of Bloody Ridge a handful of enemy soldiers penetrated deep enough to menace the headquarters of General Vandegrift, but the staff fought them off. The artillery mentioned by Spurlock, plus the small-arms fire of machine guns and rifles, killed an estimated six hundred Japanese. The three remaining much-disdained P-400s exploited their heavy firepower with a devastating assault as the surviving Nipponese struggled to retain their positions. In addition, another eighteen Wildcats from two carrier-based Navy squadrons flew in to reinforce the battered airmen. Their appearance enabled Spurlock and several other ferry pilots, without ever engaging in combat against the Japanese, to fly to their Espiritu Santo base on a Navy transport.

Two days after Marion Carl plopped into the sea, Bob Galer engaged in another free-for-all in the sky. "One guy," said Galer, "I think shot me down. I was diving and he was tailing. I went into a cloud and came back out. My engine was only sputtering. There was a [Zero] right in front of me. I unloaded on him and then went down. The Navy told me that I shot it down but I think it was one that exploded."

Unlike Carl, Galer chose to try to pancake his plane on the water. He splashed down about two hundred yards offshore and remarked that when he hit the sea, "It almost feels like you hit a wall. Just as I landed, I could see three people coming down the beach with rifles. I'm swimming and I'm pooped. I got over behind a log, got out my pistol. These three guys came up—they could obviously see where I'd been—and I said, 'Drop your rifles!' They said, 'Me friendly!' I said, 'Drop your rifles!' They said, 'Me friendly! Me friendly!' but didn't drop their rifles. Eventually, about the third time, I thought they were friendly and I captured the three. They were natives working with the Australian coastwatchers. In a dugout canoe." The local people paddled Galer to Tulagi. An amphibious plane picked up the Marine pilot to return him to his base.

As the buildings and grounds officer for VMSB-232, Hise mentioned that he and the squadron executive officer, Major Fletcher Brown, scouted the area around Henderson Field for a new campsite, one with improved drainage. Brown, however, along with Second Lieutenant C. B. McAllister, crashed at sea during heavy weather about a week after Hise was injured. The survivors of the squadron moved to the new bivouac area, which came under intense bombardment. Shrapnel ripped through the open sides of tents, killing Hise's friends Baldinus and Rose, and wounded Iverson.

The two Navy squadrons that took up temporary station at Cactus had flown off the carriers *Hornet* and *Wasp*. During the sea voyage, according to Max Brand's book *Fighter Squadron at Guadalcanal*, one sailor on the *Wasp* expressed fear that the trips by the carrier through such turbulent waters provided a prime target for submarines. Indeed the *Wasp*, with the casualties seen by Henry Hise, had been wrecked by torpedoes on September 14; it expired after a coup de grâce from American ships.

Nearly seven hundred miles away Joe Bauer, in addition to his duties as squadron commander of VMF-212, served as a kind of general factotum for the operations on Efate, code-named Roses. Between flying patrols and training his pilots, Bauer scoured his island for other promising sites for landing strips, entertained top brass visitors, and supervised the shipment of fighters and dive-bombers to Cactus. His diary recorded high and low moments. On August 31 he noted, "Got in a few more dog fighting lessons today. We flew more hours this month than last and on top of that had 8 of our boys up at Guadalcanal. Everton, King and Bastian returned today. . . . Poor Red [Taylor]—we'll miss him. Our boys got credit for eleven Japs up there but they know they got about ten more than that."

September 6: "Took a look at the night fighter strip up at Havannah Harbor. It is expected to be ready within two weeks. That will give me a place to put all these fighters."

September 9: "It sure rained a peckful today. Water was standing everywhere. The edges of the runway and most of the revetments were washed out pretty severely."

September 15: "Took the dawn patrol—getting off before daylight. We weren't raided, of course. Sent my two troublesome planes back to Roses. 15 *Hornet* SBDs were supposed to land at Button [Espiritu Santo] about dark. 5 were lost. Those boys gave us the sad news that the *Wasp* had been sunk, the *North Carolina* [battleship] damaged and a DD [destroyer] sunk by subs. That certainly changes the aspect of this south Pacific battle. Am wondering now what will become of the boys at Cactus."

September 16: "251 [the Marine squadron in which Roy Spurlock served] took the dawn patrol today. Still we weren't raided. They are bringing in 3–4 loads of wounded on the DC-3s each day. . . . I returned to Roses alone this P.M. to get a stove, some towels for Gen. Geiger, and 15 of my men on a plane for Cactus. Heard [that] Carl returned to Cactus airport after being in the hills living with natives for several days. Hooray!"

September 18: "3 of my planes and pilots started out for Buttons. One returned due to prop trouble. Our planes are approaching a rapid state of deterioration due to lack of spare parts. Doc Martin shoved off for a trip to Cactus. They need doctors or corpsmen to ride the evacuation planes to take care of injured in transit. A B-26 was lost tonite [sic]. Later heard they all bailed out at Buttons."

September 21: "Four full colonels from Cactus came through today on their way to a rest. Too bad all the aviators and troops couldn't be going thru, too. Certainly hearing a lot of rumors about replacements these days. Sent up lots of supplies to Cactus today. They'll sure be glad to see the stuff. Cots, juices, rain coats, screens, candy, etc."

Along with the flight crews exchanged between Espiritu Santo and Guadalcanal, ground personnel from the former also served at Henderson Field. Jim Law said he spent several weeks there, assisting in the repair of aircraft. During these first months, Law reported, "Spare parts were critical and when a plane was damaged beyond repair, all usable parts were salvaged to try to keep others flying."

SIX

CACTUS THREATENED

Except for the occasional infiltrator or sniper, the Battle of Bloody Ridge annihilated the ground threat to Henderson Field, and for about ten days the Americans enjoyed a lull. While the enemy restocked his aerial armada, the Cactus Air Force also added strength, although from one to three airplanes were lost daily because of weather and the abominable conditions of the rain-soaked runways. But toward the end of September, the Japanese resumed their attempts to destroy Cactus from the air and the sea.

Following a warning from a coast-watcher, on September 27 a mix of thirty-four Marine and Navy Wildcats intercepted thirty-one enemy bombers and fighters in the skies over Henderson Field. The Americans knocked down six Bettys and five Zeros. On the following day, an even greater force—well over fifty aircraft bearing the blazing sun insignia—struck.

Among those who confronted the Japanese was Joe Bauer. In his diary for the day he wrote, "I left Roses at 0200 for Cactus—arriving there about 0745. Went up in a DC-3 to clear up a few administrative problems and talked them into giving me a plane for any air raid that might materialize. The Japs came through in noble fashion. They brought over 27 bombers and about 30 Zeros. We got [a] 132-mile warning so had all our fighters up-stairs to give them a welcome. We shot down 23 bombers and 1 Zero. All our fighters returned safely—one had to make a deferred forced landing. I got credit for one Jap bomber. Am going to return in a couple of days and try to increase said total. Will try to run a rotation of 4 of my pilots at a time up there until all who want to go have had the opportunity. It was the greatest sight of my whole life to see the Jap bombers fall out of the sky like flies. I saw all the gang besides Gen. Geiger, Col. Woods, Lt. Cooley, Frank Daily . . . etc. etc."

Major Frederick R. Payne, the exec of VMF-212 who had been one of those shuttled from Efate to Guadalcanal and VMF-223, recalled in Max Brand's *Fighter Squadron at Guadalcanal*, "That day was Sunday, and Joe came out to the fighter strip and looked at the sky like a wild duck with a clipped wing. His business was on the ground, not in the air, but he had been holding himself in for a long time. He asked Major Robert E. Galer, commander of 224, if there was a spare plane around and Galer gave him one.

" 'They'll come over today just because you're here,' Galer said to him. 'I know your luck. It's your first chance to make a score, and you never waste time.' Well, it was just that way. In a minute or so, radar was telling us about a fine sky full of Japs, that were coming in. [Payne, quoting Galer, appears to be in error; the official Marine history attributes the warning of a raid to the coast-watchers.] And then there was Joe Bauer hitched into Galer's outfit and climbing into the sky. Twenty-five bombers and thirty Zeros were zooming in and were intercepted before they had a chance to damage the field. Of course, Joe got a score for himself, and it was one of those outsize Mitsubishis at that.

"He just got up there to Guadalcanal, popped into a plane, shot down a Jap, landed, and grabbed a transport plane back to Efate. It was a real Bauer stunt, a sort of game, a sort of joke, and I'll bet he was grinning all the way back to the New Hebrides. If he'd ever had a steady run of chances against the Japs, who can guess how many of them he would have had on his score? As it was, he was only four times in the air, and he grabbed eleven. Nobody ever topped that."

Bauer pressed his case for the use of VMF-212. On September 30 he flew a Wildcat to Buttons. He made his argument to the South Pacific Aircraft Command and indeed persuaded them to allow four of Bauer's pilots to report each week to Cactus for "combat experience." The following day Bauer and three from the squadron traveled by transport to Guadalcanal. That first night he noted, "It was practically impossible to sleep due to SBDs tuning up and taking off at all hours of the nite [sic]."

On October 2 the Coach saw action during a dismal day for Cactus. A flock of twenty-seven Zekes—similar to the Zero—evaded the eyes of the coast-watchers, and the primitive radar picked up the incoming traffic only half an hour out. That left little time to scramble the interceptors and get enough altitude to duel the enemy. The Japanese, high enough to compensate for a slight numerical disadvantage, quickly shot down a pair from VMF-223: Lieutenant Charles "Red" Kendrick, a Harvard law graduate and an ace, and Lieutenant Bill Lees, who like Kendrick had received a Distinguished Flying Cross from Admiral Nimitz one day earlier.

John Smith emerged from a cloud to find three Zekes dead ahead. He blasted one but the others maneuvered onto his tail and poured bullets and shells into his F4F. As the engine started to seize up, Smith artfully controlled the plane to a dead-stick landing some six miles beyond the Marine perimeter. Marion Carl, who saw the squadron leader in distress, flew protective cover over Smith until he climbed out of his ship and started to trudge toward the home team's lines. "It was just like a hike," said Smith. "There were a few rivers to ford, of course. The whole trip took me just two and a half hours." Fortunately for Smith, no Japanese soldiers were in the area.

Bob Galer also encountered trouble. For the second time in less than three weeks he was shot down. "I was up with six fighters, cruising about, at twenty or twenty-five thousand feet. Suddenly eighteen Zeros came at us out of the sun, and we took 'em on. The day was cloudy and after a few minutes, the only other Marine I could find was Second Lieutenant Dean Hartley. In the melee of first contact, I heard several Jap bullets splatter against—and through—my ship, but none stopped me. At about the same moment, Hartley and I started to climb into a group of seven Zeros hovering above us. In about four minutes I shot down two Zeros and Hartley got a possible. The other four were just too many and we both got shot down.

"Hartley got to a field but I couldn't make it. The Jap that got me really had me bore-sighted. He raked my ship from wingtip to wingtip. He blasted the rudder bar right from under my foot. My cockpit was so perforated, it's a miracle that I escaped. The blast drove the rivets from the pedal into my leg. I pancaked into the water near Florida Island. It took me an hour and a half to swim ashore. I was worried about the tide turning against me and sharks." Friendly inhabitants of the island took him to their village, and then he rode a canoe back to a Marine outpost.

A replacement pilot from VMF-121, Second Lieutenant George Treptow, was another casualty; a Navy pilot also lost his life. Four enemy planes were shot down, but the Cactus Air Force could ill afford to lose six aircraft with several more damaged. Of the original eighteen pilots from VMF-223 who arrived on August 20, only half survived. With twenty-six fighter aircraft flyable, Geiger could muster but one-third of the Japanese strength on hand at Rabaul.

One day later, signal success marked the Cactus complement—and Bauer played a prominent role. Marion Carl, who recalled the frustration of Bauer while confined to Roses, said, "He was just jumping up and down to get into the battle. But for some reason he couldn't persuade anybody to send his outfit up to Guadalcanal, and why, I don't know, because we sure could have used them.

"Joe was the type of guy that when there was anything interesting going on, he wanted to be in the middle of it. He was real aggressive and a real personable guy. Anyhow, he came up there one day [referring to the week of October 1–8], and he wanted to fly. He went to see John Smith.

" 'John, how about letting me go on a flight?'

" 'Well, you're going to have to talk to Marion. He's flight leader today,' said Smith.

"So Joe came over to me and asked if he could fly. I said, 'Hell, yes! How about taking a second section?' We only had six planes in commission. Pretty soon we got word from the coast-watchers that the Japanese were coming, to expect them in about 40 minutes. We scrambled, and we climbed, and we climbed and we climbed. It took about that long for that damned F4F to climb to 30,000 feet. No sooner did we get up there, expecting them momentarily, when we got word that the Japanese had turned around and gone back. I was just about ready to let down when I looked down and there were nine Zeros at about 10,000 feet!

"The bombers had turned back, but some of the Zeros had taken it on themselves to come on in. Normally, I wouldn't have said anything. I'd just have peeled off and away we'd have gone and bounced them. But since I had a lieutenant colonel back there in the third section, I called on the radio and said, 'Colonel, we've got nine Zeros down there.' I didn't get any answer, so I called again, and still no answer. I figured his mike was fouled up—which it was—so I said, 'We're going after them.' And down we went.

"Well, I guess we got them all, if we didn't, eight out of the nine. I got two myself, and then my guns jammed for some reason. Ken Frazier got a couple, got shot down. We were coming in to land, oh boy, Joe was so excited he could hardly stand it. He was bouncing up and down."

Bauer's diary entry for the day brims with enthusiasm for his task. "Our division (6 planes) led by Capt. Carl dove on 10 Zeros. We got 3 on the first pass. They all shoved right away, leaving me to play with the Zeros all by myself. I definitely shot down four and might have got more. At the end of the affair I noticed a parachute going down in the water when suddenly a Zero came out of nowhere and fired a long burst at the dangling pilot. This infuriated me and I went after the Zero with much gusto. I know I scored several hits on him and chased him away smoking. I'm positive he didn't get his plane back to his base. I returned to the field nearly out of gas—jumped in another plane and went back to locate the parachutist for rescue. The boy's name was Frazier."

One of the VMF-212 pilots taken by Bauer to Guadalcanal, Lieutenant Robert "Pop" Flaherty, related to Max Brand his view on the protection given Frazier. "Bauer got on the tail of that Zero and started him smoking right off. A Zero can fly around any

Grumman Wildcat that ever was, but the Coach had injured this fellow so badly that he was able to stay up there on his tail while the Jap lost altitude. The Coach kept slamming into him with his one gun [apparently his others had jammed] until he remember[ed] the man in the parachute and went back to see that he was taken care of when he landed in the sea. . . .

"The Coach was the last to land and we were waiting for him. We knew what he could do in the air, but this was the first time he'd had a chance to show his stuff to the world [Flaherty erred on this point]. When he came in, his engine was flaming out from time to time—burning gasoline was what it was. He taxied it back to the line. He cut the switch. It was still burning like a son of a gun. They had to put out the blaze with fire extinguishers. The Coach came roaring in like a happy boy, shouting that he had gotten five of the sons of bitches. He was plenty excited. . . .

"He was still explaining this when a mechanic came up to him with a grin and said that he'd landed with his high-altitude supercharger on as well as the auxiliary fuel pump. Both should be cut off under fifteen thousand feet.

"The coach didn't excuse himself. He just laughed about it. I never saw a man who loved a fight the way he did. He was drunk with it. It was shining out of him. After a fight he was always a little crazy with excitement, and it burned us up to see the effect on him. It made you want to get up there and breathe the same extra-special ozone that he always seemed to find when he was in action."

Bauer remained at Cactus several more days, in time to receive a singular honor. In mid-September the First Marine Raider Battalion under Lieutenant Colonel Merritt Edson captured a Japanese flag. Edson sent the trophy to Roy Geiger, saying, "With this flag we send our congratulations and appreciation for the magnificent work done by the officers and men of our Naval, Army and Marine Corps units under your command."

In his thank-you note Geiger promised, "This flag will remain the property of this Wing, and will be turned over for custody to the first Cactus based pilot who shoots down three Japanese planes during one raid." On October 5, Bauer told his diary, "I was presented with a historic Japanese Battle flag today for my successful attack on the Zeros on the 3rd. I in turn presented it to Group 23. It will be put on display in the Marine Corps Trophy room in Quantico, Va."

Bauer felt no individual should take credit for what was obviously a team effort. However, when he received a letter of commendation from Admiral McCain and another from Roy Geiger, he admitted, "It is a grand and glorious feeling to get patted on the back for one's efforts. Makes one really want to do things. Had the colored band [the race-conscious Marines did not even accept African Americans until August 1942] out for the boys tonite. They really enjoyed it."

While Fighter One's short, grassy strip opened for business from the Wildcats and Airacobras, Marston matting—a meshlike steel rug—paved Henderson Field to make it more hospitable to heavier aircraft and less vulnerable to weather. A trickle of reinforcements appeared. The Navy fed in portions of its VS-71 and VT-8 units—scout-bombers and torpedo aircraft. VMSB-141's complement began to arrive, and all of VMF-121 under Major Leonard K. "Duke" Davis with executive officer Captain Joe Foss boosted the fighter strength. Replacement pilots from VMF-212 and VMO-251 continued to shuttle among Buttons, Roses, and Cactus.

As understrength as the aerial defenders of Guadalcanal were, the tours of VMSB-231 and VMSB-232 had ended before the first half of October. From the latter unit, SBD pilot Henry Hise, evacuated because of his injuries when he leaped from a truck during an attack upon Henderson Field, said, "The squadron was gone within 10 days of [the] time I left. It had ceased to be a fighting force. We sunk a few ships, did our job, and mainly dispelled the myth of Japanese invincibility. The fighter pilots did great and their losses weren't as great as ours. Of the 27 second lieutenants who had departed San Diego in July 1942, there were seven of us still alive. They'd been killed in every way you could imagine— from weather and aircraft accidents to combat." One pilot had even been shot down and killed by a U.S. Navy warship that mistook him for a marauder.

Time also ran out for VMF-223. On October 10 came its final moment of glory. For several days the "Cactus Express"—small batches of Japanese destroyers and the seaplane tender *Nisshin* and light aircraft carrier *Chitose*, loaded with troops, light tanks, artillery, and other heavy equipment—attempted to land reinforcements on Guadalcanal. American warplanes, drawn from all three services, had harassed them. To help protect the Cactus Express, flights of floatplanes, akin to the Zero, shepherded the voyage. When the Grumman fighters fell upon them, John Smith, according to Max Brand's book, was heard to shout over his radio, "Jesus Christ, have I got a field day!" Having downed a number of the enemy and strafed the small flotilla, all of the Wildcats returned to Fighter One, relatively unharmed except for some bullet and cannon shell holes.

The depredations inflicted by VMF-223 and cohorts did not deter the Cactus Express. Actually, the Japanese command ordered a renewal of daylight strikes against the lair for the Cactus Air Force as well as bringing up heavyweight naval guns to bombard the island garrison. Shortly after noon on October 11, radar on Guadalcanal detected two flights of planes around 140 miles away. A motley crew drawn from Navy, Army, and Marine fighter squadrons rose to meet the challenge. Newly arrived VMF-121 and the Navy Wildcats of VF-5 never made contact, while the Army's latest version of the P-39 could not surpass nineteen thousand feet. But at twenty-five thousand feet, sixteen fighters, mostly from Bob Galer's VMF-224 (plus a few remnants of VMF-223), grappled with the oncoming raiders.

The Japanese tactics first advanced seventeen Zekes followed by a main body of twenty-seven Betty bombers with thirty Zekes as their chaperones. The Marine pilots brushed by the forward echelon and headed for the bombers, which were scattering because of poor weather and forced to dip below the clouds. They never reached their target. The fighters knocked down six of them while one, having descended to a lower altitude, fell victim to an Army P-39. A pair of enemy fighters were also splashed.

On this day John Smith and Marion Carl flew to Roses on their way to a war bond tour in the States. Within twenty-four hours,

the remainder of VMF-223 had also left Guadalcanal. Although
the Americans had been spared an aerial assault, the Cactus Express succeeded in depositing soldiers and equipment on the island. While the Nipponese unloaded their cargo and prepared to
bombard the American positions, U.S. Navy warships assigned to
protect a convoy bearing GIs from the 164th Infantry to bolster
the Marine ground forces were alerted to the presence of the
flotilla. Just before midnight, off Cape Esperance, a fusillade of
shells from American ships battered the Japanese cruisers and destroyers, sinking one of each and damaging others. Retaliatory
fire demolished the destroyer *Duncan,* killed more than one hundred sailors, and severely damaged several vessels.

Aware that the battered enemy fleet remained within striking
distance, Navy and Marine torpedo planes and dive-bombers took
off at the first light of day to search for the now retreating elements of the night sea battle. The combined air groups sank a pair
of destroyers at the gateway of the Slot into Iron Bottom Sound—
the name given to the waters between Guadalcanal and its eastern
neighbors where so many vessels had been sunk.

Hot on the heels of triumph, disaster struck. On October 13
neither radar nor coast-watchers warned of incoming aircraft in
sufficient time. The U.S. fighters were still struggling to gain altitude when the first bombs exploded upon both Henderson Field
and Fighter One. The Marston matting became a maze of twisted
steel, and great gouges pitted the runways of the fighter strip.
Only one bomber and one Zero were shot down.

The Japanese returned for a second assault that afternoon.
Among those who tried to intercept them was VMF-121's exec,
Joe Foss. "Before the war," said Foss, "in 1937 I started flying a
Taylor craft, a 40 horsepower job. I'd gotten [the] idea I wanted to
be a pilot when Charles Lindbergh flew to Paris. He came to Sioux
Falls and I wanted to get on the stand and shake his hand but
somebody removed me from the platform." A graduate of the University of South Dakota, Foss, like most Americans, was naïve
about military strength. "At the time, I heard people say we were
the greatest air power in the world. Lindbergh rated Germany as
the number one air power and Great Britain as number two. He

was right. We had good training but our equipment was down the line."

Foss enlisted in the Marine Corps in 1940 for training at the Pensacola air base. Upon graduation he remarked, "I got plowed under. I came back to Opalaka [a flight training site] as an instructor. I didn't have the patience I should have had as an instructor. You have to work hard, and I tried to escape from there.

"I volunteered for everything, including glider school. I was number 13; they took the 12 ahead of me." [The Marine Corps never developed an airborne organization.] Thank you Lord. I volunteered for photo school. The people going there know all about photography. I was a farm boy. I didn't know [anything] about it. But it was required of officers that you be in the upper 10 percent of the class or you get an unsatisfactory report. That's not good for the home team if you want promotion. I had to work at it night and day. I joined VMD-1, a photo-reconnaissance squadron. In 1942, we had two airplanes and a whole squadron of people. I was the most junior man, number 40 in that squadron. Twice every day I went to headquarters and picked up the mail. And then I just sat around studying books on aerial photography. But I didn't want to study. I wanted to get with the war. I thought there's gotta be a way out of this situation."

When Foss heard of an aircraft carrier training group he asked his CO if he could get assigned to that school. He was told they did not accept Marines. Foss argued that in a photo reconnaissance outfit somebody should know fighter tactics and persisted, volunteering to sweep hangars and organize funerals for the growing numbers of casualties. Eventually the authorities relented. When he finished the course with the highest gunnery score ever recorded, he pestered the Marine brass for assignment to a fighter squadron.

Colonel Perry O. Parmalee, a veteran of the Midway experience and in the Marine aviation hierarchy, on August 7, 1942—the day of the first landings on Guadalcanal—offered Foss the post of executive officer for VMF-121. According to Foss, Parmalee said, "You're too old for the job [he was twenty-eight] but due to your enthusiasm, and we think you know what you want, we'll give you the job."

When Foss reported to Camp Kearney at San Diego, he found a few tents, ninety-six lieutenants, five Brewster Buffalos, and two F4F Wildcats. "It was a great outfit, ready to go to war. The Buffalo was a great airplane. Those who [have] flown it know it's an enjoyable vehicle. It has especially great visibility when you're taxiing, and good visibility for circling the field." As obsolescent as the aircraft were, the tactics taught were up to date. During a voyage to the South Pacific, Foss said they talked about combat and the Thach Weave. Matters improved on their arrival at New Caledonia, where the squadron received F4Fs.

"The big day came in October 1942. They said we were going to head north. We went on a carrier. After we got within about 375 knots south of Guadalcanal they told us there were a number of enemy submarines in the area and we were going to have to launch. The Skipper of the squadron, Major Duke Davis, a great pilot and a gutsy guy, said; 'I'll go off first, you go off last.' Meanwhile the carrier was doing evasive action because it wasn't safe there. They didn't want one of the fish in the side. . . . Then I had a good take off. I got my crew together, one half of the squadron. We got together and headed for Guadalcanal.

"When we reached Guadalcanal I could see the war was for real. When you see those pock marks all over the place, when you see the air bomb holes, it's entirely different from what you saw in the newsreels. When we landed there were all of those happy people, they were really enthusiastic about seeing us. They just cheered. These people had the enemy on three sides. Then we met the pilots; they all looked tired—Maj. John Smith, Maj. Marion Carl. We planned on getting some good instructions from them. Maj. Davis said 'You veterans will be able to show us around the area tomorrow.' Ole Smitty looked us straight in the eye and says, 'After one day you'll be a veteran.'

"They showed us where they left the airplanes. They were not taking anything with them except what they had on. They kissed us goodbye and left. Smith had 19 [victories]. Marion Carl had about 16. We couldn't get enough word of what to do. The next day we were on our way. After a couple of days there we felt like veterans. We got shot at immediately. Some of the boys did get to shoot some down on the first mission, one Betty bomber and three Zeros. All I got was shot at."

On October 13 Foss seized his first opportunity. He described the event: "A bird got in my way and I managed to knock the plane down. That was the first one. For an instant it felt great to get rid of an enemy. But it upset all of the other enemy in the area and they were after me. I heard that if you dove straight down full throttle and then made a turn, it would pull the wings off a Zero. Whoever wrote that was a fiction writer. I'll guarantee you they poured the lead into me. They already had the oil cooler out and the engine froze. [Was I] scared? I really was, I thought boy this really is tough. I came down and hit the field, too fast to get the flaps down and the prop was just windmilling. There was nothing to do but sit there and wait. At the end of the field I gave it [a] little left brake and I sat in a palm grove there. Somebody counted 258 holes, whether they were coming in or going out, I don't know. As I sat there waiting to get out of the airplane I thought why did I ever leave the farm.

"It all happened directly over the field. Some of our boys on the ground had opportunity to see it; they were slapping me on the back, telling me how great I was. I didn't dare tell 'em how scared to death I was." Japanese records indicate that all of the Zeros in this engagement returned safely. The discrepancy between Foss's version and that of the Japanese emphasizes the dubious nature of claims and statistics for both sides who staked claims amid the hurly-burly of battle.

The Imperial Navy command, rather than leave the subjugation of the Cactus Air Force to artillery units and aircraft, decided to protect its convoy of reinforcements by means of its own heavy guns. That night the Japanese brought two battleships close enough to hurl 918 rounds of fourteen-inch shells that shook the earth, shattered buildings, toppled palm trees, and ignited five thousand gallons of gasoline stores, turning Henderson into "a sea of flame," said one observer. To add to the pummeling, Japanese artillery, including 150-millimeter howitzers, lay down barrages while overhead Washing Machine Charlie dropped his bombs. Among the forty-one killed that terrible night was Major

Gordon Bell, who had brought VMSB-141 to the island little more than a week before, and four of his pilots. Bombs and shells wrecked the radio shack and left the Pagoda a shambles. As many as twenty-six airplanes were ruined; only seven out of thirty-nine SBDs could function the following day, and not a single torpedo plane was operational. The damage was so extensive that temporarily all flight operations shifted to "the cow pasture"—Fighter One. Geiger, long suspicious that the Pagoda provided the enemy with a convenient landmark and aiming point, ordered the structure bulldozed in favor of a less conspicuous headquarters.

Joe Foss cringed under the nocturnal ambuscades from enemy ships and artillery. "The shellings were terrible. They began right off the bat when we arrived. On the 12th, the Japanese Navy sailed through the Slot and sat there from a little after 9 o'clock in the evening until 4 in the morning with no let-up, I can still hear the screams of men getting hit. We were in an impact area, and hadn't dug in too well. We were lying with our shoulders flush to the ground." Foss, in his biography, admitted to the same uncontrollable shaking that afflicted Henry Hise. He said, "During barrage, the 14- and- 15-inch shells hit the dive bomber squadron across the trail. A lot of them were killed, including the doctor who had his spinal column severed. My former instructor Ed Miller was killed. From the time the firing started till it stopped, the ground vibrated. They shot star shells that lit up the place and destroyed most of our airplanes that were on the ground."

When dawn arrived, the air arm on Guadalcanal had been whittled down from forty-two Wildcats to twenty-four; thirty-nine Dauntless SBDs were reduced to seven, and not a single torpedo plane remained flyable. The Army's Sixty-seventh Squadron counted only four of the substandard P-400s available, and just two of the improved model P-39 Airacobras were operational. When Vandegrift pleaded for reinforcements, Rear Admiral Aubrey Fitch, who had replaced McCain as commander of the South Pacific Air Forces, ordered eight dive-bombers from VB-6, housed on the *Enterprise*, to report to Guadalcanal while pilots from Joe Bauer's VMF-212 flew in another nine SBDs, spares at Espiritu Santo. After they dropped off the aircraft, the fliers would return to Efate by transport and then the entire squadron could check in for duty on Guadalcanal.

Even with the hasty reinforcements, a dire emergency gripped Henderson and Fighter One. The bombardment during the night had wiped out almost all the aviation gasoline. As part of the normal supply system, huge special-purpose barges with thousands of gallons of fuel, towed by tugs, had been under way from Espiritu Santo. As a supplement, the *McFarland*, an aged destroyer, loaded 750 drums of gas and steamed toward the Solomons. Until these ships arrived, the only source lay in what could be drained from wrecked planes.

As night fell on the fourteenth, the already sleep-deprived Americans hunkered down in dugouts and shelters, anticipating another battering. In the predawn hours the first flares, dropped by floatplanes, illuminated portions of the fourteen square miles of the island held by U.S. forces. Through the flickering light, the two Japanese battleships belched 752 shells that blasted both Henderson and Fighter One while artillery whistled in round after round.

When the barrages slacked off as the first rays of the sun parted the darkness of the sea, the defenders saw transports busily disgorging some four thousand Nipponese soldiers into landing craft. Above the scene fighters confidently patrolled against any American interference, although the Japanese believed their naval and artillery bombardments had rendered the Cactus Air Force impotent. Two of the three SBDs from VMSB-141, still operational after the nighttime pummeling, tried to take off. Both ran afoul of craters, and Lieutenant Robert Patterson—who with his gunner escaped injury in the second crash—took off in the third dive-bomber. Hampered by a hydraulic leak that prevented him from retracting his wheels or using his dive flaps, Patterson still claimed to have planted a bomb on one of the enemy ships before staggering back to the base.

Duke Davis led five fighters in a strafing mission against the enemy transports. One of his companions, Lieutenant (J.G.) Elvin "Smokey" Stover, nominally a member of VF-5, literally bumped into a Japanese floatplane. As Stover maneuvered to blast the biplane head-on, he pulled up a bit late. His right wing hit the fabric-covered upper wing, causing the aircraft to smash into the ground. When Stover checked in at the airfield, the ground crew removed a yard of Japanese insignia wrapped around his wingtip. However, one of the other Wildcats also went down.

Without gasoline, the Americans seemed all but grounded, and they engaged in a frantic search for more fuel. Someone recalled that Colonel Louis Woods, Geiger's chief of staff, cognizant of the shaky nature of the pipeline to Cactus and the consequences of bombardment, had ordered hundreds of fifty-five-gallon drums buried in the earth around the perimeter. Two staff officers painstakingly searched the area and discovered underground lodes adding up to 465 barrels, enough to keep the planes in the air for two days. Woods had actually written a note to Geiger detailing the arrangement. Unfortunately, the Marine aviation commander had simply stuck the memorandum in his pocket without ever reading it.

The defenders, gas-rich for the moment, and with mechanics having repaired some of the damaged aircraft, launched a coordinated attack with four of the Army's Airacobras, twelve Dauntless SBDs, and eight Wildcat F4Fs. In addition to the twenty-four combat planes, Major Jack Cram, Geiger's personal pilot, joined the mission in the *Blue Goose*, a PBY-5A amphibian. When not flying Geiger, Cram packed everything from toilet paper to beans into his PBY, but he had landed on the fourteenth with a cargo of two torpedoes, requested by the VT-8 squadron.

In his book *Devilbirds*, John De Chant, the Marine Corps combat correspondent and also a pilot who saw duty on Guadalcanal, quoted Operations Officer Joe Renner's briefing to Cram: "They've got our backs molded into the wall. We've had a permanent Condition Red all day. No sirens now unless at least 15 Jap planes come in. The F4Fs can't meet all the raids. We haven't enough gas or ammunition to send them up each time.

"What did you bring up this time? Torpedoes? What in the hell good are they now? Every one of the TBFs got smashed up in the shelling last night. Good Lord, what a show that was! They must have had the whole bastardly fleet out there! It was like kicking a wounded guy in the groin time after time to see if he'd yell 'Uncle.'

"They frisked the place like a pickpocket. There were BBs [battleships] out there in the channel with a flock of cruisers and destroyers in support. The insolent stinkers just stood off and plastered the place like they were in a free shooting gallery. Some of them walked searchlights up and down the shore picking out targets. The rest of them went over the place like a fine-toothed rake. If they ever try to break through what's left today . . . God help us, Jack . . . it'll be bad."

After digesting the information from Renner, Cram persuaded Geiger to allow him to make a torpedo run on the enemy vessels. De Chant said that one of Geiger's staff remarked, "If ever I saw a man with sheer guts, it was Jack Cram. He knew it would probably be his last flight but he jumped at the chance. As long as he had to, he was going out in a blaze of glory."

Mechanics hung the tin fish on the wings of the *Blue Goose*. Cram, who had never made a torpedo run, received a quick course in tactics from Lieutenant Commander Roy Simpler, a Navy fighter pilot, equally inexperienced, but whose brother-in-law was a torpedo man. Cram conferred with Marine Air Group Fourteen's CO, Lieutenant Colonel Al Cooley, and Duke Davis and they plotted an approach in which the dive-bombers would occupy the enemy's attention long enough for the *Blue Goose* to dive down and unleash its torpedoes at a transport.

Normally a PBY cruised at a torpid ninety knots per hour and had all the maneuverability of a lump of coal. With the Japanese sailors and pilots momentarily diverted by the dive-bombers, Cram shoved the yoke forward and headed toward the ocean in a long dive. Focused upon his target, he suddenly noticed his airspeed indicator hovering around 240 knots, far exceeding the maximum of 160 specified by the manufacturers and, indeed, his wing appeared to be fluttering in protest. He eased back somewhat and sailed over a screening destroyer at about two hundred feet before pulling the torpedo release. Cram and his crew thought one struck the ship, although the damage may have been from a dive-bomber.

As the PBY slowly turned for home, enemy fighters pursued the slow-moving Catalina, speckling it with bullets while Cram's gunners and Duke Davis's Wildcats sought to fend them off. Lifting and then dropping like a roller coaster, Cram, who flew without a copilot, tried to evade his tormentors. The amphibian lumbered past Henderson on its way to Fighter One, with a single persistent Zeke continuing to attack. Simultaneously, Lieutenant Roger Haberman of VMF-121, with his F4F gear down, banked for his final approach. He saw the threat to the *Blue Goose* and applied full power to his badly shot-up Wildcat, although he was unable to hand-crank his wheels up. He still managed to yank himself behind the enemy fighter whose pilot was so intent on knocking down the *Blue Goose*, he never realized his own peril. On his second pass Haberman blew up the Zeke. Cram landed, followed by Haberman, who had just shot down his first foe. In subsequent action, Haberman would be seriously wounded and evacuated while protesting he should be patched up and allowed to continue in the fight.

The *Blue Goose* had barely survived, riddled with 175 bullet holes, the tail surfaces generously perforated, the gunner's blister shattered, and the starboard engine showing signs of multiple wounds. Geiger summoned his aide and proceeded to chew out Cram for his destruction of the plane and threatened him with a court-martial. Outraged at the denunciation, Cram considered an epithet-laden retort but then noticed one of Geiger's staff choking down his laughter. He realized that the general was only joking, as Geiger then invited him to lunch and later wrote out a citation for a Navy Cross.

During the furious attack and defense, three sizable Japanese cargo-passenger ships burned up, incinerating most of the supplies aboard. However, about forty-five hundred soldiers clambered up the beach to aid in the offensive designed to wipe out the American forces.

It was fortunate that Woods had the foresight to stash the gas and that it was found. One of the fuel-laden barges with its tug and destroyer escort had already turned back when marauders from the Imperial Navy's Carrier Division One swooped down upon the remaining barge, its tug, and the destroyer *Meredith* just as the commander of the expedition decided they, too, should retreat. In short order the destroyer went down, leaving many sailors in the water tormented by strafers, a searing sun, salt water, and ravenous sharks.

While the resupply expedition led by the *Meredith* ended dismally, another effort that featured three converted destroyers steamed toward Guadalcanal. The *McFarland* arrived on the morning of October 16 and unloaded a cargo of forty thousand gallons of gasoline, torpedoes, and other ammunition onto barges at Lunga Point. That afternoon nine Japanese dive-bombers, Aichi-99 Vals, unable to locate the *Hornet* whose fighters were interfering with raids and striking at Imperial Navy ships, headed for the immovable target of Henderson Field. When they spied the *McFarland* handing over its last 350 drums of fuel to a barge, they immediately dove on the two vessels. The antiaircraft guns of the old destroyer knocked out one Val, but a bomb ignited the barge into a fiery wreck. A second one exploded on the fantail of the *McFarland*, killing twenty-seven sailors and some ground crew who had boarded the ship for evacuation.

Just at the moment when the Aichi-99s struck, Joe Bauer and the remainder of VMF-212, finally summoned to Cactus as a squadron, came upon the scene. Mel Freeman, at the controls of a VMF-212 Wildcat, recalled, "The day we flew our entry into Guadalcanal, we had to fly from Santos. We had those belly tanks, two 50-gallon belly tanks. I was Skipper's wing man this flight, on the way out trying to climb, every once in a while my engine would cough, and finally it fouled out. I couldn't get gas out of one of the tanks. We had strict radio silence. We made that long flight, I was out of gas, I tried to hang onto one tank, hoping whatever was blocking the flow by sucking on that tank I would get it clear.

"We got up there and coming in the field was under attack. The aircraft were going in all directions. I was right by the colonel [Bauer] trying to get into position to land. We were in the landing pattern and this son of a bitch, a Jap, came right down out of the sky. It was a Zero and hit me from behind. Here I am, with that goddamn tank. I dropped the tank and maneuvered out of harm's way. In that melee I lost the colonel, I saw him going off towards the water.

"I'm out of gas and we'd been told the whole purpose of this mission was to get those airplanes there. I had one of those decisions. If I go after him I am going to lose this airplane because I was out of gas.

"I landed and I ran off into the weeds because the field was being strafed. I ended up backing into a hole near Huckleberry Watkins who was in our squadron. Huck and I were lying there, and a Grumman comes in really smoking. He was going fast, maybe [his] flaps didn't work. He hit half way down the field, and rolled off the end. The next thing Huck is running like a son of a bitch. He ran the whole length of the field to get at that pilot. He thought it was one of our guys, but it [was] one from another squadron. He helped haul that guy out as the plane caught on fire. He said, 'I did that and that son of a bitch was from the other squadron!' I stayed in the hole."

While the members of VMF-212 sought refuge at Henderson Field, Bauer stayed in the air. Alone, and with little gas remaining, he charged the slow-moving dive-bombers. Within a few moments Bauer had shot down four of the enemy, right in sight of those who had just landed and hunkered down. These were fliers from his squadron and the other residents of the base. When Bauer completed his work and the surviving enemy had fled, he set down at the field. Max Brand reported that to the first pilot he saw from VMF-212, Bauer yelled, "Chamberlain [Lieutenant Clarence C.], where the hell were you? There was the table all set, and enough for the two of us! The least you could have done was count 'em for me."

In Freeman's version, Bauer upbraided him for his absence. "I tried to explain what happened, and he allowed, 'Well, maybe but you sure missed a lot.' I think today, if I would have gone with him, I might have gotten one or two. They were dive bombers, sitting ducks."

Bauer's feat uplifted morale mightily. Quick to recognize his singular triumph, Geiger nominated him for a Medal of Honor.

Freeman testified to the appalling conditions that prevailed at Henderson Field. "When we went up there as a squadron—it was absolute devastation. There wasn't a tree left in [the] area; the tops had been blown off every one. It looked like a site on the moon. The old Pagoda was gone and there were no hangars."

The dearth of supplies jeopardized operations. The command pressed into service all available R4Ds, the twin-engine Navy version of the Army Air Corps's C-47. Unarmed, they shuttled back and forth through the dangerous skies with stocks of bombs and drums of fuel.

The scores rung up against Japanese planes did not halt the almost daily raids by bombers and fighters. For that matter, the U.S. forces seemed unable to prevent Japanese attempts to install more reinforcements, artillery, and antitank pieces while removing some of the wounded and sick. The destroyers that convoyed transports to the Guadalcanal beaches also seized an opportunity to hurl shells at the Americans, beset on the ground, in the air, and from the sea.

SEVEN

CACTUS PRESERVED

With the full complement of VMF-212 on Guadalcanal, the fatigued, stressed members of VMF-224 left the island, except for Major Bob Galer. He remained on station for two more weeks, long enough to splash down for his third watery landing and rescue. Then he, too, headed to the States where, like John Smith and Marion Carl, he toured the country to help sell war bonds. At the time Galer departed Guadalcanal, he had been credited with thirteen planes shot down and subsequently received a Medal of Honor.

On the day following the *McFarland*'s delivery of gasoline and Joe Bauer's stunning performance, Admiral Fitch alerted Cactus of an imminent raid. Instead of radar or coast-watcher detection, this time the Pearl Harbor code busters had intercepted an enemy message detailing two separate strikes. When the first mix of thirty-six dive-bombers and fighters bore down on Guadalcanal, eight Wildcats from VMF-121 hovered above them. They were led by Duke Davis and registered impressive results, six dive-bombers (two by Davis) and four Zekes, with one American plane downed.

In addition, SBDs acted as spotters for a pair of U.S. destroyers, which blasted much of the ammunition and other supplies deposited two days earlier at considerable cost. Some of the Army Air Corps's Airacobras as well as B-17s flying out of Espiritu Santo also ravaged the enemy storage dumps. In the evening, however, the Japanese again ran the show, a galaxy of cruisers and destroyers peppering both Henderson and Fighter One without opposition. A final batch of infantry reinforcements trudged from the beach to bolster the Japanese forces, scheduled on October 20 to begin a major offensive aimed at the capture of Henderson Field.

Meanwhile, Joe Bauer took command of Fighter One. His domain included not only the Marines but also the resident Navy and Air Corps aircraft and airmen. At the same time, Vice Admiral William F. Halsey relieved Vice Admiral Robert Ghormley—a man deemed insufficiently aggressive, if not altogether timid—as head of the South Pacific Area and South Pacific forces.

In his new capacity, on October 18, Bauer, in the words of Max Brand, announced, "Twenty-four bombers are coming down. They've just pulled out of Bougainville. Be here in about an hour. Operations just called up to say so. I want you to get up there, dodge the Zeros, if you can, and get at the bombers. That's your mission; they're the only part of the flight that can hurt Henderson Field. But if you can't dodge the Zeros, turn into them. Make head-on passes. You've got every advantage doing this [more firepower, self-sealing fuel tanks, and armor protecting the pilot and other vitals]. Don't be afraid. Turn right into them and mop them up. Go on, now. Beat it upstairs. You're going to get half a dozen of them today, and every damn one of you is coming home to me again." While Bauer was not one to avoid skirmishes, he was also aware of his responsibility to act as a commander, rather than an individual combatant. Furthermore, his remarks and his tone obviously sparked confidence in his naturally anxiety-ridden subordinates.

The reception committee for the incoming traffic consisted of six from Bauer's 212 under his exec, Major Frederick R. Payne; five from VMF-121 under Joe Foss; and two from the Navy's VF-5. When the donnybrook ended, the enemy had lost considerably more than Bauer predicted—seven bombers and thirteen Zeros. While two Marine pilots were listed as missing, both turned up later, after surviving crash landings.

On occasion the defense fell short. Those failures stemmed from inexperience or lack of aggressiveness. On his second tour at

Guadalcanal, Mel Freeman recalled a Bauer pep talk. "The Colonel said, 'This is our chance, when we can show what we can do as a squadron. Be aggressive.' I flew with Chick [Captain Charles] Quilter quite a few times. Quilter was trying to maneuver us into advantageous position. But the bombers were getting through. The bombers were ahead of us down below. It happened two or three times with Quilter trying to catch up with 'em, make a run at 'em. I'm ass-end Charlie when these Zeros swoop down and sweep around us. We got hit in a big way. The Zeros are coming at us from the side while the son of a bitch [Quilter] is diving out. That happened about two or three times."

Freeman explained that because of a natural lag from the moment, the flight leader dove and, before he could react, "I can't get down there as fast as the others. If anybody was going to get clobbered, it's me. I ain't going to stay up there and fight all by myself. About [the] third day, the colonel saw we were in rough shape and asked what's the matter. I answered, you told us what we were here for ["anything that wore a red dot on it was the enemy and must be fought"]. I'm not interested in strategy of getting in position, and Quilter was diving out on me. I don't like it. The Colonel agreed with me. He went and asked some of the other guys. I'm not saying Quilter was chicken and a coward, but he was not acting in accord with instructions. He was unnecessarily jeopardizing his flight."

Henderson Field shut down operations for several days because of frequent but sporadic artillery bursts from the nearby Japanese. When shells also exploded a bare five hundred yards from Fighter One, that strip's future seemed dubious. A sudden clearing of skies on October 23 enabled the Japanese to dispatch sixteen twin-engine Betty bombers with an escort of twenty-eight Zekes to add to the damage. VMF-121 put up a pair of flights under Duke Davis and Joe Foss, while Major Fred Payne led the F4Fs from VMF-212. The Japanese fighters confronted the two echelons of VMF-121. Foss burned two of the attackers while absorbing enough punishment to his engine to force him into a dead-stick glide home. It was the fourth time that Foss, during his brief stay on the island, brought home a badly shot-up aircraft.

Within a few days Lieutenant Robert "Cowboy" Stout, a Wyoming native, had replaced Quilter as Freeman's flight commander. "Cowboy was a real scrapper," said Freeman. "He brought us the leadership we needed. A couple of days after he took over, we were climbing, heading north. It was a beautiful sunny day, nice big clouds. I was on the back end and just as we turned to come back, Zeros came out of clouds on our tail. They went right through that formation except for their back end. By this time I'm pretty much by myself because of the time lag when they start to move ahead. Alone, this Zero came down alongside of me. He pulled up and hung on his prop, almost in a stall on the right side of me, waiting to come and slip on my tail while I'm moving ahead. It was a beautiful Zero. In the sunlight the big red ball showed. I turned a little bit toward him. That screwed him up and he moved right back over my head. I got in behind his tail. I blew the shit out of him. He burned in a whole helluva lot of pieces, I got him out of the way and while making a turn, here comes a Zero from my left. I went for a full 90 degree deflection shot. He ran right through those bullets, caught on fire and blew up.

"Down on my right was a Jap making a run on one of our guys in a white parachute, theirs were green. There must have been three of us made a run on him. Somebody got there before me and got him. That time we knocked down a lot of planes. I got two. I really felt good."

For the Japanese, the night of October 24 marked the start of a long-expected offensive aimed at nothing less than the annihilation of Henderson Field and the ouster of the Americans from their purchase on the island. When "Dugout" Sunday, the twenty-fifth, dawned with Henderson again closed due to constant shelling and Fighter One so swampy that every takeoff was fraught with risk, frustrated airmen squeezed into their foxholes. Only half a dozen SBDs from VMSB-141 got off the ground at dawn to hunt for enemy ships. They found three destroyers, only thirty-five miles away and rushing at a speed of twenty knots toward Guadalcanal.

On the ground, the vanguard of the enemy soldiers penetrated close enough to Henderson to send an erroneous report to the Japanese high command, claiming capture of the base. Very quickly their reconnaissance aircraft, under a fighter shield, flew over to determine whether the field was suitable for Nipponese planes to land. None of the Americans could take off to challenge the intruders. One of the Japanese became so bold as to survey Fighter One right down on the deck. From every corner of the strip, machine guns, rifles, and pistols opened fire on the aircraft. It crashed and exploded in a grove of trees.

By nine thirty in the morning, Fighter One had dried sufficiently for Joe Foss to lead four other fighters against the raiders. Throughout the day, the two sides engaged in a series of bloody and destructive brawls. Foss accounted for four more of the raiders, giving him a total of eight in three days.

As shaky as the fliers' existence was on Guadalcanal, Mel Freeman and his compatriots were aware that the grunts manning the perimeter endured far worse. "I shot down one Zero right near the field. A day or so after that, these guys in the field came in with a piece of it [from] about where I saw him go into the trees. They wanted to give me this. I felt here are these guys taking time to walk in and give me this. I had some whiskey and gave 'em whatever we had, it was real close contact with these guys. Another contact with ground guys [was] a battery of Long Toms [155-millimeter howitzers] right by our camp. During the Battle of Bloody Ridge around October 23 to 26, they kept going. The rain helped them cool the barrels. We couldn't sleep. We'd go back and see these guys. They were absolutely dragged out, could hardly stand up. Whoever ran that battery was one of the world's greatest artillerymen, he had a real crew. Later on we heard they captured some Jap back in the hills who wanted to see these automatic artillery pieces [because the battery fired so rapidly].

"On October 26, that's the day we felt they [the Japanese] were going to really break through. We couldn't get off because we were stuck in the mud. Somebody threw a carbine at me and said they'd broken the lines. I was told to get out there and take care of that airplane as long as you can. I had three or four grunts with me, we lay around that airplane, facing towards the jungle. We were sure they were going to try to get those airplanes, throw grenades at them." The perimeter held, however, and Freeman was soon able to take off.

"There were two Jap destroyers off the beach, shelling us, guns going off in all directions. I was on [the] end of that flight taking off, we climbed but didn't get very high when we started making runs on the destroyers. We got credit for sinking two destroyers because they didn't make it back." Several other Japanese warships had succumbed to attacks by Navy dive-bombers operating from Henderson.

"That day," said Freeman, "we couldn't get any altitude. I got one late in the afternoon, found him in the trees. He came by me, diving. I was in and out of the airplane all day long. On my second flight, we just barely got up over tops of trees. There were Zeros swarming all over us." Freeman on this occasion was with several other VMF-212 pilots, including Lieutenant Jack Conger. This was Conger's second tour on Guadalcanal; he had been one of those who had flown in from the ill-fated *Wasp* in September. At that time Conger recalled his excitement: ". . . it was hard to take the time for that checkover [preflight preparations] because I was so eager. Just eager to get in there; and it was tense, like waiting for the first whistle of a football game."

According to Freeman, during the fracas on October 26, "A Japanese guy was making a run on us. Jack was out of ammunition, after strafing, but he wasn't going to let that keep him away. This guy made a run at him, Jack dipped under him and pulled up, chopped his tail off with his prop—damn near wrecked his airplane. Jack jumped; the parachute made about two swings and he was in the water. Jack landed right near a Japanese pilot. They were dropping like flies."

In Conger's 1943 description of the incident to Max Brand, a Higgins landing boat ignored the enemy pilot as it came to fetch Conger. He believed valuable intelligence might be obtained and persuaded the Marines to go back and rescue the Japanese flier. When they neared the pilot, Conger motioned for him to climb aboard. "He simply kicked himself away from the boat. It made me feel a little queer. I suppose it's all right for a fellow to be willing to fight until he dies, but war shouldn't be just murder. In a way it ought to be just a game that you play extra hard. And as I looked down at the Jap there in the water, I didn't admire him. I didn't respect him at all. I simply felt that there was a lot of the ornery devil in him.

"I took a grappling hook and reached over the side of the boat and got the hook fastened right under the shoulder of his life jacket. I started lifting up on it with a sailor helping me and we hoisted the Jap waist-high out of the sea. And then the son of a bitch pulled a gun out of his belt! I didn't see it, but a Marine yelled to me to look out and the next thing I knew, that bastard had the gun right in my face and pulled the trigger. There was just a click; the cartridge was wet and didn't explode. Me? I did a sort of backflip to get away and landed on the other side of the Higgins boat.

"They say he tried to shoot himself next, but still the gun wouldn't work. I scrambled back to the rail where several Marines were taking aim, and believe me, they looked as though they were enjoying themselves. I yelled and made them put their guns down. . . . I took one of those five-gallon jerry cans [used for gasoline or water] and I reached over and slugged him over the head with it. I wanted to stun him, but if I had bashed in his brains it wouldn't have broken my heart completely. However, a Jap's skull is made of India rubber. The blow just knocked him about twenty feet down under water, and when he drifted up again he was still wearing that mean look and wouldn't get in the boat.

"I picked up a boat hook and whacked him over the head and opened a gash half a foot long in his scalp, and a sailor whanged him with a grappling hook. All this before his lights went out and we could drag him on board the boat.

"There he was, looking wet and soggy and small and we gave him first aid and admired the way he was dressed. His togs were damned smart. He wore a heavy gabardine flying suit, dark brown and over this was a tight-fitting kapok life jacket. He had on leather flying boots and a leather helmet when I first saw him land, but he'd taken these off and they were lost. Under his flying suit he had a warm cloth jacket, but to keep his damned neck warm, he had on top of a turtleneck sweater a scarf about five yards long of the finest silk. His pistol was a very neat Mauser automatic."

In addition to his weapon, the prisoner also carried his airplane clock and a set of maps with courses marked for his missions. "After we'd picked him like gifts from a Christmas tree," said Conger, "we turned him over to Intelligence to see what they could get out of him. I got the scarf and shirt as souvenirs. What I really wanted was that fine pistol, but good things like that just evaporate when there are handy American Marines and sailors around."

A few days later Conger visited the downed pilot in the prison camp. Although treated with ointments for burns and bandaged from injuries, he showed no signs of gratitude for being rescued but "just stared at me, very mean, his eyes never shifting, as though he were picking out the place where he'd like to put a knife into me." However, Conger was able to converse in English and learn that he was twenty years old and had seen combat in China, Java, and the Battle of the Coral Sea. "In that fight he'd shot down an American plane. I remember how he grinned when he said this."

During the period covering the Japanese offensive on Guadalcanal, a momentous air–sea battle erupted off the Santa Cruz Islands, some five hundred miles east of the southern Solomons. No Marines were involved, but the Japanese fleet—which included carriers, battleships, and other powerful vessels—expected to support their comrades on Guadalcanal. Admiral Halsey ordered his task forces with two carriers, the *Enterprise* and *Hornet*, to attack. Although the Japanese sank the *Hornet* and a destroyer, as well as damaging the *Enterprise* and another destroyer, the U.S. Navy carrier pilots rendered enough harm upon the enemy flattops to remove them as factors in the struggle for Guadalcanal.

On the island itself, the embattled leathernecks and the GIs, buttressed by their artillery, repulsed the determined Japanese offensive. Having sustained a fearful number of casualties, the Imperial Army, handicapped by the inability of the Navy to put ashore sufficient reinforcements and supplies because of the unremitting assaults by the Cactus Air Force, paused after October 26.

However, the Japanese had no intention of abandoning the quest to conquer Guadalcanal, and the high command organized a new plan for a prodigious reinforcement of soldiers already on the island. The script outran reality but, nevertheless, the Nipponese scraped together bottoms that could carry as many troops, artillery pieces, and other gear as they believed necessary to defeat the Americans. Almost nightly the Japanese ships operated their reinforcement program, which the Marines labeled the Tokyo Express. The Nipponese plotted to begin their offensive in mid-November.

As October drew to a close and the Japanese air raids on Guadalcanal temporarily paused, Geiger approved a mission against the Japanese base at Rekata Bay, on the island of Santa Isabel, southeast of the U.S. positions. The target was home for Zero float aircraft that performed recon for the Japanese and occasionally nighttime heckling sorties. Freeman said, "We were supposedly flat on our asses, unable to do any more than get up and fight when they came over. But Joe Bauer wanted to launch an attack." Freeman was among the seven VMF-212 pilots (led by Cowboy Stout) assigned to the task, along with three Army P-39s. "We were told that there was a float plane base there and they wanted us to go in and get the airplanes. Joe Bauer picked Cowboy to lead this attack. We didn't know anything about the weather. We got kicked out of bed early, took off in the dark, no lights, complete radio silence. It was to be a real surprise attack. We didn't know exactly where it was, but had a compass heading from a map. Jeeze, it was black. All you could join up on was exhaust, tips of wings, a blue glow about as big as a silver dollar. We were trying to fly in a formation, but not too close to the island because that might tip them off. Finally Cowboy turned in after flying over the ocean, toward what was supposed to be Rekata Bay. We're trying to keep track of each other and right ahead of me, Cowboy flamed the first [enemy plane] up. Some of them got off, in the dark while it started to get light in the sky. We got one or two of them in the air. I'm trying to pick out [the] silhouette of [a] Jap plane and not shoot one of our own. We're milling around there. Cowboy sent a couple of us down to get 'em on [the] ground. I went in and I got one in the water as he tried to run along [the] water and take off. We shot that place up, antiaircraft wasn't too shabby there. We started for home, we managed to make it back, I was last or next to last to land. Cowboy hugged me. He was afraid that in the dark he had shot down one of our own. We went up there again. Huckleberry and I saw this float plane, he was down low and we went in and got him. That's when Huckleberry and I flipped and I lost [credit for destruction of an enemy plane]." During one of the forays to Rekata Bay, Jack Conger shot down his tenth plane, making him a double ace.

In the first days of November, portions of five more Marine combat squadrons—VMSB-132, VMF-112, VMSB-142, VMF-122, and VMSB-131, which included the corps's first torpedo planes—enlarged the aviation contingent to 1,748, almost 90 percent of whom were Marines.

To supplement the existing fields, construction crews hacked out Fighter Two. The Marines also stationed their first four-engine PB4Ys—the Navy version of the B-24 Liberator—on Espiritu Santo, from where they ferried supplies and fuel when not engaged in photo reconnaissance. The Army Air Corps began to heave its weight around as it brought up more B-17s and B-26s. The air transport system added two more squadrons, one from the Marines and the other an Army troop carrier unit. C-47s now hauled out the wounded and sick while bringing in the precious stores of gasoline, machine guns, and ammunition, including mortar shells.

Numbers, of course, add only part of the equation of forces. The newcomers, in some instances, were ill prepared for their role. Major Paul Fontana, who was born in Italy in 1911 and grew up in Sparks, Nevada, commanded VMF-112. A graduate of the University of Nevada at Reno, with a degree in electrical engineering, Fontana had resigned his Army Reserve commission for an appointment as a Marine second lieutenant. After sea duty aboard the USS *Salt Lake City* and a stint at the base on Mare Island, California, Fontana attended flight school. Upon obtaining his wings in 1940, he served with several units before taking over VMF-112.

"We trained for two months and deployed to the South Pacific in October of 1942. Our training, of course, had been very limited. Except for myself and one captain, the other 22 pilots were second lieutenants and sergeants with very few flight hours of training. We were in the Grumman Wildcats which we received just about one month before we deployed. Up until about a month or so before we were flying Brewsters. The junior sergeant pilot of my squadron at the time we deployed had 24 hours in the F4F. I regret to say he did not survive."

While the Cactus Air Force received fresh raw talent, change rocked the top of the command. According to Thomas G. Miller's book *The Cactus Air Force*, "By early November, it was clear to all that Roy Geiger, the rock-hard old airman, was suffering from a bad case of combat fatigue. Two months and four days of seeing his always outnumbered young men killed or evacuated, unable to fight any more, had finally broken down even his constitution." Another veteran of World War I but not an aviator until the 1920s, Louis Woods, who had been Geiger's chief of staff, took charge as Commander Air, Guadalcanal, while an unhappy Geiger continued to hold the post of commander of the First Marine Air Wing, housed on Espiritu Santo. The shift meant nothing in terms of strategy or tactics. Geiger did not go quietly. He raged at Woods as disloyal, a reaction that indicates how distraught was the ordinarily warm and friendly Geiger.

Notwithstanding the strengthening of the Cactus air arm, during the first half of November the Tokyo Express—with its destroyer-borne troops—added a considerable number of soldiers and equipment to their Guadalcanal forces. The warships ran a gauntlet of PT boats and raids by fighters and dive-bombers. One of the more heroic figures of the defense, Lieutenant Commander John Eldrige of VS-71, along with a pair of Marine lieutenants, Melvin R. Nawman and Wayne Gentry, from VMSB-132, disappeared during a mission against the Tokyo Express, victims most likely of a vicious squall that raged during their night attack against about twenty destroyers. Roy Geiger had actually grounded Eldrige, who had led fourteen raids by SBDs in his brief thirty-five days on Guadalcanal, "because he had already done so much."

On November 7 the alert sounded upon a sighting of a cruiser and nine destroyers 125 miles north of Guadalcanal, obviously intent on arriving after dark to disgorge their human cargo. A host of aircraft scrambled to confront the warships, whose less-than-adequate air cover consisted of float Zeros and even biplane seaplanes. SBDs, led by Major Joseph Sailer Jr.—a Main Line Philadelphian and graduate of Princeton—swooped down on the destroyers while three torpedo planes from VT-8, a Navy squadron, glided low enough to loose their tin fish. One bomb fell on the cruiser, and torpedoes hit both the cruiser and a destroyer.

The fighters from Guadalcanal included some P-39s, which, going up against floatplanes, for once were not overmatched. They put down five of these while twenty-three Marine F4Fs not only hosed the ships with machine-gun fire but also shot down nine more planes, including three for Joe Foss.

However, the executive officer of VMF-121 also encountered more than his share of trouble. Passing over Florida Island, Foss spotted the enemy aircraft. He and seven other fighters peeled away from the formation to deal with the floatplanes while the remainder of the Grummans remained to guard the SBDs and TBFs as they headed toward the flotilla. For their part the Japanese pilots, apparently unaware of the threat from Foss and company, crossed the Americans' path en route to providing protection against the dive-bombers and torpedo planes. Foss, as the leader, caught up with the first victim and, in a deflection shot from a sixty- to seventy-degree angle, blew his target to pieces. The enemy pilot suddenly appeared, drifting toward the water in his parachute. Others from the sections under Foss had also engaged the Zeros with deadly results—but one Marine, Lieutenant Danny Doyle, whom Foss had glimpsed chasing a plane down near the sea, disappeared.

Foss signaled for his flight to regroup and make simulated

bomb runs on the ships, thereby preventing the antiaircraft gunners from concentrating on the dive-bombers. The Grummans, in a reverse order that placed Foss at the rear, maneuvered for their dives. Foss saw another aircraft approaching, and when it closed on him he realized it was a two-seater, an enemy.

The Marine barely missed a collision, and as he banked to his right the other pilot cunningly throttled back, giving his rear gunner a good shot at the Wildcat. Thumps and jolts informed Foss his airplane was absorbing countless hits, including a walnut-sized hole in his canopy.

Despite the punishment to the cowling, wing, and fuselage, the Grumman engine continued to roar. Foss easily outmaneuvered the slower foe for a decisive burst from his six .50-caliber machine guns. Smoke, then an outburst of yellow flame, poured from the doomed floatplane, which exploded while plunging toward the sea.

Seemingly oblivious to the American above, another two-seater droned below Foss. He quickly dove down and, before the rear gunner could react, blew up his third victim. With his fuel low, Foss found a companion Wildcat, also considerably damaged, to join him in the trip home. But now some more Zeros began to hunt for the American fighters. They noticed the two cripples staggering toward Guadalcanal. Foss ran for the nearest clouds but his engine began to misfire due to the first rear gunner's bursts. The power cut out, then started again, allowing him to dive into the nearest cloud bank. The sputtering engine cost altitude and Foss, alone in the sky, sought the nearest land, the elongated island of Malaita.

Foss recalled, "Holes in [the] canopy caused a whistle and the radio wasn't working. I couldn't tell anyone, not anyone of my group that I was shot down." The Wildcat crunched into heavy chop and the canopy, which he had pushed back to ease his departure from the plane, slammed shut. As he later admitted, he had failed to follow procedure for ditching, jettisoning the canopy before landing on water. The cockpit flooded while the pilot struggled to shove the cover open. With waves slapping against the hood, Foss managed to yank its handle hard enough to slide it back again. He fumbled with his parachute chest strap, unbuckling as he exited the cockpit, but he forgot about the leg straps. In the water the chute floated to the surface, but the attachments to his legs forced his head underwater. He succeeded in pulling the cord of his life jacket, and the Mae West popped him to the surface.

Said Foss, "I thought I was a goner. The Lord got me out of the airplane." When darkness cloaked him, he became aware of the things moving in the water around him. Foss immediately started to crack open the capsules containing shark repellent. "They don't like chlorine any better than we do," he remarked. "I don't know how to swim. Working my arms I got awful sore as I rubbed against the Mae West. Hours went by. I didn't know whether land was that way or that way. It was pouring rain, after it got dark.

"Something came right at my head. [I] pulled myself down. I went right under the outrigger of a canoe. I was convinced it was enemy. I heard a voice that didn't sound like anything I knew. Then I heard a voice say, 'Let's look over here.' I said, 'Yeah, right here.' They could see me in the dark and had these Solomon island clubs ready to part my hair. I said 'Friend, American, pilot, birdman.'

"A hand reached down and I grabbed it. Father Dan Styvenberg was in the canoe. Father Dan brought me back to the mission. One native saw me go into the water, told them at the mission. Tommy Mason, a saw mill operator hiding there, came out with Father Dan. The enemy had said if they ever saw them outside [the] mission they'd kill them."

When daylight came, Foss spread out his parachute—which had floated ashore—to signal anyone searching for him. A Wildcat scouring the area spotted the chute and Jack Cram flew a PBY to the site, landed in the water, and taxied to shore to pick up Foss. Back on Guadalcanal, Foss was ready for duty one day later.

While on Guadalcanal, Foss was informed he would receive a Navy Cross. "I told them I didn't want any medal," he said later in an interview with *Naval History* magazine. "I didn't know one cross from another. And I'd have to dress up, which I didn't want to do. All I was interested in was fighting the enemy. But my boss ordered me to dress up, which meant putting on clean clothes. I did look like a tramp, all sweaty and dirty. . . .

"As I arrived, somebody said, 'We have only two Navy Crosses here.' It was a bunch of colonels, see. So they said, 'Would you be happy with a DFC [Distinguished Flying Cross]?' I told them I'd be happy with anything, as long as we could get it over with. Then it came time for Admiral Halsey to hang the medal on me. . . . A half-dozen of us were getting decorated, but when he came to me, he stepped back and said, 'I know the Marines don't like the United States Navy, but I can tell you that from now on, there's going to be some fighting.' Boy, oh boy was he right."

The period of November 10–16 witnessed some of the most savage air battles of the entire Solomons campaign. Like their counterparts, American transports had steamed to Guadalcanal bearing fresh troops and equipment. On the eleventh, Japanese carrier-based fighters and dive bombers had attacked in one wave and then some fifty twin-engine bombers and Zekes tried to ravage Henderson Field. While thirteen of the attackers were destroyed, the Marines lost seven Wildcats, with four pilots killed and VMF-121's commander Duke Davis wounded.

Two days later, a coast-watcher, ensconced high in the mountains of southern Bougainville, radioed word of a coven of Betty bombers cruising toward Guadalcanal. Radar confirmed the approach of intruders, and the ships off the beach readied their antiaircraft stations. In an atypical tactic, the nineteen Bettys began their attack from twenty-five thousand feet, diving down to attain a speed of three hundred knots while breaking up their formation.

Foss, leading a posse of six Wildcats, saw them as they burst from cloud cover over Iron Bottom Sound and dove toward the ships. His flight, which had been hovering at twenty-nine thousand feet, zoomed down, airspeed indicator needles passing over the forbidding red lines at three hundred knots. Foss's canopy cracked, and the wind whisked away small walkway strips on his wings. He never wavered, and when he reached wtihin a hundred yards of a bomber, he shot up its starboard engine. The Betty's wing caught the water and cartwheeled into oblivion. About to fire on another plane, Foss saw a Zero attempting to intervene. He switched his attention to the newcomer and destroyed it. He scored his third victory, flaming a Betty.

The Marines in the air and the ships' guns successfully routed the marauders. Not a single vessel incurred serious damage, and the antiaircraft batteries knocked out eight of the enemy. The fighters received credit for seventeen bombers and six Zeros, with the loss of a P-39 pilot and four planes. Only one of the incoming aircraft escaped destruction.

In the early morning of November 13 the Americans fared less well at sea in a furious battle that pitted a Japanese armada—replete with two battleships, one light cruiser, and fourteen destroyers—against an inferior U.S. Navy task force of only five cruisers and eight destroyers. In a twenty-four-minute exchange of shells, three of the American cruisers reeled from heavy blows that killed the admiral in command and fatally injured a fourth cruiser. Half of the destroyers were sunk and three damaged. On the following day a torpedo blew up the cruiser *Juneau*, which foundered with 690 of its 700-man crew. Among the victims were the five Sullivan brothers. Only two destroyers of the Imperial fleet perished, but eighty-five hits on one battleship, *Hiei*, wrecked the steering gear. At daylight flocks of Marine SBDs and torpedo planes from the *Enterprise* fell upon the disabled *Hiei*, eventually forcing the Japanese to scuttle it. The loss of the battlewagon crimped the Imperial Navy's plan to hammer the American supply ships and batter the facilities of Henderson.

On the night of November 13–14, it was a weaker bombardment force that struck at the Cactus airfields, and although they lobbed a thousand shells at the targets, the results fell well short of the big blasts during October. Unknown to the other Nipponese naval force shepherding transports carrying reinforcements, the bombardment from the sea did not weaken the defenders' air arm. At the first morning light, dive-bombers from VMSB-132 and 142 under Major Joe Sailer and Major Robert Richard joined with the entire air group from the *Enterprise* to bomb, torpedo, and strafe the transport group. Even B-17s and B-26s from the Army base in the Fijis participated.

Wildcats engaged Zeros seeking to protect their fleet and splashed seven of them. Late in the day Joe Bauer insisted on taking part in a mission aimed at wiping out several of the troop transports reported still afloat. Foss wrote in a letter, "Just before I took off, Colonel Joe told me that he was going along to see just how my boys worked. He said I wasn't going to get all the fun alone, so we all took off. Upon arriving, we found several troop transports dead in the water and smoking. Some warships were cruising among them to pick up survivors and ward off our air attacks. Tom Furlow and I followed the colonel and circled high above. The three of us circled for some time and watched our planes attack and start to leave. All the surrounding air seemed clear from enemy air activity, so down we came and strafed the ships below. We came right out on the water and headed for home. All of a sudden, tracers shot over my head. Upon looking back I saw two Jap Zeros diving on us, shooting. At once Joe turned and headed straight for one. Both he and the Jap were shooting everything. Then—bang! And the Zero blew up, and Joe zoomed and made a turn for home. Tom and I chased the other Zero towards Tokyo but couldn't catch him. Upon returning to the scene of Joe's action (twelve or fifteen miles due north of the Russell Islands), I was unable to spot him. I saw an oil slick about a mile south of the spot where the Zero had gone in, and upon circling it saw Joe swimming with his life jacket on. I went right down to within a few feet of him, and he waved both arms and jumped up out of the water. Then he waved me toward home. He was in good shape—no visible cuts. I tried to give him my life raft, but it wouldn't come out, so I gave full throttle toward home. I landed and took off at once in a Duck [J2F utility amphibian] with Major Joe Renner. We were within about ten miles of Joe and it got pitch black, so we had to return home."

Foss did not disclose that the attempted rescue was delayed because a squadron of Army B-26s, short on fuel after a flight from Noumea, was landing. He and Renner could only wait in the Duck until the incoming aircraft completed their arrival. By the time they got off the ground, it was already after dark.

Foss continued, "At daybreak the next morning [November 15]

we were on the scene of the colonel's landing with my flight of eight and the Duck. The only thing in sight were two Jap planes, which we shot down at once. We searched and searched the area, but no sign of a soul. We sent up a plane that landed and talked to the natives on the Russell Islands and told them to be on a sharp lookout for Joe. They found a sergeant pilot who had gone down about five miles farther out than Joe at the same time. It took him about forty-nine hours to make the trip [to the islands], so there is no doubt but what the colonel had the stamina and the heart to make such a swim. So in my way of thinking, one of the following two things happened—either the Japs happened upon him and took him prisoner, or the sharks got him. If the Japs have him, he is safe, in my mind, as he wore his lieutenant colonel's silver oak leaves. . . .

"To me, Marine Corps Aviation's greatest loss in this war is that of Joe. He really had a way all his own of getting a tough job done efficiently and speedily, and was admired by all, from the lowest private to the highest general. I am certain that wherever Joe is today, he is doing things the best way—the Bauer way.

"I am hoping that some day Joe will come back—I'll never lose hope, knowing Joe as I did." Foss wrote this letter to Bauer's family shortly after he disappeared. Bauer was never found. In just four combat flights, the man his squadron called "Coach" had destroyed eleven enemy aircraft.

Mel Freeman expressed some bitterness over Bauer's death. "We were really upset about that. He [Bauer] didn't have to fly. Why did he do that, why did he go when we weren't there? They would never have gotten him, and if he had landed in water, we'd have gone in and got him, even if it meant landing a plane in the water. One way or another we would have kept rotating patrol over him."

Rear Admiral Tatsuhiko Tanaka, commander of the Tokyo Express fleet with transports, wavered about continuing his mission after a patrol plane confirmed that Vice Admiral Willis Lee's force (which included the battleships *Washington* and *South Dakota*) would be in attendance when the Imperial Navy vessels reached their destination at Guadalcanal. Orders from Fleet Admiral Isoroku Yamamoto, architect of the Pearl Harbor attack, directed Tanaka to proceed. Vice Admiral Nobutake Kondo of the Second Fleet, with the battleship *Kirishima*, two cruisers, and some destroyers, would provide protection.

Kondo's warships engaged the Americans at 11:00 P.M. on the fourteenth, and again the Japanese proved superior in night sea battles. Torpedoes blasted a pair of Lee's destroyers, and the three biggest vessels in the Imperial forces, firing by the light from the burning destroyers and their own searchlights, hammered the *South Dakota*. A cannonade from the sixteen-inchers of the *Washington* that wrecked the *Kirishima*, however, prevented an all-out disaster. After the crew scuttled the *Kirishima*, Kondo decided to retire rather than risk the bigger guns of the foe's two battleships.

With only a single destroyer, Tanaka realized that his only hope of completing his mission lay in beaching the four transports before they could be sunk. In the early-morning darkness of November 15, the quartet plowed onto the shores at Doma Cove and Tassafaronga Point on Guadalcanal while the destroyer fled the scene to avoid the inevitable assault from the skies. At first light Sailer and Richard brought the fury of SBDs down upon the hapless cargo ships. Bombs demolished the vessels and struck nearby supply dumps. That afternoon the Cactus airmen intercepted a flight of Japanese aircraft well shy of Guadalcanal and drove them off, claiming six splashed.

Altogether the combined efforts of the three services sank seven ships; the remaining four, crippled by the onslaught, beached themselves. Of the ten thousand troops destined for Guadalcanal, just four thousand reached the island. Others drowned, but the accompanying destroyers rescued an estimated five thousand.

Foss himself did not remain on Guadalcanal much longer. A severe attack of malaria brought evacuation to New Caledonia and Australia for treatment. He said, "I had 20 some serious attacks of malaria, thought I would die of it, or Black Water Fever. Last attack I came out at 143 pounds." Within the period from October 9 to November 19, Foss had shot down twenty-three enemy planes and seriously damaged others. His record for such a concentrated period of time was unmatched by any other fighter pilot during World War II. In addition to the DFC, Foss would be awarded a Medal of Honor. A modest individual, Foss wondered how he survived. "All missions were tough. It was like putting a rattlesnake in a black bag on a dark night. You just don't want to get stung."

EIGHT

FIRST OFFENSIVE STRIKES

Battles on land, at sea, and in the air during the first half of November initially stalemated the Japanese in their efforts to oust the Americans on Guadalcanal and then slowly shifted the balance of power until the Nipponese became the defenders. Although Tokyo refused to concede the island, the perimeter manned by leathernecks and GIs included some thirty-five thousand increasingly better-supplied troops, while the twenty thousand Japanese soldiers faced scant rations and dwindling stocks of combat wherewithal. No more transports could risk the gauntlet of U.S. warships and aircraft; only swift-moving destroyers supplemented with barges attempted to bring troops or supplies. In desperation, the Japanese resorted to floating barrels that contained rice and other items ashore. In contrast, the Americans dined on turkey and some holiday foods on Thanksgiving.

The First Marine Aviation Engineers had debarked on November 11 and, with the Seabees, improved the landing surface at Henderson while expanding facilities. Work soon began on a second fighter strip. As early as November 22 Admiral Chester Nimitz, the overall Pacific Fleet commander, notified Halsey that he believed Guadalcanal "past the most critical period." In early December the exhausted remnants of the First Marine Division—the original invaders of Guadalcanal—hauled themselves up cargo nets to transport ships as fresh army soldiers and the Second Marine Division replaced them. At the same time, the inven-

tory of combat aircraft available to the command of Brigadier
General Louis Woods totaled 188, ranging from F4Fs through
Army P-38s, which were more of a match for the enemy fighters
than the substandard Airacobras. Even B-17s now called Guadalcanal home. A flight of OS2U Kingfishers now performed antisubmarine patrol and air–sea rescues, while the Royal New
Zealand Air Force contributed a reconnaissance squadron. The
pipeline of both pilots and aircraft pumped enough men and machines to enable almost wholesale rotation of flight personnel.
Ground crews generally served a longer tour on the island. General Woods turned over his command to Brigadier General Francis P. Mulcahy, the veteran of World War I aerial combat over
France.

The change in status for the two sides, however, did not mean
the Solomons were less dangerous. On December 3 dive-bombers
and torpedo planes from Marine squadrons VMSB-142 and 131
achieved minor damage against some enemy ships 160 miles
from Henderson Field. Four days later, when Major Joe Sailer led
a flight of SBDs two hundred miles up the Slot to pummel a destroyer flotilla, they damaged three of the vessels—but Sailer, the
Ivy Leaguer who flew twenty-five missions in only five weeks, had
gone to the well once too often. Antiaircraft fire rendered him unable to close his flaps after he dove on a bomber. Straggling home
at reduced speed, he was overtaken by a Zero and shot down.

VMO-251, which had been one of the units that fed batches of
pilots to Cactus, moved as a whole to Guadalcanal on December
1. Roy Spurlock, who previously visited the island as a ferry pilot,
recalled that despite the best efforts of engineers and Seabees, the
thick mud of Fighter One following rains swallowed Grumman
wheels up to the hubs. Under these conditions takeoff became an
adventure. "You would chug chug down the runway, splashing
mud and pull the stick back. But it couldn't come off and you
soon realized you had all the speed you could get. The usual practice was to throw the flaps down and you'd get some lift, then pull
up the wheels for less drag. But there were some tall trees at the
end of the runway and that could be a problem. You would have
to fly between them." Eventually the solution was to move opera-

tions to Fighter Two, which lay right at the edge of the water. According to Spurlock, living conditions remained Spartan, with pilots and ground personnel housed in tents on a ridge overlooking Fighter Two. Behind them, as in earlier days, howitzer batteries lobbed shells at the Japanese, who responded sporadically. Japanese snipers targeted those foolish enough to drive perimeter roads at night with headlights on.

As a morale booster, Spurlock said Admiral Nimitz sent the Marines two cases of Old Crow whiskey. "Operations officer, Major Paul Fontana, stuck the cases under his bunk bed. He would issue one fifth a night to the fighter pilots on Guadalcanal. There would be a one ounce jigger to give every pilot one drink. A couple of the men got two. We had a Guadalcanal cocktail, made of ice, unsweetened grapefruit juice and Old Crow. It was set up around a table. You'd go in strung [tight] like bow string, tired, nervous. As people drank talk began and started a feeling of good fellowship. We'd ease up and by 8:30 or 9 everybody was asleep.

"On Dec. 7, 1942," continued Spurlock, "we were listening to Tokyo Rose, blatting our brains out, how the skies over Guadalcanal would be black with Japanese planes on the anniversary of Pearl Harbor. The operations people decided the best thing to do was get everything airborne by daylight. When the Japanese planes came down we'd be up there ready to meet them. There was a pre-dawn takeoff scheduled that morning. The Officer of the Day Harry Sweetham, expediting matters, was driving around in a jeep. When I got over to the flight line around 4 or 4:15, I discovered I'd left my sidearm, hunting knife, first aid kit, extra ammunition, all carried on [my] web belt, hanging on the center post of the tent. I asked Harry to go back and get it.

"Since they couldn't launch everybody at the same time, I told my wing man, George Kobler, I'd rendezvous with him over Kobi Point. I waited around and Harry got back with my .45 which I strapped on. It seemed like the one day guys didn't take a .45 they ended up either with engine failure or being shot down and you didn't want to be on an island without your sidearm. I taxied out. It was one of those mornings when you had to pop the flaps to get out of mud, and made it between trees, went down to rendezvous around Kobi Point. I didn't see him; I circled around down there four or five minutes. It was pitch black while waiting for him to join up but [he] never did show. Soon as it became daylight, I started looking for someone. Anytime you're alone against a Zero you're out numbered. You had a better chance if you joined up with somebody and used the Thach Weave, taking advantage of the F4's strong points.

"I looked around, found another lone plane, joined up, flew at altitude, waiting for Japs to show up but they never did. Weather probably kept them away. I saw a couple of quite hot fires down on Fighter One. When I landed, I found out one of the planes was George Kobler's plane. George, on take-off, somehow swerved off [the] runway, mistook runway lights, and smashed into another airplane, and caught fire almost immediately. The planes were so entangled George never got out."

Although immediate succor for the soldiers now trapped on Guadalcanal could not be achieved, the Japanese started to amass a huge number of troops at Rabaul with the intention of a February 1, 1943, massive invasion of the island. However, that strategy postponed a planned drive through New Guinea. When the Allied forces—Americans, Australians, and others from the British Empire—opened a surprise offensive on New Guinea that defeated a Japanese contingent in the seemingly impenetrable Owen Stanley Mountains, the Japanese abandoned the objective of Guadalcanal in favor of establishing a new defensive position anchored by a line from Munda and Kolombangara in the New Georgia group. The assets in Rabaul now would be plugged into this front and future operations for Guadalcanal aimed at evacuation of as many men as possible.

Indeed, the condition of the Japanese on the island had become desperate. Robert Sherrod's *Marine Corps Aviation* quoted a Nipponese soldier's December 26 entry: "We are about to welcome the New Year with no provision; the sick are moaning within the dismal tents and men are dying daily." And like others he bemoaned the absence of any friendly aircraft.

At the same time, the Japanese felt it imperative to create a base that would forestall their enemy's strikes at Rabaul and the newly established line. Late in November the first big convoy of Japanese vessels arrived at Munda Point on New Georgia Island, only 175 miles from Henderson Field. Engineers and labor crews began to lay out an airfield. The shortened distance between the adversaries meant that Japanese aircraft would no longer be severely restricted by fuel requirements when they confronted the Americans. Within two weeks the Munda strip neared completion. Although the Japanese expertly camouflaged their efforts, photo recon equipment from VMD-154 revealed the advanced state of the project.

Starting December 12 the Munda field endured almost daily raids. Fighters, dive-bombers, carrier-based aircraft, the Air Corps's B-17s and B-26s all visited their particular ordnance upon the site. They blew up revetments with planes, hangars and shops, fuel dumps and barracks while gouging huge holes in the runway. But this last could be quickly repaired, and Japanese fighters rose early and often to challenge the raiders.

On the day before Christmas, the Allied air arm struck hard. With no effective early-warning system such as aided Cactus, the Japanese were caught with only four Zeros in the air while another twenty awaited their turn to take off. The quartet that had already gotten off the ground quickly fell victims to the F4Fs and P-38s, and as the Japanese fighters scrambled for the sky ten more were almost instantly shot down. Major Donald Yost of VMF-121 destroyed four while a VMO-251 compatriot of Roy Spurlock, Lieutenant Kenneth J. Kirk Jr., Yost's wingman, scrubbed three. The attack included nine SBDs whose crews claimed they demolished the ten fighters still on the runway. Later in the day a flight of nine SBDs, accompanied by Wildcats and Airacobras, dove on thirteen troop-carrying barges near Munda and smashed nine of them, killing or drowning many of the soldiers.

Guadalcanal itself saw little aerial combat during the final month of the year. According to Robert Sherrod, the Imperial Navy, having been severely taxed by its efforts to support the army on Guadalcanal, sought to turn responsibility for support of the starving, malaria-afflicted soldiers over to the generals. To placate the aggrieved admirals, some one hundred Japanese aircraft and pilots, veterans of the victorious campaign in Malaya, traveled to Rabaul to provide support for an evacuation.

As the new year opened, Dauntless dive-bombers performed ground support, smashing an area believed to contain the enemy headquarters on Guadalcanal. The next day B-26s from the Army accompanied by P-38 Lightnings and Wildcats pounded antiaircraft emplacements and other targets around the Munda base. Late in the day dive-bombers with fighter cover harassed enemy destroyers in the vicinity of New Georgia and claimed to have sunk one and left another in flames. On January 5, the first Japanese Army planes engaged B-17s targeting Rabaul. That afternoon aircraft from Navy carriers also bombarded the Munda strip. As the ships retired from the area, enemy dive-bombers attacked. Wildcats from Guadalcanal helped drive off the foe. Ten days later, as a Tokyo Express of nine destroyers challenged the screen around the island, a melee in the sky cost the Japanese Army eight Zeros—but five American fighters and one dive-bomber also went down.

During the day's combat, Joe Foss scored three knockdowns, giving him a total of twenty-six. He had returned to Guadalcanal with the rest of VMF-121 earlier in the month under the rotation system. Ten days later Foss led a flight that intercepted a huge aerial armada of sixty enemy planes. Rather than engage the much superior force, Foss kept his small band of fighters circling above until Cactus dispatched a host of planes that discouraged the Japanese from attempting a raid. It was Foss's final mission from Guadalcanal, and ironically he never fired a single shot. Four days later the entire squadron left Guadalcanal for good.

In his interview with *Naval History*, Foss, speaking of Admiral Halsey, the Navy's South Pacific commander, reported, "When he decorated me, he said, 'If there's ever anything I can do to help you, just let me know. . . .' When I came out of combat, I had my flight of seven guys behind me, headed for Australia. On the way, we stopped in New Caledonia. I was having lunch with two city government officials and Ben Finney, a non-flying officer in my outfit. Up came an AP [air policeman] who said, 'Are you Captain Foss?'

"I said, 'Right.'

"He said, 'Would you, as soon as you finish lunch, come down to the shore patrol station? We have your boys in lockup. They say they're your boys.'

"And I said, 'You mean you've got seven pilots?'

" 'Yes, sir. We have seven of them down there.'

"So I hurried and finished lunch, and we drove to the station. Then I looked up and asked the driver, 'Is that Admiral Halsey's flag?'

"He said, 'Yes, sir.' . . .

"I said, 'Stop the show.' I got out and walked in. Everybody recognized me. I had a fire-red beard at the time and I had black hair. I said, 'I want to see the admiral.' I just walked right in.

"And the admiral greeted me with open arms. 'Well how the hell are you?'

"I said, 'Right now, I need some help, sir. You've got my boys over here in lockup for some reason or other.'

"He got on the line to the station himself and said, 'I want the commander and those men over here right now.' Next came the funniest sight I saw in the whole war. Here came my boys, all in Aussie uniforms, with U.S. Marine emblems on them and shorts. I hate shorts. I'd rather see ladies' legs than men's any day of the week. And here were these guys all in shorts. Halsey couldn't stop laughing. The Navy captain—or commander, whatever he was— tried to tell the admiral the story behind all this.

"So the admiral says to my men, 'Be my guest. Sit down.' He met them all and asked each one how many planes he had shot down. My flight alone had 78, that group of guys right there. [Altogether VMF-121 was credited with 164 planes in 122 days of combat while losing twenty of its own pilots.] So then we just started talking war games. Then he said to the commander, 'How long have you been over here, sir?'

" 'I just got here last week.'

"Halsey said, 'I'll get you some orders so you can get into combat and find out what it's all about.' Poor guy."

According to Foss, his pilots, fresh out of the jungle, hit upon the idea of shorts while in a bar and completed the outfit with

Aussie green flared jungle jackets and pith helmets, all replete with Marine Corps insignia. He contended that his colleagues were pioneers for a sartorial style that became common in the Pacific.

Foss's twenty-six was a high-water mark for Marine pilots. The record of twenty-eight listed for Greg "Pappy" Boyington included six claimed while he served with the Flying Tigers in China, and four of these were destroyed on the ground. Unlike the European Theater, in the Pacific only knockdowns in the air were added to a pilot's score.

Paul Fontana, who achieved ace status during his time with the Cactus Air Force, explained, "By being the squadron commander I was up front and got the first shots. If you look at the list of aces in the Marine Corps, in the Air Force and the Navy, you'll note that squadron commanders and flight leaders are some of the top aces, because they got the first shots."

Foss, in an interview recorded by the Marine Corps Historical Center, explained, "I never wanted to settle for one of the just ordinary spots down the line. Why not ole Joe, making it all the way." At the same time he knew his limitations. "I wanted to be world champ in boxing. I got to the semifinals in the Golden Gloves. My boxing instructor said this guy is big and fast but he's green. Knock him out in the first round. I made two mistakes. One was getting in the ring with this gorilla. And then hitting him, because he got mad and in the next three rounds, he knocked me down 11 times. My Mother said what did you get out of it. I said being smart enough never [to] get in it again."

Spurlock remembered an evening in which the Marine pilots were "chewing the fat in their tent. We knew Joe Foss was our leading ace at the time and figured he would have some inside skinny on how it was done. I asked him how he was able to run up that kind of a score."

Spurlock said Foss replied, "I track trouble. Other people can go out and never see a thing. But for some reason it comes right to me."

Spurlock offered his own analysis of aerial combat success.

"Disparity in records is no sort of indicator of relative capability of pilots themselves. You have to have talent, be able to shoot guns accurately, maneuver your airplane to become the shooter instead of the shootee. A lot of people had those skills, most people were aggressive, ready and able enough. But as Joe said, you've got to be plain lucky. You've got to be where they are, or they've got to be where you are. If they miss the first interception hit the second." Regarding his personal scorecard, Spurlock—whose only victory occurred on a mission to Rabaul—insisted, "I didn't have the opportunities."

He also conceded that not everyone measured up to even the minimum standards. "For all the heroes we produced at Guadalcanal," he noted, "some became averse to taking off against Japanese. There were cases when pilots were given information to man planes [through the coast-watchers] and supposed to get to 30,000 feet. If you'd didn't get off within minutes of the scramble signal, if you didn't get off right away there was no point to you taking off. We'd have pilots rush out, and strap themselves in, look out, find [the] planes didn't have a wing, didn't have engines on them. These were cannibalized planes or hangar queens. When this happened more than once, became a pattern, you begin to suspect their actions [deliberately choosing machines that were not airworthy]. They would check their mags [magnetos] and find some problem. Others would take off, immediately head for San Cristobal, next biggest island and farthest from Rabaul. We called them 'Giggle Girls,' and they were not well regarded by their compatriots. They didn't last long, usually were shipped out."

Back on Espiritu Santo, Jim Law worked on the latest aircraft shipped to the area. "The Grumman TBF Avenger torpedo bomber [which replaced the highly vulnerable TBD Douglas Devastator] was assigned to some of the Marine squadrons which were then redesignated as Torpedo Bombing Squadrons. The planes carried two rear gunners in addition to the pilot. Shortly after the planes arrived, we received kits of parts and instructions for installing launching rails to carry the five-inch aircraft rockets. These proved to be very effective weapons for ground attacks. I got to fly as a gunner on a few patrols but never got to shoot at any enemy aircraft."

Charles Conter from the small town of Cascade, Iowa, born in 1921, had been a member of the Civilian Conservation Corps and a factory worker. In mid-February 1942 he enlisted and chose the Marine Corps for his military service. Within a month he boarded a troop train that brought him to San Diego, where he entered boot camp. In an unpublished memoir, he wrote, "We marched everywhere together including the head [toilet]. After drilling all day under 2 DIs [drill instructors], we were ready for the sack but many times we had to go to a movie or to a stage show and the DI would ask if anyone wanted to stay in the hut and woe if you raised your hand to stay. You would be scrubbing the hut with a toothbrush, so we learned early never to volunteer for anything and always go with the group. We saw no newspapers, heard no radio and it was a life like you can't believe. We were required to write home whether we wanted to or not and mail call was always a welcome time. On Sundays we were all required to go to the church of our choice but we had better go. It was a day to catch up on letter writing but there was no place to go. We were never allowed to go anywhere except to the head by ourselves. . . . We were required to shower, shave and brush our teeth every day. It was funny for some of the 17-year-olds to have to shave the little peach fuzz they had but you had better shave whether you needed it or not.

"We used to have to run on the sandy ground and beach where the camp was located. It was hard going but built leg muscles. I gained weight with the tight regimentation and good food and when I left boot camp I had gained from 148 pounds when I went in to 160–165 lbs.

"In our platoon were two big game guides from Alaska, a number of Southerners still fighting the Civil War, men and boys from the cities and hill country of Kentucky and Missouri, all molding together in a fighting unit."

Although Conter said he wanted to serve as a rifleman, a friend in his platoon and a drill instructor helped persuade him to request the aviation branch. After passing an examination for that duty, Conter entered training for gunnery. He attended a school for that skill and then reported to Goleta, a base near Santa Barbara. "My first ride and really first dive in a dive bomber was there. It was an old two-wing job, held together with struts. The pilot peeled off around 10,000 feet and we dove straight down with the air howling thru the wires and struts. Boy, I never dreamed of anything like that. . . ."

Having completed his training, in September 1942 Conter boarded a Danish ship at San Diego while a band played "Goodbye Mama, We're Off to Yokohama." At Pearl Harbor he glimpsed the wreckage of the sunken battleship *Arizona* and the bottom of the *Oklahoma* before reporting to the Marine base at Ewa. "Our barracks were still full of holes from Jap strafing. . . . The ground was still littered with the spent shells and clips for the machine guns on the Jap planes."

Conter became a rear gunner with VMSB-234, a dive-bomber squadron. "Our squadron leader was shot down in the Battle of Midway and him and his gunner were in a life raft three days before being rescued. The gunner was also wounded and received his Purple Heart.

"I flew a lot at Ewa with different pilots . . . as we were trying to become a unit. One hop we were on we tried to go as high as we could. We got up to almost 28,000 feet . . . we could go no farther up. It was one of the few times I had to use the oxygen tank and mask. . . . We had a stick we could put in to fly the plane in an emergency. Many times when we were on a hop going no particular place, the pilot would let us fly the plane, land on clouds, etc. We had no other instruction. We also had an altimeter that would [keep] reminding the pilot in a dive when we hit 1,500 feet . . . to pull out and by the time we would get straightened out we would be about 50 feet over the water. At 28,000 feet I could see the whole Hawaiian chain. . . . Every dive was a thrill and I was always thankful when we pulled out.

"One day we were in a building close to the field when we got word a plane was coming in with wheels up so we all went out to watch. He came in with a beautiful landing and we started to run out to congratulate him. He was starting to stand up in the seat when all at once the plane blew up right in front of us. It was a terrible sight and a couple of the gunners decided they saw enough and quit flying then and there. . . . I would always dread a belly landing on land after that sight."

In the following weeks Conter saw a number of other fatal crashes but remained a gunner. On December 1 his squadron and VMSB-233 sailed on a transport to Espiritu Santo, a place he and his colleagues had never heard of. While fascinated by the tropical vegetation, Conter coped with omnipresent hordes of flies and a diet of Spam, dried eggs, and dehydrated potatoes. Papayas, knocked off trees with well-aimed shots from .45 revolvers, supplemented the menu. Occasionally an earthquake rattled the island, and twice Japanese aircraft raided the area without inflicting significant damage.

Conter became the permanent rear-seat occupant for a dive-bomber flown by Lieutenant Carl Brorein, a veteran of Midway. He noted, "Started out for Cactus on 29 [January 1943], turned back, started out twice on the 30th and made it. Brorein and me, and Wilcox and Showell flying wing on DC-3 landed at Henderson Field after 4:30 hours."

Bivouacked in a tent at Skunk Hollow, site of the ferocious Battle of Bloody Knoll, Conter said, "Even as we dug foxholes we ran into dead Japs everywhere we dug. The stench was awful with the heat and rain most every day." When two acquaintances died in a practice-dive crash, Conter reflected, "I always feared going straight in in practice. I didn't mind dying diving on a Jap base or ship but I hated the thought of dying in a practice dive . . . the thought was in the mind every time we peeled off: our life was in the hands of a pilot and he might get target happy and dive too low to get out of the dive."

In a diary entry at a later date, Conter noted, "We always carried a code book that was supposed to be destroyed if we went down. Also a survival kit. If I knew for certain we were going in, we were supposed to unlock the wing machine guns and dump them in the ocean so as not to get hit in the head with them when you crash landed. We also carried a carbine and ammo in the backseat. The big problem was it was so hot on the ground and yet you had to dress for the cold weather 16,000 feet up as you sat in an open seat. You could shove the middle part of your hood [canopy] to keep out the cold but you couldn't maneuver your machine guns as well so you generally left both hoods open and froze until the dive and then it was too hot with all of the gear on."

Conter had arrived during a period in which the intensity of the Japanese air assaults matched the peaks during early October. Robert Sherrod noted that VMF-112's war diary reported, "Pilots are flying 5–6 hours per day and Wing Operations is still dreaming up more."

In this context, First Lieutenant Jefferson DeBlanc of that squadron took off on January 31 with an escort section for a strike force of dive-bombers and torpedo planes bound for the waters off Kolombangara Island where a number of Japanese ships had been observed.

A large batch of Zeros attempted to intercept the Americans. The dogfights began at fourteen thousand feet, but when DeBlanc received word of a formation of floatplanes attacking the SBDs and TBFs, he dove down to disperse them while the dive-bombers and torpedo planes completed their runs and escaped for home. Although he knew he was running low on fuel, DeBlanc still splashed three of the floatplanes. When he headed back to Cactus, he discovered a pair of Zeros closing on him. He outmaneuvered both and shot them down. However, the encounters left his F4F badly damaged, and DeBlanc bailed out near treetop level over Japanese-held Kolombangara. Fortunately for DeBlanc and a fellow downed pilot, Staff Sergeant James A. Feliton, a coastwatcher found them; after thirteen days they were retrieved by a Duck from Guadalcanal. DeBlanc also received a Medal of Honor for his exploits at Kolombangara.

Charles Conter reported that in his first bivouac at Skunk Hollow, the foxhole for protection during raids was actually inside the tent. "It was very muddy, very crowded when we all had to get in it. . . . On the front of the tent was two poles and on each pole we had a skull of a Jap soldier. As we went out of the tent we would pat the skull on the head. It sounds very macabre now but at the time life was so cheap and nobody ever knew who would be the next to go. There were plenty of skulls around [because] the Battle of Bloody Knoll was fought here."

On February 1 Conter's VMSB-234 made its first raid on Munda. Conter did not participate but "felt the war was on when two planes failed to return. Afterwards, we got word of task force coming down the Slot. We took off in an old SBD-3 but the whole division turned back when our fighters left us to attack Jap dive bombers that were diving on our destroyer off Cactus. Jap planes sunk destroyer *DeHaven*. . . . We landed and after a half hour of waiting, took off again in a good SBD-4, flew 2d position in a division . . . found 20 destroyers just off New Georgia Islands, went in for attack as our fighters kept 15 Zeros above us busy. Good dogfights. We went into dive and got direct hit on destroyer leader. [Captain Richard] Blain also hit it; it sunk in about 10 minutes. I confirmed hit for which Brorein got credit. The ack ack they threw up was terrific but we came through without a scratch."

In his present-tense diary he noted, "Williams and Hawks failed to return and are still listed as missing. [Lieutenant Abram] Moss is dead for sure. [Gunner Gilbert] Henze bailed out near Russells, Moore and Reed parachuted out over Munda. . . ." After his pilot was killed, Conter said, "Henze, a good friend, from State Center Iowa, put in the stick in the rear and flew the plane back with fighter escort. We had no way to change gas tanks in the rear so when the gas ran out, Henze had no choice but to parachute. The plane was in a dive sort of when he jumped and the rear stabilizer cut his leg off at the knee. He landed in the water near the Russell Islands, then still in Jap hands. The natives of the islands picked him up and stopped the blood and saved his life. He was brought back to Cactus later in the month where we saw him off on a plane. We learned later he died in a San Francisco hospital."

On February 4 Conter participated in another attack upon Munda. His diary read: "I watched docks blow sky high, plenty of ack ack. The bombs also hit near runway and in revetments area. Capt. [Richard] Blain [a Midway veteran] led, made glide bombing dive to about 5,000 ft., ran into ack ack from Vila too. In afternoon 20 more cruisers and destroyers were reported coming down the Slot. 1st attack went out after them. I was on 2d attack, but Williamson had borrowed my flight jacket. Half hour later 2d attack was also sent out and met the task force off New Georgia Islands. Saw a destroyer burning about 3 miles behind the task force, knew that our first attack had scored. We came in at 13,000 [feet] and peeled off about 10,000. We had no radio, went down on destroyer leader after Capt. Blain. [Captain] Blackmun following. Saw Zeros tangling with F4F above me, nearly collided with Blain in peel off. Blackmun passed us up in dive when flaps didn't open, saw him release his bomb. Ack ack concussion threw us off target in dive, we got back and dove low before releasing. Brorein got credit for a hit on forward deck, heard .50 calibers chattering as we pulled out of dive, later learned it was my pilot shooting a Zero off another guy's tail.

"Saw my first close range Zero a second later when it peeled off right near my tail, about 50 yds away. Got about 150 rounds away at one a second after that when he came in about 7:30 high. I chased him off and chased another coming in, out of the sun at about 4:30 high. After we were in formation I watched Zeros and SBDs tangling, saw one SBD hold off 3 Zeros. Learned later it was Barr-Cechal. We sank 2 ships, left 4 damaged, our gunners got about 4 Zeros. We also lost 3 TBF on raid. Our motor conked out about Savo Island, but we made it back OK. Got in and learned we had lost Russell and Stanley on raid and had lost Murphy and Williamson. Williamson had my flight jacket on. Other planes were shot up bad. On 2d raid Blair, gunner for Lt. Thrasher, was shot in head by Zeros. Thrasher made swell one wheel landing on Henderson Field and Blair got to hospital in time to be saved and sent back to [the] States. Our plane was untouched but Zero bullets came close." Brorein received a DFC for his hit on a destroyer.

In his recollections some years later, Conter added, "I loaned [Warren G.] Williamson my flight jacket as he was going on the raid and I had just been on one so I didn't think I would be going again that day. They took a direct hit in the engine on their dive and landed as far away from the task force as they could in the water. You had 30 seconds to get the life raft out. It was the gunner's job and it was stored just back of the rear seat but you had to . . . stand on the wing to get at it. The task force took a couple of long range pot shots at them after they landed in the water but they were in too big a hurry to get to Cactus to take a couple of prisoners.

"They spent 3 days in a lifeboat [the raft] and made their way to Choiseul Island where a coast-watcher got to them and hid them in a village." Two weeks later they were rescued by a PBY. However, neither Russell nor Stanley was ever found. The casualties for VMSB-234 multiplied. By the third of the month, four of Conter's eight tent mates had been lost, with telling effect upon the survivors. "I remember Britton, a big lad from Minnesota, reading the Bible by candlelight and nobody laughed. Entwhistle, a preacher's son, learned how to cuss a blue streak. It was rather comical after never [having] heard him cuss. And Bechel, who held off the Zeros when they got separated after the dive, started smoking for the first time.

"[One night] We heard rumors of Japs in the camp area and we had just had an air raid. We all slept with the loaded .45 under our pillow. Anyway we were all a bit nervous and we hadn't lit our candles yet after the raid when I saw a figure coming toward the tent door. I reached under my pillow and aimed the .45 at his chest. As he neared closer, my finger tightened on the trigger and just when I was about to finish the squeeze, he said, 'Got a light?' I recognized Cohen, another gunner from another tent. To this day he never knew how close he was to death."

After a week or so Conter and four squadron mates, desperate for improvements in their diet, took some rifles and their .45s on an expedition to an Army food dump. "We found it and picked up gallons of [canned] pineapples, peaches and pears. We lugged all we could and when the Army soldiers on guard hollered at us, we threatened to shoot if they came any closer. They followed us for awhile but that was as close as they cared to come. I ate so many pineapples, peaches and pears that it was years and years later before I could sit down and eat [them] again."

Starting in February, the Marines introduced a truly significant new and formidable weapon, the gull-winged F4U Corsair. Able to climb at a rate of three thousand feet a minute—faster than any of the Japanese planes—and with a range twice that of the Wildcat, it promised to be a superior aircraft. But in its earliest versions, the Corsair manifested discouragingly numerous bugs. Hydraulic, oil, and fuel leaks, and a balky ignition system plagued the F4U-1. Originally ticketed for use by the Navy, the Corsair's poor visibility during taxi and takeoff from a flight deck, and a tendency for the landing gear to buckle when the heavyweight fighter touched down, dampened enthusiasm. After experimenting with F4Us, the Navy signed away its rights to the Marines, who welcomed an opportunity to deploy a high-performance weapon. Some Marines, dubious of the Corsair's qualities, called it the "Bent Wing Widow Maker," but the Japanese knew the plane as "Whistling Death."

As early as September 1942 Marines in VMF-124 had begun to fly the gull-winged fighter. When VMF-124 arrived on Guadalcanal on February 12, 1943, however, the Corsair seemed a dubious choice. According to author Bruce Gamble, Corsair crashes from noncombat causes destroyed more aircraft than the Japanese during VMF-124's entire tour.

The presence of Corsairs along with Army P-38s allowed a tactical change designed to better protect the bombers and torpedo planes. The P-38s, able to operate at extreme altitudes, held positions at thirty to thirty-four thousand feet. Below them, layers of F4Us or Wildcats guarded the space between twenty thousand and thirty thousand feet; down at twenty thousand feet where the bombers cruised, P-40s monitored the skies for interceptors coming up from below.

All of this was not enough to overcome skillful enemy fliers. On their third day in the battle zone, the F4Us along with P-40s and P-38s chaperoned Navy PB4Ys on a strike at Kahili Field in southern Bougainville. Japanese Zeros knocked down two Corsairs, two P-40s, all four P-38s flying top cover, and two of the big bombers while only losing three of their own ships. The painful experience, on February 14, became known as the "St. Valentine's Day Massacre."

Even so, the Japanese now recognized Guadalcanal as a lost

cause. On February 4 another flotilla, twenty-two destroyers and a cruiser, sailed from Shortland Islands, part of the northern Solomons. Covens of Zeros hovered overhead for the inevitable clash with American dive-bombers, torpedo planes, and their fighter cover. The attackers disabled one destroyer, damaged three others, and shot down seventeen Japanese planes while losing ten of their own. Still the convoy steamed on and eventually evacuated 11,706 soldiers, according to statistics compiled by naval historian Samuel Eliot Morison.

It was estimated that about twenty-four thousand Japanese died of combat wounds or disease while one thousand became prisoners. Casualties for the combined Marine and Army ground forces amounted to almost sixteen hundred dead and more than four thousand wounded. Both sides lost considerable tonnage on the sea, including a pair of aircraft carriers for the United States and two battleships for the Japanese. The fifteen Marine combat air squadrons counted 94 pilots killed or missing in action with another 177 evacuated due to casualties, sickness, or being otherwise unfit for combat flight duty. Total figures for Japanese aerial losses during the Guadalcanal campaign were never calculated.

While the flag of the Rising Sun set upon the Japanese presence on Guadalcanal, the island became more intensely populated with aircraft and crews assigned to lead the offensive against enemy holdings. A set of newcomers to Guadalcanal's air arm was VMF-214, formed on July 1, at Ewa. Major George F. Britt assumed command shortly after the squadron's activation. Britt, the son of a World War I naval lieutenant and born in Portsmouth, Virginia, in 1914, had graduated from Georgia Tech. He had majored in aeronautical engineering, been a member of the naval ROTC, and taken a commission in the Marine Corps. Britt followed three years as a ground Marine with flight training. Initially a bomber pilot, he switched to fighters immediately after the war began.

Britt trained on the F2A Brewster Buffalo and escaped the slaughter of his brother Marines in these obsolescent machines at Midway only by a fluke of fate. He had been detached for several weeks to learn the workings of a new type of gun sight and was ready to report back for duty, which would have dispatched him to Midway. However, when VMF-211 loaded aboard the *Lexington* for stationing at Palmyra, Claude Larkin, the Ewa commander, realized that the squadron's F2A-3s bore the new gun sight and Britt was the only one who had received training with the instrument. Orders for Britt to report aboard the *Lexington* were quickly cut; in place of a ticket to the Midway carnage, he was made executive officer of 211, then sent back to Ewa for duty with 214.

"When I took over," Britt wrote in a letter, "we had only two other pilots, both Midway veterans and no aircraft. For seven months, new pilots dribbled in; aircraft were alternately assigned and taken away until finally we were able to settle down with 24 new F4F-4s and about 27 pilots, mostly inexperienced and directly from pilot training. Training proceeded gradually and carefully . . . with the responsibility for supervision falling mainly on the only two experienced fighter pilots in the squadron, Ellis [Captain Henry A., his executive officer] and myself. The tempo increased, with emphasis on air-to-air gunnery and tactics. By the end of December we had reached a fairly high level of readiness." Their training experience exemplified the dangers even when not in combat. Over a six-month period ground loops, midair collisions, and mechanical mishaps destroyed ten planes or damaged them beyond repair, while half a dozen required extensive work by mechanics. One pilot was lost.

Britt declared himself gratified by the "squadron personality [that] began to develop, characterized by pride in the attainment of increased flight proficiency, congeniality, humor and high morale. . . . The four enlisted pilots fitted in with no difficulty. Three of them . . . were on my recommendation, later commissioned 2d Lts."

In *The Black Sheep*, Bruce Gamble's account of VMF-214, Staff Sergeant Jim Taylor said, "Britt made it abundantly clear that we were all, first and foremost, pilots. There were social differences but not professional differences between us. We were all of the same cloth, even though we were from different pay grades. In his welcoming address he made sure that nobody felt left out, and nobody could possibly assume that they would have an elevated position."

From Ewa, in February 1943, the squadron and two others, VMF-213 and 221, all part of MAG-21, deployed to the South Pacific, arriving on March 4 on Espiritu Santo. Ten days later Britt said, "I left Espiritu Santo with nine F4Fs [only that many replacement F4Fs were needed by Guadalcanal fighter command at the time] and proceeded to Guadalcanal in formation with a SCAT [South Pacific Air Transport Command] C-47 acting as navigational lead. All other 214 pilots rode the C-47. Fourteen TBF Avengers of VMSB-143 made up the remainder of the flight.

"It turned out to be anything but a routine flight. About midpoint, over the Coral Sea at eleven thousand feet, the C-47 pilot exercised extremely poor judgment and led the entire formation into a vicious tropical storm. With visibility so bad I could not see the transport even in tight formation, and fearful of a collision, I veered off, collected what remained of my flight, and proceeded on to our destination at an altitude of about fifty feet. Approaching Guadalcanal, visibility improved sufficiently to make landing routine.

"So heavy had been the rain and hail that the paint on the leading edges of our wings and engine cowls had been stripped clean. So ended a harrowing five-hour trip. Captain Ellis had been the tail-end man in our formation and, as we learned later, lost fuel pressure just as we entered the storm, glided to three thousand feet with a dead engine, bailed out, hit the water in heavy seas, managed to inflate his parachute seat raft, and floated around for five days before being picked up by one of our destroyers that just happened to be passing by. He later joined us. Sergeant Taylor became separated from our flight in the storm and proceeded on alone. Running out of fuel, he made a successful landing in a marshy area close to the coast about thirty miles short of Fighter Strip One, our destination. Seven of the TBFs, with crews, were lost on this flight. None were ever recovered. In my opinion using a C-47 as navigational lead was needless and in this case a disaster. My prewar carrier experience and many long over-water flights was sufficient to enable me to lead on this 550-mile flight with ease."

Actually, two TBFs showed up later in the day, leaving five unaccounted for. The Avengers normally carried a crew of three, but on this occasion radiomen did not make the trip, just the gunners on four of the ships. One pilot flew alone. The cost to VMSB-143 added up to five pilots and four enlisted men.

In the nearly six months since Marines splashed ashore on the island, little had changed for Americans except that the Japanese had been shoved well away from the airfields. Britt with his squadron settled in on Guadalcanal amid frequent torrential rains that created ankle-deep mud, the swarms of mosquitoes requiring daily doses of atabrine to ward off malaria, the stifling, humid heat that soaked khaki uniforms with sweat, the miserable food and imperfect sanitation that fostered bouts of dysentery.

The squadron commander described the operational environment as "primitive by any standard and fraught with hazards— marginal airstrip (though much improved over that used by earlier squadrons), unpredictable weather with unreliable forecasting, no navigational aids of any kind, 4:30 A.M. formation join-ups in the blackest night sky imaginable, sleepless nights caused by Washing Machine Charlie's almost nightly visits, and aircraft maintenance made difficult by parts shortages and dust, dust, dust."

Two days after their arrival, VMF-214 fighters accompanied a Dumbo (air–sea rescue plane) on a hunt for a downed flier. "Technical Sergeant Harrell Steed," reported Britt, "unaccountably left his formation . . . and apparently spun in from a low altitude." He would be the only casualty during the squadron's two-month tour, although in the first three days with Cactus the squadron had lost three planes, counting the crashes of Ellis and Taylor.

NINE

CACTUS WANES

The departure of the Japanese from Guadalcanal encouraged the South Pacific Command to advance the American holdings to Banika in the Russell Islands, fifty-five miles northwest of Henderson Field and about the same distance from the New Georgia group. On hand February 21, Charles Conter in the backseat of an SBD with VMSB-234 recalled, "I was on the 2d attack on the big day when American forces occupied the Russells. Our first attack went out at 6 and we relieved them at 9 o'clock. I watched destroyers launch Higgins boats loaded with men to the shore. We flew over the islands for 3½ hours waiting to see if there would be any resistance. There was none." At the same time that the Japanese had pulled their troops off Guadalcanal, they had evacuated those in the Russells. While the distance seems modest in terms of the huge area of the theater, the base constructed at Banika provided a boost for the range-challenged Marine air arm.

An ill-fated idea assigned Marine and Navy TBFs to lay mines around the ports servicing the Japanese. On February 14 VMTB-233 dispatched sixteen aircraft to plant mines at Simpson Harbor. Only ten returned, and the loss of eighteen airmen and six TBFs persuaded pilots and crews that aerial mine laying was excessively hazardous. Eventually the task would be handed over to four-engine bombers better able to protect themselves with their extra firepower.

While the war raged in the Solomons, the United States

manned bases at Johnston Island and Palmyra to the southeast, to protect shipping from marauding submarines. Among those stationed at Johnston was Simon LaVois "Spider" Webb. He called his early experiences during World War II "dodging the draft." The son of a father in the meatpacking business and a Boy Scout during the early 1930s in Helena, Arkansas, Webb had his boyhood imagination spurred by local Fourth of July parades that featured veterans from the Civil War, the Spanish-American War, and World War I. "I had a local paper route in 1935 and when the Italians invaded Ethiopia an 'extra' was issued. I followed that bit of news, the Spanish Civil War, and the war news after 1939."

However much military history stimulated him, though, Webb said he ignored those friends who joined the National Guard, and he did not join the ROTC in college. "When the Helena draft board began to zero in on me," said Webb, "I started looking for something that promised more future than an infantry rifle squad. I enlisted [in July 1941] in the Navy V-5 program though I had never been in an airplane, for it seemed to offer more options if 'things didn't work out.' As a youth I saw Captain Frank Hawks [a famed aviator before World War II] fly and was fascinated by Lindbergh, the Lafayette Escadrille, and *Dawn Patrol* [a film about World War I aviators].

"Flight training at Corpus Christi centered on developing abilities to fly an airplane. Early on we were told, 'We can teach a monkey to fly, but we can't teach him to think.' Sunday, December 7, 1941, found me with friends in a movie theater watching some 'do and daring' war picture when the film stopped, lights went on, and MPs came down the aisle announcing, 'All military personnel return to your bases immediately.' On the way out we heard 'Pearl Harbor has been attacked,' which didn't mean a thing to us.

"It was a watershed day in our lives. Training was ratcheted up to a seven-day week. We flew almost every day and rode the cattle cars [Navy buses] to and from the outlying fields. On base we marched everywhere in formation. Liberty was a thing of the past. Emergency passes only."

He drew assignment to dive-bombers. "In advanced squadron we were taught the current dive-bombing techniques and practiced in fleet-weary biwing SBC4s." He received his wings on June 2, 1942, and a day later became a second lieutenant in the Marine Corps. "I opted for a Marine commission because I was deeply impressed by the Marines I had contact with, from the DI [drill instructor] corporal to flight instructors."

Webb became an early member of VMSB-243, posted to the squadron in July 1942. "We were indeed fortunate to have more than a year of operations and training prior to our first day of combat." In fact, six months passed before VMSB-243 sailed to Ewa and there swapped its obsolete dive-bombers for the newer SBDs. Six weeks later the squadron sailed for the South Pacific. "Leaving Pearl was one of the more memorable times in my life. As the ship left the pier, a Navy band played the obligatory—at that time—'Beer Barrel Polka.' We were standing on the flight deck trying to look bold and adventurous with hundreds of people on the pier and in the buildings waving and cheering us on. MGM could not have produced the scene better. I for one had a lump in my throat."

From the escort carrier *Altamaha*, the squadron on St. Patrick's Day, March 17, catapulted half of its complement, including Webb, for duty at Johnston Island, 760 miles west-southwest of Oahu. Two days earlier, the other aircrews from VMSB-243 had flown to the island of Palmyra for duty there. Like most of his companions, Webb had never undergone carrier operations training. He said, "We got a lecture in the ready room and a cockpit checkout, which proved to be adequate for the occasion. It helps to be young and really not know what you are doing."

At Johnston Island, Webb met his radio-gunner, Sylvester S. Garalski from Detroit. "Sal was a corporal and aviation machinist mate who had volunteered for aircrew duty. He was armed with two flexible .30-caliber machine guns. Like Ginger Rogers with Fred Astaire, Sal was doomed to dance through the war backward. Part of our getting acquainted and forming a team was teaching him to fly from the rear seat in the event I was incapacitated and the plane still flyable. All he had was foot pedals, a removable joystick, and mini-throttle. No instruments."

For six months those at Johnston flew two-plane dawn-and-dusk patrols searching for Japanese subs that might toss a few shells at this desolate outpost of the United States. Between missions the airmen practiced maneuvers, tactics, and dive-bombing techniques. Webb still vividly recalls "the loneliness of the sea and the sight of men going to and returning from combat . . . there is no feeling quite like that of flying at about twenty-five hundred feet on a pie-shaped sector, a hundred miles from a tiny island with a single-engine plane, realizing that even though there was a plane about seventy-five feet away, you and your gunner are all alone and helpless if engine failure or enemy action occurred."

The other responsibility involved observation of submariners at the refueling dock in the lagoon outbound and inbound. "If a sub was due in for refueling we were told what bearing and distance from the island they would surface, the time and their heading. We would patrol that immediate area at least an hour before and even though they always were exact on site, time, and heading, there was always the nagging suspicion that it might be an enemy. Having the proper identification code we—in my case, Sal—would challenge them by Aldis lamp [a portable signal light] to be sure. . . . On departure we would patrol the area before they left the lagoon and continue at least thirty minutes after they submerged."

Webb described life on the island as hot and lonely but with "plenty of good food and cheap beer plus the usual volleyball contests. Once a week, a Marine R4D or C-47 brought mail, scuttlebutt, and an occasional replacement."

Richard Mulberry Jr., like Webb, entered military service well before December 7, 1941. A son of the soil in Kentucky, he and his family lived in Detroit for several years during the Great Depression, which took a severe toll on the small farmer. By the sixth grade, however, Richard Mulberry and his family were back in Sadieville, Kentucky. At age eleven Mulberry worked on a tobacco farm while attending the local high school. "There were eleven people in my graduating class," said Mulberry. "I think five of them were my cousins.

"I did not want to be a tobacco farmer, so I ran away from home at age eighteen and worked for a sharecropper. I worked one summer for a dollar a day, three hots [meals a day] and a flop [place to sleep]. I had no vices—didn't smoke, didn't drink, didn't chase wild women." In three months of this ascetic life, he saved enough money to pay the tuition for his first semester at the University of Kentucky. He secured a job with the campus police, fired a furnace in a boardinghouse where he lived in the garret, and waited on tables to pay for his meals. He completed two and a half years studying agriculture and mathematics as the summer of 1941 approached.

"I had a roommate at this boarding house by the name of Tom Cline . . . [and he] went off to Army Air Corps flight training. Tom returned to Lexington in a new uniform with gold bars and shiny, silver wings, driving a blue Chevrolet convertible with a pretty girl. . . . I thought 'That looks very adventurous and romantic.' I thought about applying for flight training and decided that I was going to go him one better and learn to fly off of a carrier. I . . . applied for Navy flight training. Furthermore, it seemed like a foolproof way to avoid the draft [induction of young men for a year of military service had begun in November 1940].

"I had been collecting signatures on a petition for the United States to become more involved in the war against Germany. I was in school, taking summer classes, and being paid ten cents per signature. . . . That got me interested in what was happening in Europe and inspired me to do something significant. I . . . passed all the physicals but weighed only 120 pounds. I think the minimum weight was 128 pounds. They said, 'Come back when you can put on that weight.' Every day I would get a big sackful of bananas and eat them all."

After he added the necessary pounds Mulberry received orders for Opa Locka, Florida, to begin flight training. Like so many of his contemporaries, Mulberry had never been in an airplane until he flew to the naval air station. On December 7, in the midst of his instruction, he was sitting in a Miami restaurant when the radio announced the Japanese attack. Accelerated training brought his wings and a commission in eleven months. Shortly before graduation, Mulberry elected the Marine Corps. He dismissed the notion that only the top 10 percent of a cadet class could make that choice. "That was a big, fat lie, but it made a great story."

After several months in a reserve pool, he was posted to VMSB-243. Mulberry said he preferred the tactics of dive-bombers to those of fighters. The squadron had only two or three experienced pilots. One was Thomas Ahern, "a 'black' Irishman from Boston College," said Mulberry. "He was at . . . Ewa on Oahu on December 7, 1941. The story was told to me . . . the Japanese [had] destroyed all their airplanes at Ewa on the ground. T. J. Ahern was out on the ramp, shaking his fist at the Japanese pilots because he couldn't get in the air."

The second veteran was Harry W. Reed, who had flown with the RAF and received a captain's commission when he agreed to transfer to the Marines. "He was the best pilot I have ever known," said Mulberry. But initially Mulberry was appalled when the squadron received brand-new SBC-4s. "I thought at that time, 'They're gonna send me to war in this fabric covered airplane that can catch afire so easily?' " He was reassured with the issuance of the new SBD-3s and -4s. He also acquired a compatible rear-seat gunner, Herbert Munn. However, the pilots who held commissions and their enlisted crews went their separate ways when not on duty.

Mulberry frankly admitted to a very keen antagonism toward the enemy. "I hated them. When I read about some of the things that they were doing and the overt bombing of Pearl Harbor, unannounced, I had pretty strong feelings about all of the Axis Powers from early summer, 1941."

After he completed the training in Hawaii, Mulberry, like Webb, embarked on the CVE *Altamaha*. But when he catapulted off the deck he was part of VMSB-243 assigned to Palmyra. "It was like Paradise!" said Mulberry. "It was beautiful." In fact the island had been privately owned before the Navy took it over for use during the war. He called the chow more than adequate, particularly since the mess officer, a former restaurateur, developed a working relationship with the small Navy base and secured fresh vegetables, eggs, and even ice cream.

The basic duty for the airmen consisted of antisubmarine patrol. "The flying was exciting because we were flying over water with almost no navigational aids except your plotting board." It was on Palmyra that Mulberry realized just how good a pilot Harry Reed was. "I flew on his wing a number of times during anti-submarine patrols. He would get in the airplane wearing a pair of cut-off khaki shorts, 'boondockers,' no T-shirt, a Mae West and a seventy-pound dog in his lap, our squadron mascot, an Airedale. He'd take off and get airborne. He was shorter than I; I'm only 5'7" and he would lower the seat so he couldn't see over the gunwale. He'd immediately go on instruments and I'd be watching for submarines. He'd fly a leg out from Palmyra, a cross leg and then a leg back to the airfield, which was a little coral airstrip. He'd get right over the tower, raise his seat, and look down. There he was, right back at the airfield!"

In an excess of zeal, Mulberry said he competed with another pilot to see who could fly the most missions and pile up the most hours every month. "I was what they called a 'hop grabber.' I was getting fatigued and didn't know it. I returned to the island one day after an antisubmarine patrol and the wind was not blowing from the usual direction. It had reversed. The control tower was at one end of the runway, but we were landing from the other. I forgot to lower my landing gear, and the control tower could not see the airplane to tell whether or not my landing gear was down. I landed on the depth charge. It's a wonder it didn't blow sky-high because it was a coral runway and you could go through the thin skin of the depth charge pretty readily.

"I realized after I came to a screeching halt what had happened. I turned around to Munn and told him to get out of the airplane and run like hell because I knew that depth charge could go off at any second, and I did the same thing. Fortunately it did not.

"Between flying stints, it was rather boring. We were so disappointed that we could not get into combat and see the enemy face-to-face that we devised our squadron logo, which was never accepted officially by the Marine Corps. We called ourselves the 'Flying Gold Bricks' because we thought we weren't contributing." Much of the off-duty hours were spent gambling and playing poker. They also picnicked and sunbathed.

According to Amos Kay Belnap, another one of the freshly minted second lieutenants to report to VMSB-243 at Santa Barbara, the *Gold Brick* name originated in the States where the pilots spent much of the time carousing in Santa Barbara. The first CO for the squadron was Major James Booth, whom Belnap described as a "soft-spoken, kind, understanding CO [who] did not compel his gold bricking officers and men to shape up to the task of learning the skills of war." When Booth was replaced by Major William Hudson, Belnap said he and his comrades were "outraged at our skipper's release as we pilots considered ourselves to be the best flyers of the Air Group." Their complaints went unheeded, and Hudson made it clear that unless they shaped up, they shipped out.

Shortly after the change in command came the word to select an insignia. "We, the junior officers, had lots of pride, esprit de Corps, loyalty, and perhaps submerged hurt feelings and guilt to be part of the reason for Major Booth being relieved. Whatever the reason, we considered it to be a badge of honor to be called 'The Gold Bricks' and we chose the Flying Goldbricks to be our insignia.

"The squadron and group brass were aghast. They counseled us that this was not a good name. It did not give a positive image. We, however, were adamant and would change it only under direct orders. In the end, the junior officers won out; the Flying Goldbrick name was adopted, the insignia was ordered."

Like Mulberry, Belnap found patrolling off Palmyra monotonous. However, he endured one frightening experience. While on antisubmarine patrol with a wingman, Belnap kept watch on a merchant ship some thirty to forty miles southeast of Palmyra. All went smoothly until he headed toward a very black squall. "[It] stretched east and west as far as the eye could see and blocked our course. With some misgivings, I flew ahead of the ship and at sea level, penetrated the storm hoping to quickly emerge on the other side.

"Within minutes I realized it was the worst storm I'd ever encountered. Since I was unable to see anything, I took a 180 degree turn and headed for my point of entry. The rain was coming down extremely heavy making for zero visibility, and I was skimming the ocean. Since I wasn't coming out of the storm as I expected, I was getting nervous but I really panicked when the electrical instruments went dead. There were no radio, no gyro and no lights. I presumed they had all shorted out as the rain penetrated the aircraft cowlings.

"When I finally broke out into the clear blue sky, the merchant ship was gone, my wingman was gone, my radio was gone and my ability to think clearly was also gone. All kinds of terrible scenarios went through my mind as I tried to plot out my final leg home. Now that it was too late, I realized that while I was circling the merchant ship searching for subs, I had failed to keep data on my second leg of the search, and now I was unable to remember the hours I had spent circling, the miles that had been traveled by the ship, how far I had gone into the storm, or even where I came out.

"With misgivings I set a course for Palmyra. At my ETA [expected time of arrival] no island was in sight, so I circled up to gain altitude and hopefully get the attention of the island radar crew so that they would send someone out to rescue me. After what seemed to be a long time of circling with nothing happening, I called to Al Spring [his gunner] and said our gas was getting low and he should prepare to ditch. We talked about locking his guns down so they wouldn't hit him in the back of the head and that we had to really scramble to get the life raft out before the plane would sink.

"I set the same course again for Palmyra and started to let down. It wasn't too many minutes before the white triangular image of the beautiful coral atoll came into view just off the starboard side at 1 o'clock. It became a good teaching lesson and I never again got careless with my navigation."

Murray and Belnap survived their mistakes. Sudden violent storms, the vastness of the ocean, mechanical malfunctions, and pilot error, however, cost many, many airmen's lives. Of the seventeen casualties in VMSB-243 during its first three tours, while eight were lost in action, nine died or disappeared in operational or noncombat incidents.

VMSB-243 may have felt well removed from harm, but although the Japanese had abandoned their quest for Guadalcanal, Admiral Yamamoto was determined to scourge the air bases from which the Americans tormented the Japanese positions in the New Georgia Islands. Samuel Eliot Morison reported that Yamamoto collected the aerial components from four carriers and combined them with a land-based force of planes for a massive array of 182 fighters, ninety dive-bombers, seventy-two Bettys, and a handful of torpedo planes.

"I Operation" opened on April 1 with fifty-eight Zeros bearing down on Banika and Guadalcanal. They hoped to sweep aside fighter protection for what would follow. In the engagements of the day, six U.S. planes were shot down, but the attackers lost eighteen. Among those tangling with Japanese was a Lieutenant Kenneth Walsh. In 1933, during the depths of the Depression, Walsh, a native of Brooklyn, had enlisted as a private in the Marine Corps. He subsequently had earned his wings, becoming an enlisted pilot before finally receiving a commission. At the controls of a VMF-124 Corsair, Walsh had flown the first two missions to Bougainville, including the one that wiped out two four-engine bombers, four P-38s, and four Corsairs and P-40s. This time Walsh brought down three Zeros; Lieutenant William N. Snider from VMF-221 also accounted for a trio of enemy fighters.

American intelligence predicted massive strikes, gleaned from photo reconnaissance by Army P-38s that detected a huge buildup in aircraft on northern Solomon airfields. On Cactus the airmen waited for the hammer to fall. On April 7, in an F4F, James Swett, who had enlisted in the Naval Reserve while at San Mateo Junior College in California and progressed from seaman second class to the ranks of a replacement pilot for VMF-221, after a breakfast of Spam and peanut butter, had left Fighter Two as part of a four-plane dawn patrol. The quartet drilled routine holes in the sky, dropping Guadalcanal behind and then circling repeatedly over the Russell Islands. After several hours, with no enemy in sight, the patrol touched down at Fighter Two.

Just as Swett and his colleagues climbed down from the wings of their Wildcats, coast-watchers reported hostile planes headed toward Guadalcanal; subsequently blips on the radar screens at

Henderson Field confirmed the imminent threat. The aerial armada consisted of sixty-seven Val dive-bombers screened by an array of 110 Zeros. Cactus braced for the onslaught, notifying all personnel of "Condition Very Red."

Swett's flight quickly refueled, and the crew readied themselves for the coming scramble. To meet the raiders, seventy-six Marine, Navy, and Army fighters, including Swett, took off and engaged them. Swett's assignment was to protect targets in the Tulagi Harbor. According to the account in *American Aces*, over the radio he heard VMF-214's John "Smiley" Burnett (nicknamed for a movie pal of Gene Autry), now patrolling the Russell Islands, gasp, "Holy Christ! There's millions of 'em."

At some sixteen thousand feet as he approached Tulagi Harbor, Swett spied the oncoming dive-bombers. As he descended toward them, he heard over his earphone a colleague warn that Zeros had been sighted and they in turn were beginning to take a run at the Americans. In a calculated risk, Swett, in this his introduction to aerial combat, dove on the Vals. The young lieutenant—he was twenty-two—homed in on the nearest enemy. He said, "I got on the tail of the first one and gave it a squirt. He jettisoned his bombs and burst into full flame. I skidded and mushed in behind No. 2 while my tracers laced him. He smoked, burned and went down.

"I had trouble getting the third one boresighted. Then I relaxed and the plane flew itself into the saddle. As the Aichi nosed over in his bomb run, my first burst smoked him. When he pulled out I was still on his tail. A few more bursts and he exploded. Just as I pulled away, one of our 40 mm AA gun crews on Tulagi drew a bead and wrecked one of my port guns. They almost blew it out of my wing."

Indeed, as Swett pulled up, he saw a large hole in his left wing. The F4F, somewhat more sluggish to react, however, continued to fly. At eight hundred feet he saw a bevy of planes. Had they been Zeros, at that altitude he would have had no chance, but when their silhouette revealed them to be seven more Vals that had just completed their drop, Swett pursued them. When he closed the range he began to trip his wing guns. For some inexplicable rea-

son, the rear gunners initially did not challenge him. Methodi-
cally, Swett worked over the nearest of the flights, blowing away
four of them in short order. But as he approached an eighth possible Val for a deflection shot, that plane's rear gunner opened up,
shattering part of Swett's canopy. The two swapped machine-gun
fire before Swett's ammunition ran out and the Val, emitting
smoke, faded from his view.

More than the cockpit canopy of the Grumman had been damaged. Swett's instrument panel posted disastrous news. The oil
pressure gauge read zero, and the engine temperature climbed
into the red zone. Within a few minutes Swett decided to ditch off
Florida Island. As he slid toward the water, anxious gunners stationed on Tanambogo Island, unable to distinguish friend from
foe, threw .50-caliber machine-gun bullets his way. Before they
could hit him, he slopped down into the water. The sudden decel-
eration drove his head against the gun sight, breaking his nose.

The wreckage sank as much as twenty feet below the surface.
While the dazed Swett struggled to disentangle himself from his
chute harness, he snagged on the ejection handle for his raft. He
tore himself loose, pulling the raft with him. A yank on his Mae
West strings inflated the life vest, carrying him to the surface.
Aboard his life raft, Swett watched with apprehension as a picket
boat with rifle-toting men approached. According to John De
Chant's *Devilbirds,* someone yelled, "Are you American?" Swett
replied, "You're goddamn right I am!" That convinced the coxswain
to pick him up.

At the Gavutu Harbor, a Marine colonel poured Swett a stiff
shot of Scotch to relieve his pain before another boat collected
him for a trip to Tulagi. There, a doctor applied sulfa to his injured face and gave him a shot of morphine for further comfort.
Unfortunately, the combination of alcohol and the drug proved almost lethal.

From the tail-end slot of Swett's division, Kenneth Walsh had
fought against the many Zeros that tried to protect the dive-
bombers. He knocked down a pair before a third fighter shot up
Walsh's Corsair, forcing him also to ditch. He had suffered similar
wounds to Swett, and he, too, received the cocktail of whiskey

and morphine, with results that resembled those of Swett. Both men were hospitalized, as much for their first treatment as for their combat wounds.

Captain Smiley Burnett, the VMF-214 pilot who that afternoon had first tallyhoed the bogeys (aircraft whose identification was in doubt), led one of the four flights from that squadron. He shot down a Val but was himself forced to bail out after a Zero crept up on him from behind and knocked out his engine. A small Navy craft rescued him as he floated off Guadalcanal. Seven others from the outfit accounted for a single enemy plane while Tech Sergeant Alvin Jensen scored twice, giving VMF-214 a total of ten Japanese aircraft destroyed. They lost just two of their Wildcats, including Burnett's. One was declared a wreck after a dead-stick landing, and the squadron listed no pilot casualties.

When the Marine colonel at Gavutu first welcomed Swett, he had reacted skeptically to the flier's claim of destroying seven aircraft in a single sortie. While hospitalized, Swett had aroused suspicions over his mental state by insisting to his doctor that he had indeed scored that many victories and even a possible eighth.

Only after an intelligence officer from Guadalcanal visited Florida Island and interrogated the local inhabitants as well as the ground forces were the seven victories confirmed. Shortly after that, soldiers found a crashed dive-bomber on a small island, which may have been the eighth Val that Swett had battled. Six months later, in full recognition of his feat, Swett received a Medal of Honor.

The heroics of Swett and others notwithstanding, the huge number of Zeros kept the defenders busy enough for Vals to swoop down upon shipping in the harbors of both Guadalcanal and Tulagi. They sank a 14,500-ton tanker, the American destroyer *Aaron Ward,* and a New Zealand corvette. Robert Sherrod reported that the pilots and the ground AA between them asserted they shot down about a hundred aircraft. Air intelligence reduced the totals to twelve Vals and twenty-seven Zeros; Japanese records inspected after the war counted only twelve dive-bombers and nine Zeros lost.

Two more intensive raids as part of the Japanese I Operation pounded New Guinea bases, sinking one ship and damaging several others. Marine fighters were not involved. The Japanese airmen apparently vastly overestimated the destruction that they had wrought. Deceived by the good news, Yamamoto halted the operation and sent the carrier pilots and planes back to their carriers.

During all of these operations, Marine aviation continued to arrange rest and recuperation leaves for flight personnel. The memories of Charles Conter, the rear-seat enlisted man from VMSB-234, provide snapshots of the experience of Marine aviators when not at war.

Speaking of his first R&R leave, Conter noted, "First came a two week at Buttons [Espiritu Santo] living a life of ease, no roll call and no work." He and a friend sailed out to the *Enterprise*, anchored in the bay. "My buddy and I had .45s strapped on our hips and a bandolier of ammo on so we sure looked tough, if nothing else. We went down to the PX on board ship and bought a gallon of ice cream and a gallon of pop. It was the first time in a long time for us to eat and drink that. One day, walking through the area at the fighter strip, a jeep came along with 5 or 6 admirals and generals. As was the rule in the islands, I never bothered to salute and then the jeep came to a screeching halt. Boy, did I snap to and salute, but they just wanted to know directions to the big bomber base."

From Espiritu Santo he embarked on a furlough in Sydney, Australia, via a DC-3. From the airport, he said, "We were taken to town and dumped off and left on our own. First of course they paid us back at Buttons and we had about $500 which we turned into Aussie money. Their pound was worth $3.70 and we treated the pound like it was a dollar and spent like crazy sailors. Those taxi drivers sure liked us. The taxis ran on charcoal and every once in a while the driver had to stop and shovel in some more charcoal. Me, Miles, Lawrence and Entwistle got two rooms at the Great Southern Hotel.

"After we got our room, we started taking in the city and of course that meant bars. They had hot beer there as they drank it that way but they also had cold beer for the Yankees. All Americans were Yankees but they sure learned fast that Southern U.S. boys didn't care to be called Yankees. . . . I met Clare Brown and we hit it off right away. Clare worked in an office in the daytime and I would meet her after work and we would take off for the evening. Clare was the first girl that I really went steady with and like other times in war times you fall in love in a hurry because maybe your time together is limited.

"Clare fell hard for me and wrote every day after I left to go back to the Islands. Her love letters were something that was new to me but I never really was in love with her but did like her a lot as we were together all the time we could be while I was in Sydney. Clare talked of marriage and when I said I was a Catholic she said we would have to be married in the Sacristy then. It was a wonderful week to be able to see civilization, white women, and drink beer again. In the daytime while Clare was working I used to go in a tavern, have a few beers, where we met a lot of Aussie soldiers back from North Africa. . . .

"I saved a lot of Australian coins and paper money and we took whiskey back to the ground crew to sell. We couldn't make it the first time [the flight turned back] so I went out with Clare that night and parting again was tough. She sure was a wonderful girl and I would see her again." On his way back to Cactus, Conter paused for a week at Buttons before an SBD ferried him to Guadalcanal.

In the Solomons the aerial campaign slogged on. George Britt, the head of VMF-214, had missed out on the big April 7 brawl but on April 12 led a strafing mission against the airfield at Vila on Kolombangara. The eight-plane raid totally surprised the base; the F4Fs shot up fuel storage, ammunition dumps, and living quarters. Coast-watchers subsequently advised that the assault had inflicted great damage.

A day later Major Wade H. Britt (no relation to the VMF-214 commander) started to lead a section of Corsairs from VMF-213 off on an early-morning patrol. George Britt remarked, "You've never seen such predawn darkness as you could find there on Guadalcanal." The other three F4Us from Wade Britt's group lifted off, but the squadron CO's landing light malfunctioned. He

Marines began World War II with the obsolete Brewster Buffalo as their fighter aircraft. *(Courtesy U. S. Marine Corps)*

The F4F Wildcat fighter, flown by the Navy, replaced the last of the Brewsters in combat after the Battle of Midway. *(Courtesy U. S. Marine Corps)*

The gull-winged F4U Corsair which entered the war in February 1943, flew faster than any Japanese plane, climbed 3,000 feet a minute and possessed double the range of the Wildcat. *(Courtesy U. S. Marine Corps)*

The F4U Corsair used by the Marines initially was rejected by the Navy because of poor visibility during taxi and takeoff. By the war's end Marines flew Corsairs from carrier decks. *(Courtesy U. S. Marine Corps)*

The TBF Avenger Torpedo Bomber served both the Navy and the Marines against sea-going and land targets. *(Courtesy U. S. Marine Corps)*

Designated the PBJ, the twin-engine Mitchell B-25, the same type used for Doolittle's Tokyo Raid in 1942, worked as a patrol-bomber for the Marines. *(Courtesy U. S. Marine Corps)*

At Henderson Field on Guadalcanal, the rebuilt shack known as the "Pagoda," housed the control tower for the first Marine squadrons stationed in the Solomon Islands. *(Courtesy U. S. Marine Corps)*

Fight Strip 2 on Guadalcanal lay close enough to the sea for Japanese warships to shell the base. *(Courtesy U. S. Marine Corps)*

With Bill Nickerson at the controls of a BD Scout Bomber, a photographer used a movie camera to shoot the shorelines of islands in the New Georgia chain. *(Courtesy Eve Nickerson)*

During the invasion of Bougainville in November 1943, Bill Nickerson flew an SBD that dropped smoke bombs as markers on the beaches for landing barges. *(Courtesy U. S. Marine Corps)*

Marine aviators supported the invasion of Iwo Jima as U.S. forces pummeled an airfield, setting ablaze a number of parked planes. *(Courtesy U. S. Marine Corps)*

On Iwo Jima, Marines defended their hard fought capture of a fighter strip near Mt. Suribachi. *(Courtesy U. S. Marine Corps)*

On Iwo Jima, B-29s packed a now secure airfield. *(Courtesy U. S. Marine Corps)*

On Okinawa, the U.S. invasion fleet lay offshore after the seizure of the Yontan airfield, which became home to Marine fighters fending off kamikazes. *(Courtesy U. S. Marine Corps)*

VMF-212, which flew Corsairs, posed on Bougainville around a palm tree with rising sun flags for planes shot down. *(Courtesy Eve Nickerson)*

Alfred Cunningham, designated the first Marine aviator in 1912, learned to fly on a Navy Wright B-1 seaplane called the "Bat Boat." *(Courtesy U. S. Marine Corps)*

A Marine dive-bomber at the Ewa, Hawaii, base burned up during the December 7, 1941 attack by the Japanese. *(Courtesy U. S. Marine Corps)*

At Ewa, Hawaii, flames engulfed a Lockheed JO-2 twin-engine utility aircraft. *(Courtesy U. S. Marine Corps)*

On Guadalcanal, dive-bombers taxi on the Henderson Field airstrip. *(Courtesy U. S. Marine Corps)*

Lt. Col. Harold "Joe" Bauer described his aerial maneuvers to a pair from the ground crew. *(Courtesy U. S. Marine Corps)*

Major John L. Smith, Lt. Col. Richard Mangrum, and Captain Marion F. Carl held a reunion upon their return to the States after serving on Guadalcanal during the critical early days. *(Courtesy U. S. Marine Corps)*

After enlisting as a private, Ken Walsh flew with VMF-124 and became the first Corsair pilot awarded a Medal of Honor after he downed 4 Japanese Zeros before being forced to ditch. *(National Archives)*

VMF-223, the first Maine fighter squadron deployed on Guadalcanal, was commanded by ace John L. Smith (standing, third from left) credited with 19 victories. To Smith's left is Marion Carl with 18 ½ shot down. To Smith's right is Ken Frazier, 12 ½. *(Courtesy U. S. Marine Corps)*

VMF-121 Joe Foss (center), with 26 shot down, was the top scorer in a Marine uniform. Cecil Doyle to his right, and William P. Marontate and Roy M. A. Ruddell to his left were killed in action. Roger Haberman (extreme right), knocked down seven enemy planes. *(Courtesy U. S. Marine Corps)*

Greg "Pappy" Boyington, who flew briefly with the Flying Tigers in China, headed VMF-214, known as the Black Sheep, and registered 28 Japanese planes shot down including 6 with the Flying Tigers. He was knocked out of the sky near Rabul and became a POW. *(Courtesy U. S. Marine Corps)*

Charles A. Lindbergh (right) worked with Joe Fuss (left) and Marion Carl (center) to improve fighter aircraft performance. *(Courtesy U. S. Marine Corps)*

A flight of F4U Corsairs carried 1,000-pound bombs on a mission late in the war. *(Courtesy U. S. Marine Corps)*

Landing gear lowered to slow the aircraft and aid accuracy, a Corsair dumped napalm on a Japanese stronghold on Iwo Jima. *(Courtesy U. S. Marine Corps)*

Marine Air Group 24 assigned an air liaison team to the U. S. Army troops on Luzon in the Philippines. The ground element directed tactical strikes by Marine pilots in support of the GIs. *(Courtesy U. S. Marine Corps)*

Three aces, from the left, Lt. Robert Hanson, Capt. Donald N. Aldrich and Capt. Harold Spears with VMF-215 flew missions from Torokina after the loss of Greg Boyington. *(Courtesy U. S. Marine Corps)*

Major General Francis Mulcahy, a veteran of WWI whose gunner shot down a German plane, commanded the tactical air elements during the Okinawa campaign. *(Courtesy U. S. Marine Corps)*

A professor of classics at Princeton, Francis B. Godophin controlled from the ground Marine pilots providing ground support to many Army troops in the Philippines. *(Courtesy U. S. Marine Corps)*

Henry Elrod, as a fighter pilot with a detachment from VMF-211, fought the Japanese in the air over Wake Island before manning a machine gun post on the ground where he was killed. *(Courtesy U. S. Marine Corps)*

John Kinney, with a VMF-211, knocked down several Japanese planes in a vain attempt to defend Wake Island. He endured three years as a prisoner of war. *(Courtesy U. S. Marine Corps)*

Lofton Henderson led the VMSB-241 dive-bombers in the first attack against the Japanese fleet closing on Midway on June 4, 1942. A covey of enemy fighters burned his SBD. Henderson Field at Guadalcanal was named in his honor. *(Courtesy U. S. Marine Corps)*

Floyd Parks commanded VMF-221, a mix of Brewster Buffalos and Grumman Wildcats, to defend Midway. Fifteen of his twenty-five pilots were killed including Parks himself. *(Courtesy U. S. Marine Corps)*

As a member of VMF-214, Greg Boyington's "Black Sheep," John Bolt scored six victories making him an ace. As an exchange pilot with the Army Air Force in Korea he shot down six MIGs. *(Courtesy U. S. Marine Corps)*

Bill Nickerson flew reconnaissance missions in an SBD before switching to a fighter squadron with Corsairs. *(Courtesy Eve Nickerson)*

Amos Kay Belnap, during 1943–44, piloted a dive-bomber with VMSB-236 in the South Pacific. *(Courtesy Amos Kay Belnap)*

Frank Schwable, who became a Marine aviator during the 1920s, helped develop Marine night fighter capability. *(Courtesy U. S. Marine Corps)*

Bruce Porter led Marine Night Fighter Squadron VMF (N)-542 on Okinawa. *(Courtesy U. S. Marine Corps)*

taxied back for a quick repair and then returned to the runway. He mistakenly lined up on the position markers atop the tails of parked aircraft instead of the strip's boundary lights. Roaring forward, he smashed into parked Corsairs, triggering a series of explosions.

Captain Henry Miller from VMF-214 sprinted from his tent toward the tangled heap of blazing planes. He saw Wade Britt unconscious, slumped over in the cockpit as fire licked at his flight suit. From one of the ground crew, Miller seized a fire extinguisher and temporarily snuffed out the flames. Miller then released the harness holding Britt and attempted to haul him from the burning wreckage. Another pilot from VMF-214, Lieutenant Carol "Bernie" Bernard, joined Miller in an effort to free Britt, whose legs were pinned under the instrument panel. Machine-gun rounds from the burning planes began to cook off and fire erupted anew around the cockpit, driving away both Miller and Bernard, who sustained burns on their hands and arms.

Along with Wade Britt, a ground crew member who had been sitting in one of the parked Corsairs died before the conflagration could be extinguished. Miller and Bernard received Navy–Marine Corps medals for their bravery.

The changeover from F4Fs to F4Us accelerated. In fact, the aerial donnybrook on April 7 marked the last time during World War II that a Marine in a Wildcat would shoot down a Japanese plane.

While the Marines now manned the more formidable fighter, it was the Army Air Corps that made headlines. The code breakers at Pearl Harbor intercepted a message that Admiral Yamamoto planned to tour his air bases south of Rabaul. The analysts plotted the itinerary, determining that the Japanese strategist responsible for the successful attack on Pearl Harbor would fly in one of two Betty bombers. Interception devolved upon the 339th Fighter Squadron, equipped with P-38 Lightnings, the only U.S. fighters capable of traveling the distance necessary to intercept the Yamamoto party.

Four P-38s—an additional eleven were designated to provide high cover—took off on April 18 on a path that would carry them to a point south of Empress Augusta Bay on the coast of Bougainville. American intelligence indicated that the assassination team would catch the Bettys just as they descended toward a base at Ballale. Everything worked out precisely as planned. While other P-38s wiped out three of the accompanying Zeros at the cost of one Lightning, Captain Tom Lanphier (whose brother Charlie was a VMF-214 pilot) and Lieutenant Rex T. Barber shot down both of the bombers, killing the admiral, whose plane smashed into the jungle.

No one could immediately determine whether Lanphier or Barber accounted for the aircraft bearing Yamamoto. However, when Lanphier visited his brother at the Marine bivouac, he boasted that he had done it and reported how the interception had been planned. His loose tongue nearly brought a court-martial because the revelation that the Americans knew of Yamamoto's schedule would tip off the Japanese that their code had been broken.

The Army flier escaped punishment, but that night the Japanese sought vengeance. Raids upon Guadalcanal started at sundown and lasted until sunup. Henry Miller, in his diary, as quoted by Bruce Gamble in *The Black Sheep*, said, "On the first run last night we were all enjoying the searchlights and criticizing the antiaircraft when a stick [bombs] came down. I don't know who hit the dugout first, but I was third with Pace [Captain William] behind me (spilling a precious drink) and Scarborough [Lieutenant Hartwell] on top of him as a result of the plunge. On several succeeding runs, for some of which we did not bother to get out of bed, no bombs were dropped. At about 0400 we had a very rude awakening—not the gentle tinkle of an alarm clock but the whine of another stick. I think John [Burnett] made the hole first. As I was going over the Major's gear cot I was concerned about getting in his way, but when I hit the bottom there he was beside John."

Charles Conter also endured an anxiety-filled night. His diary entry for April 18 recorded, "Eight air raids. First raid hit ammo dump, fire and explosions half the night. 2d raid no damage, 3d raid Japs lost two planes by our AA. . . . Watched AA bursting from hill near operations, big show. 4th, 5th, 6th, 7th raids, Japs lost plane by our AA, no damage to speak of. 8th raid (early morning of the 19th) they come over low. I was asleep in sack near operations, they dropped incendiaries."

Years later Conter added details about his experience. "Six of us were asleep in the tent near operations which was next to the primary target, Henderson Field. I got woke up by the ack ack near the field. I raised the flaps of the tent and watched the ack ack guns blazing away but never bothered going to a foxhole. I went back to sleep but then I woke up with a start as I heard a bomb come whistling down and by the sound of it was coming straight down to the tent. I let out a yell and started waking up the guys and then we were crawling on the deck. It was much too late to head for the nearby foxhole. Havesack just hit the deck as an incendiary hit his bunk where he had just been. The bomb was an incendiary and where it hit I don't know. It could have burst overhead as the incendiaries scattered around our tent and set the tent and bunks afire."

From outside the tent, the men watched it burn and looked to the skies for the enemy who had almost killed or wounded them. "All at once the ack ack guns went silent. We wondered what was coming off, as the Jap plane was still up there. . . . All at once we saw the answer as a streak of gunfire came out of the black sky and the Jap plane went up in flames and came down in two parts. We had witnessed an historic event as it was the first use of a night fighter in the South Pacific."

The quest for an effective night fighter had begun three years earlier, in May 1940, during the after-dark "London blitz" when the Luftwaffe showered the city with block-buster bombs and incendiaries. Neither the antiaircraft nor fighters could prevent the tremendous damage. Both the Royal Air Force brass and the American Army Air Corps observers recognized the need for a weapon that could combat bombers hidden under the cover of night. According to a comprehensive history of World War II night fighters, *Those Few Who Dared* by Bill Odell, himself a veteran of the first raid by American bombers on German-occupied soil (July 4, 1942), the War Department, on January 30, 1941, had authorized the building of experimental night fighters. The specifications required an aircraft able to stay aloft throughout the night, yet also capable of the speed and agility to pounce on an enemy and destroy him with a single burst of fire. Five months later the twin-engine YP-61 passed its first test flights and, as Odell commented, "exceeded all expectations." Those concerned recognized, however, that the aerodynamic performance of the plane, later known as the Black Widow, amounted to only part of the equation; the means to find the alien threat was critical. During the German assault on London, the basic technique relied on searchlights to pinpoint a foe. The bombers could evade the fingers of illumination before the defending fighter pilots came within range. The answer lay in perfection of air-to-air radar.

While the Air Corps forged ahead in development of a nocturnal aerial weapon, the Navy and Marine Corps lagged behind, although the Navy was willing to sponsor research on air-to-air radar. The basic fighter planes of the Navy and Marines lacked both the endurance to maintain prolonged flight and—considering the bulky size of early radar models—probably the ability to house radar systems.

Marine Captain Ralph E. Davison had argued in January 1942, "The job of the Marines was to seize a beachhead and hold it until replaced by the Army. To do this successfully night fighters would be an absolute necessity." That said, the World War II Marine commandant, Lieutenant General Thomas P. Holcomb, authorized eight squadrons of night fighters, twelve planes each, ready for operation in 1945.

As the Guadalcanal campaign demonstrated, night fighter capacity was not "an absolute necessity" for retention of a beachhead, but the Washing Machine Charlies were far more than a mere distraction. Admiral Halsey, on December 27, 1942, as the flow of battle had definitely begun to favor the Americans on Guadalcanal, advised in a dispatch: "Current night nuisance raids over CACTUS are lowing [sic] combat efficiency of our troops through loss of sleep and increased exposure to malaria during hours of darkness spent in foxholes and dugouts. Recommend that minimum of six night fighting aircraft with homing radars and personnel now undergoing night fighter training plus ground equipment be dispatched CACTUS earliest time. Best available altitude determining interceptor radars with night fighter directing personnel should accompany."

Halsey's reference to those already training as night fighters referred to a program begun at Cherry Point, North Carolina, in October 1942. The commander of VMF(N) was Lieutenant Colonel Frank Schwable, an aviator since 1931 and participant in the Marine Corps actions in Nicaragua. As a special naval observer he toured several fronts before the United States entered the war. During his sojourn in Cairo, Schwable recalled, "I did have an opportunity to fly one night mission with them [the RAF] as a passenger so I could see what they did and how they did it. That is where I really got mixed up with night fighters. Headquarters sent me a dispatch and told me to go to this fighter director school [in England] in preparation for night fighters."

Schwable's first airplanes consisted of two SNJ trainers and some SB2A-4 scout-bombers originally consigned to the Netherlands, with instrument panels inscribed in Dutch. Early tests for the appropriate aircraft considered the U.S.-made A-20 and then the A-26, light bombers capable of housing the radar systems. Finally the British settled on their own twin-engine Mosquito as their weapon of choice. For a time the Marines considered using them. "It was a beautiful airplane to fly and for my purposes it would have been excellent," said Schwable. "The cockpit enabled the radar operator to sit right alongside of the pilot, far preferable to an arrangement that placed the radar man behind." A major drawback of the Mosquito, however, was its wooden construction, which bred a nickname of "Flaming Coffin."

While the Army Air Corps made its selection, the P-61, due for delivery in June 1943, those in charge arranged for Schwable to receive the Vega Ventura or PV-1, a two-engine, twin-ruddered bomber with a top speed of only 318 knots. With this the development of Marine night fighter capability stumbled badly, causing Schwable to submit a "mediocre progress report." The two-way communication between radar on the ground and that in the air worked poorly. Mechanical failures exacerbated by a shortage of replacement parts frequently grounded the first planes turned over to Schwable's unit.

Another factor that slowed development lay in the personnel. Schwable said, "I only had one experienced man, that was Johnny Harshberger [a major and his executive officer]. All the others—I don't think anybody had more than 500 or 600 hours and they were put in twin engine airplanes that they weren't used to flying and flying at night which they weren't used to." Schwable's pupils spent many hours learning not only what was known of night fighter tactics but also more basic things such as use of oxygen, navigation, and blind flying. The ground crew was equally deficient in experience, dealing with an unfamiliar machine and learning how to use and service the radar systems. In February 1943, at the very moment when the pleas for a weapon to combat the nightly raids resounded through the Solomons, a contingent of officers and enlisted men from VMF(N)-531 traveled to Syracuse for instruction in the newest mobile radar. At roughly the same time, another group of Marines flew to England to learn about the RAF's expertise in night fighting.

Fortunately for those cringing under the after-dark assault, the Air Corps's Sixth Night Fighter Squadron with five Douglas P-70s reached Guadalcanal on February 28, 1943, after a flight from Espiritu Santo. Nearly a month elapsed while the squadron set up housekeeping, installing its ground radios and radar before starting evening patrols. On the night of April 18–19, after Cactus had been under some seven hours of attack, Captain Earl C. Bennett with radar operator Corporal Ed Tomlinson lifted a P-70 off Henderson at 3:21 A.M. and began circling over Savo Island at twenty-two thousand feet.

From his position, Bennett saw a Japanese Betty pinned in a searchlight over the air base. The pilot instantly turned toward the target, notwithstanding a barrage of ninety-millimeter anti-aircraft fire hurled into the sky by the defenders. The Betty had escaped from the searchlight, but Tomlinson picked it up on his radar screen. When Bennett spotted the enemy plane's exhaust, he quickly closed upon the target. Shells from the P-70's four twenty-millimeter cannon flashed through the night sky, causing the Betty to explode.

The news of this first victory in the dark spurred the Marines of VMF(N)-531 to achieve operational proficiency, but Schwable remained painfully aware of the inadequacy of his equipment. He would write to an associate several months later, "It is only if the Japs are more stupid than anybody thinks they are, and come down to 15,000 ft., do we even stand a chance to knock them down—if we can go fast enough to catch them! If we lack speed, expert vectoring may put us in a position to do some good, but if the Japs fly thousands of feet higher than our planes can physically be pushed up to, there's not one damned thing on God's green earth we can do about it." Marine aviation, as it had in the past, labored under the handicap of being last in line when the newest and most improved technology was issued.

That gut-tightening night of April 18–19 signaled a distinct slowdown in the pace of Marine aviation's battles with the Japanese. The patrols and the strike missions qualified as "routine," with no spirited resistance from the enemy and a hiatus in their raids upon Cactus. For those stationed there, living conditions improved slightly. Charles Conter left the tent bivouac for a cot in a Quonset hut, slightly more protected from the drenching rains. The tedium, broken only by routine missions, induced Conter and his colleagues to seek release through alcohol. "I watched Delaney, another gunner, who could find liquor anywhere, make a still back of the hut. It was quite a trick as he had a gallon jug dripping in it. It made about a gallon a day, just enough to take care of Delaney and his buddy. Another trick was to put a hole in a coconut and mix certain sugar and stuff with the coconut milk and when fermented you had a pretty strong drink. I tried 180 proof mixed with grape juice once and once was enough. How those guys could drink that was beyond me."

Although the Japanese menace to Guadalcanal ebbed, they maintained strong aerial components at Rabaul. As the Americans attempted to expand deeper into the holdings of the Nipponese, the Marines gradually increased the number of longer missions. They often encountered stiff resistance from the enemy. While the attackers scored heavily, when U.S. pilots now either bailed out or ditched their crippled aircraft, they were much farther from home than in the earlier days of the southern Solomons campaign. Coast-watchers and the indigenous people saved many, but some endured frightful ordeals that featured prolonged exposure to sun and salt water, near starvation, and the possibility of capture.

Sherrod reported a number of cases of survival and death. The three-man crew of a TBF from VMTB-143 ditched on February 28 while raiding Kahili; one man disappeared in the sea. Gunner Private First Class Cephas Kelly helped his injured pilot, Lieutenant Alexander R. Berry, inflate his life vest, and then the pair swam toward Bougainville. Ashore they had nothing to eat and lived on rainwater collected by plants. Five days after they reached the island, natives welcomed them to their village and fed them. But during the night, a boy warned them of approaching Japanese. The Marines tried to hide, but the headman had betrayed them for a reported five kilos of rice.

Lodged in a stockade, Berry was beaten and hung by the heels while his captors poured water in his nose. Both men suffered from the squalor, lice, malaria, dysentery, tropical ulcers, and a severe lack of food. PFC Kelly was shipped to a Tokyo prison and liberated after the war. The pilot remained on Rabaul for eighteen months and died either during an Allied air raid or by execution.

Staff Sergeant William I. Coffeen from VMF-213, who bailed out of his Corsair on April 13 during an escort mission to Munda, suffered through a thirty-two-day odyssey of paddling his raft between islands before a friendly native brought him to a hut for something other than his basic diet of coconuts. Not until June 25 did a PBY pick him up.

The slowing pace of the war allowed another leave for Conter and others in the squadron. On this occasion they flew in a DC-3 to Roses (Efate) and then to a camp area in the Fiji Islands. "Played ball and got drunk, bought trinkets and souvenirs." A drunken spree brought restriction for the remainder of the stay, limiting his activities to sports with the "swabbies" and poker. To keep the men combat-ready, the command ordered gunnery hops, shooting at sleeves towed by other aircraft.

VMF-214, skippered by George Britt, ceased operations on May 13, completing a tour of two full months, which Britt said was the longest for any squadron up to that date. To his disappointment, he learned he would not return to combat with the organization. "I fell victim to a newly established policy . . . that removed a squadron CO after one combat tour. The reason . . . was the recent number of losses among squadron COs." Britt bid farewell to his men and headed for the recently conquered Russell Islands, where he became operations officer for MAG-21.

Marine aviation had begun to enlarge the cast of characters and advance to a new stage in the Pacific campaigns. The ensemble included both fresh and veteran faces. VMF-121, which had been the top destroyer of Japanese planes, returned to the scene of its earlier triumphs. Most of the earlier aces from the squadron had gone home—Joe Foss to sell war bonds and others to either instruct or command new units. A handful of veterans still flew for VMF-121, but a flood of newcomers filled the ranks.

Bruce Porter, already a captain, was not someone just out of flight school but a Southern Californian whose enlistment in the corps dated back to 1940. In his autobiography, written with Eric Hamel, Porter said he first became attracted to flying after seeing films called *Flight Command* and *Hell Divers*. When a naval aviator showed up at his University of Southern California fraternity to recruit, Porter said, "I was impressed with his self-confidence and I projected my own personality forward to a time when I might be like him. I was impressed with the uniform and, more than anything, with the level of excellence represented by those gleaming Wings of Gold."

Porter was also attracted by the Naval Reserve's promise of a bonus of five hundred dollars for four years, payable on separation from the service. He and a pal had just signed up and stepped out of the recruiting office when he saw a sign: JOIN MARINE AVIATION. Recalled Porter, "Beneath the headline was a photo of the same F3F fighter plane that had captivated me when I had seen *Hell Divers*. Wow, I thought, that's what I wanted to fly!" Just at that moment a Marine captain in a flashy blue tunic and leather Sam Browne belt, with high leather boots, stepped out of his recruiting office. He beckoned the pair inside and, when he heard they had just signed up with the Navy, obtained their papers from an obliging chief petty officer, tore them up, and convinced them to enter the Marine program.

Porter, after a very shaky start on his first flight with an instructor, passed through the various phases of training until he received his wings and second lieutenant's commission in July 1941. He, too, had been at the movies on December 7 when the program was halted and all military personnel told to return to their bases. Assigned to VMF-111, in March 1942 Porter sailed to the Pacific, but not to an active combat zone. Instead the squadron checked in at the Samoan Islands, a thousand miles from the combat that began at Guadalcanal.

Porter fumed with frustration over being excluded from the active war. His release appeared to come in February 1943, when with two other senior pilots from what was now VMF-441 he received orders to report to the Turtle Bay base on Espiritu Santo. To his dismay, the duty consisted of ferrying new F4Fs to Guadalcanal and returning to Turtle Bay on any multiengine aircraft headed that way. Finally, as the first Corsairs reached the area, Porter and associates were reassigned to VMF-121, which would transition to the F4U while absorbing replacements from the States.

VMF-121 honed its skills and tactics with Corsairs on Espiritu Santo alongside VMF-122. The commander of that outfit was Major Greg "Pappy" Boyington. His career in the Marine Corps had been extremely bumpy. Before the United States entered the war, Boyington had enlisted in Claire Chennault's American Volunteer Group (AVG), aka the Flying Tigers, to fly for the Chinese against the Japanese. The Marine Corps had not been unhappy with Boyington's departure; he was a hard-drinking brawler with matrimonial problems who violated the prewar standards for an officer and a gentleman. In the AVG, Boyington continued his pugnacious ways. While he claimed to have shot down half a dozen Japanese, other Flying Tigers cast a jaundiced eye on his alleged exploits and he infuriated some with his behavior. Chennault also was not sad when Boyington quit after a dispute. The Marines, in their hunger for qualified pilots, accepted him back.

On Buttons, Porter learned from a furious Boyington that he had just lost his flight status and been assigned a desk job. However, he gained a reprieve with an appeal to the chief of staff of the First Marine Air Wing. A celebration at a bar ended with Boyington firing his shot glass at a huge mirror. As the shards of glass showered the bar, Porter, Boyington, and two companions left and eventually wound up at another liquor-fueled festivity. Boyington challenged someone to a wrestling match and broke his ankle. Boyington's restoration to flight duty with VMF-122 lasted only a few hours as both that unit and Porter's departed for the war.

Behind an R4D navigation plane, on June 9, 1943, Porter's entire squadron logged the 450-mile journey to Henderson Field. On the very first night of this operational tour Porter said, "I sat out in the open beside a one-man foxhole and watched long cones of light from our searchlight batteries stab through the night sky while the automatic antiaircraft batteries hurled streams of gorgeous red and yellow tracer after the night's first circling Betty. . . .

"On this night I had been told several Army Air Corps P-38 pilots had volunteered to go aloft early and try to intercept the raiders. I was wondering where the Air Corps pilots could be— and what would happen to them if they were found by the searchlights or the gunnery radar. Suddenly a stream of red tracer burst out of the darkness overhead, and I could hear the distinctive steady thrum of a P-38's powerful twin high-performance engines. Before I could open my mouth to cheer my brother pilot on, the sky right over my head erupted in a great ball of red-gold flame, which slowly dropped behind the tops of intervening trees and, I suppose, into Lengo Channel. The P-38 had made a night kill! . . .

"I was utterly transfixed by the sheer complexity of what that P-38 pilot had done, and I made up my mind right then and there to sign up for night-fighter training if the Marine Corps ever announced the formation of a night-fighter program."

Three days after the start of VMF-121's tour, Porter participated in his first scramble. His rank and seniority had established him as squadron flight officer, the leader for two of the four-plane alert divisions. On this day Porter and his half of VMF-121 flew at eighteen thousand feet in the direction of the Russell Islands, about eighty miles from Henderson. Altogether Porter counted thirty-two American fighters as the leading wedge, with an almost equal number following up. Below the level of the Wildcats and Corsairs came New Zealanders in P-40s.

Seconds after the first "Tallyho!" sounded, Porter glimpsed oncoming silvery glints—about seventy Zeros on a fighter sweep. As the two forces hurtled toward one another, he had barely processed the sight of a brown smudge against the white clouds as an exploded enemy plane before a Zero suddenly started to pass him from right to left while diving on a Corsair, behind and below.

"I saw his pink tracer reach out past my line of vision, which was obscured by my Corsair's long nose. Then for good measure, he fired four 20 mm cannon rounds, which passed in front of me like fiery popcorn balls; I was shocked to see how slowly they seemed to travel.

"I never consciously pressed my gun-button knob. I had practiced this encounter a thousand times, and I seemed to know enough to allow my instincts to prevail over my mind. My guns were bore-sighted to converge in a cone about 300 yards ahead of my Corsair's propeller spinner. Anything within that cone would be hit by a stream of half-inch steel-jacketed bullets.

"My Corsair shuddered slightly as all guns fired, and I saw my tracer passing just over the Zero's long birdcage canopy. Then he was past me. I pulled around after him, to my left . . . came up with a far deflection shot and decided to go for it. I gave the Zero a good lead and fired all my guns again. As planned, my tracers went ahead of him, but at just the right level, I kicked my left rudder to pull my rounds in toward his nose.

"If that Japanese pilot had flown straight ahead, he would have been a dead man. Instead, that superb pilot presented me with a demonstration of the Zero's best flight characteristic, the one thing a Zero could do that would carry its pilot from the jaws of death just about every time. I had heard of the maneuver I was about to experience . . . but I had no conception of how aerodynamically fantastic the Zero fighter really was until that split second.

"As soon as my quarry saw my tracer pass in front of his airplane's nose, he simply pulled straight up and literally disappeared from within my reflector sight and, indeed, my entire line of sight. My tracer reached out into empty space. I was so in awe of the maneuver that I was literally shaking with envy."

Stunned momentarily, Porter recovered enough to pursue in the direction where he thought his opponent might have gone. When he caught sight of him, he tried again, yanking on his joystick for a severe climb as part of a tight loop that brought the crush of gravity upon him, threatening to blur if not altogether obliterate consciousness. At the top of the loop he entered a state of equilibrium as the g-forces fell away. His mind cleared—and just three hundred yards ahead his prey was fleeing. "Nothing else in the world mattered more than staying on that Zero's tail. I would have flown into the ocean at full throttle if that enemy pilot led me there.

"I squeezed the gun-button knob beneath my right index finger. The eerie silence in my cockpit was broken by the steady roar of my machine guns.

"The Zero never had a chance. It flew directly into the cone of deadly half-inch bullets. I was easily able to stay on it as the stream of tracer sawed into the leading edge of the left wing. I saw little pieces of metal fly away from the impact area. . . . The stream of tracer worked its way to the cockpit. I clearly saw the glass canopy shatter, but there was so much glinting, roiling glass and debris that I could not see the pilot. The Zero wobbled, and my tracer fell into first one wing root, then the other, striking the enemy's unprotected fuel tanks.

"The Zero suddenly blew up, evaporated." When he returned to Henderson Field, Porter said, he realized that "I had not only weathered first combat, I had scored my first kill. I had been baptized. I had won my spurs.

"It did not dawn on me until late that night that I had also killed a man."

TEN

CARRYING THE FLAG FARTHER

Having firmly established a military presence on Guadalcanal and then the nearby Russell Islands, the American Pacific commanders and their Allied counterparts began the island-hopping strategy that would take the war to the shores of Japan. While the European Theater featured a unified structure, the command for the Pacific had—as noted previously—been split on April 4, 1942. Douglas MacArthur, publicized and promoted to a fare-thee-well during the dismal early stages of World War II, bore the banner for the Army and as such received the title of Supreme Allied Commander, South-West Pacific. That gave him suzerainty over the campaigns creeping through New Guinea, leapfrogging the Solomons up toward the Philippines. Admiral Chester Nimitz, responsible for the rest of the Pacific Ocean areas, would supervise operations to the north, central, and south—the Gilbert, Marshall, Mariana, Caroline, Palau, Ryukyu, and Bonin islands. Under the arrangement, MacArthur drew on Navy and Marine resources while Nimitz could use Army ground and air forces where appropriate.

The Third Fleet, under Bull Halsey, acted as the naval arm for ComSoPac, MacArthur's fief. For the first major thrust, starting June 21, the plan scripted an invasion of the New Georgia Islands, with Munda as the chief objective. Halsey mustered a fleet of war-ships and transports under the rubric of the covering force, while Task Force Thirty-one would handle the amphibious landings.

The ground forces included elements of the Fourth Marine Raider Battalion and GIs from the Army's Forty-third Infantry Division. Naturally the entire affair required extensive air support, and as residents of air bases in Guadalcanal and the Russells the Marine fliers took their orders from Rear Admiral Marc A. Mitscher, who had tactical command of the land-based planes on those islands.

In the thick of these campaigns, VMF-121 with Bruce Porter had shifted its operations to Banika in the Russells. The squadron was assigned to help cover the June 30 landings at Rendova. The predawn launch began ominously. Two of the Corsairs scheduled for the flight under Porter aborted because of engine trouble. As he climbed away from the airfield known as Knucklehead with his wingman Phil Leeds, he heard a frantic Mayday call over his radio. After Porter's group assembled, he realized he was down to five aircraft; the Mayday call meant someone had crashed on takeoff.

The VMF-121 people were part of a twenty-nine-plane aggregation drawn from a number of Marine squadrons. Their foes were the first Japanese bombers about to ravage the landings. As the Americans prepared to fall upon the raiders, out of the sun, a huge number of Zeros dove on them. "Our shipborne radar had completely dropped the ball," commented Porter. "I also saw bomber formations slip through far below, but there was no way I or any other Corsair or Wildcat pilot could attack the bombers when there were so many Zeros to fend off."

Within seconds Porter targeted a Zero on the tail of another Corsair. He poured bullets into the enemy's engine and then the entire plane disintegrated, spitting pieces of metal and burning fuel at Porter. He emerged unscathed and then focused on another Zero attacking his wingman, Leeds. Porter believed he had done some serious damage when he discovered he was under fire. A cannon shell ripped into his wing, and 7.7 mm rounds punched holes in the wing. One even zipped through his canopy. The assault suddenly broke off as Leeds returned the favor, driving off the Japanese plane.

Back at Knucklehead, Porter learned that the squadron

claimed nineteen shot down, plus two probables. The elation was dimmed by the news that they had lost four men that day, two to enemy action and two to operational accidents.

For four harrowing days, Marine Raiders had trekked from Segi Point on the southern tip of New Georgia toward Viru Harbor. They fought Japanese troops in the sucking jungle mud until they encircled the objective. At that point, Marine aircraft from VMSB-132 and the Navy's VB-11 arrived, in the words of Robert Sherrod, "to see what help they could provide for the 'lost' Raiders [contact with headquarters had been broken]." The bombs dropped upon the enemy drove them from their entrenched positions in the vegetation into more open turf. The Marine Raider company, commanded by Captain Anthony Walker, cut them down, and many drowned attempting to escape. The first Navy warships entered the harbor. The battle marked an early, if unplanned, fulfillment of the responsibility of Marine aviation to support the fleet landing forces.

Army and Marine ground troops landed on Vangunu, an island that would disappear into the dustbins of history until it became part of the "coalition of the willing" supporting the invasion of Iraq in 2004. The amphibious forces moved up to Rendova and struck out across a lagoon for the assault upon Munda. That site had been abandoned as an air base by the Japanese after a series of raids so savaged the airfield that it was considered no longer viable. However, Nipponese artillery batteries on Munda Point inflicted some damage upon the support fleet for the final landings by the Americans. And although the defenses would not have the benefit of a home airfield, a flood of Japanese planes from farther up the island chains attempted to hammer the U.S. vessels. The furious aerial battles by fliers from all three American branches of air power, and the shipboard AA, boasted that for June 30, 101 of the enemy were destroyed, with four Marine squadrons listing fifty-eight shoot-downs. The official scorecard issued by the Japanese noted only thirty lost and claimed fourteen of their foes defeated. It was one more battle in which both sides appear to have exaggerated their successes.

The achievements in the air notwithstanding, it took five weeks before the invaders captured the ravaged Munda field. An effort by Marine Raiders to eliminate Japanese strongholds on Rice Island and thereby prevent reinforcement of the Munda Point garrison met such stiff opposition that the advance units were forced temporarily to retreat.

During the Guadalcanal offensive, the Allied fliers devoted their attention to fighting off enemy air and sea raids or hitting reinforcement ventures. Very few, if any, ground support missions were flown. The initial blow at Viru Harbor was more happenstance than a coordinated strike. As the New Georgia campaign developed, however, the concept of close air support (within a thousand yards of the front) moved from tactical theory into practice. Eight officers, including six Marine pilots and eight enlisted radiomen, under the command of Major Wilfred Stiles, began functioning as liaisons between the ground and air forces. The members were parceled out to the three Army infantry divisions engaged in the New Georgia campaign.

Like most new developments in military operations, the first showings fell short of expectations. There were casualties from friendly fire when the bombs fell short of the enemy lines. The reinforced pillboxes and foxholes gouged into coral by Japanese engineers withstood anything less than a direct hit. A communiqué during the New Georgia campaign noted the obstacles of terrain as well as the ferocity of the ground fighting. "The dense jungle encountered made the location of enemy positions suitable for air attack impossible until friendly troops were too close to the prospective target for safety. As 200 yards to 300 yards was a good day's advance, it was not practical to withdraw sufficiently to use air attacks. . . . The gridded aerial mosaic [combat map] which was used as standard for the operation was very poor, as no detail was shown on it other than the coastline. [Military maps in the Pacific Theater were often most inadequate.] Frequently troops could not locate their own position on the map, much less the position of the enemy." In general the air-to-ground support worked best when targeted at supply dumps, bivouacs, or artillery emplacements. Sherrod mentioned two notable successes: a strike at enemy guns at the edge of a plantation that enabled the Forty-third Division soldiers to advance, and a softening up of shoreline area by fifty-six heavy bombers.

At roughly the same time, the C-47 cargo planes of the South Pacific Combat Air Transport Command (SCAT), which included VMR-152 and 253 plus a pair of Air Corps squadrons, undertook the first airdrops of supplies to the men in the jungle. De Chant quoted an "observer" of the "Sky Train" mission. "We took off from Henderson in Douglas R4Ds. Knowing we would be without fighter protection until near the target area, the three-plane section flew about 10 feet off the water, rising only to clear the dozen small planes on our course. We were so low that the passage of the planes left three white wakes in the water behind us, like the paths of motor boats.

"Near the target area, eight New Zealand P-40s appeared over the Sky Train, scissoring back and forth as we closed in. Within a mile of the drop area, our plane pulled up and the crew could have picked coconuts as it moved inland, dead on the tail of the lead plane, flown by Lieutenant Colonel Harry Van Liew.

"As Van Liew's transport passed over the target, a few hundred yards behind the front lines, 14 black bursts of heavy AA fire exploded off his left wingtip but did not evidently damage it. Then our Douglas bounced like some giant's hands were trying to shake it apart. It was more flak necklacing [sic] us, without effect.

"Our plane made six runs over the dense jungle of the drop area. Each pass took us over enemy lines and within spitting distance of chopped-up Munda field, where a big gun was pumping AA at the formation. . . . As we came in for our last run, the entire drop area was littered with colored parachutes. They had all gone right into the infantry's lap. We heard later that not one pound of the nine tons of cargo fell into Jap hands." SCAT would eventually deliver a hundred thousand pounds of food, ammunition, and medical supplies to the ground forces engaged in this campaign.

Since the first combat aircraft took up station on Guadalcanal on August 21, 1942, the Marines and the other services had been engaged in an almost constant toe-to-toe battle in the South Pacific. Casualties, burnouts, wounds, and exhaustion had necessitated replacements, although in some instances people hung on well beyond what was considered a normal tour. With the war at times leaping forward and at other moments progressing by what seemed like inches, the demand for fresh flesh and blood in the cockpits persisted.

Phil DeLong, a native of Jackson, Michigan, born in 1919, was the son of a coal yard manager. Upon his 1937 graduation from high school, where he was elected class president, DeLong worked as an auto mechanic and coal yard manager in Ypsilanti before entering the University of Michigan. With a year and a half of academic credits, DeLong then held a job with an engineering company. Growing up in the 1930s and early 1940s, he said he remembered no discussion of world politics.

Right after Pearl Harbor, he enlisted in the Navy's V-5 flight program. After flight training at Dallas and Corpus Christi, he elected to wear the gold bars of a Marine second lieutenant along with his wings. DeLong performed the required number of landings and takeoffs on the USS *Wolverine*, a training vessel, at Glenview, Illinois, and qualified as a carrier-based pilot, although no Marine squadrons were assigned to flattops.

In April 1943 DeLong received assignment to VMF-212, Joe Bauer's squadron, which had been returned to El Toro, California, for refitting with Corsairs and new pilots. "We were all new to the squadron," said DeLong. "There was no friction in the squadron and we had Annapolis graduates, regulars, and Reserves. The instruction in tactics was very good and included the Thach Weave."

VMF-212 returned to the South Pacific in June 1943 and started to fly combat air patrols along the perimeter covering the Solomons. Unlike many others, during his first six months in the combat zone DeLong never encountered any air-to-air opposition. He also escaped any damage from enemy antiaircraft, which holed a number of his squadron's planes.

Another Marine newcomer was Roger Conant, who grew up on the Upper Peninsula of Michigan—"about as far north as you can go and remain in the USA. My dad was a photographer and kind of a nomad, traveling from town to town. He made pictures at carnivals and of baseball teams and of the lumber camps in the area. He was quite a baseball pitcher and if the team would buy his pictures of them for 25 cents each, he would pitch for them on Sunday. My mother was from a straight-laced Welsh Presbyterian family. When he pitched she would go to the game but sit facing away because he was playing baseball on Sunday."

As a teenager, Conant helped out in a photography studio opened by his father; after graduation from high school he worked as a drugstore soda jerk for ten dollars a week. In search of opportunity, he moved to California in 1936 and held a series of dead-end jobs. "Keep in mind this was the worst of the Great Depression. Seeing the futility of such an existence I decided to go to college." He hitchhiked to Madison, Wisconsin, and enrolled at the University of Wisconsin.

With aid from his parents he completed four years and graduated in 1941. The military service draft had begun six months earlier, and during his senior year Conant enlisted in the government's Civilian Pilot Training program. By the fall of 1941, he obtained a private license.

Having enlisted in the Reserves while still in college, Conant volunteered for naval aviation. When he completed the course, he said, "The Marines had very attractive uniforms and were doing the fighting in the South Pacific. The Marines were fighting the war. The idea of being a Marine pilot was glamorous. Also and perhaps most important, if you were selected to be a Marine you would be trained as a fighter pilot and fly fighters. That appealed to me. So, I opted to become a Marine."

Despite his comment, obviously not all Marines with wings went into fighters. Indeed, upon graduation from flight school, Conant drew assignment to the Navy photography school at Pensacola. "Although I attended the classes, my main job was to fly photographers around in an SNJ so they could take aerial pictures. I spent four months doing that . . . and chasing girls."

In February 1943, however, the need to fill out the complement for VMF-215—then at Santa Barbara, California—satisfied Conant's ambition to serve as a fighter pilot. Conant recalled, "I had no training in fighters, NONE [sic], and none in tactics. On arrival in Santa Barbara I was advised the squadron had been ordered overseas. Before leaving I flew a couple of flights in the F4F and one in the F4U. I had a total of 213 flying hours, one hour in the F4U when we went overseas. Fortunately, we spent some time in Hawaii and on Midway before we got into combat. We did some tactics training at Midway but that was it." While not specifically taught the Thach Weave, Conant said that they worked out a facsimile as a "necessity."

By the time he reached Espiritu Santo in early July, Conant had logged 481 hours of flying, much of the time in a Corsair. On July 5, 1943, Conant was among several who ferried F4Us to Guadalcanal. "The airplane that was leading us flew into a cloud and we got separated. I don't know how many got there and how many did not. We [were] now in the combat area. We didn't start off too great getting lost on the way to the 'canal."

During the first five months of his combat tour, Conant called four different bases home—Guadalcanal, Vella Lavella, Munda, and Bougainville. "The forward combat living conditions," he said, "were very poor. The 'canal was one large Quonset hut for all pilots sleeping on cots. Vella Lavella was the best. Each division had a tent. Munda was the pits. We were so occupied with missions and flying that we never saw our sleeping quarters in the daylight. Everyone had dysentery. Bougainville was tents again and not too bad.

"At no time in the forward areas was there an 'O' [officers'] club or anything like it. And there was no electricity so we had no music or lights, just lanterns. I had a tooth problem and the doc, not a dentist, had to drill using a drill powered by me pedaling like a bicycle as he drilled. The faster I pedaled, the faster the drill went. It wasn't very pleasant but I think I may still have that filling to this day.

"The mess attendants did a fair job with what they had but it wasn't much. We ate enough just to stay alive. Powdered eggs for breakfast, Spam and hash on toast for dinner . . . SOS ["shit on a shingle" in military slang]. The menu never varied. There was no booze. NONE. After one mission, Doc Neber gave me a 2-ounce bottle of LeJohns Medicinal Brandy but other than that there was no booze. There were no women in the combat area. I did not see a woman from the time I left Honolulu April 12, 1943 to the time we went to Sydney for R&R on September 29, 1943.

"We had movies on the 'canal. I remember we sat in the rain and watched them, even if we had seen them before. One night, another tent not far from ours started to burn. Smoke and fire came out of the top like a blow torch. We went down to see what it was. The entire tent burned up. The guys had a still and were making booze. Things just got out of hand.

"Another time, the mosquito abatement guys burnt a grass field next to our Quonset hut and it turned out to be a Jap ammo dump. The dump started burning and shells got cooked off and kept flying out. It blew a large hole in our Quonset hut. We spent the whole day in a fox hole."

A certain amount of on-the-job learning occurred. Conant explained a refinement of the weave following his first combat patrol, July 25, 1943, in the vicinity of Rendova. "I was flying wing on Bob Owens. I flew very good formation but saw ONLY Bob Owens. I did see a meatball flash by me once but that's all. I decided that flying a good close formation wasn't doing Bob or me any good. On subsequent flights I loosened up a bit . . . cutting inside of Bob as he made his turns. I slid back and forth as he weaved. This way I was able to keep close to him and still see what was going on."

A month would pass before Conant experienced aerial combat. "We made the usual escort to Kahili with Zeros all over us and then the bombers flew into the clouds. Free to roam, Bob Owens took off through the Zeros with me on his tail. [When] they tailed on him they were right in front of me. I must have shot at six or eight . . . all from directly behind. I hit a lot but probably missed a lot too, but now Bob is getting a little ahead of me and climbing. A Tony [fighter manufactured by Kawasaki] appears and is right behind him . . . and closing. He was a bit out of range so I waited. Finally, when I figured I'd better shoot or Bob would be history, I opened up. Actually, I was just about the proper range and I hit the Tony . . . hard. Pieces flew off and came by me. . . . The Tony flipped and went straight in. I didn't see him hit but someone did and confirmed him for me . . . my first victory.

"Bob kept going with me behind him clearing Zeros off his tail.

I shot a lot but didn't wait to see my results. Somewhere along this episode I went after a Zero. He climbed and I'm right after him. I finally got a shot at him but only one gun had any ammo left. But I had hit him and with the last gun working there was an explosion on his right wing. I didn't see what happened to him but someone confirmed him . . . my second victory. Finally, Bob decided to climb into the clouds. I tried to follow him but ended up just hanging on my prop . . . very slow. Then I took off to my left and there is a Zero at about my eight o'clock position. His guns were blinking and smoke was coming from his gun ports. I don't remember where they were . . . wing or nacelle but shit, he was shooting at ME. I pushed over and headed for the deck. He followed me for a while and finally gave up. Tokyo Rose later commented that the Zeros chased us and we fled for home. That much is true, since I was out of ammo."

He described a typical mission: "To begin with, we had a briefing where we were assigned airplanes, assigned coverage, named the target, showed AA areas, and generally covered anything about the mission including search and rescue coverage.

"We'd take off, join up by divisions and fly to the rendezvous area. Once joined with the bombers we'd fly a loose formation gently weaving back and forth to stay with or behind the bombers. As we approached the target the enemy would appear off to one side. Then we'd break the divisions down to two-plane sections and the gentle weave would become violent, almost frantic.

"We had three coverage areas . . . close, medium, and high, plus an assignment we called Roving High Cover [RHC]. We were a bit out of sorts because VF-17 [a Navy squadron] always seemed to get the RHC . . . the choice assignment because you could go after the enemy instead of sitting there waiting for him to start an attack. In weaving the idea was to start your turn just as another section passed you, going the other way. That way your tail was covered. We kept this weave until we got to the AA area where we'd pull off to one side . . . not far but away from the AA. It was not very accurate and we didn't worry too much about it. On one mission over Rabaul my wingman was lost and we later speculated that a stray AA shot got him.

"At first there were just a few enemy fighters but one would drop a phosphorous bomb which could be seen for miles. That was their way of telling everyone where the bombers were. After that there would be hordes of enemy fighters. Anyway, the bombers would make their run and usually miss the target . . . which pissed us off considerably.

"Fighters were sniping at anyone that got out of formation. A few would get out in front of the formation and come in making a head-on run at the bombers. They'd head straight in and once they passed the bombers, they'd flip over and head down. It was tough to catch them because if you sat out there and waited for them, you were in a very vulnerable position. We tried to time it so we could come out of our weave as they started in on their run. I timed it right one time and made a head-on run on a Zero. We both fired at each other. I know I hit him but don't know what happened to him. Keep in mind our closing speed was about 700 mph. I got no credit, not even a probable.

"By now the formation is heading home and descending at good speed. The enemy fighters are still looking for stragglers or wounded bombers. If there were any separated bombers we'd go to try to protect them as they were very vulnerable. Some of the enemy followed us for a long time but eventually they all disappeared. That is the way a B-24 escort would go. If we were escorting SBDs or TBFs it was about the same except they were slower and lower. But when they made their dive, we were able to circle down with them. That was good because we could be up to speed . . . our best defense. Only, when the dive bombers came out of their dives they were pretty well strung out . . . like sitting ducks. It was the time most kills were made . . . ours and theirs. Escorting the dive bombers I was able to scare several Zeros but I never got one. I did have some very grateful dive bombers, however, one in particular. A Zero had him bore sighted from the rear and was about to lower the boom. I came screaming out of the dive and sprayed him from long range. I doubt I hit him but it was enough. He flipped and ran. As I passed close behind the SBD, the rear-facing gunner waved at me. I guess he was pretty happy with me. He should be. I saved his life."

Some of the veterans were still on hand. George Britt's former unit, VMF-214, having undergone R&R for two months, returned to combat on July 21, operating from the new base in the Russells. Major Bill Pace, a graduate of the USNA, and who replaced Britt as the commander, led a section of Corsairs to protect the crippled seaplane tender *Chincoteague*. A flight of two-engine Mitsubishi Nells tried to finish off the warship, but Pace and his comrades splashed all three raiders.

On August 6, after Pace's engine required replacement because of a hit by a twenty-millimeter shell, the squadron commander took off for a test spin. When the engine failed, Pace began to attempt a dead-stick landing at the Banika airstrip. The silent Corsair lacked the glide power to reach the field, and at the penultimate moment Pace abandoned a notion of ditching in favor of his chute. Just as it began to unfurl, he smashed into the three-foot-deep shallows offshore. A pair of men from a nearby antiaircraft battery tried to save him, but he had died instantly from the impact.

John "Smiley" Burnett, the next officer in line and with two victories in the air, automatically moved up to command. According to Britt, "Though personable, [Burnett] could not somehow earn the respect of the pilots subordinate to him, particularly those in his flight division. His occasional erratic airmanship and irrational behavior in the air caused embarrassment and sometimes danger to those who flew with him in formation. He was senior enough to lead a division but was deficient in flight aptitude and leadership, a situation which has presented many a squadron CO with a dilemma. I have been told by others that squadron morale suffered under his leadership with the result that most pilots welcomed reassignment to other squadrons at the end of the second tour."

Whatever Burnett's faults, they did not detract from individual feats by others in VMF-214. Alvin Jensen, described by Britt as "an aggressive, intrepid, skillful pilot, personable, intelligent," and who joined the squadron as an enlisted man before Britt recommended him for a field appointment to second lieutenant, delivered a monumental blow against the Japanese airfield at Kahili.

On August 28 on Munda, Jensen awakened shortly before 4:00 A.M. for a dawn strafing raid upon Kahili. In the darkness the pilots stumbled about and searched for their assigned Corsairs. As they warmed up their engines, a Washing Machine Charlie droned overhead and to their intense discomfort dropped five bombs, which, fortunately for all, exploded harmlessly in the water alongside the strip. The script called for eight F4Us to shoot up the target while an equal number flew cover for them. But the confusion in locating the appropriate planes and the interruption by the night visitor upset the careful schedule. The Marines could not join up properly. Although Jensen and three others assembled in a division led by Bob Owens, a violent squall scattered the quartet.

The turbulence pitched Jensen upside down, and he lost contact with the rest of the squadron. When he emerged upright from the storm about twenty miles east of Kahili he thought he heard his flight leader calling on the radio, "Let's go." Rather than wait for a coordinated strike, Jensen decided to take advantage of the darkness that still hovered over Kahili. From twelve hundred feet he zoomed down to near wave-top level and skipped over Bougainville Strait before pulling up to clear some hills. Using an eight-hundred-foot-high hill as a landmark, Jensen then peeled off and, as the first fingers of dawn brushed the earth, roared down on the field. With that final salvo, Jensen scurried home to Munda, leaving two huge blazes behind him.

Jensen reported that he thought he had fired on as many as twenty-five different parked aircraft, although he never claimed he destroyed them all. Photo reconnaissance images the following day captured the wreckage of twenty-four Japanese aircraft. Whether anyone else hit the Kahili airfield that same day is a matter of conjecture. A belated arrival from VMF-214, Vic Scarborough, witnessed the fires there but believed several F4Us accounted for the damage. One possible participant, Lieutenant Charles Lanphier, the brother of the Army pilot who had shot down Yamamoto, had been with the Bob Owens division. He never returned from the flight and was presumed lost. In fact he had crashed, possibly due to AA while over Kahili, and been taken prisoner on Bougainville. From an Army B-24 pilot also captured by the Japanese, it was later learned that Lanphier slowly succumbed to starvation and the ravages of disease.

Sherrod described Jensen's achievements as "one of the great single-handed feats of the Pacific war," and credited him with the destruction of all twenty-four grounded aircraft. Bruce Gamble in his history of the squadron, *The Black Sheep*, believed circumstances indicated the number was closer to fifteen. In any event Jensen received a Navy Cross, and had the Marine policy counted airplanes obliterated on the ground, as in the European Theater, the twenty-four coupled with his seven aerial victories would have made him the top Marine ace.

Taking off from Munda, Lieutenant Kenneth Walsh, like Jensen a former naval aviation pilot, who rejoined VMF-124 in mid-August following a leave in Sydney, had knocked down six more airplanes to add to his previous total of ten. After one encounter, Walsh brought his crippled F4U into a strip at Segi, just south of Munda. Roger Conant remembered, "It landed and lost control during roll out. It left the runway and smashed into several of the Corsairs parked along the runway, totally demolishing them. The CO of the strip told Ken he wanted him to leave while he still had some airplanes left."

On August 30, with the squadron pulled back to Guadalcanal, Walsh was among the Corsair pilots assigned to escort B-24 bombers on a mission to obliterate any further threats from Kahili against the ships landing troops and supplies on the newly invaded Vella Lavella Island. The fighters, drawn from Walsh's outfit as well as VMF-123, flew first to the Russell Islands strip, where they refueled. That would allow them more time over the Japanese stronghold on Bougainville, two hundred miles distant, if the enemy sought to intercept the raiders. As planned, V-124's divisions, along with those from the other Marine squadron and a group of Army P-39s and P-40s, rendezvoused with the heavyweights in the vicinity of Rendova Island.

As Conant had described the tactics, while the Air Corps planes stayed level or below the Liberators to deal with head-on attacks, the Corsairs climbed above to meet interceptors diving upon the big planes. All of the fighters throttled back to accommodate the slower "big friends." Suddenly Walsh's F4U started to lose power as the supercharger malfunctioned. Under radio silence, Walsh waggled his wings to attract the attention of his wingman and then held his nose while pointing to his engine with his other hand. He motioned that he was going down. He intended to land at nearby Munda and replace his Corsair with another. He hoped to catch up with the armada as it droned on toward the target.

Walsh brought the plane in and quickly taxied to operations. Roger Conant was in an F4U on standby alert. He saw Walsh land. "The pilot jumped out and raced to the operations office. It was our good friend Ken Walsh. He asked Major [Jim] Neefus, the operations officer, for a replacement. They hopped in a jeep and rode to the end where we were on alert. Jim told Ken to take his choice . . . and he took mine. I'll never forget that lanky guy climbing into MY airplane. He got airborne in record time."

Neefus had ignored the protocol for time-delaying paperwork. Within ten minutes of landing, Walsh was in the air, speeding toward the combat area. He anxiously scanned the skies for the bombers and their shepherds. On course for Kahili, he saw a large clump of aircraft ahead. But instead of Americans, these were unmistakably Zeros hunting for marauders. Almost simultaneously, the Marine noticed the B-24s, seeking to leave the scene after having dumped their bombs. The Japanese also spied them and began to form for diving attacks on the lumbering four-engine ships.

From an altitude of thirty thousand feet, Walsh shoved over into a screaming four-hundred-plus-mile-per-hour dive upon the Japanese, who—concentrating upon their prey—did not notice this lone Corsair. Walsh's radio carried the excited voices of the bomber crews as the enemy fighters attacked. He caught up with the tail-end Zero. Several bursts from his .50s tore into the plane, igniting a fire; smoke wafted back. Within seconds the victim exploded. In the high speed of aerial combat, only a few seconds elapsed before a second unsuspecting Zero filled his gun sight. At point-blank range Walsh drenched the plane with bullets, and it trailed off before entering a plunge earthward.

The covey of Japanese, however, were now aware of the lone American in their midst. Walsh threw himself into a dive as they started to make passes at him. His course hurtled him through the Liberators, whose gunners, fortunately, did not train their .50s on him. By now other F4Us had joined a melee spread out over the Solomon skies. From stricken and burning bombers, men in parachutes floated down. Half a dozen Zeros doggedly pursued Walsh. One of them closed on him but the Marine cut a sharp turn, rolled out, and unloosed a deflection fusillade as the enemy crossed in front. Fatally wounded, the Zero swooned in a death dive.

Down below, Walsh observed clouds of dust on the airfield as more Zeros took off. More American fighters entered the fray, trying to provide some protection for the bombers while at the same time dogfighting a swarm of enemy aircraft. The B-24s broke into groups and separated as they attempted to escape. Over his radio, Walsh heard a call for help from one batch under assault by Zeros as they sought asylum at Munda. Walsh called for others to join him and then headed for the embattled Liberators.

When he reached the scene he saw the bombers under attack while a small mix of P-39s, P-40s, and Corsairs tried to screen them. From his position Walsh again began a diving attack from the rear on five of the enemy fighters homing in on a target. Once again they were unaware of the predator behind them. Within range, Walsh blasted the fuselage and wings of one enemy until the plane blew up. The pilots in the other Zeros instantly focused on Walsh, and all four started to stalk him.

Nevertheless, he managed to isolate another foe, and the pair engaged in a duel for firing position. Walsh gained the advantage and a brief spasm from his six .50s rocked the Zero, which fell off toward the water. Uncertain whether he had inflicted a mortal wound, Walsh followed it down until it splashed. He was a bare five hundred feet above the sea and highly vulnerable to the posse of Zeros that enveloped him. With a pair riding both his flanks, another on his tail, and at a minimum altitude, Walsh endured a succession of thumps as twenty-millimeter cannon shells slammed into the F4U. Fleeing toward Munda, he tried every evasive maneuver he could but his tormentors stuck to him, scoring hits in his wing and engine. White smoke escaped from the cowling, and his cockpit gauges announced failures of systems.

Thirty miles from Munda, Walsh appeared doomed as the Japanese continued to pound his Corsair. Then, in the distance, he spied some friendly fighters hurrying to his rescue. One of them, a P-40, started shooting from out of range. Although the bullets dropped far short of the mark, they alerted the enemy that they soon would become targets themselves. The Japanese turned away. Still, the damage to the Corsair forced Walsh to chance a ditching. He slid along the surface of the Solomon Sea rather gently. Once in the water, Walsh began to swim toward shore. At Barokama Point on Vella Lavella, Seabees constructing an air base there had seen the F4U go down. A rescue party soon pulled the now exhausted pilot from the water.

For his courage in attacking at odds of fifty to one, and his four confirmed kills, Walsh was awarded a Medal of Honor. Conant later commented, "He was rescued but he never brought my airplane back. Ken and I made much of this event in later years. That makes four Corsairs Ken wiped out in two days. We kidded him, saying he was well on his way to becoming a Jap ace."

ELEVEN

BOUGAINVILLE, THE GILBERTS, AND THE MARSHALLS

On July 31 the first echelon of VMF(N)-531, under Lieutenant Colonel Frank Schwable, boarded the aircraft carrier *Long Island* with its six PV-1 night fighters. Schwable had fruitlessly argued with the Bureau of Aeronautics to discard useless equipment that prevented the planes from gaining sufficient altitude. "We were carrying all kinds of excess weight," said Schwable. "De-icers. Can you imagine going down to the Solomon Islands with de-icers on your wings and all the machinery that goes together with those. Navigation equipment—a big navigation table with lights, big heavy brass joints. We weren't going to use them. We didn't even have a navigator.

"When I got aboard the *Long Island* the first day out from San Diego heading for Hawaii, I got our crews together and said, 'Each one of you get a monkey wrench and a screwdriver and a hacksaw and go through those airplanes and tear out everything we don't need and throw them over the side.' And they did. I don't know how many thousands of pounds of weight we eliminated this way . . . we climbed better."

On September 11 the night fighter squadron took up station at Banika, the Russell Islands base. Members commenced operations immediately, but their own ground controllers were not permitted to function until they learned the local procedures. That forced the Marines to coordinate with unfamiliar fighter directors. Banika and a subsequent stay at Vella Lavella offered pluses and minuses, according to Schwable. The coral landing fields were visible at night without landing lights. On the other hand, jittery crews manning antiaircraft at these bases frequently fired on the night fighters as they sought to come home. Danger-filled days passed before the friendly fire diminished.

While VMF(N)-531 coped with the deficiencies of the twin-engine Vega, the Navy had created a squadron of night fighter F4Us. Instead of the three-man crew of the Marine aircraft, the Navy's system relied on a single man to fly, navigate, scan the sky, and fire. As a weapon, however, the Corsair climbed higher and flew much faster. Aware of the potential, the Second Marine Night Fighter Squadron, training in the States, worked with the F4U.

Simultaneously, Lieutenant Commander Edward "Butch" O'Hare—the famous naval hero who knocked down five Japanese planes in a single February 1942 day—had begun to develop a carrier-based night fighter program using the F4F Wildcat working in tandem with a TBF that installed the radar. The available models of the F4U Corsair at the time were considered unsuitable for flattops. O'Hare was lost during the first combat test of the plan.

The Navy's VF(N)-75, a small unit with six pilots, two radar officers, plus a ground crew and six F4U-2 planes, arrived at Munda on September 23 and started patrols October 2. The Navy was reluctant to base them on a carrier for fear of a disastrous accident during a night operation. To Navy Lieutenant Harold D. O'Neill went credit for the outfit's first confirmed shoot-down of an enemy marauder at night. Having taken off around 9:30 P.M., O'Neill was steered by the ground radar operators to a bogey southeast of Shortland Island. The fighter pilot saw the exhaust from a Betty bomber two miles away. He quickly maneuvered onto its tail and sent it flaming into the sea.

The introduction of new weapons and tactics aside, the grand strategy by the Allies for the Pacific Theater plotted a campaign that would advance toward the Philippines and then Japan, not step by step up the islands but by leaps and bounds. At the Chiefs of Staff conference at Quebec in August 1943, the notion of invading Rabaul was abandoned. Instead, the huge base would be bypassed, cut off from further supply or reinforcements and neutralized by air power. In that arena, AirSoPac, the tactical command, included the First and Second Marine Air Wings, the Air Corps's Thirteenth Air Force, some American naval units, and elements of the Royal New Zealand Air Force. Tactical and operational aviation in the Solomons devolved upon a subordinate organization, Commander Air, Solomons (ComAirSols). A multiplicity of squadrons and weapons broke down into a fighter command that controlled and directed all 314 fighters involved. Two strike commands that included the dive-bombers, torpedo planes, search aircraft, and a bomber organization responsible for heavy and medium bombers drawn mostly from the Army, combined to contribute 317 more aircraft. A photo wing of ninety-seven planes devoted itself to gathering intelligence and providing transport. In this aggregation, fourteen Marine squadrons participated.

The most efficient means of achieving the desired end lay in airfields closer to Rabaul than any of those already created. The ideal sites were on Bougainville, the largest of the Solomons, 255 air miles from Rabaul. The Japanese already operated five fields there, including the one most familiar to the Marines, Kahili. In preparation for invasion of Bougainville, ComAirSols pummeled the Japanese installations on the island throughout September and October with stepped-up daily assaults starting October 15. The enemy offered modest aerial opposition, and the raiders counted only six planes shot down during this intensive campaign while destroying nearly sixty of the opposition in the skies and on the ground.

Conant's logbook for the start of September 1943 registered daily strikes at Kahili. On the first day of the month, he remembered, "We had made the usual raid on Kahili. It was a pisser as usual. I'm flying behind Bob Owens. On the way home Bob spotted a Zero down low. He, the Zero, was tailing the bombers, looking for a straggler. Bob dove down on him at a very high speed and shot at him. He probably hit him but didn't disable him, because as he passed the Zero it tailed in on him. Well, I'm behind Bob and I was able to slow down enough to stay behind the Zero. I did just that and at very close range opened fire on him. I hit him

. . . hard. Pieces flew off and came at me. After several seconds of continuous fire, a large piece came off the Zero. It came by me close and just as it passed over my head, a parachute started to stream behind it. It was the pilot . . . he had bailed out as I was shooting at him. I don't know how my bullets missed him . . . maybe they didn't. Anyway, if he survived the jump he had a seventy-mile swim home. I doubt he made it. Anyway I got my third Zero. Big deal. I've now got three and all I've done is shoot planes that get in front of me. Some hero, huh?"

Obviously, the offensive against the Japanese also involved the Marine bomber and torpedo units. Charles Conter, the rear-seat man in a dive-bomber, continued to fly missions for VMSB-234 and observe the sporadic jabs by night visitors. On August 13, he said, "I went to a movie, open air affair, with some of the other gunners. The show was stopped and we were told it wouldn't go on anymore that night on account of Jap bombers overhead. We headed back to our hut. We got halfway there when we heard a plane coming overhead low. There happened to be a bunker foxhole close by and when someone [on] the beach started shooting at [the plane] we knew it was a Jap. Some of the guys dived for the foxhole but I was too late as two of them got in a squeeze trying to get in and left me out there. . . . Anyway the Jap plane went right over our heads about 50 feet above the deck but it wasn't caring too much about us. It headed for a ship unloading supplies offshore and put a torpedo in it. I got a good view of the torpedoing of the Victory Ship, *William Penn*. A lot of lives were lost [as many as one hundred killed, and more than a hundred injured]."

A week later Conter flew to the captured Munda field. "The place was a wreck, trees bare from shelling and bombing, wrecked Jap Zeros and two-engine bombers all around [the] field, place full of shell holes and bomb craters, smell of dead Japs all over. . . . Capt. Boniske [his new pilot after Brorein had transferred to the night fighter program] and I went up by ourselves to bomb and strafe Jap artillery pieces that were giving the boys trouble near the field. It was also something else to be the only enlisted man sleeping in a tent of officers and listening to the fighter pilots tell of their dogfights over Bougainville and Vella Lavella.

Walsh, the big ace of the time, was sitting right across from me telling how he added one more that day. When I had some time to myself, I went down along the strip where the wrecked planes were and tore off a couple of pieces from Zeros."

VMSB-234, during the final days of August and into September, focused its wrath upon the base at Vila, on the southern tip of Kolombangara. Attacking the artillery and forty-millimeter guns there on August 24, Conter recalled, "It was about the closest I came to death. . . . There was a mixup after the dive on Vila and we were coming out of it in all directions. Suddenly I saw this other SBD coming right at us. I screamed into the mike to Boniske to look out but he never saw or heard the plane coming at us. It just skimmed by and missed us by a thin tobacco paper. Boniske came back and said, 'What did you say?' I said we damn near had a collision but he said he never saw it.

"The number of planes going on the attacks was tremendous compared to last February. We were gaining more and more strength while the Japs were going down hill." The ability of the enemy to intercept the bombers with fighters, according to Conter, had slackened, enabling him to write, "It was nice not being bothered by Zeros now in our strikes. [Conant perceived the situation as less benign.] Boniske was not as good a pilot as Brorein but we got along okay. Being able to strafe the targets was fun, as the pilot would strafe and lean the plane over on the side and I would get off good shots with the twin .30s."

In mid-September an eight-day leave in Sydney brought another spree—"spent $200 in a week, raised hell, took out Clare. . . . we couldn't get married in Australia without special permission from high military authorities and a lot of red tape." As replacement crews started to fill the ranks of the squadron, those with extended combat service received word they would rotate to the States. Any chances of a wedding with Clare vanished when Conter finally left the South Pacific for his first leave home in nearly two years.

Amos Kay Belnap, the dive-bomber pilot with VMSB-243, had been on Palmyra for four months when he, as a captain, and two lieutenants, Lou Conti and Noble Shepherd, "drew the short stick and were transferred back to Ewa. While at Ewa we were assigned to VMSB-236, known as the Hellraider Squadron, and again boarded ship and transport plane for combat in the South Pacific, arriving on September 4th at Henderson Field, Guadalcanal.

"My first combat target on September 9 was the Vila Airstrip on the Island of Kolombangara. This was a small circular island about two hours flight time northwest of Guadalcanal. The enemy was using the airstrip to mount air attacks on Henderson Field. . . . My guess was the high command generals thought this would be an easy first time target for a new squadron, as it had been bombed many times before. However, it was still an active airstrip and a concern to me.

"Thirty Douglas Dive-Bomber SBD-5 pilots from VMSB-236 and 24 Marine Converted Torpedo Bomber VMTB-233 pilots were up before dawn and briefed on the targets, assigned planes and trucked to . . . revetments which were scattered about Henderson Field. It was about an hour before takeoff and I used this time to make sure my plane was ready to fly. I checked the tires, ailerons and tabs, elevators and tabs, tail-fin and tabs to insure they were unlocked and in working order. I started the motor, checked the mags, instruments and radio, all of which were OK. I conferred with my gunner, 18-year-old Corporal Jim Graham from Brooklyn, New York. All appeared OK and while we were in the air, he would check and test-fire his twin .30-caliber machine guns. Together, we checked out the 1,000-pound bomb and made sure the arming wire was correctly installed. After all this was completed, the ground crew topped off the gas tanks.

"While refueling was in progress, we checked our .45-caliber revolvers, the dye markers, shark repellants, hunting knives, survival maps, American flag, machetes, water, personal camera and navigation board with target and return data. We were sure we were ready to go and I climbed into the cockpit and Corporal Graham climbed into the rear seat with his back to me."

VMSB-236's CO, Major Floyd Beard, led a parade of dive-bombers from the revetments and took off, with the others following every thirty seconds. They flew over the ocean at an altitude of five hundred feet before Beard made a 180-degree turn to the left. His subordinates then cut inside as they jockeyed into their formation positions. Once properly arrayed, the flight vectored toward the target while climbing to thirteen thousand feet. Meanwhile the torpedo bombers and the fighter cover had left their airstrips for the rendezvous point near Munda, home for enemy fighters. Belnap worried about a possible attack from there as well as from Kahili on Bougainville. "When we left Guadalcanal, it was hot and humid and when we climbed to altitude it was very cold. I was shaking quite hard and, of course, I blamed it on the cold!"

As they neared the target, Belnap forgot about the frigid temperature and his shakes to concentrate upon his objective. "As we closed I could now pick out the airfield and the south end where my target should be. The Skipper began leading the formation into a 20 or 30-degree shallow turning dive and we began to pick up speed to about 200 knots. We could see the black puffs of smoke in front of us as the antiaircraft shells were exploding all around us, with Lieutenants Noble Shepherd and Lou Conti now easing away from my wings and getting into position to follow in the dive.

"There were many times I dove on AA guns during my three combat tours, but this being the first was a very exciting experience. This time the target was a revetment protecting dual five-inch British Naval Guns. These guns were captured in the battle of Singapore and transported to Kolombangara to protect the Vila airstrip. The choice dive-bombing targets were always against combat ships. . . . Dive-bombing gun emplacements wasn't such a big deal unless you were the torpedo bomber pilot who was counting on you to knock out the guns when he was vulnerable [while] bombing the runways.

"Ignoring the exploding black puffs of AA, I found my target, steepened my dive and at about 90 degrees straight down, opened my dive flaps and took aim through my telescope. Air speed was about 250 knots and I could see these five-inch dual guns shooting right at me. They went BOOM—BOOM—BOOM—BOOM— BOOM. Those gun flashes were quite unnerving.

"Concentrating on my aim I began to shoot back, firing my two front-mounted .50-caliber Browning machine guns and I could see the tracer bullets going right into the revetment. Later I would think of this action like a shootout on Main Street in a Western movie. This shootout lasted for as long as it took to dive straight down two miles at 250 knots.

"When the enemy figured out they were the target, I could see in my telescope little figures leaving the protection of the armor shell around the guns and disappearing into the revetment wall. I assumed they were headed for a bomb shelter.

"At about 800 feet, I released my 1,000-pound bomb and began my pullout and retreated to the safety of the sea, flying at tree-top level. While doing this, my rear gunner was firing into the trees, which hid the enemy with his dual .30-caliber machine guns. It took a great deal of courage to be a gunner and to fly backwards toward the ground and pray that your pilot would pull out safely.

"When an attack on the enemy is well coordinated, the dive-bombers suppress the AA fire while simultaneously the torpedo bombers drop their string of four 500-pound bombs on the run-way and parked airplanes. In this strike, 96 bombs were laid down perfectly on the runway and all our planes returned to their bases. Later, it was reported that some Zeros did attack our formation, but I didn't see them and I assume our fighters took care of them.

"I was extremely pleased to taxi into my assigned revetment at the end of the strike. My bum was numb from being strapped in for four hours and I was beginning to sweat from the heat. When I turned the airplane engine off, I wanted to, but did not, kiss the ground. What happened next was an embarrassment. As I climbed out of the cockpit and stood on the ground, my parachute seat fell to my knees. Somehow in the long pre-flight check, I failed to buckle the parachute straps to my legs. If it had become necessary for me to use the parachute, I would have slipped right through it." On the following day, his plane captain brought Belnap a two-inch piece of shrapnel that had been embedded in the leading edge of his wing.

His associate Lou Conti spoke of other incidents in that first combat flight. "I recall thinking seriously about my ability to get off the ground. We always had the 1,000 pound bomb on the yoke in the center of the underbelly of the plane, right below where the pilot and rear seat gunner sat. The yoke was used to 'throw' the bomb so it would clear the aircraft's propeller when released in a vertical dive. Many missions out of Henderson included a 52-gallon fuel tank under the left wing and nothing under the right wing. Not a very symmetrical loaded aircraft! It was full throttle, tab at full right to compensate for the exterior fuel tank, stick over right, and lots of prayer and sweat!

"Flying from a Marston matted air strip [pierced steel planking] is like going over a rail crossing with sunken rails and in poor repair. You feel every hole, and with an underpowered plane, unbalanced load, trees on either side of you, just as you get airborne, it is quite a thrill, in retrospect!"

When Conti dropped his bomb and began his pullout, he forgot to close his dive brakes. Until he remembered to adjust the brakes, he lacked the speed to join with Belnap and Noble and create a defensive posture in the event of an enemy attack. "As soon as I got the brakes closed, enabling me to catch up, still shaking from the excitement, fear and wondering what else I had forgotten, I noticed upon checking my instruments that my cylinder head temperature was high and climbing. It finally dawned on me that when going into the dive, you 'cleaned' up the aircraft to gain maximum speed which included closing the engine cowl flaps. Reopening them got the temperature down to an acceptable range."

After the squadron re-formed and was well on the way home, Conti said he calmed down and lit a cigar, informing his gunner that the smoking lamp was lit. "After debriefing and getting a 2 oz bottle of brandy from our flight surgeon, I felt like a drained dishrag. I believe most of us did not drink the brandy at that time, but saved it for a squadron 'happy hour' when we knew that we were in a 'stand down' basis."

Unlike Belnap and Conti, Bill Nickerson, a native of Arizona, joined VMSB-132 not from another squadron but out of the replacement pilot pool. In October 1939, as an eighteen-year-old student at the University of Arizona, he was accepted into the first

CPT program in Phoenix. Two weeks after the Japanese attack on Hawaii, Nickerson volunteered for naval aviation pilot training. With a diploma from Arizona State, in June 1942 he started pre-flight instruction in California. Ten months later he earned his wings and a Marine commission at Corpus Christi, Texas. A day after he pinned on his new insignia, Nickerson married the former Eve Kirkman.

Although he had hoped to serve as a fighter pilot, Nickerson drew the front seat of an SBD. He, too, carrier-qualified on the USS *Wolverine* before sailing to New Caledonia and his slot with VMSB-132. When he reported in at Espiritu Santo in August 1943, he recalled for the Marine Aviation Association's *History of Marine Aviation,* "Major R. D. Rupp was C.O. of VMSB-132. He and his experienced pilots were doing their best to make passable combat pilots out of a gaggle of very young second lieutenants." Nickerson had completed one assignment chauffeuring a sergeant attempting to photograph a coastline for use by Intelligence. The camera, however, was too bulky, but a Navy lieutenant on hand had a more compact model. Rupp ordered Nickerson, "Fly him around."

For roughly five weeks the Marine spent most of his hours in the air carrying the naval officer to various areas. "For the lieutenant," said Nickerson, "close meant 'closer' and low meant 'lower' and slow meant 'slower.' But there are limits. To me 105 knots was slow enough. Close and low meant you had to climb over things like headlands and trees and you should be careful not to 'dig in' a wing if you were going in and out of an inlet. This requires intense concentration and on occasion you sweat."

The Intelligence people not only scrutinized the film but also intensively debriefed Nickerson on what he saw. The purpose of much of the reconnaissance was to balk Japanese efforts to evacuate their troops from the increasingly untenable positions in the New Georgia chain. Said Nickerson, ". . . unless you have flown the coast of the Islands of the Solomons you couldn't have any comprehension of the endless miles of coasts with inlets, bays, streams and small beaches, all covered by dense tropical forest." The myriad avenues for wooden barges, undetectable by radar, would—unless pinpointed from the air—enable rescue of some of the otherwise trapped nine thousand soldiers.

According to Nickerson, by studying the photographs and his own observations while on these reconnaissance hops, he learned how to penetrate the mask of camouflage. Most notably, he became proficient at discerning the difference between natural foliage and the subtle color changes of vegetation that was cut and artfully placed over barges, guns, and other installations. But he also confessed that despite the best efforts of the Americans, the Japanese still managed to rescue most of the soldiers. The black of night and the hundreds upon hundreds of outlets to the sea thwarted interdiction.

Spider Webb and Richard Mulberry, having flown antisub patrols from Johnston Island and Palmyra for nearly six months, now moved to the front. In September 1943 VMSB-133, fresh from the States, relieved VMSB-243 on both islands. The squadron spent a month that mixed R&R with refitting in Hawaii before embarking for the Solomons. After a ten-day sea voyage they bedded down at the base on Efate, which now bore the name *Bauer Field* in honor of the commander of VMF-212. From Efate, on November 20, the flight echelon was airlifted to the recently captured Munda base to replace VMSB-236. "I found myself in the first planeload," said Webb, "and was apprehensive as well as 'goggleyed' to actually be in the combat zone. While being transferred by truck from the strip to pilots' quarters we noticed a strong putrid smell and were told it was 'dead Japs'; later we discovered it to be land crabs that had been crushed by vehicular traffic. Before we were able to get squared away in our tents, a runner came, ordering all division leaders to report to operations with full flight gear."

Webb had been promoted to captain and was expected to lead a six-plane division, composed of two three-plane sections. At the operations shack he and the others from the squadron met the combat veterans of VMSB-236 and received a briefing on a strike at the Kahili airfield. "The briefing officer was Commander 'Swede' Larson, then head of Strike Command, which controlled all tactical Marine and Navy aircraft in the forward area. Man, was I impressed. Swede had become a legend in the early days at Guadalcanal with his Navy torpedo squadron. This was the real thing."

The newcomers were assigned to fly as wingmen for the outgoing squadron on their final mission. "Nervous?" said Webb. "Yes. Scared? Yes. Afraid? Apparently not, for it never occurred to me not to go. Into a new, to me, plane serviced by persons unknown to me [the ground echelon of the squadron had not yet made the trip] to go God knows where—I'd seen it on the map and heard of it—to do God knows what—actually what I'd been trained to do—to God knows who—everyone knew in general but not specifically—was a helluva feeling."

The target for the mission was antiaircraft gun positions on a hill overlooking the air base. The objective was to destroy or disrupt the defensive fire, enabling a torpedo bomber squadron to unload on the field. Marine Corsairs would fly high cover; Australian P-40s would handle the lower altitudes.

"Pilots are known for their light banter and graveyard humor which helps ward off negative thought and apprehensions," remarked Webb. "Here I was, with a 'war machine' strapped on my back, flying with a group of whom I previously knew only two or three before the briefing, fighting my own interior battle with attitude and adjusting to reality. I don't remember being in a bantering mood—that came later after I had a few missions under my belt.

"I had learned early on that everyone gets scared at times and, in fact, never to trust anyone who brags that he doesn't for he's either a fool or a liar. I was scared at some point in every mission I flew, and sometimes often in a particular one. Later I heard combat flying described as 'Hours of boredom interspersed with moments of stark terror'—very descriptive and basically true."

As he was being driven to the flight line, Webb coped with myriad doubts—whether he'd find the correct plane; whether it would start; whether he would locate his flight leader in the air, locate the target, and remember to arm his bomb; whether the release would function, open his dive brakes, and then close them at the correct moments; whether he'd pull out to sea while avoiding a center of AA; whether he'd know the drill if he was hit.

The sight of his gunner, Sal Garalski, waiting beside the aircraft reassured Webb. Everything went as planned from the takeoff, the join-up, and the rendezvous with the fighters. "There were about forty SBDs, the largest formation I had ever been in. . . . The flight was to last about three and a half hours; just get there, hit the target, and get the hell away, then home. I had plenty of gas, the engine ran smoothly, and the weather was fine. My section was on the right side and as I was flying right wing I was able to see the target as we closed in a shallow left-hand turn. I remember we were just under twelve thousand feet when starting our high-speed approach, probably a blistering 140 knots indicated."

The protocol stated that aircrews should rely on oxygen when above ten thousand feet for an hour. But Webb noted that in the Solomons, the dive and torpedo planes seldom rose that high, and even then for short periods. Therefore the SBDs on this mission carried no oxygen equipment, leaving the pilots with one less matter to consider. Originally, advanced dive-bomber training instructed pilots to pull up and then wing over to begin a dive. But under combat conditions the airmen realized that loss of speed when pulling up and subsequent exposure of the underbelly offered enemy fighters an easy target. The standard operating procedure now called for a rollover immediately followed by the dive.

On his baptism by fire, Webb said, "About the time we started our final approach antiaircraft shell bursts started appearing in our flight path. This was certainly new but I don't recall any particular emotion for they were like dark blossoms appearing, and we could not hear them over the noise of our own planes. If there were any Jap planes around I did not see them. I remember finding my target early on and following my leader in a dive that would let us pull out toward the sea. What was new and fascinating was seeing what appeared to be blinking lights coming from the target. This was of course the source of the blossoms we were now flying through. The Japs cut each succeeding fuse a little closer so each shell exploded a little lower than the previous, which enabled them to keep us in their bursts all the way down.

"I remember a calmness in that I had 'been in combat' and had not wavered. Heck, I was too busy trying to do what we had been trained to do to have time for other thoughts before the flight home. Even though I was smoking in those days, I remember being surprised that my leader lit up a cigarette going home. . . . We were cleared at Munda for landing. . . . Here for the first time I observed what was to become routine in our squadron operations, multiple landings. Traditionally planes landed one at a time, allowing space between. Here, with a wide runway, we were landing two and three almost abreast—not in formation but singly. Later we learned the Air Corps bomber pilots thought we were foolhardy devils for their practice was to allow about a quarter of a mile between planes. In practice, we could land twenty planes to their one." Neither Webb nor the Air Corps fliers seemed to have recognized that the Army's multiengine aircraft were much larger than the Marines' single-engine SBDs and TBFs.

Following a cup of coffee and "the obligatory two ounces of brandy" at the debriefing, Webb said, "The best news was that all of our planes returned. I was told my bomb had made a direct hit and I was able to describe damage made by planes ahead of me. While I was second on my target, I was pulling out before the bomb ahead of me hit, I was amazed at the number of bomb hits I was able to see on other targets while exiting the area. Man, what a feeling to tell them [pilots who did not make the mission] we had already gotten a mission under our belts. Everyone wanted to know how it went and what it was like. I felt ten feet tall and remember a feeling of inner peace in that I had done what I had been trained to do."

On Munda, Webb lived in a four-man tent with a foxhole inside. "[It] was probably dug by the pilots we replaced. When Washing Machine Charlie first came late one night, we had a traffic jam getting into the hole when we heard the bomb whistle. Bob Boaz landed atop me just as the bomb exploded and I thought we had been hit. Luckily the bomb landed about a hundred yards away in an open area.

"The climate was strictly 'tropical.' Hot, humid, intermittent rain showers, and plenty of mosquitoes, which accounted for our 'atabrine tans' [the drug turned skin yellow]. It was not uncommon for individuals to stop where they were when a shower [rain] appeared, strip, produce a piece of soap and bathe. In the Solomons we got the obligatory two ounces of brandy after each mission [contrary to the experience of Roger Conant] and two cans of beer *per week*. An active black market on beer and whiskey thrived. No ice, so the preferred way to cool beer was put it in a plane where it would chill during a mission, and pray that the plane would return. Most of us drank it warm, particularly after being introduced to warm beer in Sydney."

Richard Mulberry's introduction to combat occurred the same day as Webb's. In fact, Mulberry said he flew left wing on Webb. He voiced similar sentiments to Webb's about fear and fascination with the sight of antiaircraft fire. He remarked that he never thought about the possibility of flak detonating his bomb; rather, "We were more concerned about the antiaircraft fire coming through the cockpit. Although we had some armor plating in the back, we were more concerned about our rear-seat gunners and the pilots getting hit than we were the bomb."

When the squadron revisited Bougainville the following day, said Mulberry, "We were going after bivouac areas where the Japanese were living. They were pretty easy to spot, and we did a lot of damage on that one. We just wiped out their bivouac area on that second strike." He noted that the fighter cover stayed above the dive-bombers until just before the start of the dive. "They [the fighters] would go in ahead of us and do strafing for which we were grateful because sometimes that would assist in suppressing antiaircraft fire. We rarely, rarely were attacked by Japanese fighters."

TWELVE

CENTRAL PACIFIC OPERATIONS

Despite the infusions of replacements like Phil DeLong and Roger Conant, during the summer of 1943 the turnover in fighter squadrons and pilots created a gap in airpower that Admiral Halsey felt he could ill afford. Among those ticketed for relief had been George Britt's former organization VMF-214, referred to in Bruce Gamble's history of the squadron as the Swashbucklers. During the six weeks of their second combat tour, they accounted for twenty Japanese planes in aerial combat and as many as thirty on the ground, the latter mostly due to Al Jensen and perhaps Charles Lanphier. Their own losses had been severe: six planes crashed during operational accidents, one of which killed the skipper, Major William Pace. Two of their number were lost in combat: Lanphier who died in captivity, and Wilbur Blakeslee who disappeared during a scrap with the Japanese.

After the usual leave in Australia, the veterans of VMF-214 expected to return to combat, but the demand for fighters caused the First Marine Air Wing and the MAG-21 command, which included George Britt, to create an entire new complement for the squadron and ship the group to Guadalcanal before the former members returned from their sprees in Sydney and Espiritu Santo. The reconstituted VMF-214 went into combat with Greg Boyington in command. Boyington, still limping from his fractured ankle, had campaigned hard for an active role, and he had the sympathetic ear of the 1st MAW's deputy commander, Brigadier General James Moore.

Distinguishing truth from fiction in the case of Greg Boyington resembles an attempt to separate a martini's gin from its vermouth. He once admitted to an interviewer, "I'm a psychopathic liar," although he probably meant *pathologic*. His alcoholism undoubtedly fueled his casual regard for veracity. Only a dogged researcher like Bruce Gamble could have uncovered so much of his mendacity. With the AVG paying a bonus for each plane shot down, the Flying Tigers may all have exaggerated their claims, but Boyington's flights of fancy flew higher than others. When he recounted his adventures with VMF-214 in a postwar book and then as part of the TV series *Baa Baa Black Sheep*, he distorted and embellished events, enraging many of his former colleagues.

The legend he spun about VMF-224 asserted that he took over a squadron of neophytes with only three veterans of combat. Actually nine of the new aggregation had seen a fair share of combat with from one to four victories. Boyington had little to teach them. Gamble pointed out that of the others, four—while virgins to air battles—had been instructors with countless hours in the cockpit.

Henry Bourgeois, age twenty-two, assigned to VMF-214, already had shot down three enemy planes during tours with VMF-122 and 112. "My father worked in the shipping business for the Port of New Orleans. He and several businessmen arranged for the first airmail service to New Orleans. That was 1928 and the day the biplane arrived, the men were offered a ride around the city. There was enough room in the cockpit for a little seven-year-old boy to ride. From that day on all I wanted to do is fly airplanes.

"He [his father] arranged for a Reserve Air Force officer to teach me and I soloed at age thirteen. I attended Louisiana State University, majoring in aeronautics. I worked at the Baton Rouge airport on weekends to earn flight time. I was not doing too well at school and in the spring of 1941, a Navy recruiting team came to the university, and I decided to become a Navy officer and pilot." Once accepted, Bourgeois passed through an elimination flight school and finally entered the aviation school at Corpus Christi. "My instructor and check pilot was a Marine captain. I thought I was a hotshot pilot but he showed me how to really fly an airplane. He and another man who served in World War I with the Marines and was my Boy Scout leader inspired me to become a Marine."

Bourgeois had begun his first fighter tour with VMF-122 flying a Wildcat and then became a Corsair pilot with VMF-112. On June 30 Bourgeois, dispatched from Guadalcanal, had lost his wingman in the thick clouds near Munda when a two-engine Sally bomber blundered into his path. The two aircraft exchanged fire and the Mitsubishi, trailing smoke, headed toward the ocean. But a burst from its guns had knocked out Bourgeois's radio.

Hopelessly lost, he wandered through the sky until he suddenly saw a flock of SBDs traveling a few hundred feet above the waves. He assumed they knew the way home and began to follow the dive-bombers. Unfortunately, the formation split, heading in two different directions. The Corsair pilot chose to stick with the leader and three others, who actually were off course. They arrived in the vicinity of Rennell Island, some one hundred miles south of Guadalcanal. One by one the SBDs peeled off and landed in the water.

Bourgeois circled about for a time but then decided he, too, would ditch. He followed procedure, making his harness snug, jettisoning the canopy, and lowering his flaps. The F4U splashed into the surf a hundred yards from the beach. When Bourgeois climbed out and into the water, he discovered his Mae West would not inflate properly. Natives in an outrigger canoe, however, pulled him aboard. He spent a night in a hut before his rescuers bore him in a canoe to the main village, home of the "Super Chief."

Bourgeois told Gamble, "I was the first to get there. The other eight Marines—four pilots and four gunners—were paddled there later. When I arrived, I was treated royally, and they kept talking about Marines and Japs. They could speak pretty good pidgin English and wanted to know if I was number one. I kept saying, 'I'm number one. I'm number one' so they thought I was in charge of everything. Later the rest of the Marines arrived, and the natives did some cooking for us and fed us pretty well. Since I had said that I was number one, I got to sleep in the Chief's hut with one of his daughters."

On the following day, his hosts insisted Bourgeois accompany them to another site. There a young woman in labor lay in a hut. The villagers expected the pilot to treat her, but all he could do was to put a hand on her head, then dispense some aspirin tablets from his first-aid kit.

That afternoon when a PBY taxied in from the lagoon, Bourgeois persuaded the Dumbo's corpsman to have a look at the pregnant woman. He reported that she needed help. When the Americans returned to Guadalcanal, they arranged for a flight surgeon to fly to Rennell, and he delivered a healthy baby. "When the doctor came back, he told me that the chief was so happy they named the boy 'Boo-gawa.' "

One of the entrants to VMF-214 was a former flight instructor, John "Jack" Bolt. Born in South Carolina in 1921, he grew up in Sanford, Florida. "I was president of my class my junior and senior year," said Bolt in an oral history given to the Naval Aviation Museum Foundation. "I was not a very good student. I'd been working because my family didn't have any money. I provided my own clothes and most of my social expenses since age 10."

When he enrolled at the University of Florida, he reported, the attitude of the students was "highly pacifistic." The attempts by President Franklin D. Roosevelt to rouse the public to the threat of the Axis powers met "considerable hostility." He detected a change in feelings after a U-boat sank the American destroyer *Reuben James* on prewar convoy duty. With the family strapped for money, Bolt saw the five hundred dollars a year proffered for Naval Reserve pilots as an opportunity to complete college and attend law school. He joined in July 1941 and in November, a few weeks before Pearl Harbor, went on active duty.

Commissioned in August 1942, he started teaching others how to fly. Not until June of the following year did he embark for the combat arena. Once committed to the reincarnation of VMF-214 as the squadron prepared for its debut, he logged another forty-nine hours in a Corsair, for a total of almost seven hundred. That surpassed what even combat pilots had accumulated in two tours.

He had met Boyington earlier while both were part of a replacement pool and held a more benign view of him than many others. "Boyington was tremendously popular with all the pilots from the beginning and provided charismatic leadership even down in the pool—so much so, that we wanted to name ourselves *Boyington's Bastards*. Some public information officer said, 'No, that won't do, you gotta have something acceptable to the press.' . . . we came up with *Black Sheep*."

His many hours in the cockpit gave Bolt an appreciation of the F4U's strengths and weaknesses. "The Corsair was a great bird. It was a little stiff longitudinally; it was so long. But it was a tremendous gun platform and could always out-shoot the F6F [Hellcat] on gunnery. The F6F was short-coupled—longitudinal stability relates to fuselage length in part—and would wobble. . . . But the main thing was the F4U's engine; it had the R-2800 with water injection and about 2,500 or 2,600 horsepower. We could bang the throttle full-forward and outboard, and we would have about five minutes of 200 to 300 extra horsepower. Of course, it just ran circles around the Zero and the F4F.

"The Corsair had a poorer radius of turn and we realized that we'd never try to turn with a Zero. Essentially, we almost had to surprise the Zeros. They apparently didn't have 360 degree visibility behind them and you could surprise them. We could get a deflection shot sometimes, if one of them saw us and broke away before we got to him. I would bet that 75 to 90 percent of the kills that we had were from shooting the guy who never knew we were there." Bolt noted that for both the Corsair and the F6F, "rearward visibility was nil.

"The old Thach Weave tactic was great in theory, but the fact is, when we made an attack in the Corsair, we seldom came out with any tactical integrity. Every man was a shooter because the shooter could not protect the wingman, and the wingman wasn't going to sit out there doing nothing when he saw that nobody was watching him. The Thach Weave sounded good, where everybody watched everybody else, but the fact is an attack required strong concentration forward, and the wingman just had his rear end sitting out there in the open."

Bolt modified his dismissal of the tactic. "We used a four-plane section. If we were fleeting an attack, it worked for the initial attack. (Sometimes we had to go into an area and the Japanese fighters were up above us.) If we were defending bombers, it was effective there too. (We were not supposed to leave to chase an attacking Zero away from the bombers; we were supposed to stay in our weave.) But if we were taking the offensive, the position of the Thach Weave concept, in this case, didn't work."

Boyington had taken VMF-214 to the Russells on September 12. Contrary to what he claimed in his memoirs, the squadron did not immediately engage in a huge melee with the enemy. Instead two escort missions passed without aerial contact. On the third mission the Black Sheep became part of a conglomeration of Corsairs, Hellcats, P-40s supplying fighter cover, and torpedo and dive-bombers targeting Balldale, an island base just off Bougainville. From the clouds over Balldale, a flock of thirty to forty Zeros or Zekes sought to intercept the raiders.

VMF-214 benefited from its designation as high cover and struck with the advantage of altitude, diving down upon the foe. Jack Bolt, in his initiation to war, recalled, "The first time I saw a 'Meatball' [Zero] it was a full deflection, and he just zipped by: a great big 'Meatball' with the sun over my shoulder. I was just in a state of shock. It takes a while to develop real expertise in a combat situation. You're not very effective on your first few contacts with the enemy." Bruce Gamble's squadron history said that Bolt encountered another Zero head-on but again failed to trigger his guns.

Bolt's slowness to react might be chalked up to buck fever by a neophyte. But even a veteran like Boyington could err. During one engagement he had placed himself in a prime position on the tail of a Zero. However, he forgot to throw the master switch on his guns and never got off a shot. He also succumbed to a lapse in judgment when he followed a clearly fatally wounded foe in his death dive, putting himself in a highly vulnerable position.

In the turmoil and tumult of the excursion to Balldale, Boyington believed he shot down one enemy plane, and perhaps two others. His subordinates claimed five definitely destroyed and six probables. Who did what and where frequently became highly contentious. With multiple squadrons from different organizations participating in free-shooting brawls spread over many miles of sky, it became difficult to resolve conflicting claims. Adjudication of credits—whether by higher authorities or plain bluster—often left parties unsatisfied. Duplications also increased kill counts above the actual numbers.

One highly successful late-afternoon mission sent about a dozen from VMF-214 to shoot up the Kahili base on Bougainville. Arriving at twilight, a four-plane division led by Henry Bourgeois swooped down upon the strip. Overhead, the remainder from the squadron, along with representatives from other units manning P-40s and P-39s, blanketed the raiders in the event of an attempted interception. Wrote Bruce Gamble, "The four shooters (Bourgeois, Bill Heier, Sandy Sims and D. J. Moore) spread out and dropped to just fifty feet, then opened fire at a thousand yards and held down triggers as they crossed the facility. Their twenty-four machine guns totally surprised a bivouac of encamped Japanese and then lanced through a cluster of Zeros parked on the south end of the strip, hit an AA position just beyond it, and finally chewed through a group of boats and personnel two miles to the west at the mouth of a river."

Heier nearly became a casualty when the strafing caused an unknown object to suddenly appear in front of him. When he pivoted his F4U he clipped a palm tree, shearing off a wingtip and damaging his propeller and oil cooler. The wounded bird continued to fly but obviously could not limp all the way to Munda. Near newly acquired Vella Lavella, Heier decided to bail out. But when he rolled his Corsair over and opened the cockpit, instead of falling out, he discovered g-forces pinning him to his seat. Only when he shoved the stick forward did he suddenly eject. His chute opened with its straps cinching painfully tight around his groin.

Heier told Gamble, "The airplane spiraled down and hit the water, and it was gone: no pieces. I got into my rubber boat, and here comes a Japanese landing barge. I took out my .45 and got in the water by my boat. I was going to kill as many of them as I could and then let them do me. Then I heard some guy say, 'The sonovabitch is around here someplace, there's his parachute!' It was the Seabees, and they were using [the barge] as a garbage scow. So I yelled, 'It's me, fellas!' "

To provide the airmen an extra cushion of flight time to targets, VMF-214 left its more comfortable station at Banika for the primitive accommodations of Munda. Under the rough-and-ready circumstances at this base, no attempt was made to preassign aircraft. Not even Boyington had his own airplane. In the predawn darkness, jeeps rolled by the waiting Corsairs; when a plane captain signaled with a thumbs-up, a pilot dropped off the jeep and climbed aboard. Record keeping fell to a minimum; the fliers on return from a sortie mumbled to mechanics about any obvious malfunctions and left it to the technicians to inspect for subtle defects. In light of the bugs that bedeviled the early models of the F4U, the haphazard maintenance resulted in high rates of grounded aircraft and, worse, breakdowns in the air.

A typical example of this problem manifested on a September 23 assignment to escort SBDs and TBFs against AA emplacements near Kahili. Five of the twenty Corsairs listed for the 8:00 A.M. takeoff either never got off the ground or else aborted almost immediately after becoming airborne. Boyington brought the fifteen still airworthy to a rendezvous with the bombers and a union with Army P-39s and New Zealand P-40s.

Well before they even reached Bougainville, the Allied forces bumped into an assortment of enemy fighters chasing a flock of B-24s that had finished their strike at Kahili and now were fleeing for home. One of the Black Sheep, Lieutenant Bob Alexander, aware of a malfunctioning cylinder, had elected to stay with the flight. But at a most inopportune moment, when he dove at top speed to evade a trio of Zeros, the engine conked out. Fortunately the maneuver discouraged his pursuers, who quit the hunt. Alexander restarted his Pratt and Whitney but with minimal power. Having abandoned the mission, Alexander staggered toward Vella Lavella. Unable to advise by radio of his emergency status, he approached an airfield littered with construction equipment. He could only pick out a less populated area of the strip, a stretch of soft earth. When the F4U slammed into the marshy ground, it flipped over on its back. Only because Alexander at the penultimate moment pitched himself forward under the instrument panel did he survive the impact, which crushed the canopy.

While Alexander escaped destruction, a melee raged in the sky, with the Americans absorbing considerable punishment. Captain Stan Bailey, the exec, with two confirmed bombers shot down during previous tours with VMF-122, barely made it home, low on gas and with hits from four cannon shells and thirty bullets. First Lieutenant Paul "Moon" Mullen, another alumnus of VMF-122 who had shot down a Zero previously, coped with a swarm of as many as ten fighters. Bullets slashed his cockpit and canopy; one of them cut his shoulder. But in a one-on-one duel he outflew his opponent until able to pour a deadly stream of fire into the Zero. The Japanese plane caught fire and fell from the sky.

Lieutenant Denmark Groover endured the worst punishment. Battling a pair of Zeros, he told Gamble, "I had one of them smoking and was trying to make him catch on fire. We were in a turn, and while I settled in on the left one and had him smoking, the one on the right pulled up sharply. I kept trying to get this other one on fire. I read a story about the atrocities the Japanese had committed on nurses, and like a damn fool I let my feelings take off, saying, 'You sonuvabitch, you'll never mess with another American woman.' About that time, I wondered where the other Zero went, and made a sharp turn. As I made that turn, BAM! My right arm and leg went dead and my left wing was on fire."

While Groover had fixated on one of the enemy, the other Zero and several companions had gone to work on him. A twenty-millimeter shell through the cockpit sprayed shrapnel that lacerated his right arm, leg, and ankle while trashing the instrument panel. Tongues of fire sprouted in the cockpit and along his left wing due to additional cannon bursts. With his good hand Groover beat down the fire in the cockpit; his dive (to get away from his attackers) snuffed out the other flames.

Groover tottered toward home, forced once to restart his engine while medicating his bloody wounds with sulfa powder slipped through the tears in his flight suit. With his instrument panel destroyed, he had no means to figure his airspeed. Aileron and rudder controls were gone, and the radio no longer functioned. Still, he elected to run for Munda. Over the field, he manhandled the gear down and made a perfect landing. But, too weak even to climb out of the cockpit by himself, Groover was lifted from the Corsair, then trundled onto a stretcher to the ready tent for a quick examination by flight surgeon James Reames. The almost instant diagnosis put the wounded pilot on a transport to the hospital on Guadalcanal. Although riddled with seven blows from cannon and more than a hundred bullet holes, the F4U, so often mechanically temperamental, brought him home. When sound, the Corsair showed a remarkable toughness under fire.

In this same engagement Jack Bolt knocked down a pair of the enemy. In both instances, as he had recounted, he came upon the enemy unnoticed. He slipped behind a formation and, taking advantage of the Zero's poor hindsight, crept within two hundred yards before burning it. Almost immediately afterward another Zero unwittingly cut across his path, and Bolt circled behind before disposing of it. Only a cannon shell that smacked into his wing discouraged him from chasing a third victim.

Although Bolt expressed admiration for Boyington, like others he occasionally found his commander arbitrary in his decisions. He recalled a mission to escort B-24s. When the bombers disappeared into thick clouds, Boyington led the flight down through a hole in the overcast over Kahili and Ballale. After they started for home, they noticed considerable surface traffic on the water below. "Clouds were down to about a thousand feet," said Bolt, "a good day to move [ships]. Nobody was going to bother them; nobody was up there. And we just chugged along at cruise speed. Boyington said, 'Nobody shoot.' "

After putting down at Munda, Bolt was chagrined at not having attacked the barges and would have gone on his own despite Boyington's orders, but his gun sight was defective. At the airstrip, Bolt urged, "Come on guys; let's go back up there and shoot up those barges—this is perfect! If we get jumped by Zeros, all we have to do is pull up on instruments, get in the cloud cover and we're safe." His companions, however, were reluctant to risk Boyington's wrath. One of them loaned Bolt a gun sight replacement.

"I got in the same plane I had before and went back up by myself. It worked just as I thought it would; I got in there, shot up three or four barges. More important still, in making a run inland on one of the barges, I found a barge staging area. . . . I roared up the harbor, did a wingover, came back out Tonolei Harbor, and shot up a few barges and one tug boat. I was just taken under fire from one gun. I saw only one gun shooting at me. It was on the tug boat, I think, firing 20 mm ammo which just floated by. It was a low velocity 20 mm, big orange tracer, recognizable. . . . I had plenty of fuel and went on back down to Munda.

"When I had returned, Boyington was mad about it and chewed me out. A day or so later, I got a telegram from Bull Halsey. It said, 'Congratulations on your one-man war in Tonolei Harbor.' That was the end of the criticism for having done it. All the Marine brass, and Boyington specifically, were put at ease over that."

The first wave from the Third Marine Division was scheduled on November 1 to hit the beaches at Cape Torokina. Strategists, prior to this venture, ordered two preliminary efforts designed to deceive the enemy of the real objectives for the gathering Allied forces. On October 27 New Zealand troops, veterans of North Africa, waded ashore on Mono and Stirling, Treasury Islands, outposts halfway between Vella Lavella and Torokina. The Japanese rose to the bait with an estimated thirty-nine fighters and ten bombers. They actually penetrated the Army fighter cover for the invasion forces. The official Japanese report insisted their planes sank two transports and two cruisers, but the only serious damage was to a fighter-director destroyer. Sherrod listed twelve of the enemy lost. As soon as the beachhead on Stirling had been secured, a Seabee bulldozer started to carve out another landing strip.

That same day about midnight, a Marine battalion led by Lieutenant Colonel Victor H. "Brute" Krulak struck on the west coast of Choiseul. The leathernecks engaged the Japanese garrisons at a number of places, making, said Sherrod, "a big noise." The entire operation was a feint, with Krulak's people withdrawn after nine days. The landings and evacuation drew strong support from air cover.

In the first hours after dawn on the day the Marines would invade Bougainville, Spider Webb flew from Munda with a naval fire control officer in the rear cockpit. "[We were] circling fairly low over the Torokina invasion area, while he directed cruiser and destroyer fire onshore. We had a panoramic view of the entire operation and a distinct feeling that the Japanese were trying to terminate our mission; plus, since it was a new experience for me, a fear that we might be hit by friendly offshore fire. He [the Navy man] was on a different frequency than I so I heard none of his exchanges. All went well (another squadron pilot on a later similar mission experienced his spotter being shot in the arm by ground fire)."

Bill Nickerson of VMSB-132, who had been flying photographic missions from Munda during the run-up to the attack on Bougainville, suddenly shifted to VMSB-144. He reconstructed his experience and conversations from that invasion day. "The commanding officers reviewed the charts once more and indicated some individual assignments for the planes we had operational. 'Ripper Two' [Nickerson's designation], said Major [Frank E.] Hollar, 'Stay. Everybody else dismissed.'

"I waited, surprised. I was a newcomer to this squadron, if not to everyone in the room. My CO went back to the chart and waved me over. 'Let's take a closer look. The landing fleet's out there, inside the ring of cruisers, destroyers and the two aircraft carriers. You've flown low level photo missions over those beaches inside Empress Augusta Bay. You're going to drop the smoke bombs on Cape Torokina to guide the landing craft onto different beaches along the shoreline.'"

Nickerson responded that the beaches were narrow, the sea rough, and conditions therefore difficult for landing barges. His superior answered, "Yes, but few enemy troops. And the Navy's big guns should take out the shore batteries. We've pretty much located where they are. You shouldn't run into much AA if any.

Dive in close to get your smoke bombs right on those beaches. Not a piece of cake."

According to Nickerson, while the number of enemy defenders at the beach was not large, they were determined to repel the amphibious force. "And I found that the guns protecting the beaches had not all been knocked out."

His SBD loaded with the smoke bombs and machine gunner in the rear seat, Nickerson began his assignment. "We stayed low over the waves and hugged the treetops, glancing up at our fighter pilots thousands of feet above, mixing it up with enemy planes. As we closed in on our targets, the cruisers' and destroyers' big guns were finishing their last barrage and the assault troops were climbing into landing barges. I identified each landing site and dove down steep and close enough to drop the smoke bombs. The CO was right: the big guns seemed to have knocked out the Jap artillery, at least temporarily.

"As I dropped the last smoke bomb, tracers began streaming past my gunner and me. I pulled up fast and made a wide circle to spot the hidden enemy artillery. They were positioned at the far end of the arc of beaches and had a well hidden spot, perfect to mow down the Marine landing forces in a murderous crossfire."

Nickerson scurried for home. As soon as he landed, he said, "I leaned out of the cockpit and yelled for the armorer. 'Load on a 500-pounder. We've got some Japs to take out, fast.' We were back in the air in record time. As we flew over the fleet, the landing barges were headed in to shore. 'You poor sons-o-bitches,' I thought. 'I'd never want to trade places with your guys, but here's a present from us.'

"I calculated the position of the hidden guns from where I'd dropped the last smoke bomb, and went into a steep dive. As we headed down, I could see the enemy gun and me, waiting for those Marines to be sitting ducks on the beach before they opened up. They swivelled their gun barrels up and bullets zipped by us. I was damned if I was going to miss, and was practically on top of them when I released the bomb. As we pulled out sharply, we turned and looked back at the explosion. Smoke and flying debris, pieces of men and metal, were all that were left. We'd hit them dead center."

During the first hour of the operation, not a single Japanese plane challenged the Allied forces whose cordon of fighters awaited them. Not until after 7:00 A.M. was an alert sounded for the approach of enemy aircraft. They were initially met by P-40s manned by New Zealanders. In the low-altitude dogfights, the New Zealanders shot down seven without a loss. Shortly after, it was the turn of P-38s from the Air Corps, which claimed eight enemy bombers. VMF-221's Captain James Swett, who during the battle for Guadalcanal had notched seven victories in fifteen minutes while protecting U.S. ships, joined up with the P-38s and accounted for a pair of dive-bombers. VMF-215 engaged a flock of Japanese fighters and splashed five; three of the kills belonged to First Lieutenant Robert M. Hanson, who himself ditched. A destroyer with the screening force off Torokina rescued him as he paddled his rubber dinghy toward the warships.

Nickerson, of course, was not the only offensive weapon at Cape Torokina. Aside from the offshore bombardment by naval vessels, a total of thirty-one TBFs and eight SBDs bombed and strafed the beaches. ComSoPac described the aerial attacks as "excellently timed and executed," but the ground command qualified its praise: ". . . not considered to be in sufficient strength." While Nickerson apparently annihilated one threat, the estimated 270 Japanese defending the site killed seventy-eight and wounded more than a hundred during the first three days. Nickerson noted, "The surf was higher and many of the landing craft broached on the beach."

Phil DeLong reported that during the fight to extend the Marines' hold on Bougainville, his squadron engaged in combat air support, "protecting our perimeter." He remarked that this was not the usual duty and noted that during the Korean War almost ten years later, most of the time the flying was combat air support (CAS).

However, Spider Webb reported that he led a six-plane ground support mission from Munda. "[I] was in direct radio contact with the unit we were supporting in the heavily wooded Torokina River area southeast of Torokina Point. We followed their instructions by bombing and strafing sites identified by smoke bombs. I recall strafing Japanese barges along the riverbank and bombing a specific wooded area across the river from our Marines." On the other hand, through his career—which included two tours in the South Pacific—he flew only three ground support missions.

The massive effort against the Japanese on Bougainville placed heavy demands upon the ground crews to repair damage from hostile fire and maintain the aircraft. Richard Barrett, born in Brooklyn, New York, in 1920, graduated from Jamaica High School. "At the height of the Depression in 1937, I was fortunate enough to get a job as a brakeman on the Long Island Rail Road. As far as world affairs were concerned, as a typical teenager, the war in Europe and the turmoil in the Far East were just something happening on the other side of the world. When Pearl Harbor happened, everything changed dramatically. Having already been registered for the draft, it was decision time. I applied to become an aviation cadet in the Air Force but was eventually rejected because of a slight discrepancy in my depth perception. I was physically and mentally ready to serve, but where? I had an older brother in the Air Force and a younger brother about to be drafted who wound up in the Rainbow [Forty-second Infantry] Division.

"The decision was made for me twelve thousand miles away. The Marines landed on Guadalcanal on August 7—my birthday. I went to the local Marine recruiting office and signed up and was given a date to report. At some point during boot camp at Parris Island we were given aptitude tests. At the end of the tests there were little boxes to be filled out as to your choice of infantry, artillery, tanks, aviation, etc. Naturally I chose aviation first.

"After boot camp I was sent to Cherry Point Air Base to go to school to become an aerial gunner. While waiting to be placed in a class, late one night, we were all rousted out of our sacks and put on a train for the West Coast. I wound up at MCAS [Marine Corps Air Station] at Mojave, California. My designation was general duty. After the dust settled I and three others were told we were the hydraulic crew under a staff sergeant who had the formal training in that work. After about six weeks at Mojave, the squadron [VMSB-236] was sent to Ewa where we went through about four months of intensive 'on the job' training. From there we went to Guadalcanal to relieve VMSB-234.

"From there we went to Munda Point on New Georgia. The ground crew was flown there in DC-3s with a fighter escort. That's when we knew we were in the thick of it. It was on Munda that VMSB-236 did most of its work in the counteroffensive, from the softening up of Bougainville prior to the invasion, to supporting the ground troops when they went ashore. It was a round-the-clock operation and kept everyone very busy. The way the SBDs held up was nothing short of phenomenal. They were extremely rugged and came from raids with half a rudder, wings full of holes, belly landing, because hydraulic lines were shot up and just about everything terrible you can think of—including wounded pilots and gunners.

"That's when the ground crew took over. Every plane was patched up, checked out from stem to stern, refueled, rearmed, and made ready for the next strike. It was not unusual for engine mechanics to be replacing parts, sheet-metal men repairing holes in the wings and fuselage, ordnance men rearming the .30- and .50-caliber guns, and hydraulic crews checking the brakes, struts, landing gear, and diving flaps all at the same time on the same plane. With this kind of dedication, it was not surprising that almost every plane was ready every day for every strike.

"While the planes were off on their raids, the ground crews did not just sit around waiting for them to return. There were plenty of other duties . . . digging latrines, driving trucks to resupply the mess tent, supervising local natives in spraying the camp area for mosquito control. Living conditions on Munda were not too bad, if you didn't mind the monthly migration of the land crabs. We had large open-sided tents that held six to eight men. Each man had a cot with a mosquito net. The nets were mandatory. A full night's sleep was almost nonexistent. Nightly bombing raids kept us running for the shelters. The camp had been set up in what used to be a jungle with many huge trees that had been shot up during the preinvasion barrages. Whenever a monsoonlike squall came up, the air raid warnings were sounded—not for enemy planes, but we had to clear the camp area to avoid falling trees, which flattened many tents. A special crew was created . . . [with] the job to cut down as many of the damaged trees as possible." Barrett would spend eighteen months "in the field" before rotation back to the States to attend advanced courses in aviation hydraulics and serve as an instructor.

When reconnaissance and intelligence detected a Japanese armada forming near Rabaul to disrupt the Bougainville beachhead, rather than the Marines supplying the opposition, the Navy brought up the carriers *Saratoga* and *Princeton*. The flattop aircraft inflicted sufficient damage to discourage a seagoing thrust at the leathernecks ashore at Cape Torokina. After November 8 the Japanese seemed to have written off any ambitions to expel the Americans from Bougainville. The aerial attacks petered out, although on November 13, VMF(N)-531—which had flown three hundred hours protecting ships and installations—scored a successful interception of an enemy plane. Amid scattered clouds and a full moon, Captain Duane Jenkins was vectored out to intercept an estimated six bombers menacing a naval task force off the Solomons. Emerging from a cloud bank, Jenkins saw the enemy formation some fifteen hundred feet beneath him. He descended slowly to creep behind the trailing plane. A burst from his .50s ignited a fire in an engine. The five others quickly retreated while Jenkins followed his victim in a shallow dive. His bullets ripped into the flaming bomber, which exploded as it crashed into the sea. Several weeks later Jenkins recorded another kill, but as he pursued a third airplane, the radar operators watched in horror as the blips marking his Vega and those of the enemy merged. Both then disappeared; it was presumed that he had collided with his target and plunged into the ocean, killing Jenkins and his crew.

The secured enclave on Bougainville, combined with successful landings on the opposite end of New Britain from Rabaul and advances in New Guinea, increasingly isolated Rabaul. It lost much of its effectiveness as a base from which to strike at the developing American installations throughout the Solomons. The Japanese believed that Allied strategy would involve seizure of the stronghold and as a consequence garrisoned the island of New Britain with nearly a hundred thousand men. Four airfields surrounding the port served more than 370 aircraft. MacArthur did not intend to overrun Rabaul and its staunchly defended bases. But in order to prevent Rabaul from hosting raids against naval operations aimed at the Gilbert and Marshall islands, the Marines and other Allied forces delivered constant blows to deflect any interference with the fleet.

THIRTEEN

LEFT BEHIND

Historian Robert Sherrod wrote that the Bougainville campaign marked the first sustained progress in the concept of close air support. Although the original mandate for Marine aviation had been to buttress the fleet landing forces, the Marine fliers had mainly devoted themselves to defending against Japanese air strikes or in offensive missions attacking enemy ships and installations not directly in contact with the ground troops. General Francis Mulcahy, the Marine veteran of World War I who also had commanded all Guadalcanal aircraft for a period and then those on New Georgia, remarked that despite the principle enunciated in 1933, during World War II Marine aviation was expected "to support naval operations. That was actually the first thing in practice and by necessity. We had no more control than the man in the moon of what our aviation was going to do in some circumstances. It was whatever the Naval Amphibious Force commander directed until the target was secure. It was his responsibility."

Nevertheless, cognizant of the usefulness of combined efforts by amphibious units and those in the air, the Marines began a program to develop air-liaison skills some three months before L-day, the invasion of Cape Torokina. Not the least of concerns was the fear of friendly fire. On Guadalcanal and New Georgia infantrymen frequently complained of being bombed or strafed by their own side. Three bomber pilots and six enlisted radio specialists, led by Lieutenant Colonel John Gabbert, studied the best ways to communicate support needs and to fulfill them. Training exercises coupled with battlefield experiences led to specifications on how close to the ground troops' front lines bombs in varying sizes could be used. These ranged from a closest-possible seventy-five yards for hundred-pounders to seven hundred yards for the heavyweight two-thousand-pound ordnance. In practice the separation yardage was usually increased about 25 or 30 percent.

Marine aviation had provided a form of close air support on November 1 during the invasion of Cape Torokina on Bougainville. During L-day, however, the airmen pounded enemy positions on the beaches ahead of the amphibious forces and then withdrew. A little more than a week later, the ground forces requested more strikes against the entrenched enemy positions. On this occasion there was a more coordinated effort. As the Third Marines prepared to attack Piva Village on November 10, ground troops marked their forward positions with colored smoke bombs. An air-liaison party with the troops maintained contact with the dozen bombers from VMTB-143 and 233. Each TBF bore twelve one-hundred-pound bombs, which were dropped within 120 yards of the front lines. The strike routed the enemy in the area, who fled, leaving behind some thirty to forty dead. Three days later two Navy squadrons were credited with having scored 95 percent hits in the target area, again driving off the defenders, but they operated without the use of ground-to-air controllers.

On December 13 the Marines began struggling against some three hundred well-dug-in Japanese at "Hellzapoppin' Ridge." From barely a few miles off at the newly completed Torokina airfield, a batch of bombers tried to help. One plane missed the target by six hundred yards, killing two and wounding six. This was the only such incident in the Bougainville campaign, but it and similar accidents stoked the Army's antagonism toward close air support, a duty habitually disdained by its Air Corps. The Marines involved in the Bougainville battles persisted with such operations. Two more attacks by a total of thirty-four Grumman Avengers did not dislodge the deeply entrenched enemy. VMTB-134 struck with time-delay-fused bombs that would explode after penetrating the earth a scant seventy-five yards beyond the leatherneck positions. As the TBFs followed up with dummy runs over the defenders, the foot soldiers advanced with grenades and bayonets to overrun Hellzapoppin' Ridge. In this instance, the executive officer of the Twenty-first Marine Regiment flew with Lieutenant Colonel William K. Pottinger in an SBD to spot enemy positions and direct the attack from the air.

Major General Ralph J. Mitchell, a 1915 Naval Academy graduate who became a pilot in 1921 and served as director of Marine aviation for the first fifteen months of World War II, took command of the First Marine Air Wing in April 1943. He received responsibility for the reduction of Rabaul once the Marines secured their foothold on portions of Bougainville. The construction of an airfield at Torokina paved the way for fighter sweeps calculated to obliterate their opposite numbers, rendering Rabaul defenseless against air attacks.

As the First Marine Air Wing girded up its wings for the assignment, Colonel Marion L. Dawson, a newly arrived staff officer, expected to experience firsthand what was involved. A 1927 graduate of the USNA, which he described as "a school for wayward boys," Dawson took his commission in the Marines. After duty as a foot soldier in Nicaragua, he won his wings in 1930. By the time of the Pearl Harbor debacle he had been involved in a stillborn program to develop a paratrooper and glider-borne Marine unit. "The Marines had no transport planes for them and the Navy wouldn't provide them either."

Dawson noted that shortly after his role began in the Pacific Theater, "We were going to have an extra big attack on Rabaul with bombers and fighters and I was going to lead the fighter echelon and find out what was going on. In the early stages down there we lost several senior pilots, although not as senior as I was. [Someone] issued a decree that no senior officers—lt. colonels or colonels—would do any combat flying, which in my opinion was a horrible mistake, because here we were trying to direct combat operations about which we knew nothing, we had no experience." Called in by a superior, he was told, "Dawson, if you take off on that flight, you will be court-martialed when you get back." Dawson stood down, to his regret.

Although he denied his upper echelons an opportunity to eye-witness the operations, to carry out the strategy General Mitchell brought four Marine fighter squadrons to Torokina. In addition, the Black Sheep and Greg Boyington, who with the others from VMF-214 had recently returned from a sojourn in Sydney, based on Vella Lavella would fly to Torokina. From there they would easily attack Rabaul. Mitchell designated Boyington to lead these sweeps. On December 17 a total of seventy-six Allied fighters gathered over the target. The Japanese showed only a modest inclination to meet this massive force.

Boyington, flying high cover and using a radio frequency available to the enemy on the ground, snarled, "Come on up and fight." From Rabaul, said Gamble, a former Japanese baseball player and native of Hawaii, Chikaki Honda, answered, "Come on down, Sucker."

The results of this sortie disappointed Mitchell and Boyington. Out of the handful of opponents, two aircraft were knocked down by a Navy Hellcat and a Marine Corsair. The latter victory belonged to 214's Lieutenant Bob McClurg, who broke from formation to destroy a meandering floatplane. When McClurg returned to his assigned place, Boyington shook his fist at him for breaking formation. According to Jack Bolt, however, Boyington did not practice what he preached. "He got most of his kills by attacking the enemy when they were taking off. Frequently, he was supposed to be weaving, in close cover of the bombers. They would sometimes identify the cover of the bombers as 'close cover,' 'medium cover' or 'high cover.' Generally, the close cover was supposed to be almost whipping right through the top of the bombers; the medium cover was supposed to be 3,000 to 4,000 feet higher and the high cover was supposed to be 6,000 or 7,000 feet above them. There was more freedom with high cover. Boyington took the high cover himself and wandered off and attacked the Japanese as they took off. It was a good tactic, and he got a lot of kills. But the rest of the 'peasants' were supposed to stay where we were put."

The two New Zealand squadrons, in their P-40s, at low altitude, claimed five enemy at a cost of three of their own. Postwar research indicated only two Japanese aircraft were destroyed, with one pilot rescued. Boyington contended that the superabundance of Allied aircraft effectively discouraged the Japanese from an engagement, thereby defeating the purpose of fighter sweeps. A week later, he led forty-eight to Rabaul, and on this occasion a significant number of the enemy grappled with them. That may have had less to do with the reduction in the sweep's complement than with a bomber attack shortly before. Japanese interceptors had risen to meet the bombers, and when Boyington and company arrived on the scene these fighters were still milling about.

In the hurly-burly that followed, the American fighter pilots abandoned the discipline of formation in favor of a pursuit of targets of opportunity. Boyington blew away a Zeke, whose pilot exited in a parachute. Boyington happened upon two more, one obviously staggering from previous wounds. He set it afire, and again the cockpit occupant bailed. When his companion tried to hover over the parachute as it neared the water, he became an easy prey and crashed into the water. Cruising the sky, Boyington spied a group of enemy fighters and exploited their poor rear vision as he jockeyed behind the rearmost plane and destroyed it.

Jack Bolt recalled, ". . . up over Rabaul, where we had lost our tactical integrity . . . I was by myself and picked up a Zero that had a phosphorus bomb on it; they used to try to 'throw' those bombs at the B-24s [the tactic was mostly unsuccessful]. They turned them loose, and the bombs went 1,000 or 2,000 feet and exploded. They were pretty spectacular when they went off. I saw two or three more used against the B-24s. None of them had any effect; they didn't bring down any planes. With this kill, I started chasing him, and I think he knew I was back there. I'm not sure, but he must have. He jettisoned his bomb, and then I got him."

Bob McClurg, Boyington's wingman for the day, had separated from him. He hounded a Zeke down toward the water until a burst from his guns splashed the victim. McClurg climbed rapidly and soon downed a second plane with a deflection shot. Others from VMF-214 also scored victories, which added up to twelve confirmed and two probables. Overall the Marines listed nineteen downed and five probables. Navy pilots were credited with four kills. The Japanese figures for casualties were considerably less and their own score an exaggerated eighteen American fighters plus four bombers. The final tally by the U.S. command showed three of the Black Sheep and one Navy flier missing.

Boyington with twenty-five victories was now only one behind the score of Joe Foss. His background and behavior had already attracted the media of the day, and the publicity about his feats obviously added to the pressure upon him. John De Chant, as the public relations officer for MAG-21, put together a script for cere- monies that would celebrate Boyington's ascension. The Marines set up a mobile radio trailer for a broadcast. The object of this at- tention continued to drink excessively and display a bellicosity that frightened some associates. Gamble cited an instance in which he challenged a subordinate to a wrestling match on a piece of the Marston matting near a shower. The lieutenant, aware that the pierced steel planking would lacerate the bare skin of anyone foolish enough to tussle on it, talked Boyington out of the idea.

On December 28 the increasingly testy Boyington took off with eleven other Black Sheep for another charge at the Rabaul-based air forces. Bruce Gamble flatly declared that "permission for [the] fighter sweep was sought in order to give Boyington another crack at the record." In this instance the all-Marine strike of forty- six Corsairs flew under the leadership of VMF-216's Major Rivers J. Morrell.

Major Frank Walton, the exec for VMF-214, later criticized Morrell's tactics for approaching the target in a fashion that al- lowed the enemy plenty of time to climb to altitude while another formation of Japanese fighters rose behind the American forma- tion. Morrell's mistake was apparently compounded by one divi- sion leader who tried to climb on a straight-ahead course that exposed them at reduced speed to the interceptors flashing down out of the sun.

Two of the four Americans, including the division leader, per- ished in a hail of cannon and machine-gun fire. The surviving pair destroyed two Zekes while their F4Us trembled from numerous hits, eventually forcing them to abandon the battle. Boyington's four-plane group also met a skilled and well-positioned foe. One of his division vanished during the dogfights, and he came away from the engagement empty.

After the First Marine Division crossed the beaches of Cape Gloucester at the western end of New Britain, opposite from Rabaul, it brought up artillery. Major General William H. Rupertus, the commander of the division, created the first leatherneck artillery spotting squadron. He acquired ten beat-up Piper Cubs from the Army, and his staff recruited men in the ground forces with enough flight experience to pilot the single-engine planes. The fliers, none of whom had wings or received flight pay, logged a thousand hours in reconnaissance, transport of specialists, and calling in fire on targets. The ersatz observation unit functioned for almost nine months before an official squadron assumed the duties.

As New Year's Day, 1944, dawned, the Commander Air, Solomons (ComAirSols), reported fighter sweeps had shot down 147 of the enemy in the past two weeks. Navy Hellcats and Marine Corsairs, complemented by New Zealanders, on January 1 knocked out another thirteen. Major Marion Carl, after about a year away from combat, had returned to the South Pacific as the CO of VMF-223. He had been scheduled to lead an attack on December 30 but agreed to give his post to Boyington, a slot that would offer the best opportunity to achieve the record. Poor weather, however, aborted the mission, and when Boyington sortied again on January 2, a massive oil leak eliminated his chance to grapple with the enemy.

On the morning of January 3, Boyington—in tactical command of a forty-six-fighter sweep, the majority of them from Marine units—left Torokina for still another whack at Rabaul and his personal goal. En route, four of the eight from VMF-214 dropped out because of mechanical failures. Some seventy Japanese fighters, alerted to the incoming traffic, rose to challenge the Americans.

With Captain George Ashmun as his wingman, Boyington attacked about a dozen Zekes, still climbing from their airfield. Several of his companions witnessed an enemy fighter erupt in flames from Boyington's guns. Almost immediately he and Ash-mun disappeared in a haze that hung over the area. The battle over Rabaul broke off fairly quickly, and the Americans straggled back to their Vella Lavella base. Over his radio, one member of VMF-214 heard a voice report he was going to ditch. Other than that, there was no sign of either Boyington or Ashmun.

At Vella Lavella the rest of the Black Sheep, other Marines, and a cluster of reporters awaited the return of Boyington. The news-men had gathered themselves around the revetment ordinarily used by Boyington. Frank Walton had De Chant's interview script ready for the radio hookup. Navy and Marine photographers stood by with their cameras. About five hours after the flight had left at 6:30 A.M., word came that Boyington had indeed tied Foss with his twentieth victory while in Marine uniform. (He had been credited with six from his Flying Tiger period.)

As time trudged on without any sign of the hero, the assembled crowd of celebrants realized that Boyington, as well as Ashmun, could no longer be airborne. In fact both men had been shot down, the wingman killed and the Black Sheep commander forced to bail out because of an inferno consuming his plane.

Some nineteen months later, Boyington surfaced in a Japanese prisoner-of-war camp. He then described, as reported by De Chant, what had happened to him. "Halfway up to Rabaul, my en-gine started spewing oil over the greenhouse [canopy]. I throttled back, leaned out and wiped it off with my handkerchief. When we got over Rabaul at 20,000 feet, the weather was good. Sixty to eighty Jap fighters were rising to meet us from their airfields below. When they reached about 12,000 feet, I told the boys to wait a second and get set. I took one quick look around and hollered, 'Let's get the bastards.'

"Ashmun and I picked out two Zekes flying at 15,000. He took one and I the other. I made an overhead run on mine. He was a dusty brown color, I closed to 400 yards and fired one short burst. That was pretty far out for me. I'd rather get in to about 100 yards. But the Zeke flamed and went down. It surprised me.

"As I pulled out of my run, Ashmun yelled: 'You got a flamer, Skipper!'

"George and I circled for a few seconds, then picked a large formation of Zeros and dove. We caught them at 12,000 feet, but before we could open fire, we were surrounded by Zekes. We scissored, crossing back and forth over one another. We cut across three times and in those few minutes, we both got flamers.

"Suddenly George stared nosing down, with smoke pouring out of his plane. I kept screaming, 'Dive, for God's sake, dive!' But he was hit, apparently, because his plane kept gliding down at the same 45 degree angle.

"It was the old story of the Nips piling in on the guy who can't fight back. About ten of them ganged up on him in a sort of 'Banzai' charge. I got behind that procession and kept kicking the rudder back and forth, firing short bursts into the mob. Ashmun's Corsair burst into flames with smoke pouring out of his wing and fuselage. Then one of the Nips in front of me went down in flames.

"All the way down while I was trying to chase them off Ashmun's tail, the rat race was complete with a flock of Zekes riding right behind me. When George's plane smashed into the water, I leveled out low and gave it full throttle.

"I went about half a mile wide open when my main gas tank burst into flames. Right then I didn't have a Chinaman's chance. I flipped over on what I hoped was my back. The fuselage burned like an inferno. It was like looking into an open blast door. I grabbed my safety belt in one hand and the rip cord ring in the other. If I'd had a third hand, I would have grabbed the hood. About two or three hundred feet over the water, I kicked the stick forward and catapulted out.

"Thank God, the chute worked. I felt one tug and then slammed into the water without even time to swing once. I hit on my side, so hard that the impact crushed the canteen on my belt and even one in my back pack.

"I spent the next 15 or 20 minutes duck-diving while four Zekes expended their ammunition strafing me. One would make a pass and pull out while another came in, firing, from the other direction. Their 20 mm stuff was kicking up all around me. I finally got so tired, as they closed in, that all I could do was lay my head on the water . . . and hope. Finally the Zekes gave me up for dead and went back to Rabaul.

"After treading water for two hours to make sure they didn't sneak back, I reached down for the raft dangling between my legs. It wasn't hit, so I popped it and crawled aboard to examine the damage.

"My scalp was dangling down over my eyes. My left ear was about chewed off. My throat was cut open and the left ankle torn up. My hands were full of shrapnel holes and my left leg hurt badly. It must have hit the stabilizer when I bailed out. Generally, I was pretty much of a mess.

"I had hope all the time that Dumbo [an air–sea rescue plane] would pick me up. . . . Just at dusk when I felt very safe, a submarine broke surface right alongside of my raft. I thought it was one of ours until I saw the tarpaulin on the conning tower with the big red meatball on it. Then the little yellow men with funny hats climbed out through the hatch. I remember thinking, 'Oh, oh, Boyington, here we go!' "

For his exploits, on April 12, 1944, Boyington, in captivity, was awarded the Medal of Honor. After his liberation he received credit for the last two shoot-downs he described in his statement. That placed him at the top of the list of Marine aces with twenty-eight victories, including the six he claimed from his days with the AVG. Bruce Gamble, in his authoritative history of VMF-214, refused to accept the statistics of the Marine Corps, dismissing three from the AVG records as having been planes on the ground and calling the final two described by Boyington as unsubstantiated.

The personality of Boyington and his legend that he created the Black Sheep out of a motley of green pilots, which the publicity-conscious Marine Corps exploited, drew the attention of the media. VMF-215, the prosaically named Fighting Corsairs, actually inflicted more damage upon the Japanese during the northern Solomons campaign. First Lieutenant Robert M. Hanson, born in India, shot down twenty enemy aircraft over a seventeen-day period.

De Chant reported that "Butcher Bob," as he was known to his mates, had already become an ace in his previous two tours. On January 14 he had escorted a bomber mission directed at Rabaul's Simpson Harbor when seventy Japanese fighters attempted to interfere. Hanson knocked down five of them. During his next five sorties to Rabaul, he destroyed one Zero, three Zeros, four Zeros, three Zeros, and finally four more. His record stood at twenty-five, and he was on the threshold of surpassing Foss when, during a strafing run at Cape St. George, he died at age twenty-three as his F4U crashed. On August 1 he was named a posthumous Medal of Honor recipient, the last of this decoration to be issued to a Marine pilot during World War II.

Two of Hanson's associates with the Fighting Corsairs, captains Donald N. Aldrich and Harold Spears, also preyed upon the Japanese opposition over Rabaul. Aldrich completed his tour with twenty downed, and Spears had fifteen. The squadron, in large part due to the achievements of this triumvirate, became the first to receive the Navy Unit Commendation.

Upon the loss of Boyington, Captain Henry Miller, a Harvard Law School graduate and former practicing attorney, became the acting commander of VMF-214 for the remaining few days of the tour. On January 4, the day after Boyington disappeared, Miller—along with Captain Moon Mullen, a Notre Dame graduate with a degree in English and holder of a Purple Heart from his earlier tour with VMF-122—had fruitlessly scoured the waters near New Ireland and New Britain in search of Boyington and Ashmun.

After they returned, Miller and Mullen led two divisions against whatever Rabaul might offer. Jack Bolt added one more enemy fighter, giving him six. Denny Groover, hors de combat in the midst of the squadron's first tour, had recovered to splash one and leave another smoking. On January 6 the Black Sheep flew its final fighter sweep over Rabaul and Lieutenant Harry Johnson alone brought down an adversary. The two-tour record for VMF-214 listed ninety-four of the enemy destroyed in combat with another thirty-two as probables and twenty-one smashed on the ground. They sank four small ships and twenty-three barges, strafing 125 ground positions. For their more than two hundred missions, the Black Sheep counted a dozen pilots missing in action and half that number wounded.

As VMF-214 readied itself for leave, Miller entered a complaint in the squadron war diary. Of the sixty Americans airborne for the January 4 attack, he noted in his diatribe, only about half actually arrived over the target. The comment quoted by Bruce Gamble read: "About 50 percent of the formation returned to base because of various mechanical difficulties, fancied or real. It seems to be becoming increasingly difficult to get fighter planes to fight. It's a matter that would bear some examination. It's one thing to insist on your plane being in proper fighting condition to fight—but quite another when fighter pilots dream up a series of fancied motor troubles and return to base before the strike gets started. Others don't even dream up a mechanical difficulty—just start calling, 'Let's go home' as soon as the formation enters the St. George Channel. VMF-214 pilots are anxious for the opportunity to go on these strikes. They even cut cards to see who gets to go. It seems that some of the other squadrons could use a little more aggressive approach."

Whatever failings Greg Boyington may have had as a truth-teller, he obviously knew how to get his people to fight. However, following the customary recharging of human batteries in Australia, the veterans of VMF-214 received transfers to VMF-211. When pilots like Jack Bolt returned to the combat area two months later, they found few enemy aircraft to fight. Instead they engaged in a series of strafing missions. Bolt remarked, "We were fanatics at shooting trucks." In place of the original Black Sheep, VMF-214 welcomed a fresh contingent of newly trained pilots and a few veterans of other squadrons. The sole atavism from the era of Greg Boyington was Major Stan Bailey, who assumed command.

The absence of VMF-214 hardly brought a decline in the punishment meted out to Rabaul. Throughout the remainder of January and the first three weeks of February, thousands of sorties by Allied aircraft hammered at the Japanese installations. The raids culminated on February 19 when, in a final gasp, fifty Zeros met a massive sweep. The defenders lost twenty-four planes while the attackers counted only one casualty.

A fortnight earlier, on February 4, a pair of Marine PBY4s (B-24 Liberators) from VMD-254 executed a photo reconnaissance of the massive Japanese naval base at Truk in the Caroline Islands. The planes, piloted by Major James R. Christensen and Captain James Q. Yawn, with ten-man crews, took off at night from a new airstrip on Stirling Island for a thousand-mile journey to the northwest. In the morning hours they arrived over Truk at twenty thousand feet. Against limited opposition from several fighters and AA from a battleship, their cameras recorded the warships and transports in the harbor, along with the aircraft packed onto the fields awaiting pilots to ferry them to Rabaul.

Armed with this intelligence, Admiral Marc Mitscher directed Task Force Fifty-eight, the Fast Carrier Force, with a total of twelve full-sized carriers and six light flattops, to strike Truk. The target was too distant for any of the land-based Marine squadrons to participate. One unhappy witness, however, was Greg Boyington.

He later recounted, "On February 17, they took six of us to Truk in a transport plane on our way to Japan. We landed at Truk right in the middle of our first naval carrier strike. They shoved us into a concrete slit trench at the end of the field just as a Hellcat fighter roared over and blew up our DC-2.

"Our slit trench was at the foot of a hill, just 50 feet short of the aiming point for a target nearby, where several dozen Jap planes were parked. Those Navy torpedo planes kept coming in over the hill and dropping their bombs as they passed over us. One 1,000-pounder exploded about 15 feet away and shot the trench apart, but didn't hurt any of us. Things were so beat up at Truk by that raid that they couldn't get a plane in there for ten days to take us out."

The devastation wrought by TF-58 included 325 aircraft either demolished or damaged, and doomed any further attempts to reinforce the airpower at Rabaul. However, that did not mean the American positions on Bougainville were no longer in harm's way. Pilot Richard Mulberry, the Kentuckian who flew a dive-bomber for VMSB-243 and had flown out of Palmyra on antisubmarine patrols, had begun combat flying at Munda.

From that New Georgia field Mulberry had attacked a number of targets before March 17, 1944, when the squadron followed the landings on Cape Torokina, Bougainville, to the base constructed on that island at Piva. "This tour," said Mulberry, "had two objectives: air strikes against the Jap complex of airfields at Rabaul, approximately 210 air miles from Cape Torokina, and to support the perimeter defenses as necessary.

"The Japs had moved troops and artillery from Buka-Bona, at the northwest tip and Kahili at the southeast tip of Bougainville, to apply pressure on the airfields. They were periodically shelling the strips, as well as launching harassing raids on the perimeter twenty-four hours a day. Our first night there was interrupted by artillery bursts, both near and far, as well as sporadic firefights accompanied by the shouting of friend and foe alike. About 2:00 A.M. Washing Machine Charlie flew over and dropped a bomb close to the pilots' camp, which contributed to a restless night."

There were roughly forty thousand Japanese soldiers on the island, and General Harukichi Hyakutake, an alumnus of the battle for Guadalcanal, concentrated his forces upon the American perimeter, with the ultimate goal of capturing the main airstrip on the Cape Torokina beach and two adjoining ones, Piva Uncle for bombers and Piva Yoke for fighters. Marine Air Group Twenty-four, when not engaged in aviation, organized itself into infantry-type battalions to add its strength to defense of the air bases. It was supplemented by an Army heavy-weapons company.

To reach a position from which the artillery could strike at the American positions, the Japanese had organized two-man work crews to laboriously haul each hundred-pound shell through the jungle to the gun pits. On March 8 the first of hundreds of shells began exploding along the Torokina perimeter, also striking the airfields. They blew up three fighters and a B-24 while damaging nineteen other aircraft. There were also personnel casualties.

Over the succeeding ten days artillery continued to pound the Americans, and the Japanese jumped off in a series of infantry charges. The local strike command, using Army P-39s and Marine

F4Us, strafed and bombed the enemy lines. The preoccupation with holding the Cape Torokina turf denied fighter cover for some bombing missions bound for Rabaul. The action became so intense that the South Pacific Air Command directed evacuation of all airplanes overnight to nearby bases. During the morning they would return to Bougainville with a load of bombs and bullets to douse the enemy lines before landing. A concentrated effort on March 10 squelched the opposition sufficiently for an entry in the Solomons Strike Command war diary, "where Pistol Pete [a single-engine night raider] has brought in all his relatives in the past two or three days no shells fell."

Two days later fury rained down upon the Piva strips, chewing up the Marston matting and doing considerable other damage. But the work of the SBDs and TBFs with bombs and machine guns, and—equally importantly—spotting for artillery and offshore destroyers with five-inch guns, silenced many of the enemy artillery pieces. The infantry repulsed a banzai charge, while Lieutenant Colonel Frank Schwable, the night fighter specialist, temporarily installed as strike commander, kept a portion of the air fleet home from missions against Rabaul in favor of perimeter defense.

Richard Mulberry flew in a thirty-six-plane strike at Rabaul the morning after he arrived at Piva. "It was our first encounter with well-established antiaircraft fire on a large scale. We were on stand-by the next day. Stand-by meant many things, which did not include a lazy day in the ready room. I drew the predawn artillery spotting job. That was an attempt to spot Jap artillery gun flashes when they shelled the strip.

"My day started around 4:00 A.M. with hot coffee and a lukewarm 'something' for breakfast, followed by a briefing at Strike Command on the mission. Sergeant Munn, my radio-gunner for the past year, and I met at the plane after a blacked-out jeep ride, during which time the Japs started shelling the far end of the strip. We crouched for cover until the shelling stopped, and then pulled an abbreviated inspection of the plane in the dark. That is when one must have full confidence in the plane crews!

"After crank-up, the tower gave us taxi instructions, and we were guided to the end of the runway by a blacked-out jeep and a hooded flashlight. I reported in position and was told to wait, as the other end of the runway was under fire. During the taxi period, I was aware that planes, probably fighters, were taking off . . . by this time there was a definite pre-dawn appearance to the sky. I remember thinking that if we didn't get up soon, the mission stood a 90 percent chance of failure.

"Luckily, the tower told me to prepare for takeoff, and I pulled into the center of the runway, applied full brakes, checked the 'mags' and was ready to go. Just at that moment, a Jap shell hit an ammunition dump not far from the other end of the runway, and the place lit up like a fourth of July celebration, which I could not hear [because of] my engine noise. The tower told me to hold. After a few minutes the explosions had not stopped. The runway was closed and dawn was upon us. I was instructed to return to the plane revetment area."

Mulberry parked his dive-bomber, attended a debriefing, and then returned to his tent to find the bivouac area deserted with all of the Marines at the runway edge, some fifty yards from the encampment. "I joined them to discover that our defensive positions were a series of recently scooped-out slit trenches parallel to the strip. We were armed with .45 automatics or .38 revolvers. Mine was a .38. Throughout the day we heard firefights in several locations.

"That night, March 19, 1944, the Japs broke through the perimeter across the runway from our camp, and we immediately assumed our defensive positions. This was my first clear view of a night firefight. Tracers flew everywhere! Small arms and heavy weapons firing sounds were rolling like thunder, punctuated with occasional cannon or howitzer firing; all accompanied by shouting and yelling. I remember thinking that my .38 was little firepower if they started across the runway. Luckily, there was enough moon for the coral strip to be bright enough to provide contrast. We could make out the trees on the far side. At one point I thought my world had ended. A mobile Bofors 20-millimeter gun opened fire about twenty yards behind our positions. It was an antiaircraft weapon, depressed to fire over our heads and into an area outside the break in the perimeter. Finally the firing slacked and ceased. We were told the next day that the Japs had penetrated as far as the SeaBee camp across the runway from us. There was not much sleep.

"The next morning, we were awakened by firing within our camp area and calls to take cover. . . . The firing was an infantry squad spraying the trees in the pilots' camp area, following an infiltrated Jap sniper, who shot Major John Flickinger of VMSB-236 in the neck when he stepped outside his tent just after dawn to relieve himself. Luckily it was just a flesh wound. The Jap sniper was killed before he did any more damage."

During the succeeding days, Mulberry sortied on short missions, acting as a spotter or bombing and strafing the Japanese who threatened the turf occupied by the Americans. Not until the end of the month did he undertake a trip to Rabaul. Although the antisubmarine patrols often lasted longer, the three and a half hours to the target area and return wearied Mulberry. After the fighters suppressed AA with strafing runs, he said, "We went to about 12,000 feet, peeled off and started our dives from about 10,000 feet. The supply dumps were fairly easy to find and pretty easy to hit because they were so extensive. We'd see revetments, but no airplanes in them. Whether they wheeled those airplanes back into the jungle or if they had any at all I don't know, but it [his first strike at Rabaul] was very successful. We did a lot of damage. The rear-seat gunners had a lot of fun, too, strafing after the dive.

"There was a lot of ground fire and small arms fire. I think they used a .30 caliber gun . . . it may have been a little smaller but we got a lot of holes in airplanes from that small-caliber rifle fire from the ground. It's amazing that we didn't get more damage or lose more airplanes."

The attackers were vulnerable to the weapons of Japanese infantry because, Mulberry explained, the aircraft flew at treetop level as they came out over the water. The actual raid lasted from three to five minutes.

Although the ground-to-air coordination for tactical support debuted on Bougainville, and official histories describe the program as a great success, Mulberry, who flew a number of missions aimed at aiding the American foot soldiers, reported, "We had very little communication with the Marines on the ground. . . . We would get a briefing where our Marines were. The Marines on the ground would try to mark their positions so that we wouldn't be strafing or dropping anything on them. There were panels that they would put out on the ground. [The panels] were made of cloth in frames. They would arrange them so they would point toward the enemy lines." Mulberry also noted that communications air to air were "abominable." Radios malfunctioned, breaking off contact with other aircraft during strikes or even with the flight leader.

Bill Nickerson, who had flown an SBD during the campaigns against New Georgia and the Russells, and dropped smoke bombs to help guide the invasion forces to the Bougainville beaches, had been transferred from the dive-bomber squadron to fighters, to his great satisfaction. After undergoing a short familiarization course in the F4U Corsair, he was assigned to VMF-212, Joe Bauer's old squadron. Nickerson returned to Bougainville with the unit.

In his absence, Nickerson said the Japanese had slowly mobilized a concentration of men and gear atop a ridge that overlooked the American positions. "Our defensive perimeter wasn't far from the airfield. The jungle was so dense that it wasn't a continuous perimeter. Fiji Islander scouts were employed to keep track of any Japanese activity. Those tall, dignified men with their high topped hairdos were the best scouts any armed force could ask for.

"They'd been out on patrol and discovered that the enemy had taken up threatening positions. There was practically no flat land up there, but nevertheless they [the Japanese] had set up their artillery on our side of the ridge, well within range to fire down on us. Making their way through the jungle, the Fiji scouts had found them the hard way, from directly beneath the guns. They'd gone up a ravine and were caught in the middle of the field of fire, preventing them from escaping back down the ravine.

"The scouts had a carrier-pack radio. These were bulky and

heavy, and they didn't always work well. However, they were in line of sight to the airfield, so they could contact our base. They called in and described their problem.

"A rescue mission was mounted. Someone chose me to fly an SBD dive bomber and take out the enemy artillery so the scouts could get out. I talked to them by radio and got what descriptions I could to pinpoint where they were, but this left a lot to be desired. They were on the ground under a canopy of jungle, and I'd be in the air looking down on relatively featureless green. In addition, they had no signaling devices to show exactly where they were, because they traveled very lightly. There was also the language barrier.

"First, I put a couple of 100-pound bombs on an SBD. I planned to drop these small bombs where I thought they were, without killing them, so they could respond and pinpoint their position. That worked all right. Most of the Japs were uphill of them, but there were a few who'd worked their way down below them and were closing in on them. Their ammunition was almost gone, again because they traveled so light. They told me where to put bigger bombs in relation to where I'd dropped the 100 pounders. I loaded three 500-pound bombs and dropped them in a line parallel to the ridge where they said they needed them. I didn't want to drop 1,000-pound bombs because the drops were very close to where they were, and they might be killed by the concussion.

"Then they asked for more bombs a little closer. I loaded up three more 500-pounders and took off again. I could now see exactly where the other bombs had exploded so I was able to judge the position better. The Japs were getting a lot of target practice on me, but I was diving steep and low and pulling up as fast as that old plane would go.

"By then I could see how the scouts were situated in the ravine cutting down the side of the mountain ridge and I thought that my last drop had cleared the way for them. I landed back at the airfield and immediately learned that the scouts were still in trouble. This time I loaded two 500-pounders and a 1,000-pounder (more load than an SBD normally carried) and climbed up to eight or nine thousand feet in order to make as vertical a dive as I could. I put the thousand pounder just at the upper end of the line I'd made with the earlier bombings, and the two 500-pounders just at the other end of the line. After that we didn't hear from the scouts for three days. The concussion from the thousand pounder, we later learned, had shattered the short wave radio tubes, but hadn't hurt those scouts.

"They came walking into the airfield carrying the radio and a string of ears, traditional trophies harvested from their enemies' heads. They wanted to meet the guy who flew the airplane, so I walked over to the scouts' tents. All five of them hugged me and patted me and shook my hand. Grinning widely, they said, 'Boom! Boom! Big boom! Big boom TOO big!' Then one of them handed me a large folded bundle of rough cloth with black and red marks on it. They all bowed as he gave it to me."

Later, Nickerson showed the gift to VMF-212's engineering officer, Captain Walt Johnson. He explained to the pilot that this large tapa cloth appeared to be one used by a chief to wrap himself in during ceremonies. Their tribe had given them the cloth to advise the gods of their bravery and goodness and confer protection. By handing it over to Nickerson, the Fiji scouts had donated the safety and protection granted to them by their gods.

FOURTEEN

THE GILBERTS AND THE MARSHALLS

At the Quebec Conference in August 1943, Allied leaders, including Roosevelt and Churchill, along with their top military commanders agreed upon the strategies in the various theaters for the coming year. In the Central Pacific, the route toward Japan specified the Gilbert, Marshall, and Mariana islands. Douglas MacArthur, who received considerable credit after the war for an island-hopping strategy, had in fact demurred, issuing a public statement that read, "My strategic concept for the Pacific contemplates massive strikes against only the main strategic objectives, utilizing surprise air and ground striking power, supported and assisted by the fleet. . . . Island hopping . . . is not my idea of how to end the war as soon and as cheaply as possible."

At this point in the war, the distances and logistics involved in carrying out the rather vague parameters of MacArthur's idea were beyond the resources available. He apparently feared that his zone in the Southwest Pacific would be pinched off with the seizure of New Guinea. He was reassured by word that, along with a drive into the Central Pacific under Admiral Chester Nimitz, he would command an advance from New Guinea through the East Indies into the Philippines. There was a line drawn down the middle of New Britain. To the west side of this line lay the area ceded to MacArthur. On the other side sat Rabaul and the rest of the responsibilities of the Navy and Marines.

To maintain a secure lifeline for those engaged in the operations against the enemy earlier in the Solomons and then as attention turned toward the Gilbert Islands, fourteen hundred miles away, the United States had established bases in the Samoans. In April 1942 the first Marine squadrons arrived at Tafuna, on Pago Pago. Subsequently detachments set up shop at other Samoan outposts, and units from the Air Corps shared the fields. For the Marines, duty here was almost entirely devoted to training and patrols in the event of a Japanese strike at the right flank of Guadalcanal. Small raids by Japanese bombers, perhaps once a month, kept the residents aware they were in a war. The only offensive endeavors involved the Army airmen whose B-24s, starting late in April 1943, called upon Betio Island, half of the Tarawa Atoll 704 miles from the Samoan strip at Funafuti. That was the overture to what would become a full-scale assault upon Tarawa as part of the Gilberts campaign.

When the amphibious force of the Second Marine Division struck at Tarawa on November 20, there were no Marine fliers to support them. The preinvasion preparation depended upon Army bombers and carrier-based Navy planes. The latter also provided the close support for the fiercely contested atoll. That held true for the invasion of nearby Makin Island by the Army's Twenty-seventh Infantry Division. After the islands had been secured, Lieutenant General Holland M. Smith, the commander of the Marine ground forces, dismayed by the stiff resistance of the enemy and the possibility that better close support from the air might have helped, suggested a Marine aircraft wing be specifically assigned for this duty in future landings. His recommendation failed to change the minds of those in charge of deployments on aircraft carriers.

After construction crews rebuilt airstrips on Tarawa, Makin, and Abemana, a Marine dive-bomber outfit, VMSB-331, put in a brief appearance but played no significant role in operations. As Americans seized other dots that made up the Gilberts, more Marine squadrons were housed there, but they served largely to defend against nuisance attacks. Weather and pilot inexperience wrought an operational disaster for VMF-422. Briefly ensconced on Tarawa, the squadron left on orders to report to Funafuti in the Samoans. En route, the twenty-three brand-new Corsairs, traveling without an escort plane acting as navigator, ran into a series of squalls. Several pilots separated from the main group; the remainder blundered through the tropical storms until the leader of fifteen of the F4Us decided they should all ditch together. Most of them endured two days drifting in their rubber dinghies. Six pilots were lost, along with twenty-two aircraft.

When the invasion forces advanced to the next chain of islands, the Marshalls, the Marine airmen again sat on the sidelines while others covered the responsibilities for softening up major targets and then aiding the troops going ashore. There were two exceptions. First was the Green Islands, flyspecks between Bougainville and New Ireland. New Zealand infantry stormed ashore February 15, 1944, shielded against aerial strikes by VMF-212. The defense was minimal, and the Corsairs shot down six enemy planes. Phil DeLong accounted for half of them.

On Bougainville, VMF(N)-531, led by Colonel Frank Schwable, endured some frustrating nights awaiting an opportunity to demonstrate their prowess. On February 16, the controller at Torokina vectored Major John Harshberger, the squadron exec, in a PV-1 toward bogeys over Empress Augusta Bay. Harshberger picked up the night raiders on his own scope and quickly obtained a visual sighting of a pair of Betty bombers. Both of the enemy spotted the hunter and spewed twenty-millimeter shells from their tail guns. They silenced five of Harshberger's six nose guns and punched a big hole in the nose of his aircraft. Harshberger doggedly pecked away at one Betty with his only remaining nose gun while his turret gunner fired bursts at the other, which broke off and fled. Harshberger and his gunner concentrated upon the one within range, and soon it spiraled down in flames. Harshberger barely escaped destruction when he sought to land without having made radio contact. Searchlights on the field probed for him, and AA greeted his return. However, he was recognized and the ground fire ceased.

Several nights later Schwable and Lieutenant Jack M. Plunkett, guided by the fighter-director radar, shot down a snooper. On his second victory Schwable flew so close to the victim, a reconnaissance floatplane known as a Jake, that oil from the fatally wounded aircraft splattered the Marine's windshield. The turret gunner, Sergeant William Fletcher, remarked that he felt he came near enough to have hit the enemy pilot with his gun butt. On another sortie, Harshberger returned with debris from the enemy aircraft snagged in his own engine cowling.

A month later, the Fourth Marine Regiment (Reinforced) landed unopposed on Emirau Island, only seventy-five miles from the enemy base at Kavieng, a subsidiary of Rabaul on New Ireland. Here the First Marine Air Wing provided protection. Both sites became operational bases for punishment of Rabaul. Marine fliers also ensured that the Japanese still on Bougainville did not dent the perimeter that protected the airfields used by the Marines.

Once the garrisons on the Marshalls succumbed, Marine air units could step farther into the Pacific, deploying to Roi, Kwajalein, and Eniwetok. From there they could strike at the fringes of the Carolines. In an escort mission against Ponape, Major Loren D. Everton, a veteran of the early going at Guadalcanal, added three more Zekes to bring his South Pacific total to twelve. Engagements of this intensity, however, were few. The Marine aviation continued to grind down bypassed Japanese forces on isolated atolls.

For fighter pilots, the absence of aerial combat generated frustration. Joe Foss had returned to combat in February 1944 as commander of VMF-115 after a bond-selling excursion in the States. Foss participated in the effort to fumigate the bugs that plagued the Corsair. In particular, he had complained about the engine quitting above twenty-three thousand feet during aerial gunnery. "When I had nine engine failures," recalled Foss, "I went to see General [Charles] Fike who said, 'I'll send you up an expert.'" Foss continued, "There was a knock on the door. A man walked in with no insignia. He said, 'I'm Charles A. Lindbergh.'" The Lone Eagle had become a troubleshooter for military aviation and traveled to the Pacific to help cure mechanical problems. Foss remembered that in 1927, as a boy in Sioux Falls, he had tried to shake Lindbergh's hand during his cross-country tour, but someone had chased him off the platform. What Lindbergh contributed to the solution is unknown, but the performance of Corsair engines did improve. Later Lindbergh also brought his expertise to problems with the Air Corps's P-38.

When Foss returned to the wars in the cockpit of a Corsair, he never had an opportunity to shoot down another enemy plane. "There was no aerial combat; it was all ground support, dive bombing, strafing, chasing trucks at night. That's a wild escapade, to try to follow a truck with those little peeper lights on mountainous country. Then when you fire, a slight flash in the cockpit from guns blinds you for a moment."

Corsairs, like the Navy's F4F-6 Hellcats, had been fitted with bomb racks, and on March 18 eight F4Us from VMF-111 dumped thousand-pounders on AA installations on Mille in the Marshalls. Additional experiments demonstrated the ability of the Corsair as a dive-bomber that could add devastating power by triggering its six .50-caliber guns during the dive. Major William E. Classen, the squadron honcho, said, "This type of bombing is an art, not a science, it's like playing a violin. In the last analysis, you can't tell a man how to do it. He's got to experiment until he works out his own individual technique."

The accepted approach for dive-bombing in an F4U instructed neophytes to keep the entire target in view, just above the engine cowling. At the moment the target disappeared under the cowling, they were to release the bomb and then either flee or fly right through the target.

The night fighter capacity of the Marines also proved itself. F4Us from VMF(N)-532 knocked down a pair of nocturnal enemy interlopers and scored a probable third.

Runs at vehicles on the ground such as Foss described offered a dash of excitement, but the almost daily parade of planes to Rabaul became routine. Still, there was always a risk in any mission. Upon return to base, Richard Mulberry described the atmosphere as one of elation and relief, particularly if they had not lost any airplanes. A former pediatrician serving as flight surgeon dispensed small bottles of brandy. Mulberry recalled the procedure if an airman was missing or confirmed shot down. The squadron commander would appoint a fellow officer to inventory and gather up all of the casualty's personal gear. "He'd box it up and be ready to ship it back to his family. I had the occasion to do that one time . . . it was a traumatic experience. The guy I did that for was an NAP [naval aviation pilot] by the name of John Schreibak [shot down over Rabaul]. We were good friends. He was just a great guy. He had been in the Marine Corps much longer than I. I boxed it [Schreibak's belongings] just the way I found it. I often wondered later why we didn't at least launder his flight suit and his uniforms. Of course the commanding officer was the one who wrote to his family. They didn't leave that to first lieutenants."

The bulk of those in uniform during World War II were young men. When they were not occupied by humdrum military duties or engaged in a desperate struggle to survive, their natural attraction for the opposite sex emerged. The life-and-death atmosphere, the separations with no time limits, the glamour attached to service—particularly aviation—fostered liaisons. In the South Pacific, the Marines, except for a few service units late in the war, were white. A frequent lament of those in the islands counted the number of months that passed "without sight of a white woman." Not surprisingly, some on leave plunged into the fleshpots of Australia or Hawaii (where prostitution was allowed for most of the war by the provost marshal of Honolulu). Others, like rear gunner Charles Conter, entered into temporary overseas romantic relationships.

Shortly before he shipped out to the Pacific, Bruce Porter said, "I did what many thousands of young men have done since war was invented. I became involved in a whirlwind romance that resulted in a wedding I only dimly desired. The girl was wealthy, sophisticated, smart and fun to be with. She dazzled me and I dazzled her; we swept one another off our feet. It was great fun to be together. And it was great fun when the time came to dress up in my white formal dress uniform and leave the church beneath the crossed swords of my fellow pilots."

When he returned home after twenty months overseas, he was taken aback after his wife informed him that she had not been faithful and said, "I was not, after all, the man for her. She was fond of me, but she was definitely not in love with me. . . . I was a man of my time. I had had no qualms about shacking up with Samoan lovelies and neither had I held back an ounce of desire during my madcap leave in Sydney. In my heart, I knew that she was right. I had had an inkling during my many months overseas that she had fallen for the dashing aviator in his dashing uniform, and that I had fallen for her considerable charms and sophistication."

While still in flight school, Richard Mulberry had fallen in love with Jane Denny, a Kentuckian like himself. At the time he embarked for service in the South Pacific, Mulberry said, "I was so much in love with Jane and had so much confidence in her that, when I got orders overseas . . . I had a part of my pay sent directly to her. Every penny of that went into a savings account. By the time I got back, there was about $10,000 in that savings account. She opened the account for me, and she was a signatory on the account. She could have spent the whole thing."

Beyond serving as his banker, Jane Denny, to whom he sent letters almost daily, bolstered his morale. "One of the most favorite sights . . . was seeing that R4D come in with supplies and mail, which would be about weekly. She wrote quite frequently . . . and I'd get four, five or six letters at one time, which I really coveted." During World War II the stories of Conter, Porter, and Mulberry, with infinite variations, were replicated ten-thousand-fold.

For the Japanese penned up in Rabaul, letters to and from home must have been as rare as a day free of depredation from the air. According to Sherrod, morale did not waver until very late in the war. Ample stocks of food, soap, toothpaste satisfied mundane needs, and five to six hundred Korean and Japanese women, imported early in the war, served as prostitutes. However, long after the ground war bypassed New Britain—in fact, until V-J Day—Allied fliers and occasionally warships blasted the harbor and installations of the city. High-flying heavy and medium bombers from the Army Air Corps, Navy planes from carriers, and Marines who began operating from the Green Islands and Emirau all piled ordnance upon the residents, their storehouses, and their emplacements. Of the nearly hundred thousand on the island, some ten thousand perished.

By mid-1944 Rabaul had become a Marine responsibility, largely by default. As the war shifted west and northwest, ever farther across the Pacific, there were few places the Marines could attack. The Army's bombers all had much greater range than the standard single-engine fighters and dive- and torpedo bombers of the Marines. Aircraft carriers, bearing the Navy's equivalents, brought their aircraft well beyond the range limits of land-based operations.

Many of the Marine pilots, particularly those schooled before or early during the war, had carrier-qualified, but no Marine squadrons were assigned to carrier duty. Marion L. Dawson, as a senior officer in Marine aviation and who was privy to the thinking behind the decisions, explained, "The Marines, ever since we were on the *Saratoga* and *Lexington* in the early 30s, had been fighting to get some sort of agreement with the Navy to have a certain number of Marine squadrons permanently based aboard the carriers to support Marine landing garrisons and the Navy never would agree to it. They had agreed in principle and said, 'When we have a spare carrier, we'll see what we can do about it.'

"[Actually] they would not agree to assigning a carrier to Marine squadrons or even a portion of a carrier to Marine squadrons, with the idea that Marine squadrons were going to support the amphibious forces that were going to land on some distant shore and take up housekeeping, because, as the Navy pointed out—and I couldn't help but agree with them—if all the Marine squadrons went ashore, what was the carrier going to do for planes? They didn't come right out and say it officially, but they made no bones about it unofficially. This doesn't work for us. They'd have to bring airplanes out to resupply the carrier and the pilots coming out would . . . take several weeks to get organized and it was right in the midst of war."

With the capture of several of the Gilbert Islands, Marine squadrons advanced to bases such as that on Majuro. Among the units there was VMSB-231, the Ace of Spades and the oldest squadron in Marine aviation, having been activated in 1919. VMSB-231 had been at Midway and then Guadalcanal. One of the virgins to combat was Princeton undergraduate Tom Hartmann. He sprang from a socially conscious mother, an immigrant from Scotland who took over the family hardware supply business after his father died in 1932 when Hartmann was ten.

"[My mother] was a superpatriot (American) but she believed that we should go to war against Germany whenever the UK was under threat. We talked about it often. We also talked about Hitler from 1932 on. Japan was seldom mentioned until Pearl Harbor. . . . On December 7, 1941, she drove me back to my dorm. Some townies were sitting on Brophy's [a shoe store] steps and announced to us that the Japanese had attacked. My mother grimaced but said nothing. I went up to my room and decided to join as soon as possible." However, when the university president asked the students not to make rash decisions, Hartmann deferred enlistment.

In his sophomore year he read in the *Daily Princetonian* that naval aviation had lowered its minimum educational requirement to one year of college. Almost immediately Hartmann boarded a train for New York City, where he could apply and undergo the tests for admission. When one eye seemed a bit weak during the physical examination, he was required to come back for a second look. "A Navy corpsman was to be the examiner. His first question was, 'Are you another college boy?' I thought I should drop through the floor. Princeton was like the kiss of death in that milieu. But I admitted my status. He said, 'Princeton, that's great.' He told me he had worked as an usher at the Chicago Opera House and the only show, passing through, which invited the ushers to their cast parties was the Triangle Club [the Princeton student drama organization]. He was so excited he never gave my eye a look, and he signed my clearance."

Hartmann reported on June 10, 1942, having received the blessings of the dean to forget about his finals at Princeton. A former Navy football hero and coach, Captain Tom Hamilton, had persuaded his superiors to create a preflight school for all cadets with an emphasis upon physical conditioning. At Iowa Pre-Flight,

Hartmann, on the basis of his freshman football at Princeton, received orders to play for the program's team. He practiced with alums from the National Football League and all-Americans and made the team. Just before the first game, however, he and another cadet were shipped to primary flight training in Minneapolis.

He trained to become a carrier pilot in single-engine aircraft, and the Navy assigned him to dive-bombers. "Then they asked us to choose between the Marine Corps or the Navy. The Marines sent the most gung-ho officer in the corps. We were on our feet cheering when he finished. I rushed over to sign up." Wings on his breast, gold bars on his shoulders, Hartmann carrier-qualified, although Marines were not flying from flattops, and reported to VMSB-231 at El Toro, California.

Under Major Elmer Glidden, a survivor of Midway and Guadalcanal—where he earned two Navy Crosses—freshmen like Hartmann learned their craft before settling down. Hartmann arrived at Majuro on February 4, 1944. "By the time we got there," he recalled, "all of the ships and planes had either been destroyed or evacuated to Truk, etc. Our job was to bomb the bypassed islands in the Marshalls.

"The first mission was one of apprehension, but only because of the unknown. We knew how to dive our planes at the target; to release the bombs at a certain altitude; to pull out against many g's of force; how to close the dive flaps immediately in order to ensure a maximum rate of speed at our low level; how to join up in close formation on the way back in case any fighters suddenly appeared. The SBDs were so well armored and so underpowered that they were slow. We had to fly in tight formations so that all of the rear-seat machine guns could fire almost as one against enemy fighters.

"We had trained so often that it was a relief to go on a mission. I was apprehensive but, like all young guys, I thought I was indestructible. We bombed antiaircraft placements, barracks, and other buildings. The return fire was intense and a number of planes were hit, but there were no casualties. If one is well trained and in a unit with experienced leadership . . . fear was never my particular concern. Our equipment was superb. My radioman-gunner [Ed Quint] was a cool customer and very good at everything. He trusted me as he had to—there were no real controls in the backseat. The strategy and tactics were absolutely appropriate for the task.

"We dove from ten thousand feet at an angle of seventy degrees; we opened our dive flaps at the top—they helped us control the planes and limited the speed (350 knots) in a steep dive; we released the bombs as we passed through fifteen hundred feet as I recollect. We were also an accurate dive-bombing squadron. We practiced hitting circles 150 feet in diameter.

"By the time I reached the Pacific, Japanese naval strength was seriously depleted. Coral Sea, Midway, Guadalcanal had been losses from which they never recovered. U.S. strength had been recovered in a few months with new carriers and other ships. I remember flying the early-morning search mission one day on Majuro, and, much to my amazement, the lagoon was filled with Task Force Fifty-eight, which had sneaked in during the night after raids on Truk and the Marianas. There was nothing but ships of all types. It was the fleet in all its glory. This was 1944, less than three years after Pearl Harbor."

Major Elmer "Iron Man" Glidden, his squadron commander, strung together seventy-seven consecutive combat dives against the atolls with his gunner Master Technical Sergeant James A. Boyle. Coupled with the 27 runs Glidden had made while on Midway and Guadalcanal, the leader of VMSB-231 established an unpublicized record of 104 plunges against flak and machine guns.

The limited targets available for dive-bombers also affected the flow of battle for Marine fighter aircraft. With VMF-212, Bill Nickerson, having returned to the war reborn as an F4U pilot after his initial tours at the controls of an SBD, escorted the bombers from Bougainville to Rabaul. Since Japanese interceptors no longer offered resistance he noted, "When we flew cover missions for SBDs, we were flying directly over the dive bombers, not up high. . . . In order to approach Rabaul with any success, the SBDs (and our Corsairs with them) skimmed the wave tops to try to avoid detection. Marine dive bombers always dived at a steep angle into targets and didn't pull out until directly above their targets. We strafed the opposing antiaircraft to give the low, slow SBDs a chance to get in and out. Having flown SBDs [during] earlier days in the South Pacific, I knew how those guys felt."

Although some influential Marine commanders, such as General Holland Smith, had recommended stationing Marine squadrons on carriers in June 1943, the policy against such deployment was reemphasized. The Commander for Aircraft in the Pacific, Admiral John Towers, declared the practice of carrier qualifications for Marine pilots wasteful. General Ross E. Rowell, director of Marine aviation, concurred, and as a result the Marine pilots in training no longer practiced landings and takeoffs from flattops.

As the war moved deeper into the Pacific, the top echelon responsible for setting aviation policies (General Louis E. Woods— who had replaced Rowell—and others) read the tea leaves. Without the ability to follow the action, the air arm would atrophy. They began to lobby for reinstatement of Marines aboard carriers. Several admirals, including John S. McCain (who traded places with Marc Mitscher) and Frank J. Fletcher, a commander in the early days of the Guadalcanal operations, boosted their argument. In the summer of 1944, after General Alexander Vandegrift, the corps commandant, met with Admiral Ernest J. King, Chief of Naval Operations (CNO), the latter agreed to the assignment of Marine fliers to carriers as the best means for supplying close support during amphibious missions. As a compromise, Vandegrift also accepted a reduction of the Marine air wings from five to four.

Prior to adoption of this program and six months before squadrons could actually start flattop duty, Marine aviation extended its reach with the development of medium bomber squadrons. Robert Sherrod suggested that impetus to the formation of these units derived from the Army Air Corps's surplus of B-25 Mitchell bombers and the hunger of Marine aviation for anything that would involve them in combat. The first PBJs, equivalents of the Air Corps's Mitchells, belonged to VMB-413. Most of the complement were recent graduates of flight schools and required considerable training not only with the B-25 but also in the navigation, radar, and radio that missions of long duration would entail. At the same time, the corps was endowed with an abundance of qualified personnel. In March 1942 the Marines had counted only 885 aviators, but a year later, when the PBJs became part of the arsenal, there were 3,191 men listed for flight duty.

Irwin Deutscher, from East Rockaway, New York, and born in 1923, was a charter member of VMB-413. "My father had lots of professions, electrician, refrigerator repairman, motion picture operator which was a great job in the depression because the movies kept going. I was a rich kid, got two pennies every day I went to school to buy candy. We were a working class family, but not poor. My parents believed in education. I started college, got three semesters, at [the] University of Missouri when Pearl Harbor happened. I wanted college life, fraternities, beautiful campus, drinking beer.

"I was a student at Missouri on the day Pearl Harbor was bombed. A bunch of us were listening to the radio. We didn't know where Pearl Harbor was, hardly knew where Hawaii was, somewhere in the Pacific. I had seen too many John Wayne movies, so I ran home and joined the Marines. For an 18-year-old it was a dramatic, romantic thing to do. War was [a] very romantic thing. We didn't think people disappeared and got killed. There was a lot of gung ho heroism. I was a miserable student, just in school for the fun of it. I would have been thrown out of college if the war hadn't been on.

"When I went into the Marine Corps I had no idea I was going to fly. They sent me to radio/gunner school out of boot camp. At naval air gunnery school, my college background came up. The Marines had gotten hold of these PBJs and they needed recruits. They pulled a bunch of us out for bombardier school at Quantico. They could teach people to navigate on the ground and for bombardier training they had a platform with the highly secret Norden bomb sight. You'd sit up there and practice hitting things on the ground."

After several weeks of ground instruction, Deutscher and others reported to the Cherry Point Air Station for training on the B-25. "I had never been in an airplane before." Following his learning at Cherry Point, Deutscher entered advanced training in the Florida Keys, then traveled to the West Coast from where he flew overseas. "We had refitted B-25s with spare gas tanks that looked like a big wooden box." At this point Deutscher was a boot sergeant—three stripes.

The first stop was Oahu. "We were twelve hours in the air. Everyone else had someone to relieve them. There was no radio allowed, no direction finder. You really had to navigate. I never stopped. I did everything I had learned in school and then did it all over again. I used a drift meter. You would look down through a pipe and from triangulation, read your drift from the white caps, calculate your wind speed and direction. I wanted to do that every hour. The pilots didn't like it because it meant you had to go off course and then back on course. This was the first time I ever said no to an officer, our copilot. I gave him some headings, three minutes on this one, then three minutes on that, he said it's a waste of fuel. I said I've got to do it. It had clouded over so I couldn't shoot the stars."

VMB-413 began its missions from Emirau, on the very northern tip of New Ireland. "Coast-watchers would tell us about targets. We would go in at very low altitude. We did daily and nightly harassing and went after any shipping, any unidentified airplanes. The Japanese had little air strips on Kavieng. They were so badly bombed, but the Japanese would still fix the air strips at night. The next day we'd drop 100 pounders, from medium altitude. You were supposed to use the bomb sight, but I never bothered with that so I never hit anything. We quit medium altitude bombing, went down, did low altitude bombing, strafing and used small bombs.

"When we had emergency landings a couple of times, I smelled gasoline and feared the airplane was going to blow up on you. It was scary. The pilot always told me to get up in the nose, but I didn't want to be there in [an] emergency landing. I'd rather be behind the armor plate. They never shot anybody down from our outfit.

"The planes were old and broken down. An engine would stop and you'd have to land. I remember going down on water. The Dumbos were always hovering around, because somebody was always going down. I remember coming in without any wheels. The hydraulic system had been hit and we couldn't manually get the wheels down. We came down between Emirau and New Ireland. A Dumbo rescued us right away. The plane stayed afloat five or ten minutes.

"I wasn't with my regular pilots on this mission. They didn't have trained navigators but everybody else got replaced. Pilots got to looking younger and younger, smaller and smaller, like grade school kids. I had to trick new young pilots, had to pretend to be navigating, taking star shots. I always knew where we were, could spot something and didn't have to navigate anymore.

"There wasn't any doubt that we were going to win the war. You just didn't know when. You get used to things. This is life and it is going to go on forever. There seemed no end to it. I didn't have the worst of it. We flew back to secure air strips. Mostly you were back someplace where you lived comfortably, tents on platforms. It was not a bad war." Because of the shortage of airmen with his skill, Deutscher would continue to fly missions that took him to the Philippines campaign while the crewmen who started with him enjoyed rotation home.

Many of the initial assignments for VMB-413, flown from Stirling field in the Treasury Islands, specified precision strikes after dark. Just as Washing Machine Charlie harassed soldiers hoping for some relief at night, the PBJs disrupted evening meals and sleep. While the top brass commended the effort and that of other units banging away at Rabaul, many Marine airmen lamented their role away from more active contributions.

With VMF-212 one of the first squadrons to settle on the newly acquired Green Island base, Bill Nickerson accompanied PBJs from VMB-413 on a raid. "Vanakanau was one of the airfields on Rabaul. I [led on April 2, 1944,] the flight of Corsairs. We strafed antiaircraft around the area—less than 100 feet off the ground, flying at treetop level before the bombers unloaded."

A few days later, a Japanese fighter did suddenly appear. "This is the time when Bob Soule (my best friend [from] Phoenix Union High School) says I saved his ass. Bob was flying TBFs (Grumman torpedo bomber) off the carrier *Independence*. I shot down a plane that was on Bob's tail when he was attacking Rabaul."

In mid-March VMB-413 had been the first of the twin-engine bomber squadrons to enter combat, and it suffered significant losses. On May 5 the unit was relieved by VMB-423. In the pipeline, four more of the PBJ squadrons that had been activated in September and October 1943 were about to join the war.

Born in 1920 in Arkansas, Bill Lindley moved with his family to Kansas City, Kansas, where he graduated from high school. He married in 1939 and the couple had a son, but after his wife died in 1942, Lindley decided to enlist in the Marines. "After boot camp," recalled Lindley, "they wanted to send me to OCS, I said no, I just want to fight a war. They said you're supposed to go, but I said no way. Finally they shipped me to Memphis and an aviation ordnance school. From there I went to Purcell, Oklahoma, and gunnery school and then Florida for advanced gunnery."

At Cherry Point, North Carolina, he became a tail gunner in a new PBJ squadron, VMB-423, activated September 15, 1943, with Lieutenant Colonel John L. Winston as the CO. En route to the Pacific, the gunners traveled on the carrier *Hornet* while the pilots flew the planes to Ewa.

"We were there about five weeks," said Lindley, "while modifications were done to the tail areas of PBJ-1." The original gun sight would not stay synchronized with the gun.

The mid-May odyssey of VMB-423 carried it to Palmyra, Canton, Tunafuti, and then Espiritu Santo. The bombers would fly from there to Green Island, refuel, and go on to bomb Rabaul, New Ireland, and Kavieng. Once established on Stirling Island, Lindley reported, "We hit Rabaul rather frequently—every night there was coverage. I flew every fourth or fifth day, did a lot of day and night work. I didn't like that night work too much. They'd have these bogeys up there and they'd fire these phosphorus type antiaircraft at you, weird thing to see at night, wasn't very nice of those people to do that. We only lost 36 people while I was with that organization.

"On the island, we had two wild pigs as pets, Franklin and Eleanor. They were nice little pigs, like little dogs, very clean. They would follow you to the mess hall for a hand-out. One morning after I'd been heading to the flight line to clean the guns, I heard this rustle off in [the] weeds. I thought this was a wild pig. But right at the side of the road I saw this big, old Monitor lizard, tongue flashing out at me. He looked as big as a man doing push ups. I got into my jeep, put that thing in gear and I was gone!

"After we were there for a little while, we picked up a new CO. Winston moved up to a group commander. We took on Norman J. Anderson, a fine officer and a gentleman. (In fact, Anderson set a record with 107 missions in PBJs.) One of our tail gunners, Randolph J. Massey, decided that if he went on a scheduled mission, that was the day he was not coming back. He said I'm not going, and I don't care if they court-martial me, and put me in the brig. I was in charge of tail gunners. I said, 'If that's the way you feel, Randolph, I'll go in your place this one time. But if [it] ever happens again, I'll hog-tie you, put you in the tail and go with you.' We had no problem on that flight, we were shot at but I don't remember getting any holes. He never refused to go again.

"One time, we were out looking for targets of opportunity when [we] noticed this convoy [of] trucks on New Ireland. We saw a bridge and decided let's hit that first, to see if we can't stack 'em up. We had this 500 pounder aboard. I could see that bomb went right through the bridge. It tore the dickens out of it, then it hit the water, skipped up into the air and went off under our tail. It blowed [sic] a hole in our tail, I bumped my head but we got home all right.

"[During a target-of-opportunity sortie,] usually there were two planes. One would fly high cover, while the other went in. We went [first,] dropped our bomb and then started back up to high cover. The [second] plane went in, but before he could even drop his bomb, they hit him and he was on fire. He jettisoned his bombs over the beach, and set her down in the water, a half mile off shore. They all got out and got on this raft. [The Japanese] started shooting at them from shore with a five-inch gun or its equivalency. We started hitting that weapon area but after dropping our bombs, all we had left was our machine guns. On our last pass as we ran out of ammunition, we got hit. We'd already called a Dumbo [PBY rescue aircraft] for them. They were already on their way. The [ground fire] hit our oil line, up front. We had to close one engine down—oil was blowing right out of the cowl—so it wouldn't catch on fire. They sent a second Dumbo for us. But we didn't need it.

"After a daytime run on Rabaul, we were tail end Charlies, I didn't sleep going back but kept on looking around, even down on the water. I saw a life raft. I saw'm waving. We called the leader of formation and got permission to drop back and circle to see what was going on. Sure enough there was a pilot waving like frantic. They got a Dumbo for him and he was all right.

"Borpop on New Ireland was a place we'd already beaten . . . down pretty good. The air field was no longer operational but occasionally they'd take some shots at us. Coast-watchers told us there were quite a few Japanese there who were very active. Late in the afternoon was when they'd bivouac and cook their meals right out on the strip. They'd light little fires to cook their rice. We thought we'd take a little run on 'em, pulling a little surprise on 'em. We carried those bombs known as parafrags [small bombs that floated down in chutes and then exploded above ground, like a hand grenade]. First we flew over them like we were going on to Rabaul. We went over at about 12,000 feet, then dropped down behind the mountains before coming back to drop those parafrags. We also used our machine guns on 'em. You could see them falling every which way. Later we got word from the coast-watchers that we killed so many in that one raid, they didn't have enough people to bury their dead. Many years later I have thought about it and am kind of remorseful now but you have to live with it."

Another crewman on a PBJ, Harley Redin began his long journey to the combat zone in the Texas panhandle, where he was born in 1919. After graduation from Silverton High School in 1936, he entered John Tarleton Agricultural College, a two-year school, which he chose mainly for its reputation in basketball. From there he matriculated at North Texas State, majoring in business administration and enrolling both in the Civilian Pilot Training (CPT) program and as a naval aviation cadet.

He was allowed to complete his college studies before being called up in June 1942. In his last months of flight training, Redin chose to become a Marine. "I always had kind of a fantasy about the Marines. Part of it was the fact that we'd heard about twin-engine bombers coming to the Marines. We had a chance to be on the ground floor of that. I wasn't real fond of aerobatics. I could do them, but I just felt like I would like multi-engine planes better than I would fighters."

He was introduced to this type of aircraft in the form of twin-engine Beechcrafts and then began to fly PBYs, which he found quite agreeable. "I liked the landing and taking off on water. Of course, it was real slow and cumbersome but it was a lot of fun to fly." Unlike the single-engine fighter and dive-bomber pilots who, upon graduation, reported to bases where they received advanced instruction from experienced Marines, Redin checked in at the American Airlines Flight School in Forth Worth. There, he said, he received comprehensive training in precision flying, navigation, and radio work with exceptional attention to details. His teachers were retired American Airlines pilots and Redin learned in the cockpit of a DC-3, the workhorse of commercial aviation in the late 1930s and 1940s.

Transition to the PBJ went smoothly. "[It] was real easy to fly. It was real stable. Its reliability was great. Its maneuverability was real good. Maybe it was not as fast as the A-20 [Douglas Havoc attack bomber, a lighter machine] that the Air Force had but it was a real good, stable airplane." While familiarizing himself with the PBJ at Cherry Point, Redin became an original member of a new squadron, VMB-433. As one of the earliest chosen for the bomber program and a graduate of the American Airlines school, Redin, along with Travis Lattner Jr., a fellow Texan he had met when inducted, checked out newcomers.

Not until January 1944 was the training in navigation, formation, and cross-country flying complete enough for the squadron to head for the base at El Centro, California. There the fliers worked on gunnery practice and practice in dropping torpedoes.

Redin's crew consisted of a copilot, an officer, and four enlisted men—a navigator-bombardier, a radioman-gunner who handled the top turret, and two gunners. One of the latter triggered the .50-calibers in the tail while the other, as waist gunner, manned two positions, going from side to side. Four months later, the PBJs took off singly over a period of days, stopping first in Hawaii before hopping to Espiritu Santo via Palmyra, Canton, and Funafuti, until finally reaching Green Island.

Redin happened to be one of the last to arrive, and the squadron had already flown several missions. His first taste of combat, carrying twelve bombs, each a hundred-pounder, was one of the night heckling sorties. "If it had been a daylight mission, it would have been a lot better. But taking off there [at] night and not knowing a thing about it except what they told me, I wasn't too comfortable. I was very worried about the navigation because there were no lights and very few radio aids of any kind. You just depended upon your navigator. If [he] told you a certain course or certain time, you had to do it. If you didn't, you and he both were in trouble.

"I was really uneasy about finding Rabaul. . . . When you found it, the only reason you knew was because the searchlights came on you. You didn't know where you were because at night it was real dark and real black. All of a sudden there were searchlights, and you knew that they were firing at you. . . . The first thing I did was try to get out of the searchlights with evasive action. You couldn't get out of them until you got a little distance away."

His colleague from Texas, Travis Lattner Jr., grew up on a farm during the Depression. After he graduated from high school, he entered North Texas State Teachers College, living with an aunt. "She kept three cows and delivered milk around the neighborhood. I milked those three cows morning and night, the first year to pay my way through college." He, too, learned to fly through the CPT program. Motivated by both patriotism and a thirst for adventure, after December 7, 1941, Lattner enlisted as a naval aviation cadet rather than go home to farm, an occupation that early in the war brought exemption from the draft.

He requested assignment to twin-engine aircraft, explained

Lattner, because "I knew that in a medium bomber, a twin-engine plane, I would never have to fly off a carrier, I never thought I would be too hot about that." His instruction on the PBY, however, was not to his taste. "It had some bunks in the back of it. It'd take six of us out at once to practice landings. You got to fly for an hour and then you had to spend the other five hours back there laying down and trying not to get sick as it landed and bounced around on the water. I don't ever remember getting sick, but it certainly was dull and boring for the five hours you spent in the back." Nor did he enjoy his cockpit hours in the Catalinas. "It was really hard to fly. It was slow and cumbersome."

Basic flight training emphasized navigation and instrument flying. "They would put a hood over you and then you had an instrument. There was a line with a little airplane that, when you turned, the wings of the airplane would turn. The solid line was the horizon. That was the main thing we used in instrument flying. Also you had to learn how to maintain your altitude." In addition, Lattner spent hours on the ground in the traditional Link trainer.

Like his friend Harley Redin, Lattner opted for the Marine Corps because he wanted to continue to fly twin-engine planes. He, too, attended the thirty-day course under the tutelage of retired American Airlines pilots. "The ground school was tough and those instructors were tough. I probably learned more about flying in those thirty days than I did at other times of my training."

He heartily endorsed the PBJ. "It was an excellent airplane . . . one of the safest airplanes ever built . . . we enjoyed flying it. . . . It had a lot more power than any other plane that I'd ever flown." Another charter member of VMB-433, Lattner said the squadron insignia summarized the triple threat of the aircraft: "a picture of this devil riding a torpedo, with a machine gun in one hand and a bomb in the other hand."

In California the squadron practiced torpedo runs at the Salton Sea. "There was a simulated ship and we'd drop the torpedo and see how close we could get to this target." Bombing exercises also featured runs at a Salton target. They honed their strafing skills, firing machine guns at sleeves towed by another aircraft. Lattner described the tight formation drills, "almost wing-tip to wing-tip," as "a lot of fun."

The Marine PBJs, like the Air Corps bombers, employed the Norden bombsight, originally developed for the Navy but discarded by that branch as unsuitable for its dive-bombers and torpedo bombers. In the system developed by the Air Corps, when the pilot reached the target, the bombardier controlled the plane for a few seconds while he plotted the exact moment for the drop. High security enveloped the Norden device. Said Lattner, "We never left it in the plane. When we would return from a flight, it was taken out of the plane and checked in. When we went on another flight, it would be reinstalled." Usually when a group of PBJs attacked, a lead bombardier would drop his ordnance and the bombardiers in trailing planes behind would follow his cue. On single-plane missions, however, the Norden came into play for each aircraft.

As the moment approached for VMB-433 to go overseas, Lattner, like most young men, felt little concern over the possibility of his death. "It never crossed my mind. I just had a lot of confidence that nothing like that was ever going to happen to me." Unlike Redin, who flew to the war zone, Lattner sailed on an aircraft carrier, a voyage from San Diego to Espiritu Santo that lasted thirty days. After their aircraft arrived, portions of the squadron, in July 1944, moved to Green Island. Lattner described the living conditions as comfortable enough, better in fact than those at Peter Point Field near Cherry Point.

On his first mission, planned as a night heckling raid, Lattner had just taken off when the control tower asked him to investigate an unidentified vessel. He picked up the ship on his radar and obeyed orders to circle it. "Finally, the tower did call and said they'd identified the ship and we were to proceed to Rabaul. I turned around and started flying west and climbing. I had gotten up to about 10,000 or 11,000 feet and thought I was over New Ireland. We'd fly over this portion of New Ireland to get to Rabaul. I looked down and saw some runway lights. I discussed it with my co-pilot [Lieutenant Emil Mennes], and circled it a time or two. I said, 'Maybe we ought to drop a bomb or two here just to wake this bunch up.'

"Your radar would usually outline these islands, so actually you didn't need to navigate. I had no idea that the navigator was trying to keep up with where we were. When we were circling and discussing whether to drop a bomb on what we thought was a Japanese-held island, he told the copilot [who] told me that I was circling over Green Island. I came pretty close to dropping a bomb on my home base.

"Then we did proceed to Rabaul. The weather was bad, a lot of thunderstorms up around 10,000 or 12,000 feet. It was hard to even look and find out where Rabaul was. I finally made up my mind, 'To heck with this.' I just dropped all twelve bombs and turned around and headed home." Normal procedure on this type of run called for dropping a bomb every fifteen to thirty minutes to harass the enemy.

Henry W. Sory, a native of Dallas whose family eventually settled in Sherman, Texas, also became a pilot for VMB-433. While at Austin College in the spring of 1942, he, too, completed the CPT course and received a private license. He believed the naval aviation pilot program superior to that offered by the Army and began his preflight experience at the University of Georgia.

During his first phases of instruction, Sory said he found the acrobatics aspect of flying less to his taste and was more at home when he flew the twin-engine SNV—known as the Vultee Vibrator because of its shaky performance—or a Beechcraft. When the moment to choose his branch of service came in June 1943, Sory said, "At the time I thought the chances and the opportunities for advancement were going to be much greater in the Marine Corps. It didn't turn out to be that way. They were turning out lots of Marine pilots by the time I graduated."

Assigned to what became VMB-433, Sory, like Lattner, heartily endorsed the PBJ or B-25, "a good safe airplane. It was a stable, easy-to-fly airplane." Among its virtues, it could get off the ground on a single engine in the event one failed. Sory, who had PBJ experience dating back to the operational training squadron that preceded VMB-433, became the man in the left-hand command seat, while a newer member of the squadron, Lieutenant Mike Lewis, drew the copilot's right-hand position. The crew called six different states home. Lewis was from Tennessee; Staff Sergeant Gerald Hoff, a Pennsylvanian, served as navigator-bombardier. Vince Montie from River Rouge, Michigan, operated the radio and radar. Arthur Boulton, a son of New Jersey, was a gunner, and Glen Albright from Ohio was the tail gunner. Except for Montie, Sory was the youngest man.

In contrast to Redin who actually flew from California to Espiritu Santo, and Lattner who traveled on an aircraft carrier, Sory sailed on a destroyer escort as far as Hawaii. From there he expected to pilot a PBJ to the squadron's base. Obviously, VMB-433 went to the war zone in piecemeal fashion. But before Sory caught up with the rest of the unit, he spent three months at Ewa as head of a twenty-nine-man group detailed to ensure the aircraft were fit. "The plane had a lot of trouble passing gas consumption tests, and the Air Corps wouldn't let them leave because some of the blades on the props were an inch shorter than the other two. It was a three-bladed prop. They just didn't think that planes could fly like that. But the Marine Corps didn't have a lot of spare parts at that time. We were glad to get the planes. They [had] stripped these planes back. I mean that they took all of the guns off, took the turret out, even the radar to fly them out. It was a twelve or fourteen hour flight. In the bomb bay they would put auxiliary gas tanks. The turrets and all of the guns were packed in Cosmoline [the trade name for a rust preventive]." Sory's people labored to clean the equipment and unpack the radar. They also modified the tails of the aircraft to afford the tail gunner a better view. "Lieutenant [Dan] Collins [the radar officer] and I spent three months there before we got all of our planes through."

Sory finally caught up with the squadron in time for his first mission, August 14, over New Ireland. It was a tactical mission in the company of several other aircraft and involved some night flying for the return. He had been reunited with his original crew.

On his second mission Sory flew a night heckler against Rabaul. Like Redin, he also became lost, even though he had maps, radar, and radar officer Dan Collins with him. "We finally found something that corresponded to our maps, that looked the same on radar. We went back to Rabaul, dropped one or two bombs and before we got lost . . . we jettisoned the rest and went home to Green Island."

Clearly, the campaign against Rabaul had lost importance.

FIFTEEN

FROM THE MARIANAS TO THE PHILIPPINES

Working over Rabaul and bypassed atolls became a matter of diminishing returns, but the raids enabled Marine pilots to refine their techniques against ground targets. The Corsair's ability to carry a heavy payload and to function as a dive-bomber begat a new hybrid, the fighter-bomber. To add to the arsenal, the Fourth Marine Air Wing perfected the napalm fire jelly concoction.

The strategy developed by Admiral Nimitz and his Central Pacific Command outflanked another Japanese stronghold, the huge base at Truk in the Carolines, neutralized by carrier-borne strikes. Instead amphibious forces, backed up by massive armadas of carriers and capital ships, zeroed in on the Marianas, Saipan, Tinian, Rota, and Guam. From here long-range bombers—the new B-29s that had started operations against Japan from deep in China—would find the home islands of Japan more accessible.

The decapitation of Truk and the struggle for dominance in the air over the Marianas relied on the Navy's planes on flattops and the Army's bigger bombers. The Marines banging away at the remnants of the Japanese on bypassed islands could only wait for new airfields in the Marianas before they took a bigger role in the war. On a particularly momentous day, June 19, 1944, an avalanche of carrier-based Navy fighters swept away a huge number of Japanese aircraft, 383 total. Japanese fighter capacity was shoved back to the Philippine Islands. As the amphibious forces secured portions of the Mariana Islands themselves, a small Marine contingent drawn from observation squadrons flew artillery-spotting missions and evacuated wounded.

VMO-2 in single-engine Stinson Sentinels took off from carriers and then operated from roadways on Saipan to pinpoint emplacements and guide the big guns. Once airfields were captured, the "Grasshopper" squadron bore observers just two hundred feet off the ground searching ravines, caves, and cane fields for enemy positions. Frequently the small planes—with fabric-covered fuselages and wings—returned pockmarked by bullet holes, but VMO-2 lost not a single pilot, including subsequent missions on Tinian. However, a brother squadron, VMO-4, engaged in the same type of operations on Saipan and Tinian, reeled from accurate fire by the Japanese with five planes wrecked and two pilots killed.

The invasion of Guam by Third Division Marines and GIs from the Army's Seventy-seventh Division also depended mainly upon the Navy for air support. From Saipan, VMF(N)-532 performed combat air patrol from dusk to dawn. Two weeks after the first troops clambered onto the Guam beaches, VMF-216, 217, and 225 joined with VMF(N)-532 to aid the ground forces. Again, the Grasshoppers played an integral role in the direction of artillery. Nevertheless, considering the frenetic pace of Marine aviation during the days of Guadalcanal and the first battles moving up the Solomons chain, Robert Sherrod described the period as "the doldrums of 1944."

Tom Hartmann, flying an SBD with VMSB-231, recalled that he and his comrades had been told they should prepare themselves to join the Marines on Saipan once a third of the island was secured. "We were to fly close air support for the Marine troops. We had not been trained in close air support but our accuracy was legend and we knew we could hit within 150 feet of any target. Then, late one night, Elmer [Glidden—the CO] called us together to tell us that the orders were changed because the Army wanted to use P-47s for that purpose. This change caused the decision to break up the squadron into thirds, thereby ruining morale. We were senior in length of overseas duty, so they did not wish to deplete one squadron of its experienced pilots."

Hartmann had also gradually come to learn, personally, of the prevalence of death. "I was a very close friend of a former Penn student. He was probably mortally wounded in his dive. My best friend from Somerville [New Jersey] lost his brother on the *Quincy,* sunk off Savo Island. The brother was four years older than I. He was a ninety-day wonder from Annapolis after graduating from Lehigh. I really liked him. He was always terrific to me. His death shook me to my roots even before I saw combat. Then his next-door neighbor, also a good friend, died in the invasion of Saipan as a Marine lieutenant, and the neighbor on the back of their properties was killed at Normandy. [The] losses in a war need not be in one's presence to have an impact on one so young and gung-ho."

Henry Sory from VMB-433 was similarly affected. On the day after he helped find a downed Australian pilot floating on a raft, Sory's brother was KIA in France. Sory said he was comforted by his chaplain, and the fate of his brother heightened his empathy for foot soldiers. "Lord, have mercy! They really know about war."

The breakup of Hartmann's squadron gave him a new skipper. "[He] was an alcoholic while Elmer didn't drink. [He] was in the tank all day long on Makin Island. The morale in all of the squadrons was shot but [he] made it worse. He instructed us to fly one plane *above* the other when flying in a line rather than a formation. You can't see the plane ahead of you! I told the executive officer, whom I knew, that I refused to fly in line. He told me to forget it. The CO was loaded. They never flew that way. I believe that [the skipper] was either fearful or he had seen combat at the Canal which essentially destroyed his effectiveness. He was relieved of his duty quietly, one day."

Hartmann completed his tour in the South Pacific striking at the bypassed Japanese. He was never wounded, but after the first twenty-seven missions his SBD had survived a number of hits. He picked up an Air Medal for putting a bomb on an active radio installation on the island of Jaluit.

While Marine fighter and dive-bomber aircraft struggled to locate opponents and targets, the PBJ squadrons took off from Stirling, Green Island, and then Emirau—captured April 29, 1944—for short flights that carried them to Kavieng on the tip of New Ireland, as well as Pondo Point and Rabaul on New Britain farther southeast. The resistance from interceptors was close to nil but the AA could still exact a deadly price, particularly if airmen made a mistake. Henry Sory, flying for VMB-433 from Emirau, remembered his worst experience. "It was on September 11 to Pondo Point, a low altitude bombing mission. We made the mistake of coming back around and we decided to make another run, and a third run even. We never should have made them at the same speed or at the same altitude.

"One of our planes took a 20 mm shell through the pilot's side of the plane. The pilot's name was Eric Terry. The copilot was a fellow named Kromka. I forgot his first name. He sat the plane down off shore in the water and we all saw him land. The navigator/bombardier was trapped up in the bombardier compartment. He and Terry died. Kromka was a great big, strong fellow. Kromka tried to get Terry out and nearly drowned himself. The top part of that [Plexiglas] over the pilot's compartment has an escape hatch that you can release from inside and throw away. If you had to land in the water, that's where the pilot and co-pilot could get out.

"We were hovering around and watching and hoping that Dumbo was going to get there and pick them up. We stayed until we saw them leave. We didn't know that they didn't get everybody out until we got back to Emirau."

According to Sory, the copilot suffered emotional problems after the war and died in an institution. "He always thought he should have gotten Terry out of the wreckage. Terry was probably already dead." Sory said that while he and his comrades missed the dead men, they did not dwell on the shadows or mortality. "I think that you've got to be thankful that you are in an aviation outfit compared to the infantry or something like that. You at least know that you are coming back to someplace that is a relatively good place to be at night. You're not slogging around in a bunch of mud and other stuff."

Travis Lattner, who often served as a flight leader, led a group of the twin-engine bombers on a strike at Rabaul and committed the same error. "As we approached the target, the bombardier informed me that there was a cloud that completely covered the target, and there was no way he could tell where to drop the bombs.

"I hated to just drop them at random, so we just didn't drop [them] and continued on. I informed the squadron that we were going to make a 360-degree climbing turn and make another run at the target and hopefully we'd be able to see the target this time. There was no reaction [from the crew] at that time. After we got back to Emirau, I supposed somebody complained because Major Cox had me in and said, 'It's all right this time, but next time don't do it again. Just go ahead and drop the bombs.' I got to thinking later that, if there had been a lucky shot that hit some plane, I imagine that I would have felt pretty bad. At least we did get the bombs where they were supposed to go. Some guys agreed with the decision, and some didn't."

Lattner faced a more deadly problem when a two-thousand-pound bomb hung up in his plane. "I reported it and called back to the tower and they said, 'Just drop out of formation and jettison the bomb and come on back to Emirau.'

"When we tried to drop the bomb, it wouldn't release. We tried everything in the world and had a lot of conversation with the tower. We'd pull down and pull up to try to get it out. Some of the crew found a pole and tried to knock it loose but we just never could get rid of it.

"Finally, we had to land with it. We never thought of bailing out and letting the plane fly off. We landed with it. When I hit the runway, it dropped out. When we turned to taxi, we looked back down the runway and could see that big bomb laying down there. That was a little scary. Of course it had a little propeller on the tail that has to turn so many revolutions before the bomb is activated. It didn't turn enough to activate it. You'd almost think that jarring would cause the thing to explode."

With the inexorable demise of Imperial Japan almost palpable, replacements included some higher-rank officers who had spent the previous years as instructors or even in staff positions. Lattner recalled pilots with senior rank starting their tours. "On one mission I was the flight leader. I had a major for a copilot and a higher-ranking officer than that in one of the planes behind us. After a few missions, they became the leaders. They didn't fly near as smoothly as some of us more experienced pilots did. That caused quite a bit of conversation."

During this period Bruce Porter, who had completed his tour as a Corsair pilot with VMF-121 and been credited with downing three of the enemy, had returned to the States. He had weathered the dissolution of his hasty marriage but achieved his ambition of assignment to night fighter duty after several months as an instructor. Porter finally reported to Vero Beach, Florida, for a course in his new specialty. Promoted to major, Porter said, "[We spent] endless hours of 'ground' flying in Link trainers . . . and even more hours in the air and under the hood aboard SNJs [trainer aircraft]. Early on, we also got time to familiarize ourselves with the Grumman F6F-3E Hellcat night fighter, a Navy model on which the Marine Corps, like the Navy, had finally settled as the basis of its night-fighter program." He attributed the choice of the Hellcat over the Corsair to the easier-landing abilities of the Grumman. The Army Air Force used the A-20 attack bomber and the newer P-61, the Black Widow, for its after-dark fighters.

The night-configured Hellcat carried a bulbous pod housing a radar system beneath the starboard wing. It worked best when used in conjunction with ground-based, more accurate radars. The F6F-3E was painted a nonreflective matte black that rendered it less visible to hostile aircraft or ships. Low-intensity cockpit lighting and red instrument panel lights protected the pilot's night vision and further lessened opportunities to detect the plane in the night sky.

Ordered to Cherry Point, Porter flew his Hellcat to the Quantico, Virginia, air base where the aircraft required modifications before it would be ready for combat. Ever ready for a good time,

Porter recalled, "I knew that the job would take at least four or five days, so I arranged to stay at the Roosevelt Hotel [in Washington, DC], which had a great reputation among fighter pilots. I had been assured by my friend, Major Joe Foss . . . that the place practically featured hot-and-cold running women. I quickly learned where Joe got his ideas; the Roosevelt hosted two full floors of woman Marines who were actually *billeted* there. Their presence, along with the presence of no end of Waves [women sailors], made for a very wild time." The sybaritic interval ended quickly as Porter, one of the few experienced combat pilots in VMF-544 and executive officer of the squadron, helped develop operational readiness.

The growing night fighter program was one area where Marine aviation could enlarge its role. A second lay in the installation of leatherneck squadrons aboard carriers. Modifications in the F4U finally made it palatable for duty aboard flattops, and the training for such duty began in earnest.

Less than a month after the annihilation of Japanese forces on Guam, the Allied forces drove toward the western Carolines and the Palau group. The latter, 1,000 miles west of Truk and only 530 from Davao on Mindanao in the Philippines, particularly Peleliu, proved to be a rock-hard nut to crack. When the first ground echelons from the Second Marine Air Wing came ashore, instead of constructing an airfield, they worked to unload landing craft and evacuate wounded. Some aviation specialists temporarily became riflemen and half a dozen were killed, eleven wounded, as part of the "air support" team.

On the third day, VMO-3 landed its single-engine observation planes on a 550-foot-long strip to begin coordinating artillery with the needs of the infantry. When the Marines, after nine days of bloody strife, finally hacked out enough of a foothold to construct an adequate air base, VMF(N)-542, shepherded by Marine transports, flew to the island. Within a week VMF-114 brought its Corsairs to Peleliu. The fighter-bombers supported a second landing and then did what they could in a grim struggle to wipe out the last defense line, "Bloody Nose Ridge," and isolated pockets of die-hard enemy troops. The entire campaign involved combat at extremely close quarters. In one sortie the pilots dropped their bombs a scant fifteen seconds after they passed over the ready tent at their airfield. Some runs against entrenched Japanese saw the Corsairs with their landing gear still down as they splashed searing gobs of napalm. For all the heroics, Peleliu proved to be neither of strategic advantage nor suitable as an air base for any ventures other than those in the immediate vicinity. In contrast, the atoll of Ulithi with its immense lagoon, in the western Carolines, soon became a massive Navy base. Once the ground forces bagged Peleliu, the Marines resumed the practice of punishing bypassed outposts—Yap, Fais, Sorol, Woleai.

Marine aviation opened up another avenue for itself with the formation of VMJ or VMR squadrons that deployed transport aircraft to haul military freight, construction gear, personnel, and mail. The operations were part of a transport air group that worked alongside Air Corps planes.

Originally MacArthur planned to make his first return to the Philippines on Mindanao. However, faulty intelligence indicated that the Japanese had all but abandoned Leyte, north of Mindanao. Possession of Leyte offered better control of the Philippine waters and a shorter range from which to hit the main enemy forces on Luzon. Unfortunately, the Japanese were on Leyte in considerable strength and determined to hold the turf. The first landings of the island struck at the eastern shores with a primary objective the towns of Tacloban and Dulag with their airfields.

When Halsey's Third Fleet sailed into position to service the Leyte landings by Army troops—no leatherneck ground forces were scheduled for the Philippine campaign—the Imperial Navy plotted a desperate gambit to engage the U.S. warships. While a "Main Body" of vessels steamed out of Japan's Inland Sea as a decoy to lure Halsey with Task Force Thirty-eight north and away from the landing sites, a "Center Force" moved from Singapore intent upon crushing the beachhead on Leyte; the smaller "Southern Force" was also expected to hurl its weight at the landings.

U.S. submarines had shadowed the Japanese approach to the Philippines, and then patrol planes began to monitor the enemy movements. The seven carriers supporting the Imperial Navy could only muster 116 aircraft against seventeen American carriers hosting more than 1,000 planes. However, land-based Japanese planes, flying from Luzon, torched the light carrier *Princeton*—which was scuttled—and heavily damaged the cruiser *Birmingham*. The Nipponese airmen paid a huge price, losing many aircraft, with Commander David McCampbell from the *Essex* splashing nine, a record for the war.

During the afternoon of October 24 dive-bombers, torpedo planes, and fighter-bombers from the American carriers attacked the Center Force. They kayoed one of Japan's two superbattleships, *Musashi*, a seventy-three-thousand-ton behemoth. After forty hits from tin fish and bombs, the ship rolled over and disappeared beneath the water. The flattop aircraft also crippled a pair of heavy cruisers.

On the night of October 24 a task force of six U.S. battleships, four heavy cruisers, four light ones, and almost thirty destroyers, plus a couple of Australian Navy ships, fell upon the Southern Force as it tried to pick its way through the Surigao Strait between southern Leyte and Mindanao. The hapless Japanese warships crossed the T, the most advantageous gunnery position the Americans could have desired. The gunfire blasted two battleships and three destroyers, damaging a cruiser and a destroyer. The violent battle cost the life of the Japanese admiral in command and forced the surviving ships into retreat. The victory over the Southern Force belonged entirely to surface vessels.

When the Northern Force dangled some patrol planes within sight of his reconnaissance scouts, Halsey snapped at the bait. Halsey would later claim that he had been misled by reports indicating near-total destruction of Japanese naval armadas approaching Leyte. He hurried north after the decoy force, which included four flattops with minimal air units, plus a pair of old battleships converted to carriers, but no airplanes. The aircraft from the U.S. flattops wiped out four carriers and a destroyer, and surface fire along with submarines added to the enemy losses.

However, Halsey's dash north had left an opening in the San Bernadino Strait, and a portion of the Center Force poured through the gap. On the morning of October 25 the covey of battleships and cruisers with a destroyer screen steamed within range of an American fleet composed mainly of escort carriers or baby flattops with some destroyers as escorts. The heavy guns from the Japanese fleet blew away several U.S. destroyers that gamely sought to shield the thin-skinned carriers. Shells wrecked two of the baby flattops, *Gambier Bay* and *White Plains*.

The besieged struck back with their aircraft—but at this moment the Japanese introduced their latest weapon, the kamikaze. Land-based planes from Luzon began diving on the American vessels. The *Santee*, designed as an oil tanker but converted to flight duty, achieved the dubious honor of being the first ship hit by a kamikaze. Even as it began to burn, a Japanese sub followed up with a torpedo. A sister escort carrier, *Suwannee*, buckled from two suicide bomber blows, but both vessels survived. The Battle of Leyte Gulf ended after three days when the Japanese Navy could no longer effectively contend with surface vessels. The remnants of the Imperial fleet withdrew to home waters to await an opportune moment.

On Leyte, MacArthur had honored his pledge to return, but the Japanese resolve to resist featured the introduction of twenty-five thousand reinforcements to buttress the sixteen thousand men already ensconced. The Commander, South-West Pacific, allowed the Navy to end its support for his operations on the island and pursue its interests elsewhere. The airfields on Leyte resembled the inhospitable conditions on Guadalcanal, as incessant rains created mushy, thick mud that wrecked aircraft landing and taking off. With the Japanese stoutly resisting on the ground and attacking the GIs from the air, and the restrictions on Army fighters because of the miserable state of the airfields, MacArthur was forced to request a return of the carrier-based fighters and bombers to assist his troops.

The advent of the kamikazes, however, made the stationing of flattops within reach of land-based enemy planes highly risky. Halsey and MacArthur agreed to introduce Marine fighters to the battle for Leyte. The former said in his autobiography, "I had had under my command in the South Pacific a Marine Air Group [Twelve] which had proved its versatility in everything from fighting to blasting enemy vessels. I knew that this group was now under MacArthur's command and I knew too, without understanding why, that when Kenney [Major General George C., MacArthur's air chief] was not keeping it idle, he was assigning it to missions far below its capacity. Kinkaid's [Admiral Thomas, commander of the Seventh Fleet] complaint of insufficient air cover prompted me to take a step which was more than a liberty; to a man of meaner spirit than MacArthur's, it would have seemed an impertinence. I called these Marines to his attention."

As a result, on December 3, Lieutenant Colonel Peter D. Lambrecht brought the F6Fs from VMF(N)-541 from Peleliu to the Tacloban field on Leyte. They replaced an Army P-61 night fighter unit that could not match the speed of the Oscar, the newest Japanese night bomber. Within a few hours four Marine fighter squadrons—VMF-115, 211, 218, and 313, a total of seventy-five Corsairs—guided by PBJs and having flown 1,957 miles with several island stops, reached Tacloban.

The Marine air units saw their first real action on Pearl Harbor Day, 1944. MacArthur, seeking to break the back of the enemy defenses by shutting down the main source of supply, mounted an amphibious operation near Ormoc on the western shore of Leyte. Totally surprised by the venture, the Japanese reacted with increasing vigor. Around 2:00 A.M. a four-engine Lily bomber, cruising over Ormoc Bay with intent to bomb the ships unloading troops and gear, met the machine guns of Technical Sergeant John W. Andre from VMF(N)-541 and crashed into the water. Andre, a six-foot four-inch NAP who had to squeeze himself into the smaller cockpit of a Hellcat (compared with a Corsair), finished the war with four victories.

The light of day exposed three destroyers and four cargo vessels to marauding F4Us vectored to San Isidro Harbor thirty miles from Ormoc. Pilots from VMF-211 brushed aside a handful of protective Zekes and dumped bombs. Near misses on a destroyer produced serious damage and strafing runs, then ignited leaking oil into a blaze that left the warship a burning hulk. The squadron mourned the loss of two pilots, one of whom had been recovered but died of his wounds. In the afternoon both Marine and Army fighters struck at the small convoy. The two services issued conflicting claims of glory, but a final assessment credited the raiders with sinking four ships.

The achievements paled somewhat against a sustained kamikaze effort involving as many as one hundred planes off Ormoc. They sank a destroyer and troop transport, and damaged two similar vessels. The increasing threat from the suicides mandated an increase in fighters able to protect the ships. The Navy began to add fighters to the carrier complements and spurred the development of F4U squadrons able to operate from flattops.

On December 11 the Japanese took their last stab at inserting reinforcements on Leyte. Morning patrols radioed the approach of a convoy with transports, cargo ships, and destroyers off Panay, bound for Leyte. They sailed beneath a thin layer of fighters. Marine F4Us pounced upon the vessels and returned home to report that they had burned eight of the air guard and laid bombs upon a transport and a cargo vessel.

That afternoon a mix of Marine fighter-bombers and Army P-40s sought out the Japanese ships. VMF-313 claimed three bombs sank a troopship. VMF-115 declared a big cargo vessel destroyed, and VMF-211 said its pilots had battered a pair of destroyers. When the Joint Army-Navy Assessment Committee (JANAC) convened it scaled down the day's achievements to only two cargo ships sunk off Leyte on that day. However, when MAG-12 F4Us and the Army's P-40s revisited the area, they blasted already wounded ships, sinking a destroyer and a transport.

On this day, a quartet of Corsairs roamed the skies over the beachhead near Ormoc. As an American resupply convoy steamed through the Surigao Strait, a swarm of kamikazes dropped on the ships. The four F4Us rushed to help stave off the gang of Zekes, a batch of which picked out the destroyer *Reid* as prey. Gunners on the DD blasted two out of the sky. Two dove into the sea within a few hundred yards of the *Reid*, while another managed to bang into the side of the ship, and one grazed the bow before smashing into the water. A final thrust from dead astern exploded against the destroyer, detonating the vessel's ammunition magazines. The warship foundered in a scant fifteen seconds.

The four Marine pilots frantically tried to aid in the defense and actually flew through a torrent of AA from the American ships as they tried to close with the Zekes. Too late to save the *Reid,* they accounted for five of the would-be kamikazes. For the day, the Marines counted six Corsairs shot down and three pilots killed. Enemy fighter fire or AA damaged seven or eight more F4Us so severely they were consigned to the scrap heap.

Combined operations by the Army Air Corps and the Marines bounced over some rough patches. Lambrecht, according to Sherrod, was disturbed when the CO of the resident 308th Bomb Wing announced that his people were not trained for the predawn takeoffs and after-dark landings necessary for the last-light and early-light patrols, essentially a duty incumbent upon day fighters since it did not involve radar direction. That levied an additional burden upon the night fighters, expected also to handle the after-dark work. Furthermore, the first ground controllers were Army specialists unfamiliar with the Marine technology. On several occasions misdirection frustrated night fighters, who lost their targets and became uncertain of their own location.

On December 12 Lambrecht's "Bay Eyes" dispatched a pair of four-plane patrols for an early-light survey. One pilot aborted, and the trio in that flight suddenly received word of a big group of enemy planes intent on savaging Ormoc invasion ships. Outnumbered eleven to one, the leathernecks—led by Captain David W. Thomson—nevertheless flung themselves at the raiders. Their onslaught knocked down five planes and dispersed the neat formations. At the same time, Lieutenant Fletcher D. Miller, leading the other four Marine Hellcats, responded to Thomson's call for help. Miller and company disposed of six more planes from a force that was described as showing poor air discipline and evading combat—the quality of Japanese aviators had declined sharply because of heavy losses.

The Ormoc vessels, which quelled their AA against the intruders once they saw the Marines rush among them, radioed a grateful, "Nice show, boys, thanks a million." VMF(N)-541 suffered no human or aircraft casualties.

Absent a mandate for nocturnal sorties, the Army commanders

paid little heed to the need for field lights at Tacloban. Sometimes night fighters circled the field for as long as an hour until enough jeeps could be marshaled to illuminate the strip. Lambrecht solved the problem by requisitioning the field lights at Peleliu complete with a crew to operate them. (The Sixth Army commended MAG-12 saying "the gallantry and fighting spirit of the Marine pilots and the skill and tireless fidelity to duty of the ground personnel, who so well carried out their arduous task of maintaining and serving the aircraft under the worst possible conditions, constituted a major contribution to the success of the Leyte operations." Inexplicably, the official U.S. Army history of the Leyte campaign totally ignored the role of Marine aviation.)

Douglas MacArthur, working with Halsey two months after he returned to the Philippines on Leyte, directed an invasion of Mindoro, two hundred miles northwest of Leyte and just south of Luzon—MacArthur's ultimate objective in the archipelago. While intelligence indicated only a thin force of ground troops defending Mindoro, the Third Fleet expected strong kamikaze attention to the warships and transports. To protect the sailors and the amphibious forces, the Army's Fifth Air Force, half a dozen escort carriers, and Marines from MAG-12 mobilized. The overture by VMF-313 began with a dirge. Squadron leader Major Theodore Olsen took off in a Corsair with three hundred holes patched from earlier missions. When the plane failed in the sky, Olsen bailed but was killed, probably when his body struck the tail. Another F4U crashed on takeoff, killing the pilot and four men on the ground.

VMF-313 never encountered the kamikazes, one of which sneaked through the screen and exploded against the light cruiser *Nashville*. Between the suicide bomber and the detonation of the cruiser's ammunition stores, 130 men were killed outright, including many of the top brass. Later that day the destroyer *Haraden* reeled from such a punishing blow that it, too, retired from the striking force.

Mindoro fell swiftly and rather easily, but the Japanese refused to fold on Leyte, clinging to ever-shrinking portions of the turf. On the night of December 22, the redoubtable Sergeant Andre took off in the ongoing efforts to extinguish a "Piss Call Charlie." Directed by the ground toward a trio of bogeys, Andre followed a pair of them as they veered off toward Luzon. When they disappeared, Andre gave up his quest and set a course for Tacloban. En route, he suddenly noticed the dinghy light of four smudge pots. He realized he was over a small airstrip still in Japanese hands, and below him he saw the two planes in a landing circle. He inserted himself into the circle, and when a white light shot up from the field to signal the aircraft to land, Andre closed up tight. He shot down the trailing enemy and then caught the other one just as its wheels touched the ground. Both planes erupted in flames as they crashed. The fire lit up the strip, enabling Andre to make four strafing runs, burning two fuel trucks and as many as three parked aircraft.

During the run-up to the invasion of the Philippines and the struggle to enlarge the American-controlled territory, VMB-433 with its PBJs performed a variety of functions. Pilot Henry Sory recalled search missions over the ocean for downed fliers, flights in which his airplane navigated for the less well-equipped Corsairs moving up to Philippine bases carrying spare equipment for the fighters in their bomb bays, and sweeps over New Ireland where enemy troops might be hiding out. Anything suspicious brought "sort of a target practice." Later he wondered whether the outpouring of .50-caliber bullets he triggered from the cockpit might not have killed some inhabitants friendly to the United States.

Life on Emirau contrasted sharply with the grim asceticism enforced on Guadalcanal. "There was a hut with a wooden floor and a tent top," recalled Sory. "There were screened sides for ventilation purposes. Instead of sleeping on a cot, [we] constructed a frame built out of wood, and we would cut rubber bands out of inner tubes and stretch those across and long ways and then put your mattress on top of that. We had frequent recreation things for the enlisted personnel. There was a beer bust every now and then." The facilities at the officer's club, nonexistent during the first months of Marine aviation in the Solomons, offered billiards and liquor. There were movies almost every day. Sory described the food as more than adequate, thanks to the colonel in charge. "He would send a plane down to Australia to pick up fresh meat, vegetables and so forth, at least for the officers' mess."

When Sory went on leave to Sydney he and his copilot rented an apartment on Bondi Beach—which, he said, "exceeds anything on Waikiki Beach and Honolulu." They also rented a sports car. Ordinarily the soldiers' pay for Marines, including officers, would not have covered the revels jammed into one or two weeks. Sory explained, "We weren't supposed to take any cigarettes, except for what you needed. Cigarettes were a great bartering item. Our little radioman had a parachute bag and he had a hundred cartons of cigarettes and he got by with nobody inspecting him." Post exchanges sold a pack for five cents, and in the combat zone troops often received them gratis. "I had four or five cartons scattered out through my luggage. When [the radioman] got ready to leave Sydney to come home, he had enough to buy a case of Scotch liquor. When we landed at Bougainville, he was able to sell that and pay for his whole trip."

While individuals enjoyed such brief respites, the war crunched ahead. On New Year's Day, 1945, Admiral Halsey steered his Third Fleet toward Formosa (Taiwan) for another onslaught at the Japanese bases from which, in December 1941, bombers had first attacked the Americans in the Philippines. Stationed aboard the carrier *Essex* were VMF-124 and 213, the first Marine Corsair squadrons assigned carrier-based duty in World War II. (During the 1943 campaign in the Aleutians, six pilots from VMO-155 from the *Nassau* flew missions in F4F Wildcats.) Later, pieces of Marine fighter squadrons went aboard four other carriers, the *Wasp, Bennington, Bunker Hill,* and *Franklin.*

SIXTEEN

SUPPORTING MacARTHUR

Marine aviation, which had languished for months, revived as it undertook the mission to provide support for Douglas MacArthur's GIs in the Philippines. MacArthur, although dubious of the value, agreed when Major General Ralph Mitchell requested permission to bring Marine Air Group Twenty-four to the campaign. Although MacArthur commanded the Army Air Corps organizations in the archipelago, he was persuaded that the Marines were more willing to engage in the nasty business of ground support. MAG-24 included four squadrons that used Dauntless SBDs and for close to a year had been battering various sites from Bougainville bases. The official designation for the Marine Air Support Group that would bed down first at Dagupan on Luzon became MAGSDAGUPAN.

Actually, the leatherneck dive-bomber pilots were not that familiar with the concept they were expected to fulfill. John De Chant quoted some as asking, "What the hell is close support?" He added that while they had the usual training, they had no experience in air infantry support. "What basic knowledge they had of Marine infantry tactics and procedures varied somewhat from those used by the army." At the same time, it had been a requirement of Marine training—particularly for those who signed up before or early during the war—to undergo some service as ground company officers. Therefore, it was somewhat easier for the Marine airmen to accept the principle, foreign to both Army and Navy pilots, that "close support aviation is only an additional weapon to be employed at the discretion of the ground commander." There would be no doubt about who called the shots.

The Fifth Air Force, the Army's outfit in the Philippines and overall commander for MAG-24's operations, did not utilize direct communications from the front lines to the aircraft in support. Instead, the Army Air Force practice was that a support air party at division headquarters would supply data and direction for air strikes. Navy policy was similar. MAG-24 tacticians proposed a radical departure. Air-liaison parties (ALPs), consisting of a radioman and pilot or intelligence officer, would use a jeep close to the front lines. The ALP, coordinating with the infantry leaders, would "talk" support planes right to the target using the radio, rocket signals, colored panels, smoke, or any other means to identify the bull's-eye. Before leaving for the Philippines, MAG-24 had developed the tactics during maneuvers with the Army's Thirty-seventh Infantry Division while on Bougainville.

On January 9, 1945, troops from the U.S. Sixth Army, led by Lieutenant General Walter Krueger, scrambled ashore at Lingayen Gulf on Luzon to open the drive for possession of the largest island in the Philippines. The Japanese had not attempted to defend at the shoreline, and by nightfall Krueger's forces had expanded the beachhead fifteen miles inland. Less than three weeks later MAG-24 and MAG-32, both commanded by Colonel Clayton Jerome, departed from Dagupan for an airstrip converted from a rice paddy at Mangaldan, near Lingayen Gulf. For the following three months, the Marines from seven SBD squadrons with 174 aircraft, 472 officers, and 3,047 enlisted men flew missions from Mangaldan. Over time, Army planes also used the field.

Initially the front-line infantry was not ready for the tactical air operations. On January 27 Major Ben Manchester of VMSB-241 led the first air strike for the Luzon-based Marines. But the target was against installations behind the lines, including Clark Field, the former U.S. air base at Manila. Four days later the leatherneck fliers engaged in the task for which they had trained on

Bougainville. The Army's First Cavalry Division, under Major General Verne D. Mudge, jumped off for a planned hundred-mile dash all the way to Manila. Simultaneously the Thirty-seventh Infantry Division, the training partners of MAG-24 on Bougainville, advanced along the western flank of the First Cavalry as part of a three-pronged attack to liberate the city. From the southwest, where they had landed, troops from the Eighth Army also headed for Manila. At the start of this campaign, Captain Francis R. B. Godolphin, at forty-two a geriatric member of the military—a former classics professor at Princeton who served as an intelligence officer and who told the university president he was enlisting in order for veterans after the war to have on the faculty someone familiar with their experiences—visited First Cavalry headquarters. There he met his opposite number, Colonel Robert R. F. Goheen, a former student of Godolphin. (Goheen eventually became president of Princeton, while Godolphin served as dean.) With others, they worked out an arrangement for a jeep with a radioman-driver to accompany those at the front line. To protect the left or eastern flank of the First Cavalry, nine SBDs kept constant watch from the air while at the same time searching for enemy strong points that lay ahead of the ground soldiers.

Captain Samuel H. McAloney, an original member of the air-liaison units, drew assignment to the spearhead for the Manila drive, the First Brigade of Brigadier General William C. Chase. McAloney said, "General Chase had no previous information about the project in detail. When he asked what equipment was sent, and found it was just a radio jeep, he merely issued the orders, 'Stay beside me and my jeep at all times.' "

McAloney discovered that the Air Corps's 308th Bombardment Wing had also dispatched a liaison party, but its complement included twenty-nine men and officers, a weapons carrier, a jeep, and a DUKW—an amphibious two-and-a-half-ton truck replete with Filipino houseboy. The unit proved too cumbersome to match the pace of the advance and too vulnerable when near the front. Furthermore, the Air Corps system involved forwarding requests through a chain of command that included division corps and Army headquarters before being passed on to the 308th Bom-bardment Wing. Chase accepted the Marines as possibly a quicker solution to his needs.

The race to Manila began at dawn on February 1. Overhead, the nine-plane patrol roamed up and down valleys, over and alongside hills, following roadways and trails seeking to detect enemy presence. Periodically they spotted roadblocks and promptly bombed them. Because the emphasis was on speed rather than confrontation, the fliers alerted the ground pounders of concentrations of Japanese and enabled the troopers to bypass opposition.

As the troops crossed a river opposite the town of Cabana-tuan—the site of a prison camp liberated in a daring raid by the Sixth Ranger Battalion—patrols by the SBDs relayed information on the deployment of the enemy soldiers south of Cabanatuan. VMSB-142 attacked targets and enabled the GIs to charge ahead.

On the second day Godolphin, accompanying the Second Brigade, learned of a full battalion of entrenched Japanese on high ground ready to stall any advance. From the skies, SBDs re-sponded to the Marine captain's instructions, and the dive-bombers swooped down, making strafing passes. Because the First Cavalry soldiers were so close, the aircraft never triggered a round, but the diversion created by the planes enabled the Amer-icans to maneuver into a position from which they routed the foe. At dusk the rapid progress achieved a union of First Cavalry troopers and the GIs of the Thirty-seventh Division.

As the First Brigade neared San Isidro, dive-bombers from VMSB-133 and 142 bombed and strafed the Japanese positions with unerring accuracy. The men on the ground reported that all bombs struck the targets and "left [them] in shambles." Air pa-trols then relayed word that a key route to Manila over the No-valiches Bridge remained intact. The troopers exploited the intelligence by rushing forward to seize the span before it could be blown.

On February 3, late in the afternoon, elements of the First Cav-alry entered the outskirts of Manila. The struggle intensified as tens of thousands of Japanese soldiers and beached sailors fought to the death to defend their Philippine prize. The air support by Marines did not end at the outskirts of Manila. As the American forces began to batter their way into the heart of the city, often in block-by-block, house-to-house combat, MAGSDAGUPAN personnel repeatedly directed the air support. Occasionally they coordinated strikes by the Air Corps, which deployed A-20 bombers.

Godolphin hooked up with the Seventh Cavalry Regiment as it seized the Balera water filtration plant. On February 8 the Japanese directed heavy machine-gun and mortar fire at the American positions from the far side of a ridge. Godolphin climbed a water tower, a position from which he could direct dive-bombers by means of a telephone wire to his jeep radio. He was broadcasting a mere 150 yards from frequent but—fortunately for Godophin—inaccurate potshots from the Japanese. On hand to witness the action were General Mudge from the First Cavalry and a visitor, Major General Edwin D. Patrick, CO of the Sixth Infantry Division, advancing on Manila from the northeast against the stalwart Japanese Shimbu Line, a chain of caves and pillboxes with interlocking fire.

Patrick had expressed doubt about close air support. When Marine Lieutenant Colonel John Smith had offered to provide the SBDs to help the Sixth Division, Patrick said he would not permit any bombs to be dropped within a thousand yards of his troops. Over Balera, Ben Manchester led the strike guided by Godolphin, and the latter instructed him to hit the enemy on the reverse side of the slope, preventing friendly fire casualties. A white phosphorus smoke bomb marked the target, and the dive-bombers started their runs. The first ordnance exploded just below the crest of the hill, on the Japanese side. The second drop detonated just behind, and all seven aircraft deftly dropped on the target while the cavalrymen on the other side of the hill cheered.

As the Marine aircraft flew off, army patrols cautiously explored the ridge. They encountered no opposition but, according to De Chant, discovered numerous enemy dead along with eight machine-gun positions and fifteen mortar emplacements abandoned. In the distance the GIs saw Japanese soldiers in full flight to safety across the Marakina River.

Convinced by this demonstration, General Patrick asked Godolphin if he could expect the same kind of air support for his Sixth Division. When General Mudge reminded Patrick that the bombs would need to fall much nearer than the thousand-yard limitation, Patrick supposedly said, "I don't give a damn how close they hit!"

On the heels of the tactical support exploit guided from the water tower, Godolphin coordinated a mission by eighty-one aircraft from five Marine squadrons, with Manchester as the air commander. The biggest raid of the Luzon campaign, the venture utilized intelligence gathered by a Filipino guerrilla lieutenant who had sneaked into the target area to plot and sketch the enemy positions. The dive-bombers ignited fires in oil dumps, blew up AA installations, and destroyed other Japanese resources.

The Marines responded to a request from General Patrick for aid to his troops starting their assault upon the Shimbu Line. In a letter to Sherrod, Captain James L. McConaughy described his debut: ". . . everything went to perfection—targets initially were 1,000 yards and more away; gradually we worked in to 500 yards and sometimes a bit under. We worked all the tricks, like dummy runs while infantry advanced under them. When the Japs caught on to this we'd bring in the first section and have them drop, then infantry would advance while the second and third sections (usually nine-plane flights) dove on the target but did not drop.

"Then when the Japs caught on to this, we'd bring in the first section and have them drop, followed by the second section which did not drop, followed by the third which did. The pilots—squadron leaders and other senior officers—usually took to coming over to our forward o.p. When the Japs started fiddling around with rockets, they took an especial personal interest in getting good targets and getting on them. I remember an especially able regular Marine officer, Major Frazer [Fred J., CO of VMSB-236], who landed his plane one day and came up forward. When the Japs let some rockets go, he hit the dirt hard, like me. While we were loving the dirt, a dogface in the same position said, 'Hey, were you one of those guys up there this morning?' Frazer grunted uh-huh. 'Well,' said the soldier, 'I'll be damned.' It was the first time he'd ever seen a flyer close-up."

Some units, however, remained resistant to the close air support; the Sixth Division's First Regiment had been strafed by Army Air Corps planes north of Manila. On February 28 a squad on reconnaissance desperately needed assistance. Their lieutenant had fallen into a ravine and broken his leg. His men refused to abandon him to the Japanese, only a few hundred yards away. McConaughy reported, "We said we could help. After a very thorough briefing, all by radio, the regimental commander [Colonel James E. Rees] said the lead plane could drop one wing bomb. It was beautiful to watch. We were on a high cliff on one side of the valley and it was a clear day. The first drop was dead on. The colonel was impressed and allowed that we could let the lead plane come in again and drop his belly and other wing bomb. It took the SBD twenty minutes to climb up again. His second dive was fantastically accurate too, and the colonel said he was convinced, so the other eight planes followed the squadron leader down. The bombing was fantastically successful—the farthest one of 27 bombs being 30 yards off the target. From then on the colonel couldn't get enough planes for his regiment. Literally, he asked for nine flights (nine planes each) as a standing daily order."

General Patrick (who would be fatally wounded in March), along with Colonel Rees, commended his Marine allies. "The close air support given this division . . . has been outstanding. The advance of our troops over difficult mountainous terrain against a well-armed determined enemy is being made possible in no small part by such air strikes."

Other army generals for whom MAGSDAGUPAN worked paid tribute. Chase, the First Brigade leader, said, "I have never seen such able, close and accurate support as the Marine flyers are giving us." The First Cavalry's General Mudge said, "The excellent close support furnished by Marine dive-bombers in advance of ground troops east of Manila . . . between February 1 and March 15 was a major contribution to the success of the operation. . . . The dive-bombers of the First Marine Air Wing have kept the enemy on the run. They have kept him underground and enabled troops to move up with fewer casualties and greater speed. I cannot say enough in praise of the dive-bomber pilots and their gunners for the job they have done in giving my men close ground support in this operation." He also commented, "I can say without reservation that the Marine dive-bomber outfits are among the most flexible I have seen in this war. They will try anything, and from my experience with them I have found that anything they try usually pans out."

General Krueger and his opposite number at the Eighth Army, Lieutenant General Robert L. Eichelberger, issued similar compliments.

Undoubtedly, the increasing respect for the Marine efforts by those up front on the ground and their commanders cheered the Marines in what otherwise was a grim, seemingly thankless task. Squadron leader Major Ben Manchester said of the operations, "It's dull as hell for a pilot. Remember he hardly ever sees what he hits. To him, the target is either a hunk of ground or a hunk of brush, unless it happens to be a building of some kind. The pilot hits it and that's all there is to it. Unless the ground forces take the trouble to tell him the results, he never knows whether he has done any good for all his sweating."

According to John De Chant, there were some compensations. "Marines agreed that operations in the Philippines were paradise compared to the aerial strangulation chore in the South Pacific. At least they saw towns and other signs of civilization, even if they had to destroy them. The ragged but ecstatic Filipinos welcomed them noisily wherever they moved up." The Marines returned the compliment with many missions in support of the bands of ragged, poorly equipped Filipino guerrillas who ravaged unwary Japanese in the mountains and fed valuable intelligence to the regular American forces. In these ventures there were echoes of Marine aviation's 1920s missions in Nicaragua.

For all of the compliments lavished upon the Marine air-liaison parties and the doctrine of close air support, word does not seem to have reached the United States. Burton Pearsall, a native of small-town Illinois born in 1922, enlisted in the summer of 1942, having completed his second year of college. After earning his wings and a Marine commission in 1944, he studied the arts of a dive-bomber pilot flying an SBD. Although the first courses in strategy and tactics for ALPs and air-to-ground aid had begun at Bougainville in the fall of 1944, Pearsall said, "We didn't run into it until we got to the Philippines. Actually, in the Philippines, we, along with these other guys, pioneered close air support. We put the finishing touches on how you do it right."

That said, he spent many hours in the States learning to control his aircraft, navigate, and drop a bomb. "You build up your confidence. You knew what you were doing. You were good at what you did. Our squadrons of pilots were trained right to the Nth degree to where if they asked us to move a bomb fifty feet, we could do it and hit the target. The big thing in those days was that you were afraid you weren't going to get there in time, that the war was going to be over and you wouldn't get your chance. That sounds kind of 'macho' but that's how you felt. You wanted to be there."

On February 12 he was "there," at Mangaldan on Luzon, where—having joined VMSB-243—he went on his first strike. Pearsall maintained his eagerness throughout his tour. He befriended the operations officer, who listed him for missions whenever possible. As a result, in April, Pearsall flew eighteen consecutive days until the flight surgeon noticed his hours logged and grounded him for week.

"The skipper was that way too. If you flew [as wingman for him] and sometimes you might miss a beat [err] or hit the wrong target, then the skipper'd say, 'I think you better take a little time off.' He watched you like a hawk. He was like a mother hen, although he was only twenty-six years old.

"Most of the time," Pearsall went on, "it was [bombing Japanese positions]. Sometimes it might be a bridge; sometimes it might be a cave that had ammunition in it or a gun position. We bombed antiaircraft gun positions around Manila. It was usually a target where one of these air control guys was down there telling you where to go, what to look for.

"The leader in your squadron might say, 'I'm going to go down and drop my bomb,' and he'd go down and drop it; and the guy on the ground would say, 'That's it! Right there!' Then everybody else would follow him and bomb on his bomb or bomb a hundred yards to the north or a hundred yards up the slope or whatever. We could start at the top of a ridge and bomb down the side while the guys [ground troops] were on the other side of the ridge waiting to come over it. That's how accurate we were. There was one time when they dropped in the wrong area and killed some Army guys but that was just one of those unfortunate things that happen in wartime."

Although Corsair pilots had begun using napalm, Pearsall recalled that on dive-bombers it was mounted on the wings and could not be controlled. "You had no accuracy with it. It was okay for fighters because they would come in down low and sling it, sort of, out in front of them, whereas the dive bomber was coming straight down and this stuff would flip off the wings and it was anybody's guess where it was going."

Enemy aircraft no longer posed much of a problem, and Pearsall fairly frequently flew with his flight surgeon as his gunner or carried other passengers. On return from a mission the fliers played tricks such as sidling up close to a companion and putting a wing under his wing, which would produce turbulence that tipped up the other plane. "It got to the point where, in order to break the monotony we'd start and get rolling down the runway and pick the gear up and roll on the tail wheel and fold the gear up and then take off from there. If you didn't have enough air speed and you landed on your bomb, it could be a wild ride."

With the battle for Manila raging at its fiercest, Pearsall and the others in his squadron dive-bombed Japanese ships in the harbor around the island fortress of Corregidor. On another mission, near Manila, Pearsall said he had pulled out of a dive and noticed that his bullets were ricocheting off the grass roof of a hut. "I said, 'That ain't right.' About that time, there was a flash in the window where they took a shot at me. It was a gun emplacement—reinforced concrete—covered with grass to make it look like a Filipino shack. I didn't hang around. I went back to the squadron and told them about it and that afternoon three of us went back down and put a few bombs through their front door and that was the end of that." For this action he received a commendation.

Compared with the rigors of life on Guadalcanal for the first Marine aviators in combat, life in the archipelago was relatively comfortable. On Luzon the tents were on the ground, but on Mindanao the officers scrounged mahogany and built a deck. A Filipino houseboy tended to many of their wants, bringing drinking water, sweeping the tent out, and taking them to his home for a feast of chicken. The local people laundered their clothes on a daily basis. The food was "adequate": Spam, fried in the morning, breaded at noon, and baked at night. "It was a lot better than the poor guys up on the front lines were getting, which was C-rations and all that crap. They were probably as sick of that as we were of the Spam." One pilot offhandedly wrote home complaining about the food. His family contacted their congressman, who brought up the subject with Pentagon brass. The Marine Corps headquarters in Washington bucked the matter back down the line until a colonel at the base called in the pilot and vigorously chewed him out. When his sister inquired whether the food had improved and volunteered to check the congressman again, her brother pleaded for restraint lest he suffer another tirade from the colonel.

Pearsall described the once deadly ground fire as little threat. "Sure you could see them firing at you, just one in front of the other as you were coming down. But all that you had to do was rattle a few .50 calibers around inside that gun revetment and those guys were over the side and gone. . . . We never got hit, but [we] could have. There was a lot of fire, but we never . . . worried about it. We figured they couldn't hit us anyway. That's how dumb we were."

From Luzon, Pearsall and his squadron moved on to the battles for the island of Mindanao. "That was a major campaign. The 41st Division went in there. There was fighting right behind us. We were sitting down low . . . up behind us the mountains rose. When I first got there, we'd take off right from the strip and . . . fly right up into the hills, drop the bomb, and come back and get another bomb."

He was imbued with the attitude that pervaded the war in the

Pacific: "They were Japs, and your job was to kill as many as you could. I mean, if you dropped a bomb and saw some running across an open field . . . we'd wind that baby around and come over and let our gunners strafe them. We had no feeling for them at all. Get rid of them. All you thought of was, 'the more of them that I kill, the less there are that are going to get after me.'

"[It] always entered into your mind—the fact that maybe you'd go down and get caught. But you knew that if you got caught, you could kiss yourself good-bye because they weren't going to take you prisoner for very long. Just like the guy on the island down there [a pilot had crashed on Panay]. They got him in the morning and killed him in the afternoon. They weren't going to give you any breaks."

While Pearsall frequently expressed his high regard for the Army "dogfaces" and had no problems with Air Corps fliers other than to stress the superiority of Marine aviators, like many leathernecks he considered the man in charge, General Douglas MacArthur, "an egotistical son-of-a-bitch who thought he was the smartest bastard in the Pacific Theater. As far as the Marine Corps was concerned, they didn't exist [for him]. Everything that he put out from his headquarters was 'MacArthur's Army' or 'MacArthur's forces.'" Pearsall allowed that the man may have been brilliant, but he doubted it.

A need for more fighter-bombers to service both the Navy and Army campaigns finally convinced the admirals and generals of the desirability of adding the Marine pilots to the fleet. For leatherneck brass, the effort to return Marines to carrier duty (during the 1930s, squadrons had been aboard flattops) had begun in mid-1944 with awareness that without a seagoing capacity, the role of Marine aviation would be substantially curtailed. Director of aviation Brigadier General Louis E. Woods, harking back to the theme of his organization as supportive of fleet landing operations, said, "The Marine aviator and the Marine foot soldier must be a team." However, that position bucked the prevalent attitudes of the day.

During the first three years of World War II, like the Army Air Corps and naval aviation, the Marine air arm focused most intensively upon combat against enemy aircraft or attacking ships. Airmen relished this role with its visible results and attendant glory. Nobody accrued glory for ground support, and it was difficult and dangerous duty. Furthermore, Marines on carriers always were subservient to the task force and fleet commanders, invariably naval officers. Marion L. Dawson, who earned his wings during the 1920s and served in various slots during World War II, recalled that in 1945, after the formation of a Marine carrier air group, he received orders to relieve Colonel Albert D. Cooley as head of a Marine carrier group. Giving Dawson the word on what to expect, Cooley said, "I was on the flagship [of a task force] and my friend was the boss, a Navy admiral. And he said [while they were on the flag bridge], 'Al, the only thing you can do in this command is hold my cigar when I ask you to.'"

Aboard the flattops, including those entirely staffed with Marine squadrons, who did what and when would remain the prerogative of the admirals. Francis Mulcahy, the Great War veteran and during World War II a boss of Marine air operations in the Pacific, noted that Marine aviation would serve "to support naval operations—that was actually the first thing in practice and by necessity. We had no more control than the man in the moon of what our aviation was going to do in some circumstances. It was whatever the naval amphibious force commander directed until the target was secure. It was his responsibility. They could support the ground troops if the naval commander would let them. But if kamikazes were going to sink his ships and his transports, instead of supporting the ground troops you'd be up there fighting the Japs [in the air]."

In fact, it was the advent of the kamikazes that forced the Navy to accept the first Marine-flown Corsairs aboard carriers. While Cooley had been training people for their assignment aboard escort carriers, the demand for more fighters to deal with the suicide planes escalated. There were not enough adequately trained Navy fighters to meet the need. VMF-124 and 213 hastily achieved carrier qualification on flattops in Hawaiian waters and became part of the complement on the *Essex*.

When Task Force Thirty-eight with the *Essex* sortied into the

South China Sea, Marine Corsairs protected Navy torpedo bombers on a strike at Okinawa. TF-38 claimed destruction of more than two hundred aircraft caught on the ground and twenty-seven in the air, including one shot down by Lieutenant Colonel William Millington, the CO of VMF-124. When the kamikazes struck severe blows at escort carriers and other warships working near the Philippines, the task force returned to the waters off the archipelago to lambaste the home fields for the suicide fleet.

The first nine days of operations, however, demonstrated that simply learning to take off and land did not prepare pilots for carrier-based warfare. In this short period, seven Marine pilots died and thirteen F4Us were destroyed. None could be chalked up to enemy guns. They were victims of weather, mistakes in navigation, water landings, and deck crashes. A few weeks of learning to carrier-qualify could not compensate for the months of instruction in navigation and flattop procedures ordinarily given Navy pilots. While the Marines mourned their severe losses, not a single F6F Navy fighter from the *Essex* went down for similar reasons.

The effort to eliminate the Japanese air force brought Halsey's Third Fleet closer to the shores of mainland Asia. While MacArthur's troops were carrying out their landings in the Lingayen Gulf, the U.S. armada slammed what was then Indochina, specifically Saigon and Camranh Bay, names that would become more familiar to Americans twenty years later, during the Vietnam War. Initially the Marine fighters provided cover for the ships, but no enemy appeared. Then they took off to accompany TBMs on a raid against Saigon and surrounding airfields. The attack sank four cargo ships, including one hit registered by Major Fay V. Domke of VMF-213 in a fighter-bomber. In addition the Marines claimed close to a dozen aircraft destroyed on the ground. Marine correspondent Lieutenant Hal Goodwin, observing from a torpedo bomber, wrote, "After our Avengers had gutted shipping and shore installations, the Marines roared in. Captain Gus Thomas [a triple ace with sixteen and a half planes] took his division and made merry with a neat line of Tojos, stubby single-engine fighters.

"Irish [Lieutenant Joseph O. Lynch] got it as he went in low to get another plane on the ground. Automatic fire pounded his engine and he was suddenly out of altitude and grating along the ground of Saigon in a wheels-up landing. The other Marines came low to cover and saw him climb from his cockpit and raise his hand in salute. They dipped their wings and left him there, a lone, straight figure in an alien land."

Lynch found refuge among some French Foreign Legionnaires until several months later, when the Japanese declared war on the Vichy French. Lynch, with half a dozen other downed fliers, helped the legionnaires resisting the Nipponese and eventually reached safety after a C-47 from Kunming picked him and his associates up and flew them to China. Other Marines who crash-landed were less fortunate. Those not killed when their plane smashed to the ground were executed by their Japanese captors.

Task Force Thirty-eight and its carrier aircraft now struck at Formosa, Hong Kong, and Swatow on the China coast. Unlike Burton Pearsall's experience in the Philippines, the AA at Hong Kong was described as "from intense to unbelievable." The profit-and-loss figures showed a deficit as the raiders counted thirty of their own planes destroyed in combat and another thirty-one wrecked in operations. The enemy figures were twenty-six shot down and twenty-one obliterated on the ground. Clearly the Japanese retained sufficient firepower to inflict severe damage to attackers.

Having battered sites on the mainland of Asia, the strategists now sought to bring the war directly to Japan. Admiral Raymond Spruance relieved Halsey and the Third Fleet became the Fifth Fleet, while Task Force Thirty-eight, led by Admiral John S. McCain, relinquished command to Admiral Marc Mitscher under the designation of TF-58. Three more carriers loaded two Marine fighter squadrons each, giving the fleet 144 Corsairs and 216 Marine pilots to go along with the naval aviators. The newcomers had undergone intensive navigation instruction in the hope of avoiding the numerous operational losses to the first complement aboard the *Essex*.

Millington from the deck of the *Essex* led the first strike at the Tenryu airfield while Major Dave Marshall, also from that flattop, commanded the escort for torpedo and photo planes bound for Tokyo. From the *Bennington*, VMF-112 under Major Herman Hansen Jr. struck at the main island of Honshu. The *Bunker Hill*, Mitscher's flagship, launched VMF-221 skippered by Major Edwin S. Roberts Jr., while VMF-216, guided by Major George E. Dooley, took off from the *Wasp* to pound airfields. For two days TF-58 pounded the home islands. Overall the fleet claimed more than 500 enemy planes destroyed, including 332 knocked out of the air. The Marines received credit for twenty-one shoot-downs and sixty wrecked on airstrips.

Attention then pinpointed the tiny island of Iwo Jima as vital for direct blows at the home islands of Japan. Its airfields posed a threat to the carrier war, and possession would provide a base to assist the B-29s bound for Japan from the Marianas. With the escort carriers exclusively designated for Marine aircraft still undergoing training exercises, the only leathernecks available to assist the Marine ground troops who would storm the shores of Iwo flew from the big flattops. On invasion day, February 19, they, along with Navy aircraft, followed up on seventy-two straight days of raids by Navy planes and the Army Air Corps.

Marine Colonel Vernon E. Megee had been named Commander Air, Iwo Jima. He discussed the tactics with Marine flight commanders Millington and Marshall, agreeing that their two squadrons would fly parallel to the beach. Supposedly, Megee instructed, "Go in and scrape your bellies on the beach." Millington led twenty-four F4Us and twenty-four Navy F6Fs, which assaulted the defenses fronting the beaches with rockets, strafing runs, and napalm for ten minutes, thirty minutes before the scheduled arrival of landing craft. The aerial attacks gradually moved inland, staying ahead of the troops by two hundred yards.

Megee recalled, "It was a very impressive and spectacular thing. Whether it did any good or not, I don't know but I know that we didn't get any fire in the initial landing. They got ashore and well inland before they started getting hit with mortars. There were no Japs during this period that were able to get up and harass the actual landing boats. I suspect it was more spectacular than effective. It had a great morale effect on the ground troops. This was the first time that they had gone in for a landing and had seen their own airplanes come right down in front of them. I had a great many expressions of appreciation from the gravel crunchers. . . ."

Whether the bombardment had destroyed defenses near the water's edge or the enemy simply no longer sought to take a stand at the beachhead, two hours after H-hour, a crescendo of mortar, artillery, and machine-gun fire would envelop the landing forces. After several days the Marine squadrons, without ever providing much in the way of close-in ground support, pulled out with the big carriers for more forays against the Japanese islands.

"The air support fell down," said Megee, "because all we had then for a few days were Navy flyers. Never enough and never at the place they should be." To provide stronger and more effective aid to the foot soldiers, the Army sent a group of P-51s. Megee recalled, "The pilots had had practically no training at all in supporting ground forces." He noted that communications had relied on a four-channel system set to handle both traffic and tactical control. The only way he could talk to pilots was on the Air Corps's frequency for landing, which meant that during a strike he could not handle any air traffic in or out of the landing strips.

Prior to the invasion of Iwo, Megee said he conferred with the squadron commanders about their training and their technique with P-51s, performing glide-bombing runs at about a forty-five-degree angle. He arranged for delayed-action fuses of about twelve seconds, which would enable the ordnance to penetrate the bluffs and hills before detonating. "For one whole day I gave them dummy runs on some little rocky islands off the coast of Iwo Jima, letting them go in and strafe those islands and answer signals. I wanted them to answer signals, to be sure that when they got out in front of the Marines, they [the ground troops] wouldn't shoot us up.

"They were very enthusiastic. . . . We got these thousand-pound bombs out in front of the troops where we suspected some concentrations underground and they started coming in from the flanks. I wouldn't let them come in over our troops from either direction and then they would bomb parallel in front of the lines instead of over and toward them [which would add to the risk of hitting friendly forces].

"Those thousand-pound bombs with a delayed action fuze acted just like a naval gun shell. They had a penetrating trajectory and they would go into those bluffs, particularly the west coast, and the airplane would be long gone before this bomb would explode and the whole damn face of the bluff would fall off into the sea. We found that it was exposing a lot of Japanese tunnels and strong points. The ground Marines were very enthusiastic about them. I got some caustic comments about why couldn't Marine aviation do things like that for them. But Marine aviation was off on the fast carriers up around Tokyo."

Marine fliers from Grasshopper squadrons VMO-4 and VMO-5 brought their tiny aircraft to an airstrip on Iwo to do artillery spotting for the remainder of the island campaign. Marine air transports supplied tons of ammunition, machine-gun parts, plasma, and even mail by airdrop. On March 4, two weeks after Millington led fighter bombers over the beaches, a crippled B-29, staggering from wounds received over Japan, made an emergency landing at Iwo, the first of hundreds in the following months that would find refuge there. And on March 16 the island was finally declared secured.

The escort carriers staffed completely with Marine aviators had steadily expanded. The *Block Island* loaded VMF-511, VMTB-233, and the utility squadron CASD-1 in February. Bruce Porter, who had come to Guadalcanal with VMF-121 as a Corsair pilot in June 1943 and yearned to fly night fighters, had fulfilled his wish, acting as commander of a new nine-plane detachment VMF(N)-544, which would operate from the *Block Island*. VMF(N)-544 became half of a hybrid squadron, VMF-511, with conventional fighters completing the complement. Porter acquired pilots flying F6F Hellcats and started a training cycle that would include simulated carrier landings at California airfields while he circulated in the movie colony's social life.

Having learned the rudiments of carrier operations, Porter and company flew aboard the *Block Island* and commenced exercises to familiarize themselves with flattop operations. On Valentine's Day, 1945, however, increasingly bad weather threatened a training mission. He and the group commander, Lieutenant John Dobbin, an ace himself, met with the ship's skipper, Captain Massey Hughes, a former PBY pilot. The two Marines suggested that in view of the deteriorating conditions, the activity be scrubbed. Hughes, however, after obtaining a meteorological report, insisted they carry on. Nine of the twenty-seven scheduled to launch, including Porter, aborted because of engine malfunctions. Those who did take off encountered worse weather than predicted and soon the *Block Island* began receiving distress messages. Hughes now canceled the affair, but the recall came too late for many. Seven aircraft were lost due to midair collisions and crashes on land or sea. Eight Marines died and nine more ended up in hospitals. A board of inquiry cleared the captain and blamed the deaths on pilot error. Porter, nevertheless, held Hughes responsible.

In the following months Marine squadrons received assignment to the *Gilbert Islands*, *Vella Gulf*, and *Cape Gloucester*. The overall plan called for another four such arrangements by late 1945 for Operation Olympic, the invasion of Japan.

SEVENTEEN

OKINAWA

Following the subjugation of Iwo and after the command rejected a proposed landing on Formosa, Okinawa in the Ryukyu chain became the next step on the march toward Japan itself. Some 60 miles in length and the biggest island in the Ryukyus, Okinawa, then considered part of Japan, lies only 325 miles south of Kyushu. It offered an excellent base for Olympic. Operation Iceberg, the invasion of Okinawa, was scheduled for April 1, 1945.

To hinder if not eliminate any efforts by the Japanese to use home-based planes against the invasion force, Task Force Fifty-eight sailed from the big station at Ulithi for a major swipe at the southernmost island of Kyushu. Navy and Marine carrier planes, beginning on March 16, smashed forty-five airfields, burning up buildings, claiming 102 defenders shot down and another 275 aircraft on the ground blasted.

On March 19 Mitscher switched attention to shipping in the Kure and Kobe harbors. While the raiders flew off, a combat air patrol kept vigil. Suddenly, from out of the two-thousand-foot ceiling an enemy plane, having pierced the screen, dove on the flattop *Franklin* and cut loose a pair of six-hundred-pound bombs. They exploded among thirty-one aircraft loaded and ready to launch, igniting a holocaust of gasoline, rockets, bombs, and machine-gun ammunition. With dead and wounded above- and belowdecks, some crewmen abandoning ship without orders, seven hundred sailors and Marines fought to control the conflagration. For four hours the big ship lay dead in the water, but although the Japanese tried to administer a coup de grâce they failed. Eventually, with the help of a tow, the *Franklin* slowly traveled toward Ulithi. The attack killed 772, of whom 65 were from Marine aviation, and although pilots from VMF-214 and 452 flew several missions off other carriers, the losses of personnel and their home knocked these two squadrons out of the war.

The strikes by Navy dive- and torpedo bombers, chaperoned by Marine Corsairs, upon the Kure and Kobe harbors inflicted serious damage upon the remaining warships of the Imperial Navy. During the sweeps on adjoining installations, Marine fighters battled flights of would-be interceptors, some of whom demonstrated great skill. Three F4Us went down and eight barely wobbled home to the *Bennington*. If the figures are to be believed, the Americans shot another 97 out of the sky and destroyed 225 at the airfields.

The experiences in the Philippines, at Iwo, and during raids upon Japanese installations on the Asian mainland and home islands, plus the kamikaze menace, escalated the demand for added power on the carriers. The adaptation of F6F Hellcats as fighter bombers, to replace dive- and torpedo bombers, strengthened the flattop punch, which became even more formidable upon introduction of the Corsair. The F4U could tote as much as four thousand pounds of ordnance. After it dropped the bombs, it was probably the best fighter in the Pacific Theater. Although several Marine squadrons equipped with F4Us now flew from some of the flattops, the Navy decided to temporarily add some leathernecks to its own squadrons. Bill Nickerson, who had done a tour as a scout-bomber pilot at Bougainville then switched to fighters, was on March 29 among a small number of leathernecks drafted to fly in a Navy squadron, VF-10, the Grim Reapers, stationed on the *Intrepid*. Nickerson and his companions had been practicing operations from escort carriers and therefore encountered no problems with the *Intrepid*'s enormous flight deck.

"As the senior officer among the eight lieutenants," recalled Nickerson, "it fell to me to report to someone and I decided the Air Group commander was the best bet. He was Commander

John Hyland, and what amazed me was that he wasn't surprised that I had no orders to present. We were assigned quarters with our Navy squadronmates and by 1500 I was part of a . . . mission [against a Japanese airfield]. I was the only Marine in the flight."

For Operation Iceberg, against an estimated hundred thousand Japanese soldiers embedded in Okinawa, the United States mustered an enormous combination of land, naval, and air forces. The ground troops would eventually include four Army divisions—the Seventh, Seventy-seventh, Ninety-sixth, and Twenty-seventh—plus the First and Sixth Marine divisions and, toward the end of the campaign, the Second Marine Division. The fleet to deliver the invaders and sustain them added up to 1,457, including 22 British vessels. Thousands of aircraft would scourge the enemy defenses and fight off the anticipated attacks on the offshore armada.

While the land contingent came under Lieutenant Simon Bolivar Buckner's Tenth Army, command of the tactical air force for that organization went to Major General Pat Mulcahy, also head of the Second Marine Air Wing. Amid a vast galaxy of aircraft, Marine aviation would contribute fifteen Marine fighter squadrons and two torpedo bomber units expected to operate from captured bases on the island. In addition, the *Block Island* and *Gilbert Islands* with their Marine air units would participate.

Prior to April 1—Love Day, the designation for the first amphibious outfits to strike the beaches—Seventy-seventh Division soldiers stormed ashore on the Keramas, a crop of small islands with excellent anchorage, close to Okinawa. The opposition crumbled quickly but the soldiers discovered 350 suicide boats armed with depth charges, presaging the expansion of the kamikaze program.

After the usual preinvasion bombardment from the sea and air, the first waves from the amphibious forces swept onto Okinawa's beaches. To their surprise and pleasure, they met no resistance and swiftly moved three miles inland, by noon capturing key objectives—the Yontan and Kadena airfields—without a struggle. So quickly had they seized Yontan that an unwitting Japanese pilot landed there; after he left the cockpit and tried to run, he was shot down. However, kamikazes had already begun to take their toll, actually striking a dozen ships supporting the invasion, including a transport and two LSTs with Second Division Marines feinting an assault on another area of Okinawa.

Artillery spotter aircraft—which needed only five hundred feet of runway—started to fly out of the captured fields on April 2. Construction and service crews quickly prepared the fields for combat aircraft. Desperate to preserve the closest outpost to the homeland, the Japanese devised Operation Ten-Go, successive mass waves of suicide bombers known as *kikusui*, "floating chrysanthemums." When a *kikusui* numbering 355 planes struck on April 6–7, Marine squadrons aboard the *Bennington* and *Bunker Hill* joined in the desperate struggle to fight them off. Along with the first big assault by kamikazes, from Kure on the Inland Sea the Japanese navy dispatched the world's largest battleship, the sixty-eight-thousand-ton *Yamato*. Accompanied by a small number of cruisers and destroyers, the massive warship headed for Okinawa where its 18.1-inch guns could ravage the Allied vessels. However, an American submarine spotted the convoy as it sailed out of Japanese waters, and then a scout off the *Essex* picked up the quarry.

Early on April 7 a pair of Marine twin-engine flying boats that took off from the anchorage around Okinawa played a small but vital role. For five hours, hovering just out of range of the enemy antiaircraft guns, the pilots from the two Marine flying boats, Lieutenant James R. Young and Lieutenant Richard L. Simms, tracked the *Yamato*. Admiral Mitscher launched a series of gigantic air strikes—the first numbering 280 dive- and torpedo bombers. The hunters swarmed over a hapless Japanese fleet bereft of any air cover.

A pilot from the *Belleau Wood*, Lieutenant (j.g.) W. E. Delaney, made his attack at fourteen hundred feet, dropping four five-hundred-pounders. As his plane passed over the battleship, he said, "There was a loud explosion under the fuselage. The cockpit filled with smoke and fumes. One wing was on fire. I was afraid the plane would explode and ordered my crew [a gunner and a radioman] to jump. They bailed out five miles southwest of the Jap task force. I watched their parachutes open, then I jumped." Unfortunately, although Delaney saw their chutes deploy, both men apparently drowned.

Delaney, after hitting the sea in the midst of the enemy vessels, managed to inflate his rubber raft. However, he stayed in the water, hanging on to the raft and hiding from the Japanese. A destroyer came within a hundred yards but veered off, apparently thinking there were no American survivors. "At first I was so cold," said Delaney, "when the Jap can approached, I thought of giving up. But I decided they might shoot me. So I stayed behind the raft."

The pilots from the two Marine flying boats, Young and Simms, still on station, saw him floating amid Japanese sailors who, having abandoned their sinking ships, clung to bits of wreckage. Simms acted as a decoy to draw off any fire from the remaining enemy vessels, and Young set down his patrol plane. He scooped up Delaney and flew him to safety on Okinawa. Within a few hours the *Yamato* blew up and sank, along with a cruiser and four destroyers.

During the slaughter of the *Yamato*, F4Us from MAG-31 catapulted from the decks of the escort carriers *Sitkoh Bay* and *Breton* for operations at Yontan. A group of Corsairs, providing air cover for the launchings, spotted a two-engine Lily five hundred feet off the water and taking dead aim on the carriers. The Marine pilots from VMF-311 dove on the intruder, lacing it with twenty-millimeter shells. It staggered forward still on direct course for the *Sitkoh Bay*. A scant fifty yards from the target, the right wing fell off and the plane crashed into the water. The four squadrons of MAG-31—VMF-224, 311, and 441, as well as VMF(N)-542—then made their way to the Okinawa base.

Earlier in the week, April 2, the forward echelon of VMF-323 had arrived at Kadena. One week later the entire squadron flew off a carrier one hundred miles from Okinawa to become one of the first combat units operating on land in the Ryukyus. George Axtell, a native of Pennsylvania, said that as a youth he yearned to work at some occupation apart from the region's industrial environment. An A student in high school, Axtell worked forty hours a week at a dairy store while devouring reports on current events. He matriculated at the University of Alabama, where he studied aeronautical engineering and joined a glider club that rebuilt the craft before soaring aloft in them. He obtained a private pilot's license while at the university and sharpened his understanding of world politics.

"I do not recall any personal animosity toward the Germans, Italians, or Japanese as a group of individuals. The philosophy manifested by the leaders of these governments, their political structure, national goals, aggressive nature of their military and in foreign affairs was, in my view, something that could not be tolerated by the democracies of the world. . . . The democracies had to resist. The United States must participate to assure the freedom of the countries that were being invaded. War was inevitable."

His convictions, at age nineteen, led him, in 1940, to volunteer for the military and become a fighter pilot. Rejected by the Army and Navy because of his age, he hitchhiked to Washington, DC's Anacostia Naval Air Station, where a Marine captain told him that the British had enlisted youngsters his age and he believed the corps should waive that requirement. In July the Marines accepted him, and by May 1941 he had earned his wings. But because he was only twenty, and ineligible for a commission at that age, Axtell briefly served as an instructor before receiving his lieutenant's bars.

Following a fifteen-month course at the Naval Academy in Annapolis, the twenty-three-year-old Axtell became the CO of VMF-323, the Death Rattlers, with responsibility for molding its members into a combat-ready outfit. But after eight months at the task he saw his pilots detached and shipped out as replacements, forcing Axtell to start afresh with novices. Promoted to major, he rebuilt the organization and with thirty-two Corsairs, on April 9, VMF-323 reached Okinawa. At Kadena, MAG-33 included three more units, VMF-312, VMF-322, and VMF(N)-543.

"We flew our first combat mission at dawn the next morning," said Axtell. "Twenty-four aircraft took off in atrocious weather—a three- to four-hundred-foot ceiling in heavy rain topping in excess of twenty-five thousand feet. We were assigned to combat fighter stations under control of the picket radar destroyers [a perimeter of warships well out to sea to warn of incoming kamikazes]. The high command wanted an early demonstration of land-based fighters to combat the large flights of Japanese aircraft causing heavy damage to the fleet. The mission was aborted due to weather conditions that prohibited visual sighting.

"My first encounter with the enemy could have been my last. With my wingman, First Lieutenant Ed Abner, I was assigned to a combat control point under radar control of a picket ship. We were at twenty-five thousand feet in clear weather, and during the first hour we were repeatedly intercepted by carrier-based Navy F6Fs. We turned into them, made identification, and each flight broke off. Because the land-based and carrier combat flight controllers operated separately, overall coordination of operations was loose. Our patrols overlapped and each flight had to identify any apparent bogey. . . .

"After several hours of these false encounters, radar control directed us on a heading to intercept a large flight of unidentified aircraft at a lower altitude, some distance to the northwest. As I added full power, we turned to the assigned heading. I made my usual visual check in all quadrants and glimpsed what appeared to be F6Fs, high above us, coming out of the sun, making an apparent pass in our direction. Since we were under a radar controller's direction, and this type of activity had been going on all morning, I told my wingman, 'Oh ****, a couple of F6Fs are making another pass. Let's press on.'

"Shortly thereafter, I noticed red flashes going all around and into my aircraft. Simultaneously, I saw in my mirrors the large insignia of the setting sun on two Franks [Japanese Army fighters]. I executed a violent snap roll. I ended up behind the two Franks while my wingman took evasive action by diving for the deck.

"I was mad, embarrassed, and determined to close on the Franks that were heading north. At full power, I was barely keeping them in range while I fired in bursts most of my ammunition at higher and higher angles of deflection in an attempt to score hits. When I finally took stock of my situation, I realized my aircraft was damaged. My engine was losing oil that streamed over the canopy. I aborted the flight and under very low power made it back to Kadena. Ed Abner had landed about an hour earlier, reported the incident, and due to no word about me had started to assume I had been shot down."

On April 12–13 the second large-scale kamikaze attack, a total of more than 180 aircraft, attempted to penetrate the screen of combat air patrols guided by the radar picket ships. Carrier- and land-based fighters splashed many of the enemy, but a combination of planes and Okas—flying bombs manned by a suicide pilot and dropped from the belly of a twin-engine Betty or Lily—sank or damaged a number of warships. Recognizing the two captured airfields on Okinawa as a source for some of the interceptions of the kamikazes, Japanese artillery on the island started to bombard the two fields and an occasional plane bombed them, damaging some aircraft.

Bill Nickerson on the *Intrepid* noted that following his arrival on March 29, "The next seventeen days were intense. I averaged two flights per day of close air support, combat air patrols, strikes on airfields in the Nansei Shoto chain [the Ryukyus], a fast carrier run north to strike fields on Kyushu, covering damaged ships struggling toward Buckner Bay, and for me, floating around, killing time in a life raft.

"On 12 April, I was leading the early morning CAP covering the northwest sector off Okinawa when the first wave of a very large force of Japanese planes found us. We had been assigned to patrol at 20,000 feet, but the 20 mm guns in the F4U-1C tended to freeze above that altitude. Eighteen Vals were flying in a very tight formation, and we had to climb to 32,000 feet to get at them. My plane seemed to climb better than the others, and though I had only one functional gun (the others were frozen) I decided to break up the enemy formation before it could get to Buckner Bay. I fired my one gun and immediately one plane fell out of formation and crashed. It was later confirmed by a destroyer. But my engine was hit, smoking and losing power, so I couldn't maintain altitude. Going through 14,000 feet I flamed another Val. At 10,000 feet I flamed a Judy. Both were later confirmed. By this time the sky was full of aircraft, none of them ours. I saw planes 5,000 feet below and I dove, catching up with a Zeke carrying a bomb. It was obvious that he was a kamikaze and an inexperienced pilot. My prop hit his tail and he went in. This was not confirmed; everyone was busy so nobody saw it.

"By then my engine quit and I went in. The plane sank like a brick. I boarded my raft only to find the emergency pack had not been attached. Just before sundown, an LCS [landing ship] picked me up. But he had a problem too; he was sinking. A bomb from one of the Vals we didn't get had damaged the hull. Fortunately, another LCS gave the ship I was on some portable pumps and that seemed to solve the problem. They dried me off, washed and pressed my clothes and flight gear, and they fed me. Soon it was dark. The CO asked if I would come to the bridge and I wound up spending the night identifying our planes and theirs, by sound. It was not my vision of a romantic Pacific cruise."

Transferred to the USS *El Dorado*, Nickerson lunched with the amphibious forces commander, Admiral Richmond Kelly Turner. "At the table sat twenty officers, none below the rank of commander, except for this tired Marine first lieutenant, four months short of his 24th birthday. The Admiral said, 'Gentlemen, this is Lieutenant Nickerson, a Marine pilot from the *Intrepid*. He shot down three airplanes yesterday morning.' I was surprised; I hadn't told him that. . . . He asked me if being a Marine in a Navy squadron created any problems. I responded that I'd flown with the Navy, New Zealanders, Australians and Army Air Corps pilots in the Solomons. I added that we were all Naval Aviators, and as long as everyone knew his job there were no problems. The fact that this was my second tour of duty overseas seemed to surprise him.

"When he asked about other problems, I told him about the F4U-1C's gun heaters. He told me that production of 1Cs had been discontinued. He asked if there was anything else I wanted to say. I told him that the previous day's air battle was so far from the fleet that we had to be careful about fuel. I thought we should be able to land at Yontan, if necessary, to take on fuel and re-arm.

With that the Admiral turned to a Rear Admiral and told him to see to the problem."

After thanking his host, Nickerson rode the admiral's barge to shore and began to hike the mile or so to Yontan, where he hoped to find a seat on a plane headed back to the *Intrepid*. As he trudged along the dusty road choked with trucks, tanks, and troops, he heard a jeep. "A deep voice yelled 'Stop!' and the driver came to a halt a few yards beyond me. A red flag with three stars was mounted on the windshield.

"As I came abreast of the jeep, General Francis P. Mulcahy [commander of all tactical aircraft in the Okinawa campaign] boomed at me, 'Nick, you sonofabitch, where the hell have you been? We were all listening to your radio when you ran into those kamikazes. Hop in, Lieutenant.'" Nickerson explained that he hoped to hitch a ride to the carrier, and Mulcahy peppered him with questions about his experiences, concluding with "how do you think this invasion is going?" And "what does it say to you about attacking Japan?"

Nickerson said he told himself to forget the august position of Mulcahy. "I described what I had seen, heard and surmised as I'd flown missions over the islands, the ships, the planes and troops. He listened without interrupting. Then I said, 'General, if it takes this huge armada to capture one of Japan's island possessions [the Japanese officially considered Okinawa a part of their island chain] I cannot imagine what it is going to take to defeat a nation whose every citizen is going to be literally up in arms. That's to say nothing of finding places to land that will be far more forbidding than this one. . . . It's going to be a long hard fight. Frankly, I'm scared.'" Nickerson reported that Mulcahy agreed with his assessment and his feelings. By that evening he was aboard the carrier and on a late combat air patrol until the night fighters took over.

Ten-Go continued to ravage the U.S. fleet for more than a month as the Japanese mobilized *kikusui* using anything that would fly, including ancient aircraft constructed of wood and fabric. As shells from a distant artillery piece intermittently exploded at Yontan and Kadena, on April 16 the third big kamikaze force struck. Throughout the day, AA from the picket ships and the CAPs battled the tide of suicide planes. Corsairs from Axtell's squadron caught up with four Japanese fighters some sixty miles from Ie Shima, a Ryukyu island close to Okinawa, and splashed two. A pair of Jacks, the latest and fastest enemy fighter, escaped.

VMF-441 from Yontan scored the most kills when it responded to a distress signal from a fighter-director vessel, the destroyer *Laffey*, under siege by some twenty-five planes and staggering from five hits by suicides. An F4U chased an enemy plane aimed at the *Laffey* that had knocked off a yardarm. The Marine pilot came so close behind him that he clipped a radar on the destroyer. Both aircraft splashed, but the American was pulled from the sea. When the engagement ended, seventeen of the foe had been downed, including four by Lieutenant William W. Eldridge, while one leatherneck was killed.

That evening, the night fighters of VMF(N)-542 from Yontan destroyed a pair of bogeys and a member of VMF(N)-543 at Kadena shot another nocturnal raider out of the sky. The final score for the April 16 *kikusui* totaled an awesome 270 enemy planes downed by fliers and AA. Nevertheless, a destroyer was sunk and the carrier *Intrepid* absorbed a severe hit.

"I was standing on the flight deck next to the conning tower," said Nickerson. "A kamikaze dove directly down through the number two deck and into Sick Bay. A navy officer was standing beside me. He dropped dead from a piece of flying metal." Out of action, the *Intrepid* steamed toward Pearl Harbor for repairs, which were so extensive the carrier continued on to the States. Although Nickerson said he had more combat time than any pilot on the flattop, while the others looked forward to home leave, he was ordered back to Okinawa to help with the close air support missions for Marines attacking on the Naha–Shuri Line, one of the last formidable defensive positions.

One week later, a school of some eighty kamikazes bore down upon the outlying picket ships. A posse of predators, Corsairs, and Hellcats swarmed upon them like sharks feasting on min- nows. Many of the Japanese pilots involved in these attacks possessed only rudimentary flying skills, and their aircraft carried neither bullets nor shells for self-defense. George Axtell accounted for five planes within fifteen minutes; Major Jefferson Dorroh, his executive officer, went him one better, burning and exploding six.

Dorroh, also a twenty-three-year-old, had been with the squadron from its inception. "I enlisted in the Navy," said Dorroh, "on July 9, 1941, after my third year in college [the University of Oregon]. At the beginning of my second college year I enrolled in the Civilian Pilot Training program and went through both the primary and advanced programs. While in training I switched to the Marines so I would be assured of receiving fighter training."

Like Axtell, he served as a flight instructor before becoming a member of VMF-323 in 1943 at Cherry Point Naval Air Station. And as in the case of his commander, Dorroh never carrier-qualified. He remarked that April 22 was his only opportunity for aerial combat. Against the slower and more maneuverable Vals, the Corsairs resorted to using their flaps and even lowered their landing gears in order not to overrun the slower enemy. He said, "Since the pilots were on a suicide mission, I doubt they were very highly trained."

Altogether the Marine hunters devoured thirty-three and three-quarters of the foe (credits were shared with Navy fighters, who splashed twenty and a quarter). The kamikazes sank a mine-sweeper and a support craft while damaging three other vessels.

During his tour on Okinawa, Axtell recalled, "My encounters after the first one, usually kamikazes, were under poor visibility and bad weather conditions. You'd be flying in and out of heavy rain and clouds. Enemy and friendly aircraft would wind up in a big melee. You just kept turning into any enemy aircraft that appeared. What [seemed] to be a big fight would be badly dispersed by the first attack of our flight. It was fast and furious and the engagement would be over within thirty minutes.

"I had the opportunity to engage enemy aircraft three times if memory serves me correctly." He destroyed one more plane in the air after April 22 when another torrent of kamikazes deluged the

Okinawa waters April 27–28. On the second day, his Death Rattlers splashed fourteen and a half. Readily admitting that the squadron did not joust with the best enemy pilots, most of whom had been put out of action previously, Axtell nevertheless noted the inherent dangers. "It was a crap roll plus the willingness to fly weather, to cruise most economically, to fly at night, and operate from airfields with minimum ceilings, utilizing primitive navigation aids."

The squadron combat against the Japanese in the air was not as dangerous as its other responsibility, ground support. The foot soldiers met fierce resistance from the enemy ensconced in blockhouses—underground bunkers connected by networks of tunnels, caves, and even concrete tombs. "My recall," said Axtell, "is that roughly half our missions were in air-to-ground support of both Army and Marine units. These were very important and were also very gratifying, as we received reports of the accuracy of the delivery of ordnance on targets and statements attesting to the effectiveness of these missions.

"The pilots made extremely low-level passes to increase the accuracy of the deliverance of bombs with ten-second-delay fuses, napalm, and rockets. The attack runs carried them through friendly artillery and small-arms fire as well as enemy small arms, mortars, and artillery trajectories directed at them, as well as antiaircraft ordnance. Small-arms fire and heavy antiaircraft fire were intense at times. We suffered considerable material damage to our aircraft, unfortunately, lost pilots and planes from ground fire." In fact, VMF-323 listed no people shot down in air battles that accounted for 124½ of the enemy, a Marine record. Six men became casualties from either air support missions or operational accidents.

The *Gunto Graphic*, the newspaper published by the Army's XXIV Corps, described a close air support mission by another outfit, VMTB-232. "The planes made a dummy run and word was received from the air liaison party that they were right on target. Then Captain [James E.] Nauss of VMTB-232 led the squadron on the wet run. He came in at terrific speed [an obvious exaggeration since torpedo bombers never attained great speed]. It appeared as though he would never come out of his dive. Observers behind the U.S. lines lost sight of his plane below the three-hundred-foot crest of the hill. Then suddenly the plane came out of nowhere with a roar, climbing almost straight up. A moment later a terrific explosion was heard. Then the rest of the squadron dived on the hill, each loosing a bomb. None of them, however, surpassed the daring dive of the squadron leader, who later admitted his plane had been within a few feet of the ground.

"A second bomb run was made. Then the torpedo bombers made a rocket strike while the Corsairs strafed. During the bomb runs, mud, trees and Jap bodies were tossed a hundred feet in the air.

"Not one plane overshot its mark. That would have been disastrous to the waiting Doughboys who, once the runs were over, advanced and seized the hill." In fact, the *Gunto Graphic* overstated the case. While the action was factually described, the beneficiaries, GIs from the Ninety-sixth Division, discovered that the dug-in Japanese had not been routed. Savage, hand-to-hand fighting ensued before they were rousted. The air attack from the deck of the *Essex* did divert the enemy's attention sufficiently for a nearby hill to be taken.

Living conditions for the Marine aviation units on Okinawa bordered on the minimal: tents, slit trenches for latrines, and makeshift laundry and shower facilities. "The food was outstanding," said Axtell, "due to our mess officer, Sol B. Mayer, an enterprising individual and a frustrated grunt. I honored his request for a week or so 'temporary duty' with infantry on the front lines. My jeep was made available, plus several cases of bourbon for his use in potential bargaining.

"Mayer had several goals. First, he wanted to prove his manhood by participating in actual combat. He was quite successful in this endeavor and performed quite professionally. Second, he was determined to obtain Japanese souvenirs with the idea that he could trade them for food with members of the fleet lying offshore. His salesmanship was outstanding. The squadron mess after the first two weeks was furnished with white tablecloths, silverware, and the fare included eggs and steak. The mess was open twenty-four hours a day and fed anyone who stopped by. Needless to say it gained notoriety islandwide."

On May 10, VMF-312's Lieutenant Robert R. Klingman, a former enlisted man in both the Navy and Marines, cruised at ten thousand feet with wingman Captain Kenneth R. Reusser. They noticed vapor trails over Ie Shima, the tiny island adjacent to Okinawa recently captured by the Seventy-seventh Infantry Division. The two Corsairs sprinted toward Ie Shima to find a Nick-type fighter engaged in a photo mission. At thirty-five thousand feet the Marines fired short bursts from their machine guns just to keep them from freezing.

Reusser closed on the Nick's tail and with his final burst damaged the wing and left engine. Klingman now slid into place, but his guns balked entirely. He decided to employ his F4U as a ramming weapon. According to the squadron war diary, on his first pass, he said, "I overshot by a few inches and my propeller nicked the top of his rudder, sliced off a foot of fabric, and chewed into the rear cockpit where a very scared rear-gunner had been pumping and pounding his guns to get them to fire."

The Nick started to lose altitude, and Klingman attempted a second collision. He severed the rudder of the plane completely and damaged the right stabilizer, but the pilot retained control. On this third try, Klingman's prop ripped away the stabilizer and the Nick spun into the sea. The Marine limped back to Okinawa for a dead-stick landing with chunks of the propeller missing, his engine and fuselage holed by the desperate rear-seat gunner, and pieces of the Nick stuck in his cowling.

Bruce Porter, who'd experienced his own baptism by fire on Guadalcanal with VMF-121 and then transferred to the ranks of night fighters, reentered the combat zone as executive officer of VMF(N)-533, which flew the F6F-5N, a Hellcat equipped for nocturnal duty. The outfit hopped from island to island in the Pacific, reaching the Yontan base on Okinawa on May 10 after a brief stopover on Iwo.

"For the time being," said Porter, "the primary mission of night fighters based at Yontan was to protect friendly vessels anchored or operating near Okinawan shores. . . . In addition to our own night prowlers, which were just getting into the business, the Navy covered the fleet at nearly all hours with smoke screens. Since the prevailing wind was from the Chinese coast, landing craft equipped with smoke generators constantly plied the waters to the west of the anchorages. Unfortunately, the smoke also masked the approaches of kamikazes from the view of our vigilant day-fighter pilots and it caused problems for our night squadrons as well."

Porter's first operational night launch on May 12 was every pilot's nightmare. After taking off and evading fire from nervous gunners aboard the friendly ships—some hit but did not badly damage following Hellcats—Porter contacted his assigned picket ship. Subsequently a controller based on le Shima, an adjacent small island, gave him directions. From that source he received a disquieting weather report.

Parked in orbit, Porter said, "The storm that overtook me was terrible. The rain was terrible and the lightning was terrible. For all my eagerness to be on my first real night mission, I could not sustain enough enthusiasm to remain aloft for essentially no reason. At length I called my controller and asked permission to fly home." The reply denied his request. Porter later learned that while all others had been allowed to land, the fleet commander demanded at least one night fighter remain on patrol.

"I continued to cut circles in the storm for another hour. It was extremely hard to maintain or properly monitor my position on instruments as my Hellcat was really getting jerked around. . . . I thought I knew where I was, but . . . I became completely lost."

At the end of this period, Porter decided he would risk an admiral's wrath rather than stay in the air. But to his dismay his radio transmissions to le Shima were blotted out by the storm's electrical disturbances. He tried a backup ground control. " 'Handyman from Muscles Two,' I kept saying into my mike. But Handyman did not answer. My sense of being lost grew and grew and so did my sense of despair. What a dumb way to go!

"Then, literally right out of the blue, a picket ship chimed in loud and clear. 'Muscles Two, this is your friend, a picket ship. We have you on radar. We will vector you on course 90 [due east].' "

Porter followed the direction and to his enormous relief, he soon contacted other controllers, who vectored him to a safe landing at Yontan.

Three missions later Porter still had not seen an enemy plane, although others had downed some night callers, including a double by Lieutenant Edward LeFavire of VMF(N)-533 and then a triple by Lieutenant Robert Wellwood from the same outfit. Both pilots were coached by ground controllers.

Marine correspondent Harold W. Martin, a very successful magazine writer after the war, described the action. Manning the microphone for Wellwood was former Stanford all-American halfback Hugh Gallarneau, who observed an unidentified glow on his radar screen. When the stranger failed to respond to a query, Gallarneau knew it was an enemy and clicked on his microphone.

"Hello, Muscles One Seven, I have a customer for you, starboard three-five-zero."

"One Seven to Poison. Three-five-zero. Roger and out."

"Hello One Seven. Target range 25 at 11 o'clock and 17,000 feet indicating 160 mph. Firewall! Poison, Out!"

"She had altitude on me and was closing fast," Wellwood said later. "When Hugh told me to firewall, I jammed the throttle forward and started to climb. We were closing fast . . . 10 miles . . . 7 miles . . . I charged my guns, just to make sure."

"Hello One Seven," called Gallarneau, "Target range 3 at 10 o'clock starboard two-two-zero. Target crossing . . . Punch! [Get him!]"

Wellwood added, "When I went into my turn, I knew this was it. If Hugh had judged his vectors right and if I'd followed him as I should, I'd be coming right in on her tail. If either of us had doped off, there wouldn't be anything out there but empty sky. As I came out of my turn, I flipped my finder and peered at the little colored gauge on my panel. There wasn't a blip [tiny light on the radar screen] on it. Then I got her signal. It came swimming down from up in the left-hand corner of the screen and I yelled, 'Contact!' so loud Hugh could have heard me even without his radio.

"I watched the blip getting bigger and bigger and coming nearer and nearer. When I thought I was close enough, I started squinting ahead and 300 feet above me . . . a vague black shape in the light of the moon. I nosed up to climb a little and swung to port to get on the dark side of the moon from her, and started closing in. The twin engine Betty didn't know I was in the sky. At 300 feet I gave the trigger a short quick squeeze. At the wing-root between the Jap's left engine and fuselage, I saw the white sparks flickering where the armor-piercing incendiaries were going in . . . little glints of light . . . dancing along the wing . . . like the sparklers the kids play with on the Fourth of July.

"I gave the Betty another squirt . . . the port gas-tank blew up in a red glare . . . and her right wing was gone. She went down in a tight spin. I followed a bit. She hit the water and her bombs blew up."

Five minutes later Gallarneau fed Wellwood a second bomber. He pursued it briefly before blasting it from the sky. He himself fell into a spin from which he recovered, shaken enough to take a nip from a small bottle of brandy he kept in his pocket. A third target appeared and as Wellwood chased it he flew into AA from the ships below. The friendly fire punched a hole in his wing, shut down his radio, and eliminated two of his guns. Still, he caught up with the foe.

"The Betty saw me the same time I saw her. The same blue blow torch flame broke out from her top turret as her gunner opened fire. I bored in and sat there pouring them into her. I must have gotten the pilot because the Betty went into a tight spin to the right. I didn't follow her. She hit—a gush of flame came up— and that was all."

Although the kamikazes offered no opposition, the entrenched Japanese on Okinawa fiercely resisted the advance of both Marines and Army troops. Two battalions from the First Marine Division as well as GIs from the Seventy-seventh Infantry Division faced critical shortages of supplies as the heavy summer rains rendered routes from depots to the front impassable. VMTB-232 and 131, instead of dumping bombs or making torpedo runs, dropped tons of food, water, ammunition, and vital gear.

EIGHTEEN

FINAL BATTLES

Bruce Porter, as executive officer of VMF(N)-533 at Yontan on Okinawa, had flown several night missions by the third week of May 1945 but had not yet even seen an enemy marauder. On May 22 he received orders detaching him to become CO of VMF(N)-542. He owed his promotion partly to dissatisfaction with the previous skipper of the unit, although the squadron had accounted for eleven Japanese after-dark raiders, a creditable score in about a month of duty. Porter now led twenty-seven pilots, only one of whom had as much experience as he did—his exec Captain Wally Sigler, already an ace.

Following a meeting with his pilots, Porter declared, "Let's try to make this the best damned night-fighter squadron in the Marine Corps. Let's prove it in the air and at night!" But action in the air continued to evade him, although his old outfit, VMF(N)-533, knocked down five intruders in another sector.

After one more fruitless sortie, a frustrated and disappointed Porter returned to the base, parked his Hellcat, and made his way to his tent. "I had no sooner sat down on my rack to pull off my combat boots," said Porter, "than I heard explosions from the field below our hill. Before anything else sank in, the field telephone beside my cot began ringing. I grabbed the handset and shouted, 'Major Porter!' A frantic voice I could not place bellowed news that all hell was breaking loose on the airfield and that the Japanese were *landing* [his italics] planes on our runways."

The strike by the Japanese consisted of a series of bomber raids that had begun at 8:00 P.M and continued till midnight. Four of the first six elements penetrated the screen of night fighters, and while antiaircraft batteries engaged them, they succeeded in dumping bombs on Yontan. The seventh flight, five twin-engine Sally bombers, approached Yontan at a very low altitude. The ground gunners flamed four, but one, with its wheels up, bounced across a runway on its belly. A minimum of eight heavily armed Japanese commandos—*Giretsu*—rushed from the wreckage and attacked the nearby aircraft.

Bruce Porter tugged on his shoulder holster, checked to see if his automatic pistol was loaded, grabbed some extra clips of ammunition, and hurried into the night. "I had already heard several new explosions and could hear small arms popping off from below our hillside bivouac. I hit the door just as a huge light flared into the darkened sky. I was certain that someone had blown up a gasoline dump.

"From my vantage point, I saw that many lines of tracer were flying across the runways and on into flight lines and tent camps on all sides of the airfield. It was totally chaotic. . . . It was evident that I could contribute nothing to events below except the seeds of more confusion. I decided to sit tight, and I ordered everyone within hearing distance to do the same. Within minutes, several coolheaded souls organized all hands to repel boarders, which was just the right thing to do."

Jack Kelly, a member of the squadron's ground crew, was much closer to the action than Porter. After the enemy started to unload on Yontan, he and others servicing aircraft took refuge in a bomb shelter. He recalled, "After a few hours, a Jap bomber crashed into one of our fuel dumps and caused instant daylight. Shortly thereafter, another bomber, loaded with *Giretsus*, came directly onto the landing strip with his gear up. The aircraft careened along the fighter strip, generating a myriad of sparks as metal mashed against coral. They ground to a halt about 100 yards from our bomb shelter. I couldn't believe what I was seeing! Out came the Nips, loaded with incendiary devices, grenades and rifles.

"In our bomb shelter were about seventeen Marines, unarmed.

Our carbines, M-1s and other small arms were all back in the tent area. The Nips were scurrying about, burning aircraft, firing their rifles and were positioned directly between us and the tent area. All we had were screwdrivers and assorted tools. I have often thought, if only one of the ground crew had taken a rifle to the flight line, many casualties could have been avoided, equipment and supplies saved. We could have picked off quite a few of the *Giretsus* as they exited their plane and staggered down the strip with their heavy loads.

"We were defenseless in the bomb shelter and at their mercy if they had seen us. One Jap grenade thrown into the shelter would have KO'd the whole group. Three Marines at the other end of the strip came to our rescue—Ordnance officer Bucket Campbell, Sgt. Chan Beasley and another Marine with small arms were a welcome sight. We pointed out several Nips nearby. They were identified as Nips and shot.

"Campbell established a perimeter defense around the shelter using a few of us out on point. I manned one, armed with a screwdriver. After being out there a short time, I heard a voice shout, 'Whoever goes there better answer up' and a shot rang out. I was hit in the foot. I had no time to answer with the password, issued fresh each day. . . .

"I hollered back, 'Hold your fire, you dumb son of a bitch!' and the firing ceased. A few buddies came running over, saw my problem and cut off my boondocker with a K-bar. They applied sulfa, dressed the wound quickly and helped me to the rear."

Bill Nickerson, assigned to VMF-441, was also stationed at Yontan. He took refuge in a foxhole with a friend, Major Mac McCall, a former car dealer who was approaching forty when he volunteered for the Marines after Pearl Harbor. Said Nickerson, "I took one look at the rifles clutched in our hands and started to laugh. 'Hell, Mac, in this crazy war I've been down in a sub [after rescue at sea], on board a carrier, flown a lot of planes and here I am with a rifle cocked in a foxhole. Looks like I've done it all, land, sea, and air.' "

Neither of the pair spotted any targets for their weapons, and when the last of the commandos had been killed, they returned to their quarters. As they neared McCall's tent they saw it had collapsed to the ground. Nickerson said, "An enemy parachutist, harness still intact, had fallen directly onto Mac's tent. His body was spread-eagled on top of it, impaled on the tent pole." Although some believed the raiders were paratroopers, the man who crashed into the tent was undoubtedly a member of a bomber shot out of the sky.

The attack on Yontan left two Marines killed, eighteen wounded. The body count of the enemy added up to ten dead on the field with three more corpses in the plane, victims of antiaircraft fire. Another sixty-nine Japanese died in the crashes of the other four Sallys, shot down by AA. The attackers destroyed or damaged thirty-three airplanes, and seventy thousand gallons of fuel disappeared in fire and smoke.

By mid-June, Bruce Porter still had yet to chase an enemy intruder in his night fighter, inscribed BLACK DEATH. On the fifteenth of the month, Porter took off for an 8:00 P.M.–midnight patrol known as a "nightcap." His hopes rose since half of the squadron's kills had been scored during this time period.

As he left Yontan and headed out to sea, nervous gunners from the fleet fired AA in the direction of the sound made by *Black Death*'s engine, but he was well out of range of the tracers. Handyman, the ground control officer on Ie Shima, contacted him and recognized his IFF signal, conveyed automatically by radio impulses. Porter advised Handyman that it was an opaque black night with a cloud cover obscuring the ground.

"Suddenly," said Porter, "my GCI [ground control intercept] officer called excitedly, 'Hello, Topaz One from Handyman. I have an unidentified bogey for you. Target range 30 miles at 10 o'clock. Angel 13 [altitude thirteen thousand]. He's indicated 170 knots. . . .'

"That started my adrenaline flowing. The intruder had 1,000 feet on me and was quickly closing. I dropped my belly tank and threw the throttle all the way forward, which added considerable power by engaging the water-injection system. This was good for an extra 15-knot burst of speed in emergencies. I also increased the engine RPM and nosed up into a steep climb. I made sure my guns [four .50-caliber machine guns and two twenty-millimeter cannon] were armed."

His guide on le Shima fed him more information, reporting the shrinking distance between hunter and prey, and vectored him onto a course of interception calculated to bring Porter onto the bogey's tail. He flicked on the screen of his radar. Pilots ordinarily left the monitor dark to preserve their night vision until they knew a target was near.

Porter said, "My eyes became riveted to the orange scope on my instrument panel. . . . This was just like a textbook practice mission . . . I was on full instruments and radar. All I needed to do was remain steady and do what my instruments and Handyman told me to do. If I trusted in the system, I would be coaxed into a perfect firing position. . . .

"Bingo! My scope indicated a tiny orange blip at the very top. I was dead on target. The body was straight ahead. It had been a letter-perfect vector.

" 'Handyman from Topaz One. Contact!' I winced slightly when I heard my voice crack with excitement. I would rather have shown a better brand [of] professionalism."

Porter watched the blip grow in size as it slid toward the center of the screen, which represented his position. He checked the ink-dark sky for a sign of the enemy. After several such brief looks he detected a "slight ripple of movement dead ahead. A second or two later, I knew I was staring at the bogey's exhaust flame. . . . I flew in a little closer in order to positively identify him as an enemy warplane and to learn precisely what I was facing. I was certain that he was a Ki45 Nick twin-engine night fighter. Thus, there was an outside chance that he would be able to find me before I could open fire.

"I climbed slightly to get right over him and then marginally increased my speed to close up. If he did not detect me and did not change course, this was going to be a sure kill.

"As I nosed down slightly to bring all my guns to bear, I decided to fire everything in my armory. When I was in the best possible position and only 300 feet from the target, I gently squeezed both triggers. My .50 calibers roared and the 20 mm cannon blew off rounds in a surprisingly slow, steady manner: *Bonk . . . Bonk . . . Bonk.*

"My initial target was the right engine and right side of the fuselage, where some fuel was bound to be stored. *Black Death*'s outpouring of lead had a literal buzz saw effect upon the enemy airplane.

"I eased off the 20mm because of a limited supply of ammunition but I kept putting .50 caliber armor-piercing and incendiary rounds in to the fuselage. I wanted him to burn so I would know beyond a doubt that I had scored a kill. Licks of flame showed up on the leading edge of the wing. Then a fiery orange tongue swept back over the fuselage. Suddenly the twin-engine Kawasaki stalled and lurched heavily to the right. My rounds poured into her vitals. I saw tracer strike the canopy. I doubt if the pilot ever knew what hit him.

"It was over in about two seconds.

"When the Nick nosed over and fell away toward the sea he was wrapped in flames from nose to tail."

Porter had now his fourth confirmed victory in the air after the GCI officer, seeing the bogey vanish from his radar, congratulated him. It was still only a little after 9:00 P.M., and he resumed circling in the night sky.

About an hour later, Handyman radioed, "I've got another bogey for you." An exultant Porter quickly picked up the track and started to chase his unknowing adversary. GCI advised that the gap between the two aircraft was diminishing rapidly, and when Porter turned on his scope, another orange blip showed. The telltale flames of the exhaust stacks betrayed the location of what was a Betty bomber that appeared to carry an Oka, or cherry blossom—a manned, rocket-propelled suicide missile Americans called a Baka, meaning "stupid."

From a mere 250 feet from the target, Porter laced the Betty with machine-gun and cannon fire. The plane exploded, with pieces showering the F6F. A secondary eruption of flames indicated detonation of the Baka's propellant. Handyman confirmed the second kill, which elevated Porter to the status of ace.

The kamikazes struck at Okinawa in the final week of May, and during June. In the first of these, organized into a series of fifty-six separate raids, from 110 to 150 aircraft attempted to smash into the ships supporting the campaign. Marine pilots claimed thirty-two downed in two days, while the Air Corps knocked out another seventeen. The fleet's AA accounted for an untold number but sui-ciders hit ten vessels, sinking the destroyer *Drexler*.

The last *kikusui* floated over Okinawan waters June 21–22. An onslaught of forty-five bore down upon the warships, damaging four. Robert Sherrod reported that Lieutenant John W. Leaper of VMF-314, having shot out of the sky a pair of bombers at the cost of a shattered windshield, suddenly saw a Zeke diving upon him. Leaper emptied his last rounds of ammunition at the foe, who now directed his fury at Leaper's wingman, Lieutenant William L. Milne, also victorious against two planes.

With no bullets left, Leaper tried to saw off the Zeke's tail with the propeller from his Corsair. He missed but on a second attempt succeeded in ripping the nose of the Zeke just forward of the cockpit, destroying the aircraft. However, the action exploded his right pylon tank, shearing off the wing. He managed to bail out. As Leaper fluttered toward the sea in a damaged chute, a Japanese fighter started a run toward him. The Marine pilot col-lapsed his chute by yanking on the shroud lines and plunged three to four thousand feet before the chute reopened. He splashed gently into the water, and, after an hour and a half, the cruiser *Cheyenne* rescued him.

When the commanding general of the Okinawa soldiers, the Army's General Simon Bolivar Buckner, was killed by an enemy shell on June 18, Roy Geiger, the Marine airman, was appointed in his place. He became the first aviator in any service ever to command an army. Three days later, General Geiger announced that organized resistance had collapsed.

As the last few hundred Japanese soldiers remaining from the hundred-thousand-man garrison either committed suicide or ac-cepted capture, the corps evaluated the close support given not only by Marines but also by Navy fliers from the nearby carriers. While the effort received general praise, some deficiencies could not be ignored. Too often planes were not available quickly enough. There was confusion about maps and grids on charts, leading to strikes at the wrong places or, worse, hitting friendly troops. In contrast with the operations in the Philippines, opportunities to deploy ground controllers who could directly contact flights were fewer. The analysts said there were too many simultaneous air strikes across a narrow front in Okinawa to permit individual direction of air support.

With the Ryukyu chain secure, Marine Corsairs began fighter sweeps over Japan. The initial raid of twenty-four F4Us, led by Major George Axtell, scourged nine air bases on southern Kyushu. The enemy refused to risk aircraft to battles in the sky, and only one plane was actually shot down. However, the Japanese admitted that the strafing Marines destroyed seventeen on the ground.

Two escort carriers, *Block Island* and *Gilbert Islands*, staffed with Marine squadrons, sailed to the waters off Borneo where they would provide close air support to a July 1 Australian landing at Balikpapan. After a flight of Navy planes bombed and rocketed areas already in Australian hands, killing several, the soldiers from Down Under declined further tactical aid from the air. The Marines then focused upon targets farther inland, bombing and strafing enemy vehicles, supplies, and troops.

Late in July, Bill Nickerson was still on the job, as VMF-441 kept up the raids on airfields, ships, factories, and other targets in Japan. His friend Mac McCall urged him to apply for R&R, but Nickerson noted that in the past, "we'd been told when it was time for upcoming leave. I didn't feel like asking.

"One day I came back from dropping a bomb down the throat of a huge factory's smoke stack. Walking away from our Corsairs, my wing man said to me, 'What the hell were you doing, Nick? I thought you weren't going to pull out in time. You were heading right into that smokestack.'

"He sounded upset. I didn't tell him I'd blacked out. The old reflexes must have handled the controls and gotten me out of there. I guess he must have talked to somebody. Two days later, the flight surgeon was waiting by a jeep on the airstrip when I landed. It was hot as the hinges of hell. He walked up to me, asked me how I was and I turned toward the jeep. I fainted at his feet." Four days later Nickerson was on a four-engine transport, headed for the States. His war was over.

As the Marines began to gird themselves for the planned invasion of the home islands, the two atomic bombs at Hiroshima and Nagasaki persuaded the emperor to surrender.

From a total of fewer than 6,467 airmen serving in Marine aviation in 1941, the Corps counted 116,628 at the end of the war, with roughly 10,000 qualified pilots. Having begun the war with Brewster Buffalos, and struggled to obtain even the earliest versions of the F4F Wildcat, Marine fliers received their greatest boon as a matter of default when the Navy originally found the F4U unsuitable for its purposes. Happenstance thus enabled the Marines to achieve a much more significant contribution to the war effort.

The mission to support the Fleet Landing Force, promulgated in 1933, initially fell by the wayside because of the nature of the Pacific war. Protection of the fleet and land-based installations from enemy warships and aircraft preoccupied Navy and Marine aviation. For that matter, despite the responsibility to provide tactical aid to the ground leathernecks, there seems to have been little attention paid to this duty in the training phases. The lack of emphasis upon this aspect of warfare was even more sorely evident within the Army Air Corps, which—if anything—showed even less interest in working with the ground troops than either the Marines or the Navy. Only in June 1943, during the battle for New Georgia, did the Marines make their first primitive attempts to provide close air support. The procedures were not much advanced beyond those employed in Central America during the 1920s. However, the tactics slowly improved, with a quantum leap through the development of air-liaison parties for Bougainville and then further refinement in the Philippines. Still, not until the Korean War did U.S. military aviation fully involve itself in close air support for the foot troops.

During and after World War II, there was considerable chatter about the comparative achievements of the three separate air forces. For example, Navy people bitterly complained about the Army receiving credit for nonexistent achievements at Midway. Old-time naval aviators still grouse about the eleven Medals of Honor issued to Marine pilots while only six naval fliers were so honored. Naval sources note that their fliers totaled far more missions than their opposite numbers in Marine aviation. The actual figures show the former with almost 165,000 sorties in contrast with the roughly 118,000 for the latter. Furthermore, the official figures for enemy aircraft destroyed in combat credits naval aviation with 7,053 while the Marine statistics are set at 2,235.

As indicated, the pace of Marine aviation operations, particularly for fighters, fell sharply after the end of the Solomons campaigns. Navy fliers can point to several battles or campaigns—Midway, the Marianas, the Philippine Seas—as critical engagements, but for Marine aviators Guadalcanal, early in World War II, stands as the high point in their combat experiences. Of the eleven Medals of Honor, five were earned on Guadalcanal and three more for service in the Solomons. Significantly, the last of the nation's most prestigious medals belonged to Greg Boyington, who was shot down in January 1944, a full year and a half before the war ended.

ACKNOWLEDGMENTS

Foremost I am grateful to those Marine survivors of World War II who allowed me to interview them or gave me access to their personal papers and memoirs. Their names appear in the bibliography but I want to give added thanks to Eve K. Nickerson, who collected the memoirs and photographs of her late husband Bill.

The Marine Corps Historical Center in Washington, D.C., in the persons of Fred Allison and Fred J. Graboske, helped me obtain copies of oral histories. Lena Kaljot from the Center supplied me with photographs. Dr. Ronald E. Marcello of the University of North Texas in San Antonio, Texas, obliged me with access to its oral history collection.

Finally, I thank my son Ted, who performs invaluable aid in gathering photographs.

BIBLIOGRAPHY

AcePilots. *Marine Corps Aces of WW II*. www.acepilots.com/usmc_aces.html.

Astor, Gerald. *Operation Iceberg*. New York: Donald I. Fine, 1995.

Axtell, George. Interview with author, 1994.

Barrett, Richard. Interview with author, 2002.

Bauer, Harold William. Diary. www.acepilots.com.

Belnap, Amos Kay. Unpublished memoir, 2000.

Bergeraud, Eric. *Fire in the Sky*. Boulder, CO: Westview Press, 2000.

Bolt, John. Oral History by Bruce Gamble, Naval Aviation Museum Foundation, 1991.

Bourgeois, Henry. Interview with author, 2002.

Brand, Max. *Fighter Squadron at Guadalcanal*. Annapolis, MD: Naval Institute Press, 1996.

Britt, George F. Interview with author, 2002.

Brown, Kent. *Lt. Col. Harold William "Indian Joe" Bauer*. www.acepilots.com.

Carey, John F. Oral History, U.S. Marine Corps Historical Center, Washington, DC, 1982.

Carl, Marion. Oral History. Interviewed by Benis M. Frank, U.S. Marine Corps Historical Center, Washington, DC, 1973, 1978.

Carl, Marion. Oral History. Interviewed by John Daniels, University of North Texas, San Antonio, 1993.

Conant, Roger. Interview with author, 2002.

Conter, Charles. Unpublished memoir, 2002.

Coyle, Jim. Oral History, U.S. Marine Corps Historical Center, Washington, DC, 1993.

Croft, Frank. Oral History. Interviewed by Benis M. Frank, U.S. Marine Corps Historical Center, Washington, DC, 1970.

Cushman, Thomas J. Oral History. Interviewed by Major Lloyd E. Tatem, U.S. Marine Corps Historical Center, Washington, DC, 1969.

Dawson, Marion L. Oral History. Interviewed by Major Thomas E. Donnelly, U.S. Marine Corps Historical Center, Washington, DC, 1970.

De Chant, John. *Devilbirds*. New York: Harper & Brothers, 1947.

DeLong, Phil. Interview with author, 2002.

Deutscher, Irwin. Oral History. Interviewed by Fred Allison, U.S. Marine Corps Historical Center, Washington, DC, 2001.

Dorroh, Jefferson. Interview with author, 2002.

Fisher, R. Jim. Interview with author, 2002.

Fontana, Paul J. Oral History. Interviewed by Major General Norman Anderson, U.S. Marine Corps Historical Center, Washington, DC, 1983.

Foss, Joe. "Naval History" (interview), Annapolis, MD, April 2001.

Foss, Joe. Oral History. Interviewed by Robert G. Webb, U.S. Marine Corps Historical Center, Washington, DC, 1979.

Frank, Richard B. *Guadalcanal*. New York: Random House, 1990.

Freeman, Charles M. Oral History, U.S. Marine Corps Historical Center, Washington, DC, 1982.

Galer, Robert. Interview with author, 2002.

Galer, Robert. Oral History. Interviewed by Dr. Ronald E. Marcello, University of North Texas, San Antonio, 1998.

Gamble, Bruce. *The Black Sheep*. Novato, CA: Presidio Press, 1998.

Gibbens, Stephen. Unpublished memoir. San Rafael, CA, 2002.

Hartmann, Thomas. Interview with author, 1998.

Hayes, Charles Howard. Oral History. Interviewed by Benis M. Frank, U.S. Marine Corps Historical Center, Washington, DC, 1970.

Hise, Henry W. Oral History. U.S. Marine Corps Historical Center, Washington, DC, 1980.

Jack, Samuel. Oral History. Interviewed by Benis M. Frank, U.S. Marine Corps Historical Center, Washington, DC, 1970.

Johnson, Edward C. "Marine Corps Aviation. The Early Years." History and Museums Division, Headquarters, U.S. Marine Corps, Washington, D.C., 1977.

Lattner, Travis. Oral History. Interviewed by Dr. Ronald E. Marcello, University of North Texas, San Antonio, 2001.

Law, James G. Unpublished Memoir. Laguna Beach, CA, 2002.

Lundley, William. Oral History. U.S. Marine Corps Historical Center, Washington, DC, 1993.

Mangrum, Richard C. Oral History. Interviewed by Major Thomas E. Donnelly, U.S. Marine Corps Historical Center, Washington, DC, 1971.

Marine Air Group Twenty-two, Combat Action Report, June 7, 1942.

Marine Scout Bombing Group 231, Combat Action Report, February 18, 1942.

MacArthur, Douglas. *Reminiscences.* New York: McGraw-Hill, 1964.

Megee, Vernon. Oral History. Interviewed by Benis M. Frank, U.S. Marine Corps Historical Center, Washington, DC, 1967.

Miller, Thomas G., Jr. *The Cactus Air Force.* New York: Harper & Row, 1969.

Mitchell, Ralph. Oral History. Interviewed by Major Lloyd E. Tatem, U.S. Marine Corps Historical Center, Washington, DC, 1969.

Morison, Samuel Eliot. *Coral Sea, Midway and Submarine Actions.* Boston: Little, Brown & Company, 1984.

———. *The Rising Sun in the Pacific.* Boston: Little, Brown & Company, 1961.

———. *The Struggle for Guadalcanal.* Boston: Little, Brown & Company, 1949.

Moskin, J. Robert. *The U.S. Marine Corps Story.* New York: McGraw-Hill, 1977.

Mulberry, Richard R. Oral History. Interviewed by Dr. Ronald E. Marcello, University of North Texas, San Antonio, 1999.

Mulcahy, Francis P. Oral History. Interviewed by Benis M. Frank, U.S. Marine Corps Historical Center, Washington, DC, 1967.

Nickerson, Bill. Unpublished Memoir. Available through Eve Nickerson.

Odell, William. *Those Few Who Dared.* Colorado Springs, CO, unpublished manuscript.

Pearsall, Burton S. Oral History. Interviewed by Sarah Canby Jackson, University of North Texas, San Antonio, 1997.

Porter, Bruce. *Ace.* Pacifica, CA: Pacifica Press, 1985.

Prange, Gordon. *Miracle at Midway.* New York: Penguin USA, 1983.

Redin, Harley. Oral History. Interviewed by Dr. Ronald E. Marcello, University of North Texas, San Antonio, 2001.

Rowell, Ross E. Marine Corps Interview, U.S. Marine Corps Historical Center, Washington, DC, 1946.

Schilt, Christian. Oral History. Interviewed by Benis M. Frank, U.S.
    Marine Corps Historical Center, Washington, DC, 1969.

Schwable, Frank H. Oral History. Interviewed by Benis M. Frank,
    U.S. Marine Corps Historical Center, Washington, DC, 1980.

Sherrod, Robert. *History of Marine Corps Aviation in WW II*. Balti-
    more: Nautical and Aviation Publishing Co. of America, 1980.

———. *Tarawa: The Story of a Battle*. New York: Duell, Sloan and
    Pearce, 1944.

Sims, Edward H. *American Aces*. New York: Harper & Row, 1958.

———. *Greatest Fighter Missions*. New York: Harper & Brothers,
    1962.

Sory, Henry White. Oral History. Interviewed by Dr. Ronald Mar-
    cello, University of North Texas, San Antonio, 2001.

Spurlock, Roy. Oral History. Marine Corps Historical Center, Wash-
    ington, DC.

Walsh, Kenneth. Marine Corps Interview, Marine Corps Historical
    Center, Washington, DC, 1943.

Webb, Simon. Interview with author, 2002.

———. Unpublished Memoir, 2001. Magnolia, MS.

Webster, Jerry. Interview with author, 2002.

INDEX

ABOUT THE AUTHOR

GERALD ASTOR is the critically acclaimed military historian and author of *Wings of Gold, Terrible Terry Allen, The Mighty Eighth, A Blood-Dimmed Tide, The Right to Fight, The Greatest War,* and *The Bloody Forest,* among other titles. He lives near New York City.

ABOUT THE TYPE

The text of this book was set in Aster, designed by Francesco Simoncini in 1958. Aster is a round, legible face of even weight, and was planned by the designer for the text setting of newspapers and books.